COLLABORATION
SYSTEMS

Advances in Management Information Systems

Advisory Board

Eric K. Clemons
University of Pennsylvania

Thomas H. Davenport
Accenture Institute for Strategic Change
and
Babson College

Varun Grover
Clemson University

Robert J. Kauffman
Singapore Management University

Jay F. Nunamaker Jr.
University of Arizona

Andrew B. Whinston
University of Texas

COLLABORATION SYSTEMS

CONCEPT, VALUE, AND USE

JAY F. NUNAMAKER JR.

NICHOLAS C. ROMANO JR.

ROBERT O. BRIGGS

EDITORS

ADVANCES IN MANAGEMENT
INFORMATION SYSTEMS
VLADIMIR ZWASS SERIES EDITOR

LONDON AND NEW YORK

First published in paperback 2024

First published 2014 by M.E. Sharpe

Published 2015 by Routledge
4 Park Square, Milton Park, Abingdon, Oxon OX14 4RN

and by Routledge
605 Third Avenue, New York, NY 10158

Routledge is an imprint of the Taylor & Francis Group, an informa business

ISBN: 978-0-7656-3845-8 (hbk)
ISBN: 978-1-03-292452-6 (pbk)
ISBN: 978-1-315-70556-9 (ebk)

DOI: 10.4324/9781315705569

References to the AMIS papers should be as follows:

Mittleman, D.D.; Murphy, J.D.; and Briggs, R.O. Classification of collaboration technology. Jay F. Nunamaker
Jr., Nicholas C. Romano Jr., and Robert O. Briggs, eds., *Collaboration Systems: Concept, Value, and Use.*
Volume 19, *Advances in Management Information Systems* (Armonk, NY: M.E. Sharpe, 2014), 42–55.

Print ISSN 1554–6152
Online ISSN 1554–6160

ADVANCES IN MANAGEMENT INFORMATION SYSTEMS

Forthcoming volumes of this series can be found on the series homepage.
www.mesharpe.com/amis.htm

Editor in Chief, Vladimir Zwass (zwass@fdu.edu)

CONTENTS

PART III. PROOF OF USE

PART IV. FUTURE DIRECTIONS

SERIES EDITOR'S INTRODUCTION

VLADIMIR ZWASS, EDITOR-IN-CHIEF

With apologies to Robinson Crusoe, productive work is largely done in collaboration with others. Defined as a joint effort toward a specified goal, collaboration underlies the functioning of organizations. Today, information technology (IT), and collaboration technology in particular, enables the effective operation of teams, groups, and communities. This technology makes it possible to collaborate asynchronously, across great distances, and on a massive scale when necessary. As teams working on projects have become the fundamental agents and units of work, organizing this work into IT-instrumented processes has become imperative to organizational well-being. Beyond formal organizations, collaboration technology is at the core of open collaboration systems: Wikipedia enables the individual to write in seeming isolation while producing a highly collaborative work; the production of open source software is made possible by the availability of collaboration systems, produced—recursively—by open source communities.

This nineteenth volume of *AMIS* is edited by the leading experts in the field of collaboration systems (CS) built around collaboration technology. The first editor, Jay Nunamaker, is the founder of the field. As we may expect from these editors and from the authors they have selected and guided, the volume gives us an encompassing view of the technology and the work systems built around it. These authors present not only the theoretical foundations and practical applications, but give you the feel of their hard-earned experience in all its immediacy.

As their well-established primary functions, CS support group decision making (in what are known as group support systems) and electronic meetings that can be distributed in space and time (via the category known as electronic meeting systems). Collaborative authoring, workflow and project management, calendaring, and team building are some of the activities supported by CS. With the move to Web 2.0 and to the mobile Internet-Web, collaborative systems have become widespread, taking on many forms and encompassing a great variety of approaches. These systems are frequently implemented on such platforms as wikis, social network systems, participative blogs, and virtual worlds. Beyond the primary "production" functions, CS should desirably support the well-being of the team, group, or community, and the roles of its individual members (McGrath and Hollingshead, 1994).

Theoretical foundations of CS are rich. They include the theories of decision making, group processes, communication, and coordination, as well as the institutional theories that help to study the context of CS use (DeSanctis, 1993). Group support systems in particular have accumulated an impressive body of research literature (Fjermestad and Hiltz, 1998–99; 2000–2001). Group decision making and idea generation are the nodal tasks supported by CS. Robert Briggs, one of the editors of this volume, and his collaborators—who are also contributors to this volume—have distilled the cognitive activities of groups supported by CS into the following six phases:

1. Expansion of the knowledge space: information gathering, knowledge sharing, and generation of ideas
2. Convergence on the ideas worthy of further attention
3. Clarification, sense making, and deeper understanding of selected ideas to produce shared understanding of meaning
4. Elaboration and organization of the relationships among the concepts and ideas
5. Evaluation and selection of the ideas for implementation
6. Building consensus and commitment around the selected and elaborated ideas

Collaboration processes can be built around collaboration technology. The construction of such processes around design patterns called thinkLets implements the above phases of collaborative decision making and ideation (Briggs, Vreede, and Nunamaker, 2003; Vreede, Briggs, and Kolfschoten, 2006). As an example of a very different collaboration context, that of co-creation of value by consumers, a set of IT components has been used to motivate the participation of enterprise-software users in idea competitions and then to conduct the competitions, in order to increase the pool of available ideas and the quality of the solutions to be adopted (Leimeister et al., 2009). The pattern- and component-based approaches lend themselves well to constructing collaboration processes for a specific work system, be it interorganizational concurrent engineering or social-media-based marketing.

Beyond supporting the immediate task at hand, collaboration systems should provide continuity of support. Therefore, they should contribute to the organizational memory through an organizational memory information system (OMIS) and thus to the continual ratcheting up of the firm's performance (Stein and Zwass, 1995). Within the setting of CS use, the rationale for decisions, solutions, and designs is elaborated, and its traces should be saved and indexed so that future decisions, solutions, and designs can be made in the context of the reasons *why* things are as they are—and modified as these reasons change. One of the factors in building an OMIS is the transactive memory of groups, as a mechanism for locating and deploying the memory of group members, invaluable particularly in activating and sharing tacit knowledge. With the use of IT, this group memory can be scaled up to the organizational level (Nevo, Benbasat, and Wand, 2012).

Group processes can be redesigned and transformed when a CS is adopted. This is particularly so in the case of knowledge-intensive processes, such a new product development; an excellent example of such process transformation has been studied at Nortel (Massey, Montoya-Weiss, and O'Driscoll, 2008). Individuals working within teams supported by CS face challenges stemming from the need to contextualize their work and can become disoriented; this evinces the need to instill collaboration know-how (Majchrzak, Malhotra, and John, 2005). With the new technological possibilities, novel system designs enable novel modes of collaboration. As one example, a collaborative visualization system enables a social data analysis, leading to collaborative exploration of big data, where social navigation can rely on usage history, annotations, and bookmarking to expand and refine navigation options (Heer, Viégas, and Wattenberg, 2009).

The more recent collaboration capabilities delivered on a massive scale by the Internet-Web compound, particularly since Web 2.0 social technologies have come on the scene, have resulted in qualitatively new and different activities. These capabilities match the needs of the new, more fluid, collaboration environment, characterized by evolving and overlapping collaborator memberships, and by external participation (Mortensen, 2012). Co-creation of value by consumers and, in general, individuals not affiliated with an organization has emerged as a potent factor in the marketplace. The two forms it takes are autonomous cocreation, where the individuals produce marketable value in voluntary activities, frequently as community members, and sponsored co-creation conducted by individuals or communities on behalf of an organization (Zwass, 2010). Here, the product aggregation facilities of the Web are of crucial importance and include progressive refinement (of Wikipedia or open source code), production of searchable corpus, folksonomy, and information markets, among others. These forms of massive collaboration across wide swaths of time and space require sustained investigation.

The effectiveness of CS has been studied for decades (e.g., Zigurs and Buckland, 1998); the shifting technological base creates excellent progress opportunities for organizational performance—and difficulties for knowledge accumulation in CS research. There are many and various intermediate prerequisites of successful deployment, trust formation among the team members being one of them (Lowry et al., 2010). The impact of CS on individual participants, groups, and owner organizations can be evaluated during the progressing system development with the use of one of the established methods (Antunes et al., 2012). Integrated theoretical approaches to the use of CS in context are emerging (Brown, Dennis, and Venkatesh, 2010). This can lead to better CS designs. The difficulties of evaluation lie in the multiple contingencies of user group characteristics, technology, tasks, and the organizational context. These are, actually, the same factors that make the implementation and infusion of collaborative systems a challenge. I hope this volume will help in both tasks.

REFERENCES

Antunes, P.; Harskovic, V.; Ochoa, S.F.; and Pino, J.A. 2012. Structuring dimensions for collaborative systems evaluation. *ACM Computing Surveys,* 44, 2 (February), 8:1–28.

Briggs, R.O.; Vreede, G.-J. de; and Nunamaker, J.F. Jr. 2003. Collaboration engineering with thinkLets to pursue sustained success with group support systems. *Journal of Management Information Systems,* 19, 4 (Spring), 31–64.

Brown, S.A.; Dennis, A.R.; and Venkatesh, V. 2010. Predicting collaboration technology use: Integrating technology adoption and collaboration research. *Journal of Management Information Systems,* 27, 2 (Fall), 9–53.

DeSanctis, G. 1993. Shifting foundations in group system support research. In L.M. Jessup and J.S. Valacich (eds.), *Group Support Systems: New Perspectives,* 97–111. New York: Macmillan.

Fjermestad, J., and Hiltz, R.S. 1998–99. An assessment of group support systems experimental research: Methodology and results. *Journal of Management Information Systems,* 15, 3 (Winter), 7–149.

———. 2000–01. Group support systems: A descriptive evaluation of case and field studies. *Journal of Management Information Systems,* 17, 3 (Winter), 115–159.

Heer, J.; Viégas, F.B.; and Wattenberg, M. 2009. Voyagers and voyeurs: Supporting asynchronous collaborative visualization. *Communications of the ACM,* 52, 1 (January), 87–97.

Leimeister, J.M.; Huber, M.; Bretschneider, U.; and Krcmar, H. 2009. Leveraging crowdsourcing: Activation-supporting components for IT-based ideas competition. *Journal of Management Information Systems,* 26, 1 (Summer), 197–224.

Lowry, P.B.; Zhang, D.; Zhou, L.; and Fu, X. 2010. Effects of culture, social presence, and group composition on trust in technology-supported decision-making groups. *Information Systems Journal,* 20, 3, 297–315.

Majchrzak, A.; Malhotra, A.; and John, R. 2005. Perceived individual collaboration know-how development though information technology-enabled contextualization: Evidence from distributed teams. *Information Systems Research,* 16, 1 (March), 9–27.

Massey, A.P.; Montoya-Weiss, M.W.; and O'Driscoll., T. 2008. Transforming the new product development process. In V. Grover and M.L. Markus (eds.), *Business Process Transformation.* Advances in Management Information Systems, Vol. 9, 185–206. Armonk, NY: M.E. Sharpe.

McGrath, J.E., and Hollingshead, A.B. 1994. *Groups Interacting with Technology.* London: Sage.

Mortensen, M. 2012. From teams to recombinant collaboration: Understanding the evolution of organizational work. INSEAD Working Paper No. 2012/02/OB. Available at http://ssrn.com/abstract=1980698 (accessed August 1, 2012).

Nevo, D.; Benbasat, I.; and Wand, Y. 2012. Understanding technology support for organizational transactive memory. *Journal of Management Information Systems,* 28, 4 (Spring), 69–97.

Stein, E., and Zwass, V. 1995. Actualizing organizational memory with information systems. *Information Systems Research,* 6, 2 (June), 85–117.

Vreede, G.-J., de; Briggs, R.O.; and Kolfschoten, G.L. 2006. ThinkLets: A pattern language for facilitated and practitioner-guided collaboration processes. *International Journal of Computer Applications in Technology,* 25, 2–3, 140–154.

Zigurs, I., and Buckland, B.K. 1998. A theory of task/technology fit and group support systems effectiveness. *MIS Quarterly*, 22, 3 (September), 313–316.

Zwass, V. 2010. Co-creation: Toward a taxonomy and an integrated research perspective. *International Journal of Electronic Commerce,* 15, 1 (Fall), 11–48.

Collaboration Systems

CHAPTER 1

INTRODUCTION TO COLLABORATION SYSTEMS, PART 1

A Brief History and Lessons Learned

JAY F. NUNAMAKER JR., ROBERT O. BRIGGS, AND NICHOLAS C. ROMANO JR.

Abstract: Collaboration systems have existed in many forms for a long period of time. It is only recently that they have empowered us with the ability to interact simultaneously and at a distance with electronic computers and data networks. This volume presents collaboration systems from three perspectives: concepts, value, and use. The first introductory chapter sets the stage for the remainder of the volume by providing a brief history of recent events and lessons learned from over four decades of scientific laboratory and field research. Neither the brief history nor the lessons learned are intended to be comprehensive but rather are based on the experiences of the editors, who have played large roles in the area of collaboration systems within the discipline of information systems. We ask the reader to keep this brief history and these lessons learned in mind when reading the remainder of the volume. Chapter 2 presents what the editors believe to be the foundations of modern computer-based collaboration systems and also outlines themes in the remainder of the text.

BRIEF HISTORY OF COLLABORATION

Even at the dawn of the computer age, hackers found useful ways to use computers to support collaboration. Collaboration systems, however, have been around much longer than computers. In the 1940s, for example, collaboration systems were based on conference tables, telephones, teletypes, shortwave radios, Morse code, even carrier pigeons, and the ubiquitous memo. Wide hallways were a critical success factor for information-intensive organizations. During World War II, the hallways in the Pentagon were so full of functionaries hustling memos from one office to another that traffic rules were established to prevent injury accidents at doorways and intersections. Winston Churchill's war room, which today is an underground museum, consisted of a large conference table surrounded by wall-sized maps. Staff in ancillary rooms monitored cable traffic and other communications and brought in the latest information. Assistants climbed tall ladders to update the maps with the latest information.

Collaborative computing had a small, almost insignificant beginning. Programmers of early systems started leaving messages in files on shared storage devices where other programmers would be likely to find them. While most computer users were still punching cards and optimizing algorithms, however, Douglas Engelbart envisioned a fully interactive, fully integrated, fully collaborative multimedia computer system for qualitative, creative, synergistic effort on complex human problems. In 1962 he released a report titled "Augmenting Human Intellect: A Conceptual Framework," which opened with this statement:

> By "augmenting human intellect" we mean increasing the capability of a man to approach a complex problem situation, to gain comprehension to suit his particular needs, and to derive solutions to problems. Increased capability . . . is taken to mean a mixture of the following: . . . the possibility of gaining a useful degree of comprehension in a situation that previously was too complex, . . . and the possibility of finding solutions to problems that before seemed insoluble. And by "complex situations" we include the professional problems of diplomats, executives, social scientists, life scientists, physical scientists, attorneys, designers—whether the problem situation exists for twenty minutes or twenty years. We do not speak of isolated clever tricks that help in particular situations. We refer to a way of life in an integrated domain where hunches, cut-and-try, intangibles, and the human "feel for a situation" usefully co-exist with powerful concepts, streamlined terminology and notation, sophisticated methods, and high-powered electronic aids. (Engelbart, 1962)

The technology to realize Engelbart's vision did not yet exist, but progress was rapid. Engelbart and his colleagues went to work to create a user interface that would integrate computers seamlessly with human thinking processes. They developed a number of approaches to let users interact with content on a screen. In 1963, Engelbart invented a mouse to control the cursor (which he called a bug) for screen selection. Extensive testing showed that the mouse had substantially higher usability than light pens and a host of other approaches. With that solution in hand, the team went to work on the first graphical user interface.

Meanwhile, at the 1964 World Fair, AT&T demonstrated the world's first video conferencing based on two analog simplex 1 Mhz video lines and one analog audio channel. In 1965, a proto-email system called MAILBOX and an early messaging system called SNDMSG were developed at MIT. These tools used a flat file approach to enable communication among people sharing the same computer. At that time computers were stand alone; they could not communicate with other computers.

In 1967, however, the ARPANET (Advance Research Projects Agency Network, the predecessor to the Internet) went live with the first packet-switch architecture. Up to that time, computers were only connected point to point. Packet switching allowed many computers to interconnect as a network. The first two nodes on the ARPANET were UCLA and Engelbart's team at the Stanford Research Institute. Engelbart's team was working on the oN Line System (NLS), the first integrated digital collaborative environment. In 1968 Engelbart demonstrated the NLS to an audience of 1,000 in what came to be called "The Mother of All Demos."

The NLS had computer-based chat, video conferencing, and screen sharing. It provided for joint interactive near-WYSIWYG (what-you-see-is-what-you-get) authoring of digital multimedia (text and graphics) documents with cut-copy-paste and text formatting, and it allowed users to annotate content. It also provided features for visible and invisible hyperlinks in text and in graphics, and it had a "hierarchical view controller" that let the users browse the hyperlinked layers of content. NLS had a directory structure for user content. It demonstrated for the first time document retrieval based on both simple keyword searching and multiple weighted keyword searching. The architecture of the system foreshadowed what we now call a service-oriented architecture. NLS was decades ahead of its time. It established the core concepts that are now integral to end-user computing. It also firmly established the potential of computers to serve as tools for human collaboration.

In 1970, a group led by Murray Turoff (now professor emeritus at the New Jersey Institute of Technology) developed a mainframe-based system using dumb terminals and long-distance telephone lines to support a Delphi process among large groups of geographically separated participants. Validation studies demonstrated that groups of twenty to thirty people could successfully contribute to complex collaborative decision processes. In 1971, they adapted the Delphi system to create the EMISARI system, and deployed it in the field to support the federal Office of Emergency Preparedness (OPE), which had just taken responsibility for President Richard Nixon's Wage and Price Freeze program.

In 1972, the first fully realized email came to the ARPANET with the formalization of the SMTP email protocol that made it possible to address a message to a specific user on any computer attached to the network. By 1976, the first commercial email packages had appeared, and email grew to account for three-quarters of the traffic on the ARPANET. Other packet-switching networks also emerged, such as Tymenet and Telnet. Each ran on its own protocols, so data could not move easily between networks. By 1977, the personal computer revolution was well under way, accompanied by the emergence of a variety of local area networking technologies like Ethernet from Xerox Park and IBM's Token Ring. As with the wide area networks, local area networks ran on their own protocols and thus data did not move easily between them. The standardization of the TCP/IP protocol in 1982 made it possible to transmit data from computers on any kind of network to computers on any other kind of network, giving rise to the network of networks that eventually became the Internet. Networked computers, in turn, provided the platform for the Group Decision Support Systems (GDSS) movement.

The GDSS movement had its roots in several academic disciplines, among them software requirements engineering, decision support systems, and the social sciences. In the 1960s, as the scope and impact of information systems grew, so too did the number of stakeholders who had a say in system requirements. In 1965, Daniel Teichroew initiated the ISDOS (Information System Design and Optimization System) project with the goal of automatically generating computer code from system requirements captured in the form of problem statements. As a first step, Teichroew and his team created the Problem Statement Language, a structured English representation of system requirements that could be read by both humans and computers. In 1966, Jay Nunamaker worked with Teichroew to develop the Systems Optimization and Design Algorithm (SODA), a program that could convert PSL (Problem Statement Language) problem statements into a system design that consisted of system architecture models and data models.

In 1973, the team tested key parts of its approach on a large inventory system for a U.S. Navy shipyard. More than 4,000 stakeholders had a say in the requirements for that system. The team suggested that the users record their requirements in PSL so that they could be automatically checked for completeness, consistency, and correctness. They were surprised to discover, however, that most of the users refused to write their requirements in the structured English of PSL, because it seemed far too technical. The Navy had to hire hundreds of analysts to sit with the users and capture their requirements in PSL. A quick calculation revealed that there would be not be enough analysts in the world to capture system requirements in this fashion.

While Teichroew continued to work on computer-aided software engineering (CASE), Nunamaker began to focus on how to support work processes by which thousands of stakeholders might be able to generate, organize, evaluate, and reach agreements on the requirements for complex large-scale systems, working in natural language without the intermediation of consultants. In 1977, Nunamaker and Benn Konsynski developed an early collaborative electronic brainstorming tool running on a VAX minicomputer as a part of the PLEXSYS system. Each participant started with a different electronic page. Each time a participant added an idea to a page, the system would jump the participant to a different page containing ideas contributed by others. There they could add another idea, and jump again to a new page. Field and laboratory experiments with the approach demonstrated that, under certain conditions, groups using the page-swapping tool could produce many more ideas of higher quality than could groups using conventional brainstorming techniques and nominal group techniques. Further, with the electronic tool, the larger the group, the more ideas it produced, up to groups of size forty (the number of terminals they had available at the time). This latter finding delayed publication of the early results for three years because it contradicted well-established evidence that groups larger than five became less productive with each additional person added to the group. Some reviewers charged that the data must have been faked. Eventually, though, sufficient evidence of the value of the approach overcame reviewers' concerns, and findings were published. The brainstorming tool was re-implemented on LAN-based PCs, and additional tools were added for generating, organizing, evaluating, and elaborating ideas.

In the late 1980s, Gary Dixon and his team at University of Minnesota began work on the SAMM (Software Aided Meeting Management) system and pioneered experimental research on social and psychological topics using group decision support systems. In 1989, the first commercial GDSS products, GroupSystems and VisionQuest, appeared in the marketplace.

In the early 1990s, the GDSS movement split into two branches: the electronic meeting systems (EMS) branch, which was later renamed group support systems (GSS), and the computer-supported cooperative work branch (CSCW). The CSCW branch focused on improving the user experience for small, unstructured groups. They developed a wide selection of tools for communication and for co-creation of texts and graphics. They noted that people engaged in computer-mediated communication lost important nonverbal social cues, and so focused on restoring what cues they could and synthesizing new cues for those that could not be restored. Among the many contributions of the CSCW community were, for example, presence indicators to let people know the identity and status of people with whom they were working; awareness indicators so that people could know immediately who was taking what actions and what were the effects of those actions; and telecursors and avatars, so that people could communicate at a distance with gestures. Some in the CSCW community were philosophically opposed to designing group processes in advance, positing that group processes should emerge naturally as the group worked to maximize creativity and satisfaction.

Researchers in the GSS branch of the movement, by contrast, focused fully on designing structured collaborative work practices that would improve the effectiveness and efficiency of complex collaborative tasks involving large numbers of stakeholders, and providing technology to support those structured processes. GSS grew into suites of five to ten highly configurable tools to support a variety of kinds of interactions in a variety of workplace tasks, and results in the lab and field were promising. In 1986, a year-long study of about 30 production-problem resolutions projects in an IBM plant showed a 50 percent reduction in labor hours, a 90 percent reduction in project cycle times, and better-quality work products. A follow-up study the following year at five plants showed similar results.

In 2001, Robert O. Briggs and G.J. de Vreede founded the field of collaboration engineering, an approach to designing collaborative work practices for high-value recurring tasks and deploying them to practitioners to execute for themselves without ongoing support from collaboration experts. In 2004, eighteen collaboration engineering researchers from around the world met for a week in a castle in Omaha, Nebraska to formalize the definition and map out a ten-year research agenda for the field. Much of that research has been conducted and published. Briggs and Vreede began work on the ThinkLets design pattern language for collaborative work practices, a collection of named, scripted techniques that predictably invoke known variations on six patterns of collaboration identified by the collaboration engineering research community: generate, reduce, clarify, organize, evaluate, and build commitment. Gwendolyn Kolfschoten advanced that work by developing a conceptual model for collaboration design patterns that made the techniques independent of the technologies upon which they were instantiated, so a designer could implement the same work practice on a wide variety of technical platforms and yet obtain the same predictable group dynamics.

The collaboration engineering research community also developed and tested theories to explain key outcomes of interest to collaborators—for example, productivity, creativity, consensus, idea quality, technology transition, willingness to change, and satisfaction. Before the advent of collaboration engineering, it typically required a year of apprenticeship for a novice to attain competence with a GSS. With the concepts of collaboration engineering, users only require about two days of training to achieve competence. While that gain is substantial, the underlying problem still remains: without training, people cannot realize the potential benefits of group support systems. In 2008, this insight gave rise to a new research question for the collaboration engineering community: "How can we package collaboration expertise with collaboration technology in a form that nonexperts can use successfully with no training on either the techniques or the technologies?" Work on that question proceeds on many fronts at a number of universities.

The mid-2000s also gave rise to a variety of new social computing systems—wikis, blogs, content-sharing systems based on tag clouds and folksonomies, and large-scale social networking systems like Facebook and LinkedIn. It may be that we are only just beginning to see potential of such systems to create value for society. The history of collaboration systems is far from complete.

LESSONS LEARNED

Hundreds of studies from dozens of universities working on a wide range of complex collaborative tasks produced similar results. A number of key lessons emerged from these studies, among them:

Anonymity Can Be a Valuable Tool for Improving Group Outcomes

Industrial and organizational psychologists at IBM initially opposed a feature that allowed people to contribute ideas to a brainstorming session anonymously, arguing that (a) it would lead to irresponsible flaming and buffoonery, and (b) their organization had a healthy, open culture, so anonymity yielded no benefit. Both lab and field studies revealed, however, that people contributed more and higher quality ideas when they were allowed to do so anonymously. An archetypal example emerged when the president of IBM participated in a GSS demonstration with his top twelve executives to address the brainstorming question, "What are the last details we must address before final roll-out of our new strategic plan?" The anonymous responses said things like, "This plan will never work. We'll spend all this money and we'll still be in trouble. This plan is doomed from the start."

The president asked, "We've been working on this plan for a year-and-a-half. Why haven't I heard this before?"

They answered, "You have! Every time you asked if there were problems, we said 'Yes, there are some problems, but don't worry, we're working on them.'"

Lacking anonymity, the executives were reluctant to criticize the president's plan, so implementation proceeded although none of them believed it could succeed. When responding anonymously, they contributed unvarnished criticisms. The company subsequently developed a new plan to overcome the limits of the prior approach, and successfully implemented the new strategy.

Participation Increased Among GSS Users

Research showed that in unsupported groups, the most vocal person typically took one-third of the air time. The next-most-vocal person took about another third of the remaining time, and so on. GSS allow all participants to contribute simultaneously; so the most vocal can contribute copiously without blocking the contributions of others.

Group-size effects are different with simultaneous input. Extensive research shows that the effectiveness of unsupported groups increases with group size up to five people, then declines with each additional member added. GSS is different because people can contribute simultaneously. They don't forget what they want to say while waiting for a turn to speak, nor do they ignore what others are saying so that they can remember what they wanted to say when they get the floor. Thus, because they need not compete for air time, many more people can contribute to the group effort without blocking productivity.

Satisfaction Did Not Correlate with Productivity

Exploratory studies showed that the most productive groups were sometimes the least satisfied, and the least productive were the most satisfied. But sometimes the reverse was true. Exploratory and theoretical work on collaboration and satisfaction finally explained that productivity is related to group goals, while satisfaction is related to the private goals of the members. There can be many paths to productivity; the same group goal can be achieved by different processes and different products. Some of those paths to productivity, however, may thwart rather than advance the private goals of team members. To get teams that are both productive and satisfied, one must therefore understand not only the group goals but the private goals when designing a work practice.

Negative Comments Can Be Positive

Conventional brainstorming techniques proscribe negative comments in order to encourage more contributions. Research shows, however, that people still withhold potentially unpopular ideas out of concern for potential retribution. A GSS, however, can be configured for anonymous input, which mitigates evaluation apprehension. Research shows that people who are encouraged to add both positive and negative comments about ideas during *anonymous* brainstorming produced more ideas of higher quality than did people who made only positive comments about ideas.

Distributed Collaboration Is Harder

Geographically distributed teams can typically generate and evaluate ideas very successfully working different-time, different-place. They struggle, however, to reach shared understandings and build consensus when they are not face to face. The loss of nonverbal social cues makes it more difficult to interpret what people mean by their words, which makes it difficult to clarify key concepts. Building consensus requires workers' getting to know one another well enough to learn one another's interests, and such learning typically takes place during informal interactions between group work sessions, rather than during sessions themselves. It is also difficult to instruct group members about the group process when they are working at a distance. In a face-to-face group, it is very easy to determine when people have misunderstood expectations. Not so at a distance, when many social cues are absent. Leaders must therefore be much more explicit, specific, and detailed in their instructions to a distributed group.

User Interface and User Experience (UI/UX) Matter

People who collaborate typically experience high cognitive load from communicating, finding and assimilating information, reasoning, maintaining their relationships with other group members, and monitoring the progress of the group to assure that the group's goals remain congruent with their own goals. A collaboration system that imposes even a modest cognitive load on group members may block them from using the collaboration system, and so realizing its potential benefits. User interfaces must be dead simple, very friendly looking, and completely predictable. This can be quite a challenge. Consider, for example, a team of thirty people contributing to the same shared outline. It would be possible for one person to be editing a contribution while another is moving it up the outline, another moving it down, another indenting it, another out-denting it, another adding things above it, another adding things below it, and another deleting it. The UI must respond in a way that makes sense to all those users. It can take ten times as much code to handle the UI/UX challenges in a collaboration system as to handle the functional requirements.

Process Structure Makes a Difference for Groups Larger Than Five People

Research shows that for groups larger than five, performance can be improved on many dimensions by carefully designing a work practice for a group before the work begins. A good design can mitigate cognitive and communicative barriers that manifest in larger conventional meetings, and can reduce difficulties relating to information access and distraction. A good design can specify a work product and a work process that not only make the group productive but also allow individual team members to attain the private goals that motivate their participation in the group effort.

Good Tools Are Not Enough

Although research shows that groups using collaboration systems can gain 50 to 70 percent savings in labor hours, and 90 percent reductions in project cycle times, those benefits usually only manifest among groups led by collaboration experts, for example, collaboration researchers and professional facilitators. There is a small subset of the nonexpert population who appear to have an intuitive grasp of collaboration, and accomplish good things with collaboration systems without training. For the rest, however, unless an expert leads the group, the benefits are minimal and the downside risk of a bad outcome increases. As a result, many installations of collaboration systems were measurable successes but operational failures. Organizations would adopt the systems, use them effectively for eighteen months to three years, and then discontinue their use in the face of overwhelming evidence that they gained double- and triple-digit return on investment. The problem turned out to be that the successful collaboration experts would get promoted to new positions, leaving behind no one who knew how to use the tools effectively.

CONCLUSION

This introductory chapter has outlined some of the history of collaboration systems since the advent of the electronic computer, as well as lessons learned from over four decades of research. The editors believe that it is important for the reader of the volume to have this background prior to reading the following chapters. The word *collaboration* has come to mean many things to many people; therefore we have qualified within this chapter what we intend to mean by collaboration and set the stage for the rest of the volume. Chapter 2 will continue the background by providing what we consider to be the "foundations" of collaboration in the context of this volume. We sincerely hope that the volume provides meaningful knowledge about collaboration systems concepts, value and use.

REFERENCE

Engelbart, D.C. 1962. *Augmenting Human Intellect: A Conceptual Framework.* AFOSR-3233 Summary Report, SRI Project No. 3578, October. Menlo Park, CA: Stanford Research Institute. Available at www. liquidinformation.org/engelbart/62_paper_full.pdf.

CHAPTER 2

INTRODUCTION TO COLLABORATION SYSTEMS, PART 2

Foundations

JAY F. NUNAMAKER JR., NICHOLAS C. ROMANO JR., AND ROBERT O. BRIGGS

Abstract: Chapter 1, Part 1 presented a brief history of collaboration and important lessons learned from decades of collaboration systems (CS) use. Part 2 presents five pillars of CS: anonymity, teamwork, business process analysis, focusing attention, and maintaining team and organizational memory. It sets the stage for the remainder of the book by discussing these five pillars through the overarching concepts that drive CS and real-world experiences.

DISCUSSION ON EQUAL TERMS REQUIRES ANONYMITY

Putting staff members in a room full of networked computers where they can express their true feelings may have about as much appeal for a project manager or CEO as joining a team-building experience. But the results shown by collaborative systems (CS) speak for themselves: shorter, more productive meetings with a freer flow of ideas. It turns out that the chance to communicate honestly and anonymously—with the use of computers—is instrumental in making online meetings productive. Even more than online mail or other team technologies such as Twitter, Facebook, GoToMeeting, and video conferencing, CS supports an atmosphere in which ideas flow freely. Because ideas enter the system and are circulated without attribution, CS frees people to spark ideas off one another or to criticize ideas without fear of rebuke from peers or superiors. It encourages people to participate in meetings without inhibition and reduces the tendency for a few to dominate a meeting.

In a CS meeting, ideas are simultaneously distributed to each participant's computing device and transferred to a shared screen or projector. People read each other's ideas, comment on them, and are inspired to come up with better suggestions. "People who are usually reluctant to express themselves feel free to take part, and we've been surprised by the number of new ideas related," a manager at a missile manufacturer observed. "We also reach conclusions far more rapidly."

After years of testing in research labs, collaboration systems have entered the workplace environment and are proving to be highly effective in corporate settings. At one high-tech firm, fifty fully equipped and staffed CS rooms (called, variously, creativity centers, meeting rooms, idea centers, etc.) were in operation and the technology reduced the number of hours needed to complete projects by an average of 50 percent. Similarly, a CS pilot project at a high-tech manufacturing firm accounted for a 72 percent reduction in project work hours. In addition, CS dramatically reduced project cycles or flow times required to complete projects.

In traditional non-technology-supported meetings, people who are worried about what other people think often do not speak up, especially with the boss in the room. Taking an unpopular or unusual stand can lead to ostracism or worse. And when meetings get too large, not everyone can contribute. With little or no hope of gaining the floor, some people withdraw, letting a few personalities dominate while good ideas remain unspoken and unpresented.

In a CS meeting, the opportunity to express an idea is never lost. Participants contribute simultaneously, so nobody waits for a turn to speak. Further, users can contribute anonymously, so people can contribute unpopular ideas without fear of retribution. They can also criticize poor ideas without damaging relationships. One can state that the emperor has no clothes without landing in the dungeon.

In one instance, the new commander of a Marine Corps base, a one-star general, found that morale on the base was very low. He set up a CS and a telephone in a meeting room and invited multiple groups of privates and corporals to use an anonymous brainstorming tool to answer the question:

"What do we have to do to turn this into the best <expletive deleted> base in the Marine Corps?"

The marines started started typing at once. The general read the ideas as they came up on his screen. The list of ideas also scrolled down the large overhead screen behind the podium. The rapid-fire key clicks were an indicator of the energy that the meeting generated. As the marines typed, the general picked up the phone repeatedly to put their ideas into action. For example, on one call he said, "Quartermaster, this is General <name withheld>. I understand my gunny boys don't have the supplies they need to keep their barracks clean. Do you think you could get them the brooms and soap they need before they get back to the barracks?" Morale skyrocketed.

Anonymity may also encourage team members to view their ideas more objectively and to see criticism as a signal to suggest other ideas. "I wasn't as uncomfortable when I saw someone being critical of someone else's idea, because I thought 'Nobody's being embarrassed here at all,'" said the president and CEO of a major financial firm. "I noticed that if someone criticized an idea of mine, I didn't get emotional about it," commented the manager at a missile factory. "I guess when you are face-to-face and everyone hears the boss say, 'You are wrong,' it's a perceived slap in the face, not necessarily criticism of the idea."

Despite the safe haven it provides for most participants, CS is not always as comfortable for the leader of a project or enterprise. It takes courage for a manager to deal with the issues that surface in an anonymous meeting. It is difficult to accept negative comments when the culture has been to repress them for years, yet if problems lie buried for too long, they may become intractable. The founder of a very successful medical technology firm called together key personnel from multiple levels in the organization for a CS session. Thirty minutes into the meeting he turned red in the face and stood up. Slamming his cup on the table for emphasis, he shouted, "I want to know who put in the comment regarding the interface for the new system. We're not leaving this room until I know who made that statement!" He glared around the room; waiting for a response. Everyone greeted his outburst with silence. After a week's reflection he returned sheepishly to the team, saying "I had no idea there was trouble. I guess I'm more out of touch than I ought to be. Let's try again."

Anonymity helps to separate ideas from the politics behind them. Ideas can be weighed on their merits rather than on their source. Each member of a team tends to view problems from his or her own perspective, often to the detriment of the project or enterprise. For example, in traditional meetings, engineers see engineering problems, sales people see sales support and marketing problems, and production people see manufacturing problems. In discussing and exchanging ideas anonymously from many different viewpoints, the big picture is more likely to emerge. CS groups often achieve a unified, shared vision of problems and solutions—something that is difficult with traditional meeting methods.

Strangely enough, CS often transforms negative comments into a positive influence on team performance. Studies at the University of Arizona and other universities showed that teams in which contributors were anonymous outperformed teams in which contributors were identified. Other studies have demonstrated that people in anonymous CS sessions keep searching for solutions until they have exhausted most possibilities and alternatives.

Traditional groups, because they accentuate the positive, tend to cut meetings short, believing they have done a better job than they really have. Groupthink sets in when participants latch onto an idea too early and completely miss other, more promising alternatives. The general attitude seems to be one of self-congratulation: Why go on if everyone likes the ideas we have already? In CS sessions, on the other hand—where anonymity is the order, no one authority prevails, and discussion is ongoing—the team can never be certain that it has found the ultimate, sure-fire answer.

By the time the team has decided on a short list of options, everyone has had a chance to think through a position and has a better sense of how the team feels. That's the time to abandon anonymity and discuss ideas openly and assign responsibility for action items. While participants are less likely to be censured during an online meeting, they are equally unlikely to win much praise. Occasionally, new online meeting participants are concerned that they won't get credit for a really good idea. Establishing a team reward structure, rather than one based on individual performance, diminishes this concern.

For all its appeal and payoff, CS technology is barely out of its horseless-carriage phase. Developers are working to integrate separate CS tools in ways that will allow groups to collaborate seamlessly any place, any time, on any kind of project. New devices such as smart phones, iPads, and tablets offer limitless opportunities for exploring new ways to improve team dynamics and team productivity.

TEAMWORK FACILITATES CREATIVITY

To stay effective in today's rapidly changing markets, businesses and governments must base their decisions on the broadest possible information from diverse sources. This is leading managers to cultivate leaner organizations with more democratic decision-making procedures. Rather than waiting for information to filter up and decisions to filter down through an organization, ad hoc teams with matrix structures are beginning to solve problems directly.

Team members may communicate across different divisions and report to managers other than their team leader. These teams, which often comprise experts of equal levels, call for democratic leadership to coordinate communication, facilitate the team process, and make sure resources are available. A leader must be sensitive to the subtle cues that indicate whether a team is approaching consensus or spinning its wheels, but it is the team itself that establishes priorities, sets goals, and decides how best to advance them.

As any leader can tell you, however, democracy bogs decision making down in endless meetings, conflicting proposals, and narrow interests. When crises arise in quick succession, a strong, autocratic leader is often needed to make rapid decisions. Such a centralized approach is not practical for most ad hoc teams, however, and therein lies the rub. Can managers have it both ways, involving more people in decisions while ensuring that those decisions are timely? Collaboration systems bring the benefits of the democratic process to businesses while letting them respond rapidly to changing conditions. Tools such as brainstorming software, online voting, and idea organizers significantly expand the scope of team members' contributions without jeopardizing the speedy response necessary in a crisis. Multi-criteria voting often leads to a different result than single-criteria voting.

Furthermore, collaboration systems permit experts from different geographic locations to participate in a discussion on a few minutes' notice. In such situations, the participants simply advise rather than decide. But their input prevents glaring oversights that might later result in severe and costly complications.

CS tools function at three levels. Individually, members use familiar applications, such as word processors, spreadsheets, graphics, and databases, to improve team productivity. At the information-sharing level, team members tap network resources, including data, text, graphics, and even voice or video. These also feed nonmeeting activities involving email, project management, team scheduling, Twitter, Facebook, and so forth. At the team dynamics level, teams use computers to fundamentally change the way they interact, both in face-to-face meetings and across time and space. These tools offer managers additional channels of communication and add structure to the often chaotic way in which teams build consensus.

Dynamic CS tools, such as brainstorming software, encourage teams to trade traditional ways of thinking for more creative solutions. Participants simultaneously, and often anonymously, enter ideas into a collaboration system. Idea organizers then help teams extract the key ideas from such meetings and other information sets, reducing information overload. Online voting and issue exploration tools can add structure and speed the decision-making process, helping team members reach a consensus by focusing on the most critical issues. Other tools support a host of team activities. For example, CS enables collaborative writing, supports decision making, and creates visual and mathematical models of key variables for team decisions.

Traditionally, the larger the team, the slower the democratic decision-making process. More subgoals must be considered and less time is available for each person to speak. One solution is to break a large team into smaller ones with narrower responsibilities. Subteams can operate democratically, but their leaders must still resolve any interteam problems that arise. It also becomes harder for individuals to see the big picture from the narrow viewpoint of the subteam.

CS increases the practical size of a democratic team from a handful to several dozen. Team members can contribute simultaneously; no one has to wait for a turn to talk. Participants type their comments into the system and view others' contributions as they are entered. People build on each other's comments, critique them, and are inspired to think in new directions. Because every entry is recorded, no ideas are lost to fallible memory. Thirty individuals can share their ideas in the same amount of time that two or three could in a conventional meeting.

In one CS session at a large tech firm, seven executives contributed ideas simultaneously. As a senior vice president at the company put it, "CS technology increased the intellectual bandwidth of the meeting." Furthermore, CS organized the information, so it could be assimilated faster and more easily than a sequential verbal stream.

A larger team size helps to keep the big picture in focus and eliminates a team leader's need to communicate separately with smaller subteams. Because all subteams are represented at an online meeting, all perspectives are included. As the team builds an understanding of problems and tasks, there is less wheel spinning, more cooperation, less chaos, and greater acceptance of decisions.

With the introduction of CS, managers change not only the mechanism for reaching decisions but usually the leadership style as well. Managers range from democratic to autocratic; situations from chaotic to static; and organizational cultures from fragmented to cohesive. The best leaders vary their styles according to situations.

CS tools support rather than replace leadership. Technology can help identify problem areas such as counterproductive executive styles. One vice president, who considered himself very democratic, presided over weekly two-and-a-half-hour planning meetings with his staff. For the first hour and a half he would let the staff speak, but then he would grab a felt marker and move to the whiteboard with the comment, "Let me see if I understand what you're saying." He would then describe his own agenda using words and phrases culled from the team discussion. This man's superiors recognized the problem and decided to try using CS to alter his autocratic management style. The staff was enthusiastic about the results, but the vice president was not; he could no longer dictate the agenda, and he ultimately decided to stop using the system. The staff, with the support of top management, refused to let him. Team morale rose quickly, and the team prospered under a new, shared vision.

Failure to make a meeting's objectives explicit can lead to disenchantment, particularly when participants spot phony democracy. If a leader includes a team in the decision-making process after the fact simply to "let them feel ownership," the team process breaks down. Leaders who merely want a team to understand a problem before they propose a solution should say so up front. If the objective is to develop a set of alternatives and recommendations, it should be so defined. Once the team has been commissioned to make a decision, however, a leader can contribute, advise, and argue, but the team will rebel against a leader who overrides its collective judgment.

False promises of anonymity are equally damaging. Any attempt to find out who said what in an anonymous session undermines the leader's credibility and defeats the purpose of anonymous input, which is to solicit unpopular or opposing viewpoints.

CS can also identify those with a stake in a project, and reveal underlying assumptions. When a national library attempted to develop a computer system, it formed a team composed of representatives from different departments such as circulation, cataloging, acquisitions, and computing. For several meetings the teams tried and failed to develop a shared vision of the project. The team leader decided to use a stakeholder analysis and assumption-surfacing tool. It turned out that the various departments had unrealistic expectations of the computer team, and the computer team had unrealistic expectations about the others. During the next few months, through vigorous and sometimes acrimonious debates, the team arrived at a common understanding and a shared vision. Until the participants engaged in stakeholder analysis they had not even been aware that fundamental differences existed. The CS allowed them to share critical information and correct mistaken assumptions, solving an intractable problem and fixing a major oversight in the process.

Any tool is only as good as the artisan who wields it. It is important to use the right CS tool for the appropriate task. This is just as true for a sophisticated collaboration system as for a screwdriver. To realize these systems' enormous potential to expand the productivity of today's team-oriented organizations, leaders must recognize both tangible and intangible benefits.

The intangibles, which depend heavily on the style and quality of leadership, include greater team cohesiveness, better problem definition, a wider range of higher-quality solutions, and stronger commitment to those solutions. The tangibles, already discussed, are dollar savings through greater productivity and reduced staff hours to reach decisions. At the bottom line, more time is free from the demands of frequent and often frustrating meetings.

CS IS THE KEY TO BUSINESS PROCESS ANALYSIS

Ask any three Information Systems (IS) professionals what CS means, and you'll get five definitions. Like the blind men describing an elephant, CS users and developers often define it in terms of the particular module in front of them, happily oblivious to its other parts.

Those who understand the entire realm of CS and how to use its various components in concert, however, stand to reap powerful rewards. The use of CS does much more than make an existing system faster or more accurate. It provides tools to implement entirely new processes and optimize them to meet organizational goals rather than simply facilitate the paper chase.

Thus, CS has much to offer managers who are looking to reengineer work processes. Collaboration systems make workflow automation feasible and the reengineering of current information systems possible. These systems are in crisis precisely because the various technologies that make up the modern business organization do not work together harmoniously. CS products bring disparate systems together in ways that enhance workgroup dynamics, melding systems and people into effective working units.

Workflow automation routes information through an application that requires the input of several people via separate processes. Thus, a process that used to entail mailing forms over several days or even weeks now occurs completely online and takes only a few hours, or even minutes. More sophisticated workflow applications automate complex paper trails, such as those found in insurance companies or banks, offering significant improvements in customer service and reducing errors and costs.

However, simply accelerating existing procedures by emulating the manual flow of work from person to person or department to department doesn't necessarily improve the process of managing information. It merely reinforces established work patterns. But the serial procedure of passing discrete elements from worker to worker remains the same. With CS, on the other hand, everyone involved in creating a document works on it, simultaneously if necessary, and changes are reflected immediately. Multiple authors and editors discuss changes as they occur. Collaboration can fundamentally change the way work is carried out, resulting in streamlined work processes.

To understand how workflow automation and CS function together to transform information systems and the organizations they support, let us consider several classes of CS technologies: communication, coordination, collaboration tools. Each contributes to workflow automation differently.

Communication

Many CS products support team communication in the form of email, Twitter, Facebook, and other social networking systems. However, recent enhancements to the technology go far beyond the simple store, copy, and forward features of their predecessors.

Some email systems include sophisticated event-driven mail routing and filtering features; others include support for mailing compound documents composed of various combinations of text, images, numbers, voice, and video. Email systems allow users to route documents to each other and even to other applications, automating traditional work processes.

All these variations on the email theme expedite workflow automation by transporting documents around the workgroup or enterprise. They do not, however, fundamentally change the process. Taken together, though, communication support tools like email and phone messaging, and information-sharing applications like Twitter and Facebook, can shorten project cycles by eliminating the need for some meetings and reducing the rounds of telephone tag.

Broad access to information is critical to the effectiveness of any organization, but groups looking to reengineer their systems virtually require it if their workflow automation application is to succeed. Team database tools focus on sharing and viewing team information and data. They help teams maintain meeting transcripts, document ongoing projects, and archive details of various company policies and procedures. The shared database is essential for any reengineering project to preserve and provide access to collective memory and information. Without such access people are unable to contribute significantly to team efforts or make the informed decisions vital to the success of any workflow application.

Coordination

"Coordination" implies keeping separate units, people, or activities in order and in sync with one another. As a category of CS, coordination tools help managers direct teams toward their goals. Products in this category often combine email capabilities with sophisticated group scheduling and project management tools. CS is particularly useful in workflow automation projects. Given that many people—potentially from several departments—will be involved in a project, and that online meetings often involve more people than traditional meetings, automatic calendar scheduling and project management tools make it easier to coordinate member schedules and keep projects on track.

Collaboration

Probably the most important and least known category of workflow automation, CS tools help groups achieve consensus, which is vital to the successful design of a system. Team collaboration tools also help team members handle the many exceptions to preprogrammed rules. Collaboration applications support teams as they reason and work together to co-create deliverables, whether they are face to face in a meeting room or dispersed across the globe.

With collaboration technologies, a team process can move easily from venue to venue. A team might brainstorm ideas from their own offices, then move to a conference room idea organization software to cluster ideas around key themes. They might separate to evaluate and elaborate their ideas, then return to the meeting room to establish priorities and clarify terminology, then move back to their own offices and use a team outliner or team editor to explore the issues in more depth and create a position paper.

These products will soon include high-level features that let managers design workflow applications by painting forms on the screen and selecting destinations from user lists. Forms will be routed to queues for both people and computer applications to act upon. The movement of any form through the system will be traced, so a transaction will never get lost or misplaced in somebody's online in-basket.

Such capabilities will allow managers to pinpoint bottlenecks in organizational processes by tracking the time a transaction stays in a particular queue. When transactions begin to stack up, this will signal a weakness in the workflow. That weakness can be technical: a computer application might need to be redesigned. Or it could be people-related: an employee might need more training or lighter responsibilities. In either case, the application immediately notifies management that a problem exists so that people can take corrective action.

As in the early days of automated transaction processing, early workflow automation tended to automate existing processes without fundamentally changing them. Yet the major benefits of CS come when organizations reduce the cost of reengineering workflow, and consequently the risk of project failure. In the traditional approach to reengineering, a team of analysts interviews potential participants, gathering requirements for the new system along the way. But with collaboration systems, organizations can eliminate the middleman: everyone critical to achieving the project goal participates in meetings.

Rather than having to work in small teams of four or five people, once the only efficient way to hold reengineering meetings, entire departments of twenty-five or more employees can work together effectively using the new collaboration systems. Discussions include all relevant viewpoints from the outset, and participants resolve many initial differences and conflicting agendas for themselves before calling in outside analysts.

In addition, the transcripts of these online meetings move into the team database to preserve a complete record of team activities. In the short term, this means reengineering proceeds even if some employees in the department are absent due to vacation or more pressing work duties. They can simply access the database to get up to date on reengineering issues. In the long term, the transcripts are available for later review. Nothing is lost to fading memory.

The CS marketplace now offers tools specifically targeted toward reengineering. Shared drawing and diagramming tools permit all the participants to contribute to a flowchart, a data-flow diagram, or some other graphic representation of complex relationships between people, processes, information, and ideas.

The finished workflow automation application can and should be integrated with other collaboration systems. The queuing system, for example, can alert the user to the presence of transactions in the queue through the same channel used for other messages such as email or the group calendar. Likewise, CS could be available on the same platform as the workflow automation, both to handle nonstandard events and to support continuous quality improvement for the workflow automation system.

It is important to realize that a workflow automation system is designed primarily to deal with the routine, the expected, and the predictable. There will always be nonstandard events that are handled outside the system. Email can be used to resolve simple cases in which the standard process fails, but team outliners, team idea-generation tools, or similar applications are better suited for reporting bugs, brainstorming alternatives for improvements, and achieving consensus. Teams can periodically evaluate results from these asynchronous activities in face-to-face sessions.

While CS provides new opportunities to create value, it also calls for new thinking on the part of leaders. The ability of managers to monitor workflow raises social issues that must be addressed in an information-based society. After all, if workers are rewarded or penalized strictly on the basis of their workflow automation numbers, that is, the average-time-in-queue or transaction throughput, managers may end up abusing the very system they had reengineered to improve productivity. Consider the analogy of hospital mortality figures: the best hospital in a given region often receives the toughest medical cases, which will mean the highest mortality figures. Something similar can happen in a workflow automation environment. Workers who give special attention to customers with knotty problems may be penalized while workers dealing with low-intensity or routine transactions receive inordinate rewards. As with any technology, the statistics generated by workflow automation should inform, rather than replace, the judgment of management. Rule One for CS should be: technology is an enhancement, not a replacement for leadership. Organizations get what they reward, not what they talk about. Use of workflow automation must be accompanied by a reassessment of the reward structure for those who participate in the new system.

Workflow automation by itself is not a panacea for lack of productivity. Providing an active, and anonymous, online forum for workplace issues on the same platform as the workflow automation system allows workers to use CS to express their feelings, and gives team members an opportunity to air grievances. Indeed, this type of forum is best used as part of a larger online meeting suite dedicated to continual quality improvement for the workflow automation system. Workflow automation may contribute most in reengineered systems that value collaboration, worker involvement, and more participative structures. Successful workflow applications employ a variety of tools, including email, scheduling, a shared database, and collaboration tools, all accessible from the same platform. Combined with easy-to-use development tools that empower users, these CS team technologies offer managers the best means of implementing the kinds of flexible organizational structures that are needed to respond to rapidly changing markets.

Smart corporations realize that they can profit when people take ownership and responsibility for how work gets done; such a workforce will propel quality products and services into the forefront of the global economy.

VOTING AND POLLING TO FOCUS ATTENTION

As corporations rely more on teams, with increasing emphasis on participative management, their need to create and measure consensus grows. A number of online voting tools are on the market, and in most cases these tools play a very different role than do conventional voice or paper ballot methods of voting. Traditional voting usually happens at the end of a discussion, to close and decide a matter once and for all. Online voting, however, supports a rapid "vote early, vote often" approach. Because it is fast, teams often use online voting to start, rather than close out, a debate. An electronic poll reveals which topics have strong agreement, and so need little attention, and which topics have little agreement, and so may need clarification and negotiation. The team can therefore focus its attention where it can do the most good. Teams find that electronic polling clarifies communication, focuses discussion, reveals patterns of consensus, and stimulates thinking. Conversations about polling results often surface unnoticed assumptions, unshared information, and hidden agendas, all of which can improve group outcomes.

The following case studies, taken from confidential research of actual events, illustrate the diversity of benefits organizations can derive using online voting.

Case 1

A management crisis loomed for a major telecommunications company. For six months, thirty-nine senior managers had wrangled to come up with an ordered ranking of 89 technical researchers on the company's payroll. When they finally completed this arduous task, a new vice president rejected the process by which they had achieved their results. This vice president didn't believe that the results accurately reflected the technical researchers' qualifications. An outside consultant was hired to engineer a new, computer-supported voting process. The new scheme required each participant to submit both a ranking of each researcher and a measure of how strongly they felt about the ranking they were giving. The senior managers then reviewed several different graphical analyses of their votes and found much confidence and consensus on some of the rankings, and a great deal of variation on others. Subsequent discussion revealed that many managers did not know some of the people they were ranking, relying instead on second-hand information and public opinion. After much discussion and information sharing, the team voted again, this time with a much stronger consensus.

After the second vote the team discussed their remaining differences, and in short order arrived at an overall ranking of their technical staff that all participants could live with. They agreed that the new computer-supported voting process was much more efficient than traditional voting methods and inspired a more open and focused exchange of ideas. More important, everyone from the vice president down felt that the new rankings were more legitimate than those obtained from the earlier process. The confidence-weighted votes and graphical representations of voting patterns provided managers with a larger picture than they had previously seen.

Case 2

Sometimes members of a team will vigorously debate issues upon which they actually agree. A startling example of this phenomenon of unneeded debate occurred in a health-care organization that encompassed a dozen hospitals throughout a major metropolitan area.

Three interest groups—doctors, administrators, and directors—set out to define a mission statement and to decide how various special services should be distributed among the hospitals. For reasons that were unclear, the process degenerated into an acrimonious battle—at which point someone noted that it had been three years since the teams had met without their attorneys present.

The teams decided that online polling might be helpful in locating the source of the conflict, and resolved to perform an experiment. Approximately 200 people attended a meeting in which every participant was given a handheld, radio-linked voting box. A facilitator projected onto a large public display screen a number of policy statements such as, "When patients need emergency care it shall be given without reservation, regardless of ability to pay." Participants voted by agreeing or disagreeing with each statement as it was displayed. Prior to the meeting, it was assumed throughout the health-care organization that doctors, as a team, were responsible for obstructing agreement and thus progress. The prevailing wisdom was that hospital administrators and directors were the peacemakers in the team, and that a good deal of their energy went into persuading the physicians to be less intractable. This assumption was destroyed by the results. Analysis of the votes by subteams revealed that, contrary to everyone's expectations, doctors and directors were in nearly perfect agreement on every issue. It was actually the staff administrators who were out of step. For three years the administrators had been telling the directors that the doctors were causing problems.

Case 3

Traditional methods of measuring consensus that do not reveal team thinking patterns can prove costly. The head of a mining company used an online voting system for the highly charged political task of allocating a budget across multiple corporate sites and projects. He asked a number of key executives for their opinion, but the results of the first poll were widely scattered. No one seemed to agree on budget priorities. The president pressed his executives in order to understand why their voting patterns were so dissimilar, given that they all presumably had the good of the corporation in mind. Finally, one vice president ventured, "None of us really knows what goes on at all these places. We can't really make an informed recommendation." The president then arranged to have online comment cards included on the ballot, and advised the team, "If you know about a project, type in what you know. If you don't know, read what the others have typed." Within half an hour, the team had exchanged a great deal of information about the various projects and sites, and the subsequent vote-and-discuss cycle resulted in high consensus on the budget allocation. As the team left the room, one of the vice presidents pointed at an item on the bottom of the budget priority list, and commented ruefully, "We dumped $5 million dollars into that turkey last year." An eager champion had pushed the project, and when no one had information to dispute his arguments, the management council had simply taken a chance. Traditional consensus building had failed to uncover people's doubts, whereas online polling had revealed people's true feelings about the project.

Case 4

Online polling can sometimes facilitate decisions that are too painful to arrive at using traditional methods. A corporation with a particularly difficult budget crunch chose to use an online polling system to help decide how best to downsize. In many previous meetings, the possibility of eliminating a large but ineffective division was raised but was set aside for fear of offending the division's head, who was a very personable and effective lobbyist for his employees. Although the division was generally unproductive, no one wanted to hurt the manager's feelings by pushing to have the division eliminated. Instead, using traditional voting methods, the team consensus indicated that across-the-board cuts should be implemented. Everyone would bleed a little, sacrificing some efficiency in the interests of harmony. When the online votes were tallied, however, it was clear to all involved that the most sensible and most widely supported alternative was to eliminate the ineffective division. In doing so, the organization did not have to make potentially crippling cuts to mission-critical functions, and at the same time it distributed responsibility for the decision among the participants.

Case 5

Not all online voting sessions are successful. Occasionally, when all the votes are in, all the terms are defined, and all the hidden assumptions have surfaced, it turns out there are fundamental and irreconcilable disagreements between parties.

A savings and loan company faced a crisis that threatened its survival. During most of the discussion, people were optimistic that they would reach a consensus and proceed accordingly. Rather than converging, however, the team diverged as online voting proceeded. An analysis revealed that the team was, in fact, made up of several factions with mutually exclusive, deeply held positions. The session came to an end with an agreement to disagree. The only thing the participants knew was that in light of the bitter disagreements they had uncovered, the viability of the current management team, and thus the company, was at stake. On the bright side, the team was now focused on the difficult problem, rather than wasting time squabbling about minor disagreements.

In addition to making face-to-face meetings more productive, online voting can play a critical role in supporting geographically dispersed meetings. Remote meeting participants lack such nonverbal cues as shifting gazes, body positions, and gestures that give speakers the sense that it's time for a discussion to move on.

Although many teams save time and money with online voting, it would be a mistake to view that as the technology's main advantage. Some teams spend more time on their deliberations when using online voting than with traditional methods. Enhanced understanding of the issues and of the work team itself remain the clearest and most sustainable advantages of online polling. But whether the purpose of polling is advisory or deliberative, it should be stated up front. The best results occur under dynamic conditions, where polling is not a one-shot affair that simply affirms a decision already made. And as with all work team tools, technology doesn't replace leadership. Polling is an attempt to win consensus, not to avoid responsibility for decisions. It provides a way to explore issues in depth.

It's a small step to move from an online voting tool used at an executive meeting to an online survey tool for gathering public opinion and customer feedback. Organizations use online voting not only to manage their own interactions but to monitor customer opinion in real time. Moreover, research has shown that teams using structured voting schemes and response analyses to clarify communication and focus discussion consistently reach higher-quality decisions than teams using traditional voting methods.

MAINTAINING TEAM AND ORGANIZATIONAL MEMORY

Individuals have memories and histories; legends and myths record the collective histories of nations, races, and tribes. But other than fallible human memories and a distributed assortment of archival documents, modern organizations can hardly lay claim to a team memory—which is odd, given this is ostensibly the age of information. Many memories that team members hold are the product of ephemeral, spoken conversations. When teams use collaboration systems, however, their communications need not be ephemeral. They can retain digital records of text, numbers, images, audio and video, and mine them as a team memory.

Imagine how useful it would be if an executive could simply ask a computer program, "What problems in the past year have involved Customer X?" and receive a printout of all relevant discussions a few moments later. Because any activity conducted online leaves an electronic transcript, many types of information once considered ephemeral can now be made permanent. This information can be a valuable asset to teams and managers long after the discussions take place. Information stored in a collaboration system doesn't get misplaced, and it is readily accessible from any node on the team network. Universally accessible information is the goal, but where, how, and what are questions that befuddle managers who are trying to cope with information overload. Team memory is a tough nut that the teamware industry has only just recently begun to crack.

The problem is not that truckloads of random, unstructured data may be floating around in an organization's collective unconscious. For corporate data, the cost of retrieval has little to do with the actual cost of disk drives and CPUs. It has much more to do with the cost in time and aggravation for a team member to find needed information. It's a bit like keeping a rotating drum filled with slips of paper on which every important piece of data is written. Everyone knows exactly where the information is in the drum—but no one's going to randomly read every slip to find the one relevant scrap of data. The cost of retrieval is simply too high. Anything that goes into the drum becomes effectively lost. Today's enterprise information systems work in a similar way.

Because teams accomplish their goals by creating, sharing, and using data, team productivity depends on readily accessible information. The requisite information usually extends far beyond the stores of financial and accounting data in the typical corporate database. Besides numbers, teams may need information about products and technology, meeting reports, informal communications, and publications, to name a few subjects. Work teams, or teams, use a great deal of information in many forms, and they often generate even more information than they bring in from outside. Team data are often difficult to manage using traditional databases. Unlike the transaction records of old, team data are unstructured and unpredictable. Text and images, scribbled notes, spreadsheets, word-processor files, and video and audio recordings do not fit comfortably into a relational database, but recent advances in teamware technology now allow teams to manage their complex and varied data sets. Whether explicit or not, there is a team memory component of almost all teamware tools, and teams are beginning to use teamware technology to prevent critical information from being lost, scrambled, or forgotten. People who join a discussion late can traverse the nodes to see what others have contributed and what supporting information is available. Participants can also refer to their maps to remind themselves and others of why and how the team arrived at a certain decision.

Although these products represent a step in the right direction, the issues surrounding management of team memory are only beginning to be resolved. What of the information that is discarded because it doesn't match anyone's current interests? What of a prescreened and presorted information set that still grows so large that the cost of retrieving a single item outweighs the value of the information stored? In other words, what do we do about well-sorted, well-organized information overload?

Electronically supported team meetings often result in thousands of lines of unstructured text. Tests suggest that semantic links may provide a practical way to retrieve ideas from present and previous meeting transcripts. Suppose a team meets to solve production quality problems at a manufacturing plant. The team would be able to augment its own experience by searching a team memory store for transcripts of any meetings over the past several years in which production quality was discussed. The semantic analyzer would return not only comments about production quality, but also comments about particular tools, plants, or processes where production problems had occurred, as well as discussions of solutions for those problems. The more specific the request, the more focused the answer. Managers attempting to implement team memory for a work team should be prepared for the pitfalls. Information is the ultimate political tool in any organization, and efforts to force changes in information access or control are often met with resistance.

Another serious difficulty may arise in organizations with a cultural bias against accountability. The map in the archives that was so useful when the team was trying to find its way through the fog of an ill-structured problem might become a smoking gun when a project dies for unexpected reasons at a later date. The same electronic brainstorming record that helped an organization make hiring and promotion decisions could also be used against it in an affirmative action suit. As with any documentation, there are social issues of privacy and security that must be addressed before the technology can gain wider acceptance. Nonetheless, work teams that already depend heavily on information exchange and are beginning to drown in information overload will likely welcome the support of team memory systems. The marketplace should encourage vendors that make it possible to sift a gem of information from the dunes of data piling up in our corporations.

OVERVIEW OF THE BOOK

The remainder of this book consists of four parts and ten chapters. Part I, Proof of Concept, consists of four chapters. In Chapter 3, "Organizing the Theoretical Foundations of Collaboration Engineering," Gwendolyn Kolfschoten and Robert Briggs discuss the theoretical foundations of phenomena that occur during collaboration. They explore two classes of theories—explanatory and predictive theory and design and action theory. They distinguish three abstraction levels from which to study collaborative effort—work practice level, activity level, and behavior level—and describe how each level addresses different approaches that explain conditions under which mutual effort and collaboration lead to goal attainment.

In Chapter 4, "Classification of Collaboration Technology," Daniel Mittleman, John Murphy, and Robert Briggs propose a classification scheme to provide a lens through which people can better understand the capabilities of, and relationships among, collaboration technologies. Their framework may help practitioners to select from among commercial collaboration software offerings, offer CS designers a range of design choices for new systems, and reveal new challenges to the CS research community. They describe methods by which they derived the scheme, and then present the details of the scheme itself, concluding with an example of how the scheme could be used, and discussing potential directions for future research.

In Chapter 5, "An Empirical Test of the Focus Theory of Group Productivity," Fang Chen and Robert Briggs report on an action research approach to investigate the efficacy of focus theory of group productivity in the context of project team interactions supported by group collaboration technology. The findings reveal that while focus theory does have explanatory power with regards to processes that consume attention, it also has theoretical limitations. Results showed that the three processes of communication, information access, and deliberation did consume attention resources, but on analysis separating the effects of each proved difficult. Feng and Briggs also discuss the implications of the study for further development of the theory, insights for researchers of collaboration, guidelines for collaboration technology designers, and everyday tips for practitioners.

In Chapter 6, "Patterns in Collaboration," Gwendolyn Kolfschoten, Paul Lowry, Douglas Dean, Gert-Jan de Vreede, and Robert Briggs argue for the need to study collaboration from three abstraction levels: effects of whole collaborative processes, emerging collaboration patterns, and collaborative effort interventions. They present the results of a literature meta-analysis and a pattern analysis of transcripts of collaborative sessions, and present six emerging collaboration patterns: generate, reduce, clarify, organize, evaluate, and build consensus. They present each pattern and its subtypes, interventions that evoke them, constructs used to measure them. They also explain how these patterns can be combined in collaborative processes and resulting higher-level patterns that emerge. Finally, they develop a framework for the explication and measurement of patterns in collaboration.

Part II, Proof of Value, consists of four chapters. In Chapter 7, "Maintaining Credibility in Group Collaboration: Detection of Deception," Judee Burgoon, Joey George, John Kruse, Kent Marett, and Mark Adkins explore deception in both verbal face-to-face contexts and computer-mediated contexts and their intersection of those two contexts. They review three deception theories and general literature on deception and its detection. They examine deception, media and team collaboration, and illustrate research at the nexus of these constructs by describing one of their experiments and its findings.

In Chapter 8, "Enabling Large Group Collaboration," Joel Helquist, John Kruse, Amit Deokar, and Thomas Meservy provide an overview of the difficulties and benefits associated with large team collaboration. They present the challenges and different methods to accommodate large teams given the current group support systems (GSS) paradigm. They present participant-driven GSS as a means to accommodate large, distributed teams.

In Chapter 9, "Mobile Computing and Collaboration," Joseph Valacich, Clayton Looney, Ryan Wright, and David Wilson present a state-of-the-art review of mobile computing architecture and emphasize the value mobile computing can deliver. They outline and discuss possible future research streams and, finally, explore trends likely to have significant impacts on anytime/anyplace computing in the future.

In Chapter 10, "The Future of Writing Together: Emerging Research in Collaborative Writing Technologies," Mark Keith, Sean Humphreys, Trent Spaulding, and Paul Lowry explain how collaborative writing (CW) has become a common part of many business activities and that understanding the process can create efficiency and other positive returns for large organizations. They discuss the fundamentals of CW, seven common CW activities, and related authoring and document control strategies. They summarize current research in CW, particularly as it relates to thinkLets and CW tools, and suggest future research in team sizes, webpage authoring, and team awareness.

Part III, Proof of Use, consists of two chapters. In Chapter 11, "Collaboration Support Technology: Patterns of Successful Collaboration Support," Gwendolyn Kolfschoten and Jay Nunamaker look back at three decades of GSS research, and elicit patterns and lessons learned on three important questions: (1) What kinds of problems are solved by collaboration support technology? (2) What characteristics of collaboration support technology create value? (3) How can collaboration support technologies be successfully employed in organizations?

In Chapter 12, "GroupSystems in the U.S. Army," James Gantt traces the use and development of GroupSystems across a period of over twenty years. He reviews early successes and failures and draws lessons on how to apply collaborative tools in an organization. Further, he examines argued that not only the CFP's equal access principle invalidated the concept of national contribution to resources, but also that mature fish stocks caught in British waters often began life elsewhere. Some countries, like the Netherlands, regarded the British fair return principle as a dangerous precedent for other Community policies which could even result in a disintegration of the whole Community (Leigh 1983, 90–91; Wise 1988, 23). This hard British negotiating position can also be explained by the re-negotiation of the term of accession[2] and the 1975 referendum, whether or not to remain a member of the EC.[3] Furthermore, Great Britain's reluctant position towards the EU has been a constant factor from the beginning. In the fisheries issue, it was also more concerned than the six original member states about the loss of economic sovereignty.

To keep the negotiations underway the Commission tried to break up the coalition between Ireland and Great Britain with a view to isolating the remaining veto player. First of all it was necessary to find out whether the two veto players had similar or different preferences on the issues being bargained. The most important issue for Great Britain was to have an early decision on the issue agreements with third countries, to empower the EC to defend the interests of its deep sea fishing fleet, in order to secure fish rights in Icelandic and Norwegian waters. The allocation of national quotas for the total allowable catches was a secondary issue for Great Britain (Farnell and Elles 1984, 82). Ireland was relatively indifferent to an external fisheries agreement, because the small Irish fishery industry had no interest in access to coastal zones beyond its own coasts (Wise 1988, 17). Furthermore, its fishing industry was considered to be a source of economical growth in poor and peripheral regions. Besides the demand for exclusive fish limits up to 50 miles, the main concern of Ireland was to obtain structural funding for the modernization of fishing vessels, financial assistance for the growth of the fishing industry, and for the establishment of producer organizations. Ireland threatened not to agree to fishing agreements with third countries as long as there was no agreement on the issues mentioned above (Farnell and Elles 1984, 33; McGinley 1991, 33–35).

In other words, the veto players Great Britain and Ireland had rich fishery grounds in common, but heterogeneous preferences on the fisheries. While for Great Britain agreements with third countries were crucial, Ireland was indifferent to this issue, because its small fishery industry only fished in its own coasts, and structural funding for the modernization of its fishing fleet was of central interest.

The bargaining game between the European Community and Ireland

Figure 6 shows a game tree consisting of different choice nodes linked in sequence representing the bargaining game between the EC and Ireland. It gives the complete sequence of the negotiations between both parties. In this figure, each node has a number of branches leading to other nodes. Here the

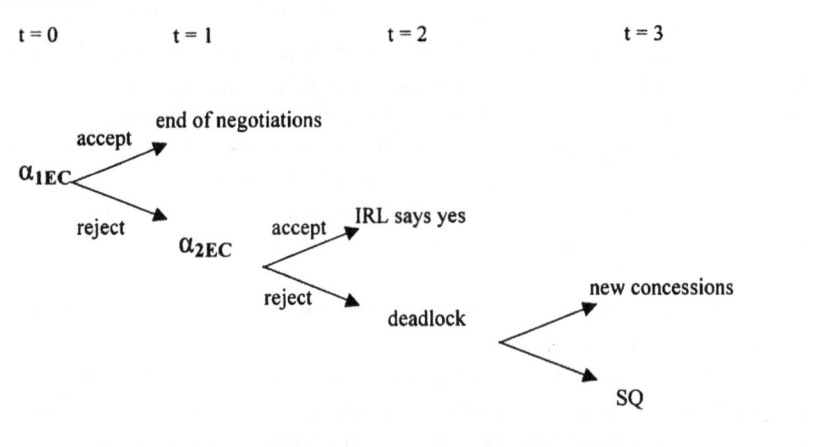

Figure 6: The extensive-form game between the European Community and Ireland

nodes represent decisions and the branches the various actions that can be chosen at each stage. As some nodes are the endpoint of the game, they have no further branches; they are the terminal nodes. The other nodes are called choice nodes, since at that point in the game a player still has a choice.

Two negotiators, Player 1 (the EC), who represents the negotiating position of the other seven member states[4] and of the European Commission, and Player 2 (Ireland), who represents the negotiating position of the Irish government, negotiate an agreement on the access to Irish waters. There are an infinite number of periods (t= 0, 1, 2, 3...), and as long as no agreement is reached, the game continues indefinitely. In the even-numbered periods Player 1 begins the bargaining game by making a proposal (α_{1EC}), which becomes the proposal of the EC at the bargaining table. Player 2 has either the choice between accepting or rejecting the proposal in the first move of the game. Each line emanating from the node represents an offer that Player 1 can put to the veto player. If the proposal is rejected, the game moves on to the next stage with new concessions (side-payments) to buy the consent of the veto player. If this first compromise proposal is accepted, as was the case with Ireland, the negotiations with the first veto player are finished.

During an informal meeting, Player 1 could persuade Player 2 to give up his/her demands for an exclusive 50 mile zone and to accept the first compromise proposal put on the negotiating table by Player 1. Ireland gave up its demand of for a 50 mile exclusive limit, and in compensation gained all the desired concessions or side-payments, for example additional fishing quotas, financial aid for restructuring and expanding the fishing fleet, and the settlement of an Irish box—a fishing area reserved for Irish fishermen– and was thus in a position to accept the proposal put on the negotiating table by the

the role of GroupSystems in preparing for year 2000 problem (Y2K) and the development of the U.S. Army for the war on terrorism in Afghanistan and Iraq.

The fourth and final part consists of one chapter. In Chapter 13, "A Six-Layer Model of Collaboration," for designers of collaboration systems, Robert Briggs, Gwendolyn Kolfschoten, Gert Jan de Vreede, Conan Albrecht, Stephan Lukosch, and Doug Dean use inductive logic to derive six key areas of concern for designers of collaboration systems, and then use deductive logic to argue that these areas address collaboration at differing levels of abstraction and so may be organized into a six-layer model, affording separation of concerns at design time. The layers are: collaboration goals, group products, group activities, group procedures, collaboration tools, and collaborative behaviors. At each layer and between adjacent layers, there are different outcomes of interest, different constructs, theories and metrics, different ways of modeling collaboration, and different design concerns and methods. Their model provides for a separation of concerns at design time, which may reduce cognitive load for designers and may help to improve completeness and consistency of their designs, yielding higher productivity for collaborating groups.

PART I

PROOF OF CONCEPT

CHAPTER 3

ORGANIZING THE THEORETICAL FOUNDATIONS OF COLLABORATION ENGINEERING

GWENDOLYN L. KOLFSCHOTEN AND ROBERT O. BRIGGS

Abstract: Collaboration has become critical to the success of many organizations. In order to design effective and efficient work processes for multi-actor systems where multiple perspectives and stakes must be integrated and reconciled, we need to understand the conditions that give rise to effective and efficient collaboration. In this chapter, we discuss theoretical understandings of various phenomena that manifest during collaboration. We will look at two classes of theories: theory for explaining and predicting, and theory for design and action. We distinguish three levels of abstraction to study collaborative effort: the work practice level, the activity level, and the behavior level. Each level addresses different approaches to explaining the conditions under which joint effort and interaction lead to goal achievement.

Keywords: Collaboration, Collaboration Engineering, Group Work

Collaboration has become a critical success factor for many organizations. A recent survey of 946 organizational decision makers from both industry and government revealed that they regard the ability of their personnel to collaborate as one of the most important drivers of the performance of their organizations (Frost and Sullivan, 2007). Collaboration may take place within or among organizations, locally or globally, in large groups or small teams. At all levels, people in organizations collaborate to create value they cannot create through individual effort (Hansen and Nohria, 2004). They work on problems of sufficient complexity that no single person has the resources or expertise to solve the problem alone.

Because of its significance to organizational performance, collaboration is an important and complex domain of scientific inquiry that seeks to describe and explain many interrelated phenomena in order to make groups more successful. In multi-actor systems, the diverse interests and perspectives of stakeholders must be acknowledged and reconciled as members make joint efforts toward their group goals. Some research focuses on making groups more effective, efficient, and productive. Other research focuses on making group members more cohesive and satisfied. Still other research examines collaboration challenges—for example, free riding, dominance, groupthink, hidden agendas, and so forth (Schwarz, 1994; Nunamaker et al., 1997; Hansen and Nohria, 2004). Early research showed that as group size increased beyond five people, productivity tended to decrease and conflicts tended to increase (Steiner, 1972). Besides group size, a key challenge is caused by the involvement of multiple actors and stakeholders in collaboration. The diversity and interdependence among interests of stakeholders increases the complexity of collaboration (Ackermann et al., 2005; Bragge et al., 2007; Bruijn and Heuvelhof, 2008).

Collaboration support may, under certain conditions, enable groups to accomplish their goals more efficiently and effectively (Fjermestad and Hiltz, 2001; Vreede, Vogel et al., 2003). Collaboration support is offered by facilitators—people who are skilled in designing and leading collaborative sessions and training—and/or by collaboration support technology (Dennis et al., 2001). It can be challenging, however, to implement such support in a way that creates a self-sustaining and growing community of collaborators. Studies on sustained use of collaboration support reveal difficulties such as lack of anchoring in an organization, dependence on a champion, difficulty of transferring skills and knowledge, and the challenge of the business case for collaboration due to the ad hoc nature of its use and benefits (Post, 1993; Briggs et al., 1999; Munkvold and Anson, 2001; Agres et al., 2005).

Improvements to group outcomes of interest, and the adoption and sustained use of collaboration support, could be improved by basing work practices and technologies designs on fundamental scientific understandings of the collaboration-related phenomena of such interventions. Researchers are beginning to find that they can obtain more useful results when they design systems and processes based on sound theories (Briggs, 2004; Briggs et al., 2008), such as theories of motivation and change, and theories of productivity, creativity, and satisfaction. An engineering approach to collaboration would be further advanced by testing designs in the field to see whether obtained results are consistent with the theoretical foundations that gave rise to the designs (Briggs, 2004; Hevner et al., 2004).

In this chapter we focus on organizing the theoretical foundations for collaboration support. Such foundations could provide a useful foundation for an engineering approach. We present an overview of several theories currently in use or under development by collaboration engineering researchers. *Collaboration engineering* is an approach to designing collaborative work practices for high-value recurring tasks and deploying them to practitioners to execute for themselves without ongoing intervention from a collaboration professional or a change champion (Briggs et al., 2003; Vreede and Briggs, 2005). This overview may offer a useful summary of current understandings of collaboration for collaboration engineers to use during the design process, and may be a useful starting place for mapping out a theoretical research agenda for collaboration support.

UNDERSTANDING COLLABORATION

The term *collaboration* comes from the Latin word *collaborare* (Harper, 2001). Collaborare means "to work with," which is derived from *com*, meaning "with" + *labore*, meaning "to work." Thus, collaborative efforts are joint, rather than individual. If collaborative efforts are joint, then they must be directed toward a group goal. A goal is a *desired state or outcome* (Locke and Latham, 1990). Thus, collaboration involves multiple individuals who combine their efforts to achieve mutually desired outcomes. Therefore, we define *collaboration* as a joint effort toward a group goal (Vreede and Briggs, 2005).

Three Layers of Collaborative Effort

It may be useful to think of collaborative efforts as consisting of three different layers of abstraction: a work practice level, an activity level, and a behavior level (Niederman et al., 2008).

Work Practice Level

A *work practice* is a repeatable process for accomplishing a specific task. At the work practice level we think of the design of a collaborative effort in terms of its interim and ultimate goals.

We ask questions like, "What goals does a group seek to attain? What deliverables must a group create to attain those goals? What value will be derived by which stakeholders through the creation of those deliverables?" At this level, we think of the work practice in terms of *why* a group has formed to make an effort. At the work practice level, we think about what effect a new work practice might have on its practitioners and on the organization after its deployment. We also focus on measures of merit that could indicate the degree to which the practitioners of an engineered work practice attain the goals they seek. Phenomena of interest at this layer pertain to the degree to which outcomes and deliverables of the work practice realize the outcomes specified in the group's goals—for example, creativity and effectiveness of solutions, successes of innovation.

Activity Level

At the activity level we focus on *what* a group must do to create its deliverables—such as understand the problem, generate and evaluate alternatives, make choices, make plans, take action, and review outcomes. We ask questions like, "What are the interim goals and deliverables that must be addressed in order to achieve the overall group goal? What sequence of actions must group members take, under what constraints must they act, and what tools will they need to support their actions in order to create each interim deliverable and the final deliverable?" In their activity designs, collaboration engineers write specific instructions to guide a group in activities that are instrumental to goal achievement.

At the activity level, we also think about *how* a group will conduct its activities. Collaboration engineering researchers have identified six general patterns of collaboration that emerge from group activities—generate, reduce, clarify, organize, evaluate, and build consensus (Kolfschoten et al., 2006; Vreede et al., 2006). Collaboration engineers and facilitators often draw upon collections of collaboration techniques or design patterns that encapsulate generally useful activities that produce known variations of the six patterns of collaboration. These packaged activities are named, and specified in terms of actions, roles, constraints, and tools. Osborn's brainstorming technique would be a well-known example. Users of that technique must add ideas to a shared list under four constraints: (1) add as many ideas as you can; (2) don't filter out bad ideas; (3) don't criticize the ideas of others; and (4) build on one another's ideas (Osborn, 1953). Among the outcomes of interest at the activity level would be goal concepts such as goal congruence, shared understanding of concepts and relationships, creativity, communication, deliberation, information access, distraction, choice, participation, preference, consensus, learning, time-on-task, or quality of deliverables. We consider the social patterns that emerge in the group as activities progress.

Behavioral Level

On the behavioral level we consider phenomena that manifest in the minds and actions of individual group members—how they act in a collaborative setting, and how they respond to the stimuli of the group environment to the guidance, structures, tools, and facilitator interventions that comprise an activity, and to the ideas, proposals, and actions of other group members. At this level we would consider, for example, the satisfaction of individual stakeholders with the deliverables and with the work practices that produced them. Another key factor is the degree to which stakeholders find deliverables acceptable, and the degree to which they are willing to fulfill the commitments they made during the work practice. At this level we would also address willingness of group members to commit to a group effort and to commit to a proposed course of action, or willingness to change

Figure 3.1   **An Organizing Structure for Theories Relevant to the Design of Collaborative Work Practices**

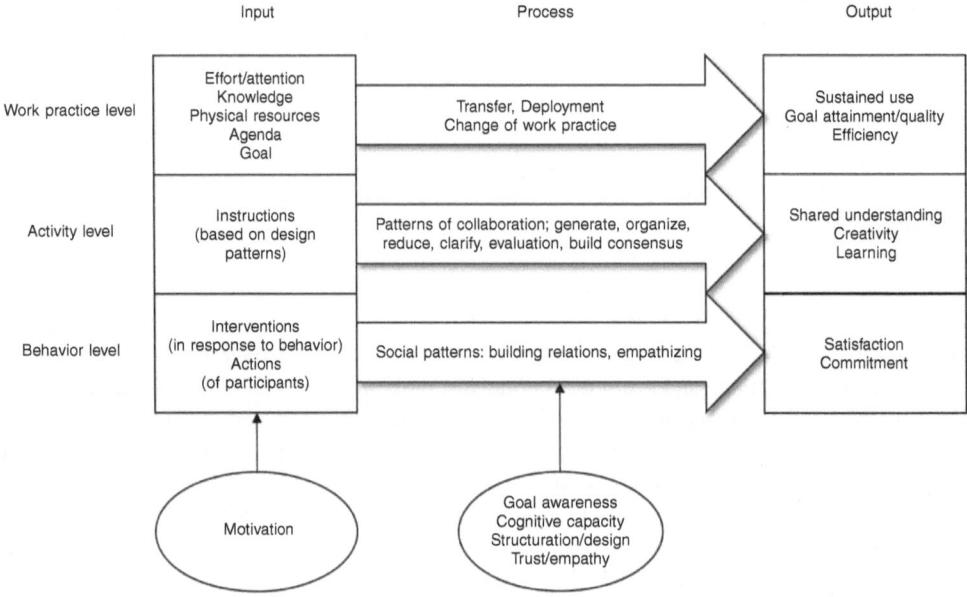

from one work practice to another. Likewise, trust and empathy are states of mind that manifest in individuals, and so pertain to this level.

The behavioral level also encompasses some phenomena that, at first glance, might appear to be group-level phenomena, like groupthink, relationship building and cohesion, and consensus. Each of these phenomena, however, is predicated on individual perceptions. For instance, groupthink manifests when individuals decide to go along with a flawed proposal for social or political reasons, while relationship building manifests when people perceive value in associating with others who reciprocate the perception. Cohesion is based on attitudes of individual group members toward other members. When groups are engaged in long-term collaborative relations and when stakes are high, the behavioral level becomes increasingly relevant, as mutual and personal interests are affected. In this case it becomes increasingly important to ensure that both the activities and the tasks included in the work practice are chosen in a way that accommodates all stakes involved. This will guide behavior to be constructive and collaborative.

Collaborative Effort: Input, Process, Output, and Constraints

Figure 3.1 illustrates how the collaboration constructs mentioned above may be organized in terms of the three levels of abstraction for collaborative effort, and in terms of inputs, processes, outputs, and constraints on collaborative effort. In this model, we create an overview of the phenomena of interest on each level and in each "phase" in the model. For instance, the process of interest on a work practice level is deployment of that work practice, while on a behavioral level, processes of interest are, for instance, groupthink or building relationships. Besides the input, process, and output there are two sources of general constraints on collaboration that emerge across all three levels:

motivation and commitment of resources, which serves as a constraint on allocating input to the process, and structuration, cognitive limitations, and goal awareness, which serve as constraints for successful transformation of input to output (Kolfschoten et al., 2010).

Collaboration Engineering

Collaboration engineering (CE) is an approach to designing collaborative work practices for high-value recurring tasks, and deploying those as process prescriptions for practitioners to execute for themselves without ongoing support from professional facilitators (Briggs et al., 2003; Vreede and Briggs, 2005). In collaboration engineering, engineers who are expert at the collaboration process design collaborative work practices and supporting tools or technologies, and transfer these to practitioners, domain experts in the organization, for use to support a recurring collaborative work practice. CE is an engineering discipline; it aims to design collaborative work practices and supporting capabilities (e.g., paper and pencil; software) and methods to increase the quality of collaboration as a process, and goal attainment as an outcome of that process.

Engineering collaborative work practices implies that such work practices can be prescribed and that, to some extent, we can predict the effects of interventions to initiate and support these work practices. The basis for this assertion is the rich body of best practices and known effect of support for collaborative activities. On a work practice level, for instance, key approaches to risk management (Vreede and Briggs, 2005), requirements analysis (Boehm et al., 2001), usability testing (Fruhling and Vreede, 2005), and strategy development (Bragge et al., 2007) are available. Further, there are several decades of experience with group support systems (Nunamaker et al., 1997; Vreede, Vogel et al., 2003). Group support systems (GSS) are suites of software tools for focusing and structuring group deliberation while reducing the cognitive costs of communication and information access among teams making a joint cognitive effort toward a goal (Davison and Briggs, 2000). The use of group support systems has been empirically evaluated to be effective and efficient to support work practices (Fjermestad and Hiltz, 2001). On an activity level, there are various methods and techniques to support collaborative activities such as brainstorming (Gallupe and Cooper, 1993; Santanen and Vreede, 2004), voting (Cheng and Deek, 2007), and filtering (Helquist et al., 2006). Collaborative activities can be captured as design patterns called thinkLets to ensure that all information to recreate the intended pattern of collaboration is captured (Kolfschoten et al., 2006; Vreede et al., 2006). When less rigorously documented techniques are compared empirically, this, unfortunately, often leads to conflicting results (Santanen, 2005; Henninger et al., 2006). Finally, at a behavioral level we also find best practices and their empirical evaluation in literature–for instance, the effect of behavioral rules to guard anonymity (Jessup et al., 1990), or to invoke social comparison (Shepherd et al., 1996). Further, Schwarz (1994) offers ground rules to support effective collaborative behavior.

In order for collaboration engineers to deliberately design collaborative work practices that facilitators or practitioners can use to produce repeatable effects on groups, rigorous documentation of collaborative activities and empirical testing of the effect of these activities is required. Therefore, theoretical foundations for collaboration engineering should focus on prediction and explanation of cause and effect and on the prescription of methods and interventions to create these effects under specific circumstances as guided by those theories.

THEORIES IN THE COLLABORATION ENGINEERING LITERATURE

In this section we discuss a number of theories that have been used or advanced to support collaboration engineering research.

Methodology/Procedures

Although collaboration engineering is a relatively new discipline, more than 100 peer-reviewed scholarly works have been published in that domain. We drew a number of the theories discussed here from that body of work. More than 400 papers have been published in the GSS literature, the domain from which collaboration engineering emerged. Several of the commonly used theories from the GSS literature also have direct relevance to collaboration engineering. Those theories have been added to the collection considered here. Having identified a collection of theories that are either now used in, or are relevant to, collaboration engineering, we extracted a list of the phenomena each theory purports to explain. We then organized those constructs into the organizing structure presented in Figure 3.1.

Gregor (2006) describes five types of theories: (1) theory for analyzing, (2) theory for explaining, (3) theory for predicting, (4) theory for explaining and predicting, and (5) theory for design and action. All design efforts presuppose principles of cause-and-effect, for design efforts always intend to produce improvements in important outcomes of interest. Theories for analyzing and predicting are less relevant to design efforts for collaborative work practices as they do not suggest answers to the "how to" questions for desired improvements. Theories for explaining do address the "how" question, but only in a descriptive sense, not in a prescriptive sense, and therefore are also less useful in the design of collaboration support as aimed in collaboration engineering. We will focus, then, on theory for explaining and predicting (category 4) and theory for design and action (category 5), explaining these theory types and their use in collaboration engineering in more detail.

Theories for Explaining and Predicting

Theories for explaining and predicting are theories that describe testable propositions and causal explanations. Such theories can help collaboration engineers understand why certain activities and interventions support collaboration and improve collaborative outcomes, while others do not. Collaboration engineering researchers have contributed theories in this category for each of the three levels. The next sections offer a brief overview of each of these theories.

Work Practice Level

On the work practice level, collaboration engineering uses theories to explain why some collaborative work practices and supporting technologies are successful and others are not. Theories to address the causes of adoption, sustained use, and successful transition of technology are the Value Frequency Model (Briggs, 2006), the Technology Transition Model (Briggs et al., 1999), and the Technology Acceptance Model (Davis, 1993). Each of these theories aims to explain why people change their behavior, their work practice, or their use of technology. A key reason for a change in behavior is the value or utility assessment of the net value of the change. When the new work practice causes additional effort, through the use or learning of new tools, it is less likely to be accepted than when it causes efficiency. A key challenge is the cost of transition. When a change requires an initial investment, in training or funds, the long-run benefits need to be in balance with this investment. When changing collaborative work practices, or when changing general work practices into collaborative work practices, part of the outcome for the individual is by definition uncertain, as it depends on the effort and input of others. Therefore, transition of collaborative technology and process support is generally challenging and requires the commitment of many.

Another key outcome to explain at this level is productivity, effectiveness, and efficiency of the work practice as a whole. For this purpose, Goal Setting Theory (Locke and Latham, 1990) and Focus Theory (Briggs, 1994) offer the basis for explanation and prediction. A key mechanism in the causality of these theories is commitment of resources, which, since effort is a key resource in collaboration, is highly related to motivation theories.

The relation between commitment and behavioral intention has been confirmed by Malhotra and Galletta (2005). We can explain the commitment of resources to a group goal using the Instrumentality Theory of Briggs et al. (2005). For participants to commit, and spend resources toward a goal, they should expect some use of that goal—it should be valuable to them and offer them some individual utility. Expected value of participation refers to expectations of the usefulness of the result for the individual and the expected resource expense (time, effort, etc.) of participation. Meyer and Allen (1991) found that there are three components of commitment: (1) affective or emotional commitment, (2) continuance commitment, a cost assessment, and (3) normative commitment, a felt obligation to continue. Emotional commitment in collaboration can occur when the group has some bond, or when there are emotions attached to achieving the group goal. Continuance commitment resembles the utility assessment also found in Expected Utility Theory (Schoemaker, 1982), which can be described as a cost-benefit analysis of the utility of pursuing the group goal for the individual. Last, continuance commitment resembles the concept of groupthink described by Janis (1972), a group pressure to keep pursuing the goal.

The idea of sunk costs also comes to mind here—the economic concept that once resources are spent (but while there is not yet a result), the pressure to continue is larger. Bishop et al. (2005) showed that perceived support from a team leads to increased commitment to this team. In such a case, the individual determines whether he expects the other group members to have the skills, knowledge, and time required, and whether they are willing to spend those resources on the group goal; it is an individual judgment of a group construct (Jung and Sosik, 2003). When both the individual and the team are willing to expend effort, this will positively influence the effort of team members and thus create a positive feedback cycle. Declaring effort is often done in combination with declaring goals.

In Goal Setting Theory, productivity is caused by goal setting. A clear goal allows people to make an effort; a challenging goal requires more effort. Another key condition for effort is goal congruence. When people have stakes in different outcomes of a collaborative task, that is, different goals, they might work against each other or disengage in the collaborative effort. Finally, a key condition for productivity is a lack of distraction. When people work toward a goal, we need to enable three key activities: communication between the participants, access to information from various sources, and deliberation and structuration of cognitive effort. These are discussed further in the next section.

Activity Level

At the activity level, collaboration engineering uses theories to explain the patterns of collaboration that emerge based on specific instructions to invoke collaborative activities and the outcomes of these activities. In collaboration engineering, six patterns of collaboration are distinguished. Some theories exist for generation, such as the Cognitive Network Model, which explains and predicts creativity (Santanen et al., 2004). For reduction, clarification, and organizing, less theoretical understanding is available, but a key source of understanding in this area should be sought in theories on cognitive load and complexity. For evaluation and consensus building, theories on preference and choice are important, such as Bounded Rationality Theory (Jones, 1999), Social Choice Theory (Fishburn, 1973), and Instrumentality Theory (Graen, 1969; Briggs et al., 2005).

A key mechanism in the causality of these theories is Cognitive Load Theory. Cognitive load can be defined as the *cognitive effort made by a person to understand and perform a task* (Sweller et al., 1998). Cognitive Load Theory is based on the assumption that our short-term or working memory is limited to seven plus-or-minus two information elements (Miller, 1956). This is the information that we can process in a given moment. Besides working memory we have a long-term memory in which information is stored, in so-called schemata (Bjork-Ligon and Bjork, 1996). The long-term memory is not limited in size. To learn we need to consciously combine individual elements of information to build schemata. Schemata in long-term memory are repositories of information that are interlinked. Schemata can be handled by our working memory as an individual component (this is also called chunking). A schema is not just a storage frame; information in the schema is automatically accessed. This means that it is retrieved unconsciously. Therefore, the larger the schemata and the better they are automated, the more information we can process at the same time, and the faster we can learn to find solutions or answers to problems. Cognitive Load Theory explains how we use our cognitive capacity to construct schemata. There are three types of cognitive load (Sweller et al., 1998; Kirschner, 2002; Paas et al., 2003):

- Intrinsic cognitive load is the cognitive load that is inherent to the task.
- Extraneous cognitive load is the cognitive load caused by the presentation and transfer method of the information.
- Germane cognitive load is the cognitive load instrumental to or evoked by processes in which the schemata in the long-term memory are constructed and automated.

As cognitive capacity is a key constraint for the success of collaborative activities, understanding how to design activities that make optimal use of this resource will improve collaboration process design. Further, a key objective in collaborative activities is learning or creating knowledge. For this reason learning and inquiry theories also provide a source for understanding collaborative activities.

Behavioral Level

On the behavioral level, we study theories to explain and predict individual and social phenomena and the effect of single interventions on behavior in collaborative settings. Relevant theories are those that explain team development (Tuckman, 1965; Janz et al., 1997), satisfaction (Briggs et al., 2008), and theories related to the effects of the functionalities afforded in the workspace, such as Media Synchronicity Theory (Dennis et al., 2008).

Satisfaction can be a judgment or an emotion. As a judgment it is similar to judgments of success; as an emotion it can differ. Emotional satisfaction is a response to a perceived shift in yield with respect to personal goals (Briggs et al., 2008). Such a yield is the result of a shift in utility with respect to goal attainment and/or a shift in likelihood of goal attainment. In addition to the group goal, many personal goals can constitute the reason for a participant to contribute in a collaboration process. Yield Shift Theory (YST) defines the satisfaction response as a balanced affective arousal (emotion) with respect to the attainment of individual goals (Briggs et al., 2008). YST posits unconscious cognitive mechanisms that automatically ascribe utility to the attainment of a goal and automatically assess the likelihood that a goal will be obtained. YST assumes a multiplicative relationship between likelihood and utility assessments giving rise to a sense of yield with respect to an active goal. The theory posits that when an individual perceives an overall shift in the yield of his or her set of active goals, a subconscious mechanism initiates an emotional response proportional to, and in the direction of, those shifts. Thus, if the individual perceives a positive shift in utility or likelihood, a positive emotion manifests; if the individual perceives a negative shift in utility, a negative emotion manifests. If people perceive that the results of a group effort produced positive shifts in yield for their sets of active goals, then positive satisfaction responses would manifest. If they perceive negative overall shifts in the yield of their active goal sets, then dissatisfaction would manifest.

The functionalities afforded to participants in a (virtual) collaboration process, and the team composition, when used appropriately, can improve communication and shared understanding. Several theories offer explanations on how certain types of functionalities and team composition affect the interaction among participants and how this in turn affects outcomes of a collaboration process. For instance, Dennis et al. (2008) describe in their Media Synchronicity Theory how media capabilities, when they fit the communication process, improve communication performance (shared understanding) and therewith task performance. In line with this, Cai and Kock (2009) explored the choice between tools with different levels of media richness based on social punishment from a Game Theory perspective. Similarly, Cooper and Haines (2008) describe how features of the collaborative workspace affect "insight awareness," the extent to which participants understand the reasons behind group member behaviors, and argue that insight awareness improves decision quality. Kock (2008) adds to this theoretical lens with insights on how certain tools for virtual collaboration affect compensatory adaptation, the way to resolve the lack of face-to-face feedback such as body language. Finally, Kudaravalli and Faraj (2008) explain in their theory how the diversity of the team and the type of dialogue members engage in affects the effectiveness of their collaboration.

Theories for Design and Action

Theories for design and action are prescriptive theories on how to perform or create certain outcomes (Gregor, 2006). Design theories are created in the context of design science (Hevner et al., 2004) and the like. Design theories can help collaboration engineers translate theory to practice and instantiate the theoretical understanding in practical interventions, instructions, and process prescriptions to support groups in achieving their goals. Collaboration engineering has design theories on each of the three levels, as we discuss below.

Work Practice Level

On a work practice level, the collaboration engineering design approach (Kolfschoten and Vreede, 2009) offers a prescription to design collaborative work practices (in which all three levels of design are involved). The collaboration engineering design approach assumes the use of design patterns—named, codified techniques to support group work. In this way it is different from a general problem-solving or design cycle. Instead of exploring or designing possible solutions, this approach offers guidelines and directions for choosing among existing methods. When choosing, collaboration engineers need to consider four dimensions: the goal and task, the stakeholders and their interests, the resources available, and the abilities of the facilitator or practitioner who will support the collaborative effort. Another critical step in supporting collaborative effort is identification of work practices that would benefit from a collaboration engineering approach (Dean et al., 2006; Briggs et al., 2008). Finally, collaboration engineering offers methods to support the transfer of collaborative work practices to practitioners and facilitators (Kolfschoten et al., 2011). This transfer method consists of a documentation framework for the transfer of a collaboration process prescription and a training method to help practitioners in understanding and experiencing the challenges of collaboration process support.

Activity Level

On an activity level we document prescriptions of activities as design patterns called thinkLets. Design patterns are descriptions of reusable best practices to solve recurring problems (Alexander, 1979; Gamma et al., 1995), which were first described in architecture and were further developed when adopted in software engineering. ThinkLets are named, scripted, reusable, and transferable collaborative activities that give rise to specific known variations of the general patterns of collaboration among people working together toward a goal (Briggs et al., 2003; Kolfschoten et al., 2006; Vreede et al., 2006).

ThinkLets are rich documentations of best practices, but their core is a very rigorous and precise description of the rules used to instruct the group in the collaborative activity. These rules describe the *actions* participants must take, the *constraints* under which they must act, and the *capabilities* they will require to execute the actions (Kolfschoten et al., 2006; Vreede et al., 2006). Actions are things participants must do individually, such as add, edit, move, delete, judge, or associate concepts. Capabilities are the means necessary to contribute, record, read, and manipulate concepts. A constraint is a limitation or guideline on how an action is to be performed (Kolfschoten et al., 2006; Vreede et al., 2006; Kolfschoten et al., 2010).

A key mechanism in most collaborative activities is communication. In Communication Theory, many different models are proposed. Craig (1999) argues that the transmission model is a useful lens to analyze communication as an intentional act to achieve some anticipated outcome, and to study distortion and misunderstanding. Communication can be described as a transmission system. The message is transmitted by a sender, who can encode the message and send it with use of a channel/vehicle to a receiver, who can decode the message. From this decoding effort, a meaning can be distilled and in response an action can be performed. A response can be either feedback—that is, the transmission of a return message—a communication effect, or any other action in response to the message (Krone et al., 1987) that will constitute a pattern of collaboration and a specific result. In such a generic system there is no predictability of the action as an effect of the message or its content. To increase predictability, conditions such as ability, absence of noise, trust, and goal congruence should be met.

Behavioral Level

No formal approach exists yet to prescribe interventions in the behavior layer. Such prescriptions are currently offered as guidelines, and some collections of these guidelines have been documented for the use of group support systems, which can be applied to most collaborative work practices (Nunamaker et al., 1997; Vreede and Bruijn, 1999; Vreede, Vogel et al., 2003). Another source of these guidelines are conflict resolution methods (Robey et al., 1993; Briggs et al., 2005). Interventions on a behavioral level are often highly sensitive and deal with power, status, and emotions. To carry out interventions at this level, it is critical that the facilitator or practitioner knows what he/she is doing. Therefore, in collaboration engineering we aim to avoid conflict and behavioral problems as much as possible by focusing on content and task aspects, and less on roles, behaviors, and relations within the group. However, these cannot simply be disregarded. Therefore some basic training and guidelines are required.

CONCLUSIONS AND RESEARCH AGENDA

In this chapter we offer an input-process-output model with three levels of collaboration as an organizing structure for the theoretical foundations of collaboration engineering. We then use that structure as a basis for discussing the relationships among the theoretical models being used in the collaboration engineering literature. We discussed important theoretical understandings at three levels of abstraction: the work practice level, the activity level, and the behavioral level. For each of these levels we considered theories for explaining and predicting, and theories for design and action.

While a rich theoretical foundation is coalescing around collaboration, this research suggests that there are areas of inquiry for which theoretical foundations have not yet been derived. First of all, Wikipedia contains the following entry under "General Theory of Collaboration," unchanged since 2006:

> Currently there exists no consolidated, general theory of collaboration (GTC). Such a theory could provide a common language and framework for those seeking to better understand and expand the collaborative aspects of any given field of human endeavor. Additionally, a GTC would provide a body of knowledge on which those developing collaborative software and other design-based enterprises might draw. (Wikipedia, 2009)

While there is theory about many phenomena in collaboration, it seems that the general principles underlying collaboration and successful group work are not yet fully understood.

Collaboration support research (e.g., facilitation, collaboration technology) has, to date, focused mainly on the work practice level. Many studies have discussed the effect of group support systems and facilitation on productivity, efficiency, and effectiveness (McLeod, 1992; Fjermestad and Hiltz, 1999; Dennis and Wixom, 2001; Fjermestad and Hiltz, 2001; Kwok et al., 2003; Vreede, Vogel et al., 2003). And many have studied the transition of collaborative work practices and collaboration support tools (Post, 1993; Reinig et al., 1995; Agres et al., 2005; Briggs, 2006). It will also be important and useful to establish the theoretical foundations for collaboration support at the activity level and the behavioral level. Ideation and creativity have been studied quite extensively. Theoretical understandings of reducing, clarifying, organizing, and evaluating ideas, and for building consensus, will be required to support theory-driven design of complete work practices.

Researchers have recently begun to explore issues of cognitive load in the collaboration domain (Dillenbourg and Bétrancourt, 2006; Henninger et al., 2006). This research may yield useful insights in a variety of aspects of collaboration. It is expected that the cognitive load of a task is one of the key predictors of cognitive productivity. Research has focused mainly on the effect of technology support and process guidance. However, we expect that small changes in the configuration of the workspace can have significant impact on the cognitive load of a collaborative task, and therefore, on the productivity of the group performing the task. It may be, for example, that the cognitive load is the most cogent phenomenon of interest when studying to reduce and organize patterns of collaboration.

Several researchers are now suggesting that a focus on precisely described interventions and their effects (activity level) is required to understand the conflicting results that are sometimes found in empirical studies (Santanen, 2005; Henninger et al., 2006). On the behavior level, a lot of work has been done in psychology and management literature. However, researchers in these domains tend to produce analytical and descriptive studies, and less understanding is available about interventions to guide behavior. For collaboration engineering to move to the next level we must drill down into the details and the distinct effects of activities and interventions on a cognitive level.

REFERENCES

Ackermann, F.; Franco, L.A.; Gallupe, B.; and Parent, M. 2005. GSS for multi-organizational collaboration: Reflections on process and content. *Group Decision and Negotiation,* 14, 4, 307–331.

Agres, A.; Vreede, G.J. de; and Briggs, R.O. 2005. A tale of two cities: Case studies of GSS transition in two organizations. *Group Decision and Negotiation,* 14, 4, 256–266.

Alexander, C. 1979. *The Timeless Way of Building.* New York: Oxford University Press.

Bishop, J.W.; Scott, K.D.; Goldsby, M.G.; and Cropanzano, R.A. 2005. Construct validity study of commitment and perceived support variables: A multifoci approach across different team environments. *Group and Organization Management,* 30, 2, 153–180.

Bjork- Ligon, E., and Bjork, R.A. (eds.). 1996. *Memory Handbook of Perception and Cognition.* San Diego: Academic Press.

Boehm, B.; Gruenbacher, P.; and Briggs, R.O. 2001. Developing groupware for requirements negotiation: Lessons learned. *IEEE Software,* 18, 3, 301–314.

Bragge, J.; Merisalo-Rantanen, H.; Nurmi, A.; and Tanner, L. 2007. A repeatable E-collaboration process based on thinkLets for multi-organizational strategy development. *Group Decision and Negotiation,* 16, 2, 363–379.

Briggs, R.O. 1994. *The Focus Theory of Team Productivity and its application to development and testing of electronic group support systems.* PhD diss. University of Arizona, Tucson.

———. 2004. On theory-driven design of collaboration technology and process. In G.J. de Vreede et al. (eds.), *CRIWG 2004.* Berlin: Springer-Verlag.

———. 2006. The value frequency model: Towards a theoretical understanding of organizational change. In S. Seifert and C. Weinhardt (eds.), *Proceedings of the International Conference on Group Decision and Negotiation,* 36–41. Karlsruhe, Germany: Universtatsverlag Karlsruhe.

Briggs, R.O.; Adkins, M.; Mittleman, D.D.; Kruse, J.; Miller, S.; and Nunamaker, J.F. Jr. 1999. A technology transition model derived from qualitative field investigation of GSS use aboard the U.S.S. *Coronado. Journal of Management Information Systems,* 15, 3, 151–196.

Briggs, R.O.; Davis, A.J.; and Murphy, J.D. 2008. An interview protocol for discovering and assessing collaboration engineering opportunities. In *Proceedings of the 41st Hawaii International Conference on System Science,* Waikoloa, Hawaii, January 7–10.

Briggs, R.O.; Kolfschoten, G.L.; and de Vreede, G.J. 2005. Toward a theoretical model of consensus building. In N. C. Romano Jr. (ed.), *Proceedings of the Eleventh Americas Conference on Information Systems,* 101–110. Omaha, NE: Association for Information Systems.

Briggs, R.O.; Reinig, B.A.; and de Vreede, G.J. 2008. The yield shift theory of satisfaction and its application to the IS/IT domain. *Journal of the Association for Information Systems,* 9, 5, 267–293.

Briggs, R.O.; Vreede, G.J. de; and Nunamaker, J.F. Jr. 2003. Collaboration engineering with thinkLets to pursue sustained success with group support systems. *Journal of Management Information Systems,* 19, 4, 31–63.

Bruijn, J.A. de, and ten Heuvelhof, E.F. 2008. *Management in Networks: On Multi-Actor Decision Making.* London: Routledge.

Cai, G., and Kock, N. 2009. An evolutionary game theoretic perspective on e-collaboration: The collaboration effort and media relativeness. *European Journal of Operational Research,* 194, 3, 821–833.

Cheng, K.E., and Deek, F.P. 2007. A framework for studying voting in group support systems. In *Proceedings of the 40th Hawaii International Conference on System Sciences,* Waikoloa, Hawaii, January 3–6.

Cooper, R.B., and Haines, R. 2008. The influence of workspace awareness on group intellective decision effectiveness. *European Journal of Information Systems,* 17, 6, 631–648.

Craig, R.T. 1999. Communication theory as a field. *Communication Theory,* 9, 2, 119–161.

Davis, F.D. 1993. User acceptance of information technology: System characteristics, user perceptions and behavioural impacts. *International Journal of Man-Machine Studies,* 38, 3, 475–487.

Davison, R.M., and Briggs, R.O. 2000. GSS for presentation support: Supercharging the audience through simultaneous discussions during presentations. *Communications of the ACM,* 43, 9, 91–97.

Dean, D.L.; Deokar, A.; and Ter Bush, R. 2006. Making the collaboration engineering investment decision. In *Proceedings of the 39th Hawaii International Conference on System Sciences,* Kauai, Hawaii, January 4–7.

Dennis, A.R.; Fuller, R.M.; and Valacich, J.S. 2008. Media, tasks, and communication processes: A theory of media synchronicity. *Management Information Systems Quarterly*, 32, 3, 575–600.

Dennis, A.R., and Wixom, B.H. 2001. Investigating the moderators of the group support systems use with meta-analysis. *Journal of Management Information Systems*, 18, 3, 235–257.

Dennis, A.R.; Wixom, B.H.; and Vandenberg, R.J. 2001. Understanding fit and appropriation effects in group support systems via meta-analysis. *Management Information Systems Quarterly*, 25, 2, 167–183.

Dillenbourg, P., and Bétrancourt, M. 2006. Collaboration load. In J. Elen and R.E. Clark (eds.), *Handling Complexity in Learning Environments: Research and Theory*, 142–163. Amsterdam, Netherlands: Pergamon.

Fishburn, P.C. 1973. *The Theory of Social Choice*. Princeton, NJ: Princeton University Press.

Fjermestad, J., and Hiltz, S.R. 1999. An assessment of group support systems experimental research: Methodology and results. *Journal of Management Information Systems*, 15, 3, 7–149.

———. 2001. A descriptive evaluation of group support systems case and field studies. *Journal of Management Information Systems*, 17, 3, 115–159.

Frost and Sullivan. 2007. Meetings around the world: The impact of collaboration on business performance. *Frost & Sullivan White Papers*, 1–19.

Fruhling, A., and Vreede, G.J. de. 2005. Collaborative usability testing to facilitate stakeholder involvement. In S. Biffl; A. Aurum; B. Boehm; H. Erdogmus; and P. Grünbacher (eds.), *Value Based Software Engineering*, 201–223. Berlin, Germany: Springer-Verlag.

Gallupe, R.B., and Cooper, W.H. 1993. Brainstorming electronically. *Sloan Management Review*, 35, 1, 27–36.

Gamma, E.; Helm, R.; Johnson, R.; and Vlissides, J. 1995. *Elements of Reusable Object-Oriented Software*. Reading, MA: Addison-Wesley.

Graen, G. 1969. Instrumentality theory of work motivation. *Journal of Applied Psychology*, 53, 2, 1–25.

Gregor, S. 2006. The nature of theory in information systems. *Management Information Systems Quarterly*, 30, 3, 611–642.

Hansen, M.T., and Nohria, N. 2004. How to build collaborative advantage. MIT *Sloan Management Review*, 46, 1, 22–30.

Harper, D. 2001. Online etymology dictionary. Available at http://www.etymonline.com/ (accessed April 27, 2009).

Helquist, J.H.; Kruse, J.; and Adkins, M. 2006. Group support systems for very large groups: A peer review process to filter brainstorming input. In N.C. Romano Jr. (ed.), *Proceedings of the Twelfth Americas Conference on Information Systems*, 116–120. Atlanta, GA: Association for Information Systems.

Henninger, W.G.; Dennis, A.R.; and Hilmer, K. 2006. Individual cognition and dual-task interference in group support systems. *Information Systems Research*, 17, 4, 415–424.

Hevner, A.; March, S.; Park, J.; and Ram, S. 2004. Design science research in information systems. *Management Information Systems Quarterly*, 28, 1, 75–105.

Janis, I.L. 1972. *Victims of Groupthink: A Psychological Study of Foreign-Policy Decisions and Fiascoes*. Boston: Houghton Mifflin.

Janz, B.D.; Wetherbe, J.C.; Davis, G.B.; and Noe, R.A. 1997. Reengineering the systems development process: The link between autonomous teams and business process outcomes. *Journal of Management Information Systems*, 14, 1, 41–68.

Jessup, L.M.; Connolly, T.; and Galegher, J. 1990. The effects of anonymity on GDSS group process with an idea-generating task. *Management Information Systems Quarterly*, 14, 3, 313–321.

Jones, B.D. 1999. Bounded rationality. *Annual Review Political Science*, 2, 1, 297–321.

Jung, D.I., and Sosik, J.J. Group potency. 2003. *Group and Organization Management*, 28, 3, 366–391.

Kirschner, P.A. 2002. Cognitive load theory: Implications of cognitive load theory on the design of learning. *Learning and Instruction*, 12, 1, 1–10.

Kock, N. 2008. Designing e-collaboration technologies to facilitate compensatory adaptation. *Information Systems Management*, 25, 1, 14–19.

Kolfschoten, G.L.; Briggs, R.O.; Vreede, G.J. de; Jacobs, P.H.M.; and Appelman, J.H. 2006. Conceptual foundation of the thinkLet concept for collaboration engineering. *International Journal of Human Computer Science*, 64, 7, 611–621.

Kolfschoten, G.L., and Vreede, G.J. de. 2009. A design approach for collaboration processes: A multi-method design science study in collaboration engineering. *Journal of Management Information Systems*, 26, 1, 225–256.

Kolfschoten, G.L.; Vreede, G.J. de; Briggs, R.O.; and Sol, H.G. 2010. Collaboration "'engineerability.'" *Group Decision and Negotiation*, 19, 3, 301–321.

Kolfschoten, G.L.; Vreede, G.J. de; and Pietron, L. 2011. A training approach for the transition of repeatable collaboration processes to practitioners. *Group Decision and Negotiation*, 20, 3, 347–371.

Krone, K.J.; Jablin, F.M.; and Putnam, L.L. 1987. Communication theory and organizational communication: Multiple perspectives. In F.M. Jablin; L.L. Putnam; K.H. Roberts; and L.W. Porter (eds.), *Handbook of Organizational Communication: An Interdisciplinary Perspective*, 18–40. Newbury Park, CA: Sage.

Kudaravalli, S., and Faraj, S. 2008. The structure of collaboration in electronic networks. *Journal of the Association for Information Systems*, 9, 10/11, 706–726.

Kwok, R.C.; Ma, J.; and Vogel, D.R. 2003. Effects of group support systems and content facilitation on knowledge acquisition. *Journal of Management Information Systems*, 19, 3, 185–229.

Locke, E.A., and Latham, G.P. 1990. *A Theory of Goal Setting and Task Performance*. Englewood Cliffs, NJ: Prentice Hall.

Malhotra, Y., and Galletta, D.A. 2005. Multidimensional commitment model of volitional systems adoption and usage behavior. *Journal of Management Information Systems*, 22, 1, 117–151.

McLeod, P.L. 1992. An assessment of the experimental literature on electronic support of group work: Results of a meta-analysis. *Human-Computer Interaction*, 7, 3, 257–280.

Meyer, J.P., and Allen, N.J. 1991. A three-component conceptualization of organizational commitment: Some methodological considerations. *Human Resource Management Review*, 1, 1, 61–98.

Miller, G.A. 1956. The magical number seven plus or minus two: Some limits on our capacity for processing information. *Psychological Review*, 101, 2, 343–352.

Munkvold, B.E., and Anson, R. 2001. Organizational adoption and diffusion of electronic meeting systems: A case study. In C. Ellis and I. Zigurs (eds.), *Proceedings of the 2001 International ACM SIGGROUP Conference on Supporting Group Work*, 279–287. New York: ACM.

Niederman, F.; Vreede, G.J. de; Briggs, R.O.; and Kolfschoten, G.L. 2008. Extending the contextual and organizational elements of adaptive structuration theory in GSS research. *Journal of the Association for Information Systems*, 9, 10, 633–652.

Nunamaker, J.F. Jr.; Briggs, R.O.; Mittleman, D.D.; Vogel, D.; and Balthazard, P.A. 1997. Lessons from a dozen years of group support systems research: A discussion of lab and field findings. *Journal of Management Information Systems*, 13, 3, 163–207.

Osborn, A.F. 1953. *Applied Imagination*. New York: Scribner's.

Paas, F.; Renkl, A.; and Sweller, J. 2003. Cognitive load theory and instructional design, recent developments. *Educational Psychologist*, 38, 1, 1–4.

Post, B.Q. 1993. A business case framework for group support technology. *Journal of Management Information Systems*, 9, 3, 7–26.

Reinig, B.A.; Briggs, R.O.; Shepherd, M.M.; Yen, J.; and Nunamaker, J.F. Jr. 1995. Affective reward and the adoption of group support systems: Productivity is not always enough. *Journal of Management Information Systems*, 12, 3, 171–185.

Robey, D.; Smith, L.A.; and Vijayasarathy, L.R. 1993. Perceptions of conflict and success in information systems development projects. *Journal of Management Information Systems*, 10, 1, 123–140.

Santanen, E.L. 2005. Resolving ideation paradoxes: Seeing apples as oranges through the clarity of thinkLets. In *Proceedings of the 38th Hawaii International Conference on System Sciences*, Waikoloa, Hawaii, January 5–8.

Santanen, E.L., and Vreede, G.J. de. 2004. Creative approaches to measuring creativity: Comparing the effectiveness of four divergence thinkLets. In *Proceedings of the 37th Hawaii International Conference on System Sciences*, Waikoloa, Hawaii, January 5–8.

Santanen, E.L.; Vreede, G.J. de; and Briggs, R.O. 2004. Causal relationships in creative problem solving: Comparing facilitation interventions for ideation. *Journal of Management Information Systems*, 20, 4, 167–197.

Schoemaker, P. 1982. The expected utility model: Its variants, purposes, evidence and limitations. *Journal of Economic Literature*, 20, 2, 529–563.

Schwarz, R.M. 1994. *The Skilled Facilitator*. San Francisco, CA: Jossey-Bass.

Shepherd, M.M.; Briggs, R.O.; Reinig, B.A.; Yen, J.; and Nunamaker, J.F. Jr. 1996. Social comparison to improve electronic brainstorming: Beyond anonymity. *Journal of Management Information Systems*, 12, 3, 155–170.

Steiner, I.D. 1972. *Group Process and Productivity*. New York: Academic Press.

Sweller, J.; Merrienboer, J.G. van; and Paas, F.G.W.C. 1998. Cognitive architecture and instructional design. *Educational Psychology Review*, 10, 3, 251–296.

Tuckman, B.J. 1965. Developmental sequence in small groups. *Psychology Bulletin*, 63, 384–399.

Vreede, G.J. de, and Briggs, R.O. 2005. Collaboration engineering: Designing repeatable processes for high-value collaborative tasks. In *Proceedings of the 38th Hawaii International Conference on System Sciences,* Waikoloa, Hawaii, January 3–6.

Vreede, G.J. de; Briggs, R.O.; and Kolfschoten, G.L. 2006. ThinkLets: A pattern language for facilitated and practitioner-guided collaboration processes. *International Journal of Computer Applications in Technology,* 25, 2/3, 140–154.

Vreede, G.J. de, and Bruijn, J.A. de. 1999. Exploring the boundaries of successful GSS application: Supporting inter-organizational policy networks. *DataBase,* 30, 3–4, 111–131.

Vreede, G.J. de; Davison, R.; and Briggs, R.O. 2003. How a silver bullet may lose its shine: Learning from failures with group support systems. *Communications of the ACM,* 46, 8, 96–101.

Vreede, G.J. de; Vogel, D.R.; Kolfschoten, G.L.; and Wien, J.S. 2003. Fifteen years of in-situ GSS use: A comparison across time and national boundaries. In *Proceedings of the 36th Hawaii International Conference on System Sciences,* Waikoloa, Hawaii, January 6–9.

Wikipedia. 2009. General theory of collaboration. Available at http://en.wikipedia.org/wiki/General_theory_of_collaboration (accessed April 27, 2009).

CHAPTER 4

CLASSIFICATION OF COLLABORATION TECHNOLOGY

DANIEL D. MITTLEMAN, JOHN D. MURPHY, AND ROBERT O. BRIGGS

Abstract: *The challenge of understanding the range of collaboration products available in the marketplace is complicated by several realities. There are currently more than 2,000 collaboration software products in the marketplace,[1] and collaboration technology vendors continue to introduce new products and upgrades at the rate of more than a dozen per week. These numbers may continue to increase as software development methods become more streamlined, reducing the cycle times for introducing new products to the marketplace.*

Keywords: *Collaboration Technology, Computer-Based Collaboration-Support Products*

Further, many collaboration software products now entering the marketplace are actually integrated bundles of several collaboration technologies, rather than single-function tools. Skype, for example, a product primarily known as a VoIP telephony product, also bundles video conferencing, Short Message Service (SMS), persistent text chat, file transfer, desktop sharing, and departmental Private Branch Exchange (PBX) services. Although major vendors are active in the collaboration technology marketplace (e.g., IBM/Lotus®, Microsoft®, Cisco®, and Google®), the vast majority of products are produced by entrepreneurial startups and open-source consortia. These products are quick to market, quick to upgrade, sometimes quick to fail, and therefore are more difficult to track than products from more firmly established commercial vendors.

These market realities impact all collaboration technology stakeholders, including consumers, integrators, developers, and researchers. To select an optimal product for a particular organizational need, one would need to know and understand the many offerings in the marketplace. Consumers of collaboration technology find it difficult to evaluate product categories, let alone particular products, and the boundaries among categories are muddied by both the fast pace of change and by the straddling of categories by many products. Collaboration technology integrators must keep pace with evolving market terminology and conventions, interoperability standards, evolving middleware platforms, and ratcheting security protocols. Collaboration researchers find it difficult to compare results when findings are based on different products. The challenge of holding technology constant makes it difficult to separate the effects of cognitive behavioral, attitudinal factors from effects invoked by technology on performance and other outcomes of interest. Likewise, developers have a difficult time relying on research findings when findings are often confounded by use of previous generation technologies. Developers struggle with user interface conventions and transnational cultural collaboration norms. Developers also find it difficult to choose which development platform to use, which interoperability standards to embrace, and which mix of technologies to bundle into a new product.

The marketplace will not stand still while these stakeholders try to make sense of it, so a cross-cutting, stable collaboration technology classification scheme could be useful to consumers, researchers, and developers. Such a scheme could provide a shared language for comparing and contrasting collaboration technologies over multiple generations of products and protocols. This chapter proposes such a classification scheme as a starting place toward that end. The purpose of this classification scheme is to provide a lens through which people can better understand the capabilities of, and relationships among, collaboration technologies. This framework may help practitioners to select from among commercial collaboration software offerings. It may offer groupware designers a range of design choices for new systems, and it may reveal new challenges to the groupware research community. In the balance of this chapter, we describe the methods by which we derived the scheme, and then present the details of the scheme itself. We conclude with an example of how the scheme could be used, and discuss potential directions for future research.

METHODS FOR CLASSIFICATION

Over the course of six years since the term "Web 2.0" was coined by Darcy DiNucci to characterize the emergence of collaboration technologies on the web (Graham, 2005) we have tracked the introduction of more than 300 new commercial groupware products through academic and trade literature searches, news outlets and blogs, and through weekly web searches. Our initial agenda was to create a taxonomy for groupware products. This proved to be unworkable because the mix of tools provided by differing classes of products tended to overlap heavily, making it difficult to defend any particular classification. We therefore shifted our perspective from products to technologies, and derived these three definitions:

- *Collaboration capability:* a specific functionality required by a group to execute their intended actions. For example, a group might require a page visible to all members upon which to record ideas during a brainstorming activity.
- *Collaboration technology:* a general software solution for providing a group with the capabilities it needs to move toward its goals. For example, a shared page capability could be provided by several different technologies—a shared editor, a chat tool, or a video link showing a whiteboard.
- *Collaboration product:* an implementation of one or more collaboration technologies offered as an integrated package, for example, current offerings by Zoho.com, Google Drive, or Adobe Connect.

The most important attribute by which collaboration technologies can be distinguished is the core capabilities they afford users. We therefore analyzed the collaboration products we had discovered in the marketplace, creating detailed functional descriptions of exemplar products. We used inductive logic to identify a set of core capabilities by which one might classify the capabilities afforded by a broad range of products. We also identified key attributes by which one could compare and contrast different products within the emerging capabilities categories. Three collaboration technology experts then compared the original functional descriptions to the capabilities and attributes to verify their completeness and accuracy. As new products emerged, we reexamined the scheme to assess fit and adjusted it to accommodate new technical concepts. We continued the review and refinement procedures over a period of three years until the scheme stabilized that could account for the capabilities of all new software products that emerged over a period of one year.

Table 4.1

Summary of the Classification Scheme

Core capabilities	Primary characteristics of a collaboration technology that provide the group with the means to take action toward attaining their goals.
Data contributions	Kinds of contributions users can add using core capabilities (e.g., text, graphics, voice, video).
Data relationships	Kinds of relationships users can establish among their contributions (e.g., collection, ordinal, hierarchical, network).
Data limits	The kinds of limits that are or can be imposed on contributions (e.g., size, duration, content).
Data persistence	The degree to which contributions can be made ephemeral or permanent.
Actions	Kinds of actions that users in each role can take with respect to contributions to a technology: add, receive/view, associate, edit, move, evaluate, and delete.
Synchronicity	Expected delay between the time a person executes an action and the time s/he could reasonably expect that other users could perceive the effects of that action (e.g., instantly, within seconds, within minutes, within hours).
Identifiability	Degree to which users can determine who executed an action (e.g., full identifiability, full anonymity, identification by role, identification by pseudonym).
Access controls	The kinds of limits that may be placed on users' ability to access a technology and act on its contents (e.g., login name, password, invitation, smart card).
Roles	The degree to which a technology affords differentiation in access and action by sub-group (e.g., leaders, participants, observers).
Awareness indicators	Ways users know who else has access to the system, who is currently present in the system, what contributions others are viewing, and what they are doing.
Interruption alerts	Ways that participants are notified that something or someone in the system requires their attention.
Instructions	Ways a technology implementation provides process guidance to users about what they may contribute, what actions they may take, and the significance of those actions.

CLASSIFYING COLLABORATION TECHNOLOGIES

When comparing and classifying collaboration technologies, it is useful to distinguish which capabilities are present, which are absent, and which can be configured to adapt to variations of need.[2] It is also useful to recognize key attributes by which one can compare and contrast collaboration technologies within and across categories. Together, capabilities and attributes of the various collaboration technologies are central to designing and selecting collaboration products. We propose a classification scheme for collaboration technologies based on capabilities and attributes. Table 4.1 lists and briefly describes each element of the classification scheme.

Table 4.2

Categories of Core Capabilities

Categories and Subcategories	Descriptions
Jointly Authored Pages	Technologies that provide one or more windows that multiple users may view, and to which multiple users may contribute, usually simultaneously.
Conversation Tools	Optimized to support dialog among group members.
Shared Editors	Optimized for the joint production of deliverables such as documents, spreadsheets, or graphics.
Group Dynamics Tools	Optimized for creating, sustaining, or changing patterns of collaboration among people making joint effort toward a goal (e.g., idea generation, idea clarification, idea evaluation, idea organization, consensus-building).
Polling Tools	Optimized for gathering, aggregating, and understanding judgments, opinions, and information from multiple people.
Streaming Media	Technologies that provide a continuous feed of changing data.
Desktop/Application Sharing	Optimized for remote viewing and/or control of the computers of other group members.
Audio Conferencing	Optimized for transmission and receipt of sounds.
Video Conferencing	Optimized for transmission and receipt of dynamic images.
Information Access Tools	Technologies that provide group members with ways to store, share, find, and classify data objects.
Shared File Repositories	Provide group members with ways to store and share digital files.
Social Tagging Systems	Provide means to affix keyword tags to digital objects so that users can find objects of interest, and so they can find others with similar interests.
Search Engines	Provide means to retrieve relevant digital objects from among vast stores of objects based on search criteria.
Syndication Tools	Provide notification of when new contributions of interest have been added to pages or repositories.

Core Capabilities

Core capabilities describe the primary functions enabled by a technology. For example, the core capability of a blog is to provide a directed text and multimedia conversation around a managed topic, whereas the core capability of voice conference is a continuous multiparticipant audio stream.

An evaluation of the products available in the marketplace today revealed that a useful approach to categorizing tool capabilities could be based on the underlying architecture of the tools. The first level of classification divides all tool capabilities into three fundamental categories: (1) jointly authored pages, (2) streaming media, and (3) information access tools. The scheme further subdivides each of these categories into subcategories by the core capabilities they are optimized to support (see Table 4.2).

Jointly Authored Pages

The most fundamental capability for all technologies in the jointly authored pages category is a digital page, defined as a single "window" to which multiple collaborative participants can contribute, often simultaneously. The data structures of pages might include text, graphics, numbers, or other digital objects. However, regardless of content, any contribution made by a participant will generally appear on the screens of the other participants who view the same page. A given technology based on jointly authored pages may provide a single page or multiple pages. In some cases the contributions to one page serve as hyperlinks to other pages, allowing for the creation of hierarchies or networks of pages. Jointly authored pages are the basis for several subcategories of collaboration technology including: conversation tools, shared editors, group dynamics tools, and polling tools.

Conversation tools are those primarily optimized to support dialog among group members. Email is a widely used conversation tool, exceeding 247 billion[3] messages sent per day (Reuters, 2009) as well as short message services (SMS) (i.e., cell phone text messaging), which has passed 110 billion messages per month (Pluckett Research, 2008). Other conversation tools include instant messaging, chat rooms, and blogs or threaded discussions. Instant messaging and chat rooms provide users with a single shared page to which they can contribute contributions to a chronologically ordered list. Participants may not move, edit, or delete their contributions. Instant messaging and chat rooms differ from one another only in their access and alert mechanisms. With instant messaging an individual receives a pop-up invitation that another individual wishes to hold a conversation, while with chat rooms an individual browses to a website to find and join a conversation. Blogs (otherwise known as Web Logs) and threaded discussion tools are optimized for less-synchronous conversations. Users make a contribution, then come back later to see how others may have responded. Blogs and threaded discussions are typically persistent (i.e., their content remains even when users are not contributing) whereas chat rooms and instant messaging are usually ephemeral (i.e., when the last person exits a session, the session content disappears).

Shared editor tools are typically a jointly authored page optimized for the creation of a certain kind of deliverable by multiple authors. The content and affordances of these tools often match those of single-user office suite tools (e.g., word processing, spreadsheet); however, they are enhanced to accept contributions and editing by multiple simultaneous users. A wiki (the Hawaiian word for "fast") is another example of joint document authoring. Wikis are simple web pages that can be created directly through a web browser by any authorized user without the use of offline web development tools.

Group dynamics tools are optimized for creating, sustaining, or changing patterns of collaboration among individuals making a joint effort toward a goal. The patterns these tools support include generating ideas, establishing shared understanding of them, converging on those worth more attention, organizing and evaluating ideas, and building consensus (Briggs et al., 2006). These tools are often implemented as multiple layers of jointly authored pages such that each contribution on a given page may serve as a hyperlink to a subpage. The affordances of such tools are typically easily configurable, so at any given moment a group leader can provide team members with the features they need (e.g., view, add, move) while blocking features they should not be using (e.g., edit, delete).

Polling tools are a special class of jointly authored pages, optimized for gathering, aggregating, and understanding judgments, or opinions, from multiple people. At a minimum, the shared pages of a polling tool must offer a structure of one or more ballot items, a way for users to record votes, and a way to display results. Polling tools may offer rating, ranking, allocating, or categorizing evaluation methods and may also support the gathering of text based responses to ballot items.

Streaming Technologies

The core capability of all tools in the streaming technologies category is a continuous feed of dynamic data. Desktop sharing, application sharing, and audio/video conferencing are common examples of streaming technologies.

Desktop and application sharing tools allow the events displayed on one computer to be seen on the screens of other computers. With some application sharing tools, members may use their own mouse and keyboard to control the remotely viewed computer.

Audio conferencing tools provide a continuous channel for multiple users to send and receive sound.

Video conferencing tools allow users to send and receive sound and moving images. Typically all users may receive contributions in both types of tools; however, systems may vary in the mechanisms they provide for alerts and access control as well as by the degree to which affordances can be configured and controlled by a leader.

Information Access Technologies

Information access technologies provide ways to store, share, classify, and find data and information objects. Key examples from this category are shared file repositories, social tagging, search engines, and syndication tools.

Shared file repositories provide mechanisms for group members to store digital files where others in the group can access them. Some such systems also provide version control mechanisms such as check-out, check-in capabilities, and version back-ups.

Social tagging allows users to affix keyword tags to digital objects in a shared repository. For example, the website del.icio.us allows users to store and tag their favorite web links (i.e., bookmarks) online so they can access them from any computer. Users are not only able to access their own bookmarks by keyword, but bookmarks posted and tagged by others as well. More significantly, users can find other users who share an interest in the same content. Social tagging systems allow for the rapid formation of communities of interest and communities of practice around the content of the data repository. The data in a social tagging repository are said be organized in a "folksonomy," an organization scheme that emerges organically from the many ways that users think of and tag contributions, rather than a taxonomy, organized by experts.

Search engines use search criteria provided by users to retrieve digital objects from among vast stores of such objects (e.g., the World Wide Web, the blogosphere, digital libraries). Search criteria may include content, tags, and other attributes of the objects in the search space. Some search engines interpret the semantic content of the search request to find related content that is not an exact match for the search criteria.

Syndication tools allow a user to receive a notification when new contributions appear on pages or repositories they deem to be of interest (e.g., blogs, wikis, and social networks). Users subscribe to receive update alerts from a feed on a syndicated site. Every time the site changes, the feed broadcasts an alert message to all its subscribers. Users view alerts using software called an aggregator. Any time a user opens their aggregator, they see which of their subscription sites has new contributions. Therefore, users do not need to scan all contents to discover new contributions.

Aggregated Technologies

While the capabilities classification scheme lists three categories of technologies, most products combine several different technologies, and so may span two or three of the categories.

Products aggregate collaboration capabilities in two fundamental ways. One, products conjoin multiple capabilities into integrated suites affording the sharing of information among the capabilities, as Skype's current offering affords a single directory of "friends" from which one can engage in audio chat, IM text chat, SMS chat, or transfer files. Or two, products merge capabilities to create task-specific collaborative environments where the whole is greater than the sum of its parts because it delivers not only capabilities, but a work practice supported by those capabilities.

Among such examples would be project management systems, academic paper review systems, and concurrent engineering systems, virtual workspaces, group support systems, and social networking systems. Virtual workspaces often combine document repositories, team calendars, conversation tools, and other technologies that make it easier for team members to execute coordinated efforts (e.g., Groove or SharePoint). Remote presentation or web conferencing systems often combine application sharing and audio streams with document repositories and polling tools optimized to support one-to-many broadcast of presentations, with some ability for the audience to provide feedback to the presenter (e.g., Webex or SameTime). Group support systems integrate collections of group dynamics tools to move groups seamlessly through a series of activities toward a goal, for example, by generating ideas in one tool, organizing them in another, and evaluating them in yet another (e.g., GroupSystems or WebIQ). Social networking systems (e.g., MySpace or Flickr) combine social tagging with elements of wikis, blogs, other shared page tools, and a search engine so users can find and communicate with their acquaintances as well as establish new relationships based on mutual friends or mutual interests. Thus, transformed technologies may combine any mix shared-page, streaming, and information access technologies to support a particular purpose. Aggregated systems deliver value which could be achieved with a collection of standalone tools. Aggregated technologies, however, provide capabilities that are not only optimized, but often also sequenced to support a particular work practice (DeSanctis and Poole, 1994).

Data Contributions

Data contributions refer to the information structures users may contribute using a given collaboration technology (Briggs et al., 1997). The structure of the contribution is informed by the architecture of the tool and, in turn, empowers or constrains the collaboration affordances of the tool. Within a given technology, contributions may be realized in a variety of ways:

- *Link:* is the ability to point to another resource (which may be of any type on this list).
- *Text object:* is a collection of text bundled into a cohesive unit.
- *Raster graphic:* media in a protocol standard organized to represent a raster object.
- *Vector graphic:* media in a protocol standard organized to represent a vector object.
- *Data stream:* media in a protocol standard to support audio, video, or other signal streaming.
- *Rich text:* a multimedia object bundled into a cohesive unit. Text pages are often implemented as rich text objects.
- *File:* an external, cohesive, pervasive object of any type listed above.

An important characteristic of collaboration technologies is that each node contains a set of pointers to nodes of similar or different atomic data type, as well as the ability to contain metadata about itself. This architecture enables the attributes listed below.

Data Relationships

Data relationships are the associations permitted among data structures. Five types of relationships are possible among contributions:

- *Collection:* an unordered set of contributions.
- *List:* an ordered collection of contributions.
- *Tree:* a one-to-many branching collection of contributions.
- *Graph:* a set of contributions associated in many-to-many relationships.
- *Matrix:* an *n*-dimensional set of contributions with prescribed ordered relations.

Relationships may be established among objects of same or differing content. For example, a list may have text pages attached to each item affording conversation about each item on the list. Tools may support only a single kind of relationship or may support several types. This variety enables a vast array of information constructions. Some groupware may articulate the semantics of the relationships represented in the content. Other tools only represent the syntax of relationships, leaving it up to group members to agree on semantics.

Data Limits

A technology may enforce a maximum or minimum limit on the size or contents of a contribution, for example, "Text contributions shall be limited to 400 characters," or, "Text contributions must have a minimum of three characters." There may also be limits on the number and kinds of relationships a user may create among different kinds of contributions. For example, "Each contribution may only have one parent." Manipulation of limits in collaboration technologies can have an impact on group dynamics. For example, if few text pages are synchronously made available to a team, a conversation may occur within each page. If many text pages are simultaneously made available to a team, it is more likely individuals will dump their own ideas onto each page without reading the contributions of others. This sort of maximum–minimum manipulation is core to the predictability of a number of collaboration techniques.

Data Persistence

Persistence is the degree to which contributions are ephemeral or permanent. In some collaboration tools contributions may disappear as soon as they are made (e.g., video or audio conferencing tools without record capabilities). In others, contributions persist only for the duration of a session and disappear when all users exit (e.g., instant messaging). Often time users may configure the degree to which their contributions persist. For example, in some systems users may decide whether session contents will be saved. Other systems (e.g., email) allow a user to delete contributions from their view, but the contributions remain in the views of others, or in a permanent record.

Actions

Supported actions indicate the activities a system allows a participant to do to the data content and the relationships between data items. These actions (already well established in the database and groupware literatures) are:

- *Add:* contribute content to the group (e.g., add a new item to a blog; speak during an audio conference).
- *Receive/View:* detect contributions made by self or others (e.g., view text contributions or hear an audio channel).
- *Associate:* establish relationships among contributions (e.g., organize ideas into categories or arrange content into an outline).
- *Edit:* modify content of a contribution (e.g., amend or change text already contributed to a session).
- *Move:* change relationships/positions between contributions.
- *Evaluate:* render an opinion on the relative merits of contributions (e.g., vote).
- *Delete:* remove a contribution from a session (e.g., delete text, erase audio).

Synchronicity

Synchronicity characterizes the amount of delay that is expected when a user executes an action and when other users respond to that action. For example, with audio conferences, participants expect a response to their contributions within a second or two, whereas with email, users expect that responses may be delayed by hours or days. In some systems (e.g., audio conferencing) participants must wait their turn to contribute and in others (e.g., group support systems, wikis) participants may contribute simultaneously.

Identifiability

Identifiability characterizes the degree to which users can determine who executed an action. Identifiability ranges from full anonymity, to subgroup identification, to pseudonym identification (so you may know which contributions came from the same person, but not who that person is), to full identification.

Access Controls

Access control deals with the configuration of users' rights and privileges with respect to entering a session and executing supported actions. Some actions may be always available (e.g., in an instant messaging, all users may always add), or always blocked (e.g., in instant messaging, no users may edit or delete contributions). Still others may be configurable on the fly (e.g., in some group support systems, anonymity may be switched on or off as needed). A range of mechanisms exist to control entry into a session, among them the requirement for a login name, password, session key, invitation, or a physical device like a security dongle or a smart card.

Roles

Roles are the classes of participants enabled by a collaboration technology. For example, many meetings have leaders and participants: two roles. Marketing focus groups often have observers, a third role. If the maximum occurrence of a role is zero, then the role is prohibited; if the minimum is one, then the role is required. Individual participants will be assigned one or more role designations.[4]

Awareness Indicators

Awareness refers to the ways in which users learn about the other people who have access to a collaborative session, the roles that they hold, and their current status. In some systems, the only indicator that others are present is arrival of new contributions. In others, people may see a list of participants who have been granted access. In some, users can learn who is currently active in a session, what they are doing, which tools they are using, which contributions they are manipulating, and in some cases, even their current state of mind (e.g., happy, confused, dissatisfied).

Interruption Alerts

Alert mechanisms are the ways in which participants are interrupted or notified that something in the system demands their attention. For example, instant messenger systems typically signal an arriving contribution by making a sound and popping up a momentary visual cue. Interrupts can range from modal queues (such as a dialog box that requires attention before the user is able to return to other activities), to passive alerts. The nonmodal interrupt is designed to attract immediate attention; however, it can be ignored or refused by the receiver. Interrupt interfaces may include: dialog boxes, flashing or colored status indicators, audible indicators, or iconic indicators. Passive alerts, like those from an RSS feed, for example, do not interrupt the user but rather require that the user deliberately seek them out.

Instructions

Instructions are the ways a particular technology implementation provides guidance to a user about what they may contribute, what actions they may take, and the significance of those actions. As products have become more sophisticated, it has become increasingly common for developers to embed meta-information to guide participants' use of the product. These instructions can relate to the use of specific features (i.e., how to invite a new participant to a desktop sharing session), or to the individual participant's designated role in the collaborative session.

USE OF THE CLASSIFICATION SCHEME

The classification scheme presented in the section "Classifying Collaboration Technologies" draws attention to key attributes by which one can compare, contrast, and select among groupware technology implementations. One can use this classification scheme to analyze, compare, and contrast the capabilities offered by groupware products while simultaneously comparing and contrasting important implementation choices in products within or across classification categories. The next two sections describe how different stakeholder groups might make use of this classification scheme.

Use of the Classification Scheme by Collaboration Technology Consumers

Consumers of collaboration technologies may use this collaboration scheme to select between different products to fulfill a need for their collaboration team. For example, a manager may need a way for his team to share ideas as they develop an outline for their corporate strategic plan. Table 4.3 illustrates how the scheme can be used to weigh the typical capabilities and attributes of three collaboration technologies (i.e., instant messaging, video conferencing, and wikis) against each other in meeting the team's needs.

The manager, using the classification scheme to compare potential technology choices in this way, could then decide that while all three options allow each team member to contribute ideas, the wiki option offers a data persistence attribute that may be valuable as the team moves forward to drafting the strategic plan. This example shows how using the scheme could help managers

Table 4.3

Use of the Classification Scheme

Attribute	Instant Messaging	Video Conferencing	Wiki
Core Capability	Creation and exchange of single text pages.	Video stream, usually paired with a synchronized audio stream.	Creation and revision of jointly authored text pages.
Data Contents	Text	A/V streams	Text, Rich text, multi-media
Data Relationships	Time-ordered list of text contributions.	Time-ordered sequence of synchronized sounds and images.	Time-ordered list of text contributions; meta-text page corresponding to each text page.
Data Limits	Maximum character limit per text page.	None	None
Data Persistence	For duration of session by default; manual or automatic saving optional.	For the duration of session by default; manual or automatic saving optional.	Persists upon save action. Version history retained.
Actions			
Add	Text	Audio and video in parallel	Text and new text pages
Receive/view	Yes	Yes	Yes
Associate	No. Contributions displayed chronologically.	No. Contributions presented chronologically.	Yes, through a link structure.
Edit	No	No	Yes
Move	No	No	Yes
Delete	No	No	Yes
Judge	No	No	No

(continued)

Synchronicity	Immediate display of contributions to all participants upon send action; users may add content in parallel.	Immediate presentation of all contributions to all participants; users will add content in parallel.	Immediate display of contributions to all participants upon save action; users may add content in parallel.
Identifiability	Identification of contributor by login-name is automatic and mandatory.	Identification of contributor typically only by cues embedded into the stream (e.g., sound of voice, face recognition).	Identification is possible; implementations vary.
Access Control	Receive by invitation only. Once invitation is accepted, all users have both add and receive rights.	Varies by system. Access ranges from browsing to dial-up access. Control ranges from open to password or access code. Once in, all users have view rights. Add rights may be under the control of a moderator.	Varies by system.
Awareness Indicators	Icon or avatar	Video content	Typically, none
Interruption Alerts	Interrupt ty invitation with sound, pop up visual cue.	Vary by system, ranging from email invitations, to audio and visual interrupts.	RSS feed or email notification may be used.
Instructions	No	No	Some implementations embed instructions into contribution structure.

Note that particular implementations of a specific product within each of the categories used in this example could differ from the configurations shown and still be essentially the same class of technology; the options depicted here represent "typical" configurations. These differences, though, could have significant impact on the degree to which the implementation serves the needs of the users.

better understand the capabilities and attributes categories of the options available and thus better match specific collaboration products to team needs.

To better illustrate this point, consider the following scenario. One of this paper's authors was consulted about a technology selection by a systems integrator who operates out of the Midwest United States to service customers nationwide. They had selected MS-LiveMeeting® as the technology platform for conducting a distributed requirements elicitation for a product under development. Without knowing anything more about the situation, the author predicted that the chosen solution would be ineffective. He was able to make that judgment based on the fact that he knew that though LiveMeeting was quite capable as a streaming technology, it lacked key technical features found in jointly authored page and information access categories that would also be important for the success of the project. This scenario demonstrates how basic knowledge of the classification scheme can help assess potential technical solutions.

Use of Classification Scheme by Collaboration Technology Researchers

A recurring problem in group support systems research has been the variance of findings across an array of seemingly similar experiments (Fjermestad and Hiltz, 1998, 2000). The problem may lie in the fact that different studies have employed similar, but not identical groupware toolsets (Briggs, 2006). Differences in tool design or tool configuration may confound attitudinal, behavioral, or performance outcomes.

The use of a collaboration technology classification scheme may aid in the description of tools employed in GSS related studies. Therefore, comparison across studies is improved and potential confounds are more readily surfaced and explored.

IMPLICATIONS AND FUTURE RESEARCH

The goal in developing these classification schemes was to address the challenge of understanding and selecting among various collaboration technologies. It has significantly reduced cognitive load for understanding the broad groupware space, particularly in trying to understand the sometimes complex "bundles of capabilities" found in current-generation collaboration products. The scheme may also help designers to identify new gaps in product offerings, understand the range of implementation choices available to them, and may help researchers to discover which of the many technological interventions account for effects observed in the field, and what groupware challenges remain unaddressed. This scheme does have limitations though, particularly in terms of accommodating the aggregated products. We anticipate that further research will be required making additions and revisions to the schemes to bring them to a state where they can account for all elemental collaboration technologies and all design and configuration choices for those technologies.

NOTES

1. Some of the lists that track groupware are shown in the chart on top of page 55. These lists total to more than 2,000 products and tools. While each site has their own criteria and categorization scheme, significant overlap exists among the tools listed. Two thousand unique products and tools is a conservative estimate. Most of these lists are updated on a regular basis.

Company	URL	No. of product/ tool listings
Thinkofit, "Web Conferencing Review"	http://thinkofit.com/webconf/index.htm	about 935
Web-based Software	http://www.web-based-software.com/	about 850
CMSmatrix	http://www.cmsmatrix.org/	about 1,080
Go2web20	http://www.go2web20.net/	over 400
Ziipa	http://www.ziipa.com/	over 400
Open Source CMS	http://php.opensourcecms.com/	about 200
All Things Web 2.0	http://www.allthingsweb2.com	about 200
Wikipedia, "List of wiki software"	http://en.wikipedia.org/wiki/List_of_wiki_software	about 66
WeblogMatrix	http://www.weblogmatrix.org/	28

2. A rich literature exists for mapping collaboration tool affordances to established group facilitation processes. Exploration of that literature, while important to a designer or user of collaboration products, is beyond the scope of this paper. However, an introduction into that literature can be found in de Vreede and Briggs, 1997.

3. Probably about 81 percent of which are spam.

4. Usually one role, but the beauty of this collaboration technology architecture is that it surfaces questions for designers such as: Does our product need to support multiple roles for a user, or will each user be assigned only one role?

REFERENCES

Briggs, R.O. 2006. On theory-driven design and deployment of collaboration systems. *International Journal of Human-Computer Studies,* 64, 7, 573–582.

Briggs, R.O.; Kolfschoten, G.L.; de Vreede, G.-J.; and Dean, D.L. 2006. Defining key concepts for collaboration engineering. In *Proceedings of the 12th Americas Conference on Information Systems (AMCIS-12),* Acapulco, Mexico, August 4–6.

Briggs, R., Mittleman, D., Santanen, E., and Gillman, D. 1997. Collaborative molecules: A component-based architecture for GSS. In *Proceedings of the Americas Conference on Information Systems (AMCIS),* Indianapolis, IN, August 15–17.

DeSanctis, G., and Poole, M.S. 1994. Capturing the complexity in advanced technology use: Adaptive structuration theory. *Organization Science,* 5, 2, 121–147.

de Vreede, G.-J., and Briggs, R.O. 1997. Meetings of the future: Enhancing group collaboration with group support systems. *Journal of Creativity and Innovation Management,* 6, 2, 106–116.

Fjermestad, J., and Hiltz, S.R. 1998. An assessment of group support systems experimental research: Methodology and results. *Journal of Management Information Systems,* 15, 3, 7–149.

———. 2000. Group support systems: A descriptive evaluation of case and field studies. *Journal of Management Information Systems,* 17, 3, 112–157.

Graham, P. 2005. Web 2.0. November. www.paulgraham.com/web20.html (accessed September 23, 2009).

Pluckett Research, Ltd. 2008. Wireless, wi-fi, RFID & cellular industry overview. Table, December. www.plunkettresearch.com/Industries/WirelessCellularRFID/WirelessCellularRFIDStatistics/tabid/263/Default.aspx (accessed September 23, 2009).

Reuters. 2009. The Radicati Group, Inc. releases "Email Statistics Report, 2009–2013." Press release, May 6. www.reuters.com/article/pressRelease/idUS119688+06-May-2009+MW20090506 (accessed September 23, 2009).

CHAPTER 5

AN EMPIRICAL TEST OF THE FOCUS THEORY OF GROUP PRODUCTIVITY

FANG CHEN AND ROBERT O. BRIGGS

Abstract: The chapter reports a study that adopted an action research approach to investigate the efficacy of Focus Theory, a general theory of group productivity, in the context of project team interactions supported by group collaboration technology. Focus Theory specifies that three processes consume attention resources to accomplish a group task: communication, information access, and deliberation. The study indicated that Focus Theory had both explanatory power and theoretical limitations. The study indicated that three processes consumed attention resources, although it was difficult to separate their effects or to measure the attention resources allocated to each. Focus Theory does not differentiate between cognitive effort and cognitive load, making it difficult to test the theory's validity. The three processes may not be equally important in all group interaction scenarios, a possibility not specified by Focus Theory. The implications of the study for further development of the theory are: the theory needs to differentiate between cognitive effort and cognitive load, specify which process is more important in what conditions, and find a method to measure attention resources consumed by each of the process separately.

Keywords: Focus Theory, Group Productivity, Collaboration Technology

A great deal of research has been conducted on how to make groups more productive through applications of collaboration techniques and technologies (e.g., Dennis et al., 1990–91; Fjermestad and Hiltz, 1999–2000), although there is a great deal more to learn. In hundreds of studies that examined the effect of a variety of electronic interventions on group productivity (for reviews see Benbasat and Lim, 1993; Dennis et al., 1990–91; Dennis and Gallupe, 1993; Fjermestad et al., 1993; Fjermestad and Hiltz, 1999–2000; Fjermestad and Hiltz, 2000–2001; McCleod, 1992; Nunamaker et al., 1991; Nunamaker et al., 1993; Pinsonneault and Kraemer, 1989; Pinsonneault and Kraemer, 1990), researchers seek to explain both success and failure of using collaboration technology such as group support systems (GSS), and several authors have offered models and theories about various aspects of group work and group support systems (see Dennis et al., 1988; Jessup and Valacich, 1993; and the 1993 November special edition of *Small Group Research* for a variety of perspectives). Each suggests valuable insights into the relationship between productivity and technology.

Many prior studies that investigated group productivity and technology explicitly or implicitly adopted an input-process-output model (Dennis et al., 1988; Nunamaker et al., 1991; Nunamaker et al., 1993) to study how input factors affect process, which in turn affects output. The model is a high-level view of group collaboration, which states that the effects of technology on group process and outcome are contingent on the interaction of four categories of input constructs. The input factors include group, task, context, and technology. *Group characteristics* are group features such as group size, group history, group proximity, group cohesiveness, and group composition. Dimensions of *task characteristics* include task type, task complexity, task clarity, and activities required to accomplish the goal. *Context characteristics* are features of a group interaction environment, examples of which include organizational culture, reward structure, time pressure, and performance evaluative tone (e.g., supportive or critical). *Technology* specifies the technology used, such as GSS, email, online chat, or manual. If a particular technology is used, the specific tool and tool features should be described. The interactions of these four types of input factors affect group process and outcome. Group outcome may include group productivity, but the model is not explicit about this.

The model seems straightforward at first, but close examination reveals its flaws as a theoretical model. First, the model specifies that four categories of input interact to affect process. However, the model diagram does not show whether and how these categories of input factors interact. In addition, the four input categories can be infinitely decomposed into other categories or factors. For example, group category can be decomposed into group size, group history, group proximity, group heterogeneity, and so on. Other input categories can be similarly decomposed and it would be very difficult to examine how thousands of different combinations of input factors might affect group process and outcome.

Therefore, a parsimonious, bounded, general causal theory of team productivity is needed to substantially advance the work of GSS researchers, practitioners, and technology designers in terms of providing more understanding of the dynamics of team productivity. Briggs proposed Focus Theory to address these needs (Briggs, 1994). Romano et al. (1999) and Walsh (1996) examined how Focus Theory could help researchers select a technology to facilitate group interactions. However, their studies were not an empirical test of Focus Theory's propositions. Walsh (1996) collected qualitative data about two constructs of focus theory: goal congruence and information access, but did not empirically examine its propositions. In this paper, we summarize the logic of focus theory, and report an empirical study of its efficacy for predicting and explaining group productivity.

FOCUS THEORY

Focus Theory seeks to explain team productivity among knowledge workers. Figures 5.1 and 5.2 are a pictorial summary of Focus Theory.

Focus Theory (Briggs, 1994) begins with the assumption that human attention resources are limited (Miller, 1956). It further assumes that groups can only be productive to the extent that team members devote their attention to attaining the group's declared goal(s). The theory proposes that the amount of cognitive effort devoted to the group task over time will be a function of *goal congruence*, defined as the degree to which the perceived vested interest of an individual in a team is compatible with and served by the goals and methods of the team. The more the individual team member perceives that working toward the group goal will be instrumental to the attainment of the team member's private goals, the greater will be the cognitive effort the group member devotes to the team effort. Focus Theory proposes further that cognitive effort toward the group goal will be in inverse function of distraction, which is defined as any factor that diverts attention from working toward the group goals.

Focus Theory posits that, in order to be productive, team members must divide their limited attention resources among at least three cognitive processes: communication, information access, and deliberation. Once a team member reaches some threshold of cognitive load, the theory posits,

Figure 5.1 **Model of Focus Theory**

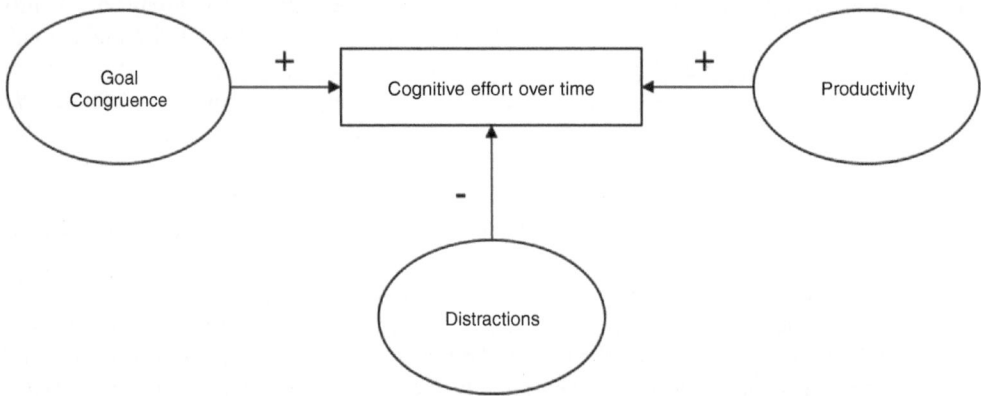

Source: Adapted from Briggs, 1994.

Figure 5.2 **Three Cognitive Processes of Focus Theory**

Cognitive effort over time

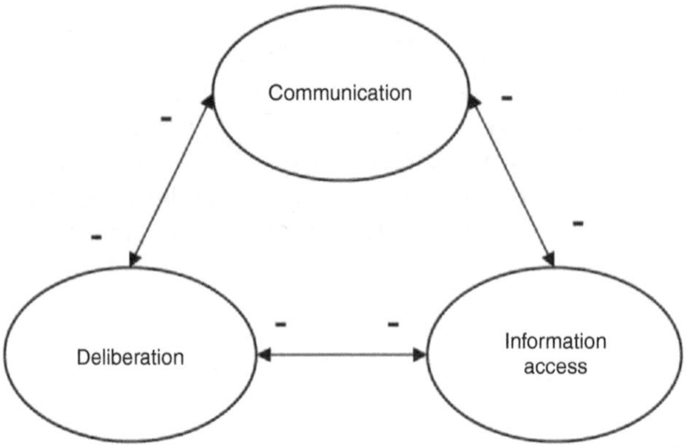

Source: Adapted from Briggs, 1994.

these three processes interfere with one another. Attention devoted to any one of these processes reduces the team member's ability to do the other two. Thus, the limits of attention become a fundamental limit of team productivity. Further, the attention focused on these processes is the direct cause of productivity. Focus Theory is so named because it attends to the focusing of team attention toward achieving team goals.

Communication takes into consideration the exchange of meanings among people, for which data communication equipment may sometimes be used. On the other hand, Focus Theory treats such equipment as a black box, and considers only how its use of such equipment might affect the attention resources of the participants.

Information is defined as knowledge about one's course of action and having more information may increase the accuracy of expectation of a certain outcome related to one's course of action. However, searching, storing, organizing, and accessing information all consume attention resources.

Deliberation, whether it is methodical or chaotic, refers to all cognitive processes except communication and information access to achieve a goal. A structured deliberation may consist of a series of processes such as defining the problem, identifying alternatives, evaluating alternatives, and choosing alternatives. A chaotic deliberation may identify alternatives before clearly defining a problem. Team productivity in Focus Theory measures the degree of goal attainment and has two components: team efficiency and team effectiveness.

If the logic of the theory holds, the three cognitive processes that it posits should be interdependent; any intervention that reduces the cognitive load for one of the processes should also make the other two processes easier.

RESEARCH QUESTIONS AND STUDY METHODOLOGY

The purpose of this study was to explore and understand the proposition of Focus Theory more thoroughly, and to develop measurement approaches that could be used in future studies to support more rigorous experimentation. This study attempts to clarify the overall model of Focus Theory as well as to examine whether and how the three cognitive processes manifest, how they are facilitated and/or inhibited during group interactions, and how these processes and other constructs may correlate with group productivity. To do this, we need to select group interaction scenarios that meet the following requirements:

First, the group task should be complex enough so that team members have to work jointly to get the job done; in other words, they have to communicate with each other, access relevant information, and think through the problem before they reach a conclusion or decision. Idea generation task is not appropriate for this study, since team members can simply generate ideas without talking to each other. Tasks that involve problem solving or decision making will be more suitable for the study.

Second, group interactions should involve different levels of difficulty for group processes so that we could see whether levels of difficulties will be manifested and how these influence group productivity. Among three processes, communication is the most observable one. Therefore, we will focus on this process and make the level of difficulty in communication different. One easy way to do this is to have groups interact in different communication modes; for instance, face-to-face (FtF) communication is easier than distributed synchronous and distributed asynchronous communication. An additional way to manipulate levels of communication difficulty is to have teams engage in distributed interaction several times. When groups interact in distributed mode, they have to rely on information technology for communication. Familiarity with technology could also be a factor that influences level of communication difficulty; in other words, after participants obtain some experience about using the technology, they may find it easier to use for communication.

To meet these specifications, we investigate the efficacy of Focus Theory in the context of project team interactions supported by GSS. When teams engage in a nontrivial project for several weeks, they have to conduct periodic meetings to check their project progress: reporting what they have done, what problems or issues that they encountered, and discussing what needs to be done in the next step. There are three advantages of using project team interactions to investigate the efficacy of Focus Theory. First, project progress tracking meetings/sessions should be complex enough to involve three processes specified in Focus Theory. Second, the discussion content is natural and substantial; given the project is nontrivial, participants should always have something to discuss. Third, team members collaborating on a large project for an extended period may work together in different ways. Some of their work may take place FtF, while other work may be asynchronous, occurring at different times and places. Some tasks, such as generating and evaluating solutions, are easily accomplished asynchronously. Other collaboration is more effective FtF, for example, sharing an understanding of key terms or building commitment to a proposed course of action.

The reasoning logic of Focus Theory allows technology to intervene in the cognitive effort and processes by reducing distraction, facilitating communication, providing group memory, and supporting the deliberation processes by structuring it into divergent and convergent thinking and by providing tools (e.g., electronic brainstorming tool, voting tool) to facilitate the thinking.

Since there has not been extensive research about Focus Theory, this study adopted an action research approach. Action research (e.g., Argyris, Putnam, and Smith, 1985; Susman and Evered, 1978) is similar to case study research in that both allow researchers to gain an in-depth understanding of the phenomena of interest in the rich context where it manifests. In case studies, however, the researcher seeks to remain as an external observer and seeks to minimize researcher impact on the phenomenon being studied. In action research, the researcher begins with a situation then intervenes actively with the goal of improving the situation, under the guidance of a theory. The dual purpose of action research is to both improve the situation and gain more understanding of the guiding theory. In our case, we want to improve project tracking session effectiveness by using collaboration technology and gain insights into Focus Theory.

Guided by Focus Theory, the study examined the ways in which these processes were manifested, facilitated, and/or inhibited during group interactions, as well as how these processes and other Focus Theory constructs affected group productivity when teams engaged in FtF, synchronous-distributed (later on referred to as synchronous), and asynchronous interactions. The objective of the study was to gain understanding of Focus Theory to offer insights into the theory.

The study addresses two research questions:

Research Question 1:   How are Focus Theory constructs manifested during group interactions in virtual teams?

Research Question 2:   In what ways is the theory useful and in what ways is it limited in terms of explaining observed phenomena? How can it be improved?

THE EMPIRICAL STUDY

Subjects and Study Design

Data were collected in Fall 2003 from two MIS undergraduate classes at a western U.S. university: class 220 (later referred to as Class 1), and class 210 (later referred to as Class 2). Participants in each class completed semester-long software projects on which the entire class worked as a team to develop or to implement a system. Everyone in a class was supposed to receive exactly the same project grade that would constitute 20 percent of his/her final grade. Students were informed of the intention of the study before data collection and had agreed to participate. Some course credits were given to participating students. The two classes had different instructors and one of the two authors worked as the coordinator and facilitator for the process tracking sessions of both class projects. Most of the students were juniors or seniors.

Class 1 helped a fictitious company implement SAP, an enterprise resource planning system. Nineteen students in the class were divided into five subteams: FI (financial and accounting), PP (process planning), SD (sales and distribution), MM (manufacture), and PMT (project manager team). All teams had three members except SD, which had six. Class 2 developed a web-based system to track their business school's courses and instructor assignments of those courses. The class had

Table 5.1

Groups and Order of Mode

Week	Group A	Group B	Group C
1	FtF	Syn	Asyn
2	FtF	Syn	Asyn
3	Syn	Asyn	FtF
4	Syn	Asyn	FtF
5	Asyn	FtF	Syn–Dis
6	Asyn	FtF	Syn–Dis

forty students who were divided into eight subteams: DES (design), SW (software development), DOC (documentation), DB (database), TST (testing), QA (quality assurance), IMP (implementation), and MGN (management). The team sizes were from three to six students (DOC and TST had four members, DES, DB, and IMP had five members, and QA and SW had six members).

The two classes first spent several weeks learning concepts related to their project. They then defined system requirements and started to design or configure a system. Classes met routinely twice a week to check project progress. These class meetings were manual FtF meetings without GSS support. Data were not collected for meetings at the class level. Each individual team had a weekly project process tracking session to check the progress of their specific tasks by using Cognito, a web-based GSS. Data were collected at the team and individual levels.

The study utilized a Latin Square design in which each team experienced all three interaction modes during a six-week period. Each team was in one of three groups: Group A, Group B, or Group C. Group A included the PMT (Class 1), SW, TST, and DOC teams. Group B included the SD (Class 1), FI (Class 1), DES, QA, and MGN teams, and Group C included the PP (Class 1), MM (Class 1), DB, and IMP teams.

Three groups followed different orders of interaction mode, as shown in Table 5.1. Each team experienced the same interaction mode for two consecutive weeks. The sequence of the interaction modes for Group A was FtF, Synchronous, and Asynchronous. The order for Group B was Synchronous, Asynchronous, and FtF. The order for Group C was Asynchronous, FtF, and Synchronous.

Even though this study is an action research, design of the study looks like an experiment in terms of layout and the random assignment of teams into different groups. However, it was not a strictly controlled experiment, because session duration, tasks for each session, team size, and the group process were not controlled. The repeated Latin Square design allowed the researcher to observe how group norms, modes, and order of mode use affected the group processes, and how processes affected group productivity.

There were no significant difference among members of the three groups in terms of age, number of full-time working years, self-rated computer literacy (computer experience), and previous GSS usage. The average age of all participants was approximately twenty-six years, and the average number of full-time working years was slightly more than four years.

Study Procedure

Training in GSS usage was provided for each class before the first week of data collection and lasted approximately forty minutes for each class. The author explained the study objective, the study process, and Cognito usage with a PowerPoint slide show. Students then logged into an FtF trial interaction session held in the computer lab in order to gain hands-on experience in use of the software. Cognito allows session leaders more privileges than regular session participants, and team leaders were supposed to be session leaders for their teams, so two additional group training sessions were held for team leaders. Some additional individual team leader training sessions were held for some team leaders who had been unable to attend the group team leaders training session due to class schedule conflicts.

Each class met at its regular time twice a week. A usual class period was seventy-five minutes. Each class tracked its project progress by checking the individual teams' progress, and discussed issues that needed to be addressed. Typically, instructors and project managers conducted these meetings. Each class had three project managers, one of whom was responsible for overall project management and coordination. The other two worked with individual teams and closely coordinated routine project tasks with team leaders. Class-level meetings were FtF without GSS support. The author attended each class meeting during the data collection period to become familiar with the students, their projects, project progress, and problems and concerns that might arise. However, the author usually did not actively participate in the meetings at the class level. The author talked with instructors each week in short informal FtF meetings about project progress and student feedback.

Teams held one formal weekly project tracking session to check their progress, solve problems, and discuss issues using Cognito. The teams also met in other times to engage in actual day-by-day work for the project. For example, although the SW (software) team might have only one formal weekly project tracking session, team members might meet more often actually to write and debug codes. Cognito-facilitated group interaction focused on project management functions, not on the actual work of the project.

One concern before the data collection was that teams may not like the distributed interaction, therefore, they might bypass distributed project tracking sessions and hold additional FtF weekly project tracking sessions. This seemed to not happen, mainly for two reasons:

1. The instructor demonstrated full support for using Cognito. In the original syllabi of two classes, students' participating in Cognito-facilitated sessions did not contribute to their final grade. Two instructors modified the syllabi to make participation in Congito-facilitated sessions as 10 percent of their final grade. The instructors also indicated to their students that learning collaboration in distributed environments is important for real organizations, so the Cognito-learning experience would be valued by job recruiters.
2. Students usually were taking three to five classes, and many of the students worked part-time. Most students had very tight schedules. It was difficult to find several time slots for the teams to meet FtF during a week's time. The author observed that students worked hard to make distributed group interactions as efficient and effective as possible and did not try to bypass distributed group interactions. Some team sessions were very short, lasting for only five to ten minutes. This is the case when no major tasks were ongoing and the team was waiting for another team's output. For example, it took the Class 2 design team three weeks to finalize the design, while the design team was working on the design, the software and database teams did not have much to do, and their sessions were very short because they did not have much to talk about.

For individual team sessions, the team leader and the author set up the session in Cognito before each session. The team leader usually filled out the Agenda Form to list agenda items for each session and entered these agenda items into the system. After the session, the team leader indicated which items had been fully discussed. The number of fully discussed items was the measure of the session effectiveness. All session participants filled out a group activity questionnaire (see Appendix 5.1) after each session. The author conducted informal, unstructured brief interviews with some participants, and all participants were encouraged to log in an online asynchronous session to provide anonymous feedback. Student interviews and participation in anonymous feedback were optional. The author had created a website for posting team session information that included PowerPoint training slides, a team's session schedule, email addresses for everyone on the team, and session notes downloaded from the Cognito server.

In FtF mode, all team members assembled in one computer room and everyone usually had access to GSS. Participants engaged in oral discussion, and entered comments and notes into the system. The author sat in the same computer room, observing group interactions, providing facilitation if necessary, and taking field notes.

For the synchronous mode, a team was split in two, with half of participants staying in one computer room and the other half moving to another. Every participant usually had access to GSS, although two participants sometimes shared a computer. Participants in the same room could talk to one another, but they could communicate with team members in the other room only through text provided by GSS. The author visited both rooms, coordinating the session, providing support, and taking field notes. FtF and synchronous sessions usually lasted for approximately five to sixty minutes.

Asynchronous sessions usually lasted for forty-eight hours. Some sessions were longer if participants misunderstood the session schedule or if some participants did not log in the system as expected. Participants logged into the system from anywhere and at any time to enter comments and engage in discussions. They were encouraged to log in four times during a twenty-four-hour period, but the actual number of logins varied by individual and session. The author logged in to the session frequently to check progress and remind participants to log in if they had not done so or if they had logged in too few times.

After the session, the author interviewed some session participants in an informal and unstructured way and took notes about their suggestions and comments on the group interaction. An asynchronous meeting also was set up to allow students to enter feedback and comments about each project process tracking session. Students were told that the comments would be anonymous in hope of encouraging candid and honest responses. All session notes were posted on the project management website for students to review.

GSS Configuration for the Group Interaction Sessions

A brief introduction to Cognito, a web-based GSS used in the study, may be helpful for understanding the group interaction procedure and structure. The Cognito server is hosted by the Center for the Management of Information at the University of Arizona. All participants have the Cognito server URL, username, and password to log in. Participants needed to download and install Cognito on a particular computer when logging in for the first time. After successfully logging in, participants saw a screen with two panes. The left pane listed topics for the group's interaction; the right pane listed subtopics associated with a particular topic on the left pane. A sample screen is displayed in Figure 5.3.

In the first week of the course, team leaders were supposed to identify whatever topics needed to be covered on the left pane. The author found that this ad hoc process of agenda setting did not work well because some team leaders set up one or two topics for the session that actually covered more topics. Content of the session might not match a topic or be confusing to the participants. It

Figure 5.3   **Project Process Tracking Main Window**

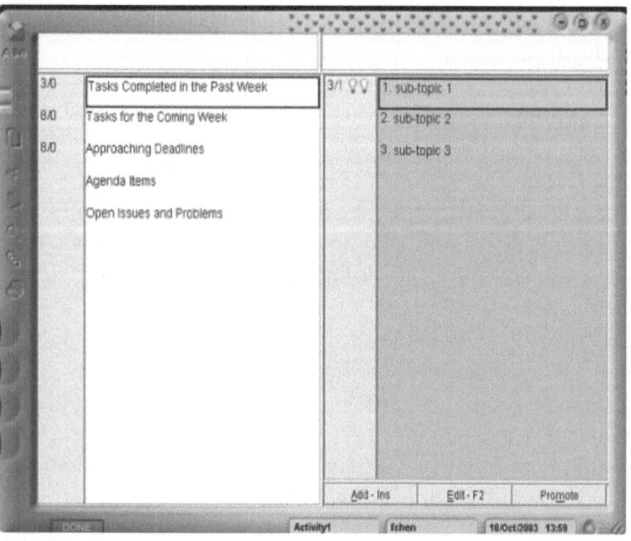

also made it difficult for participants to locate, access, and retrieve relevant information after the interaction. The author and the Class 2 instructor consulted and decided to adopt a project process tracking session template for all team interactions. The template included five general topics: Tasks Completed in the Past Week, Tasks for This Week, Approaching Deadlines, Agenda Items, and Open Issues/Problems. Open Issues/Problems referred to issues and questions that needed to be addressed, all items that were not listed under tasks, deadlines, and issues were listed under agenda items.

This session template was adopted by all teams beginning in the second week. The author created the template for each session, and the team leader logged in to the session and created subtopics for these general topics before each session. For example, to add subtopics for Tasks Completed in the Past Week, a team leader could double click the topic title, then click the "Add-Ins" button on the right pane, type the subtopic in the pop-up window, and then click the "Submit" button on the pop-up window. Subtopics for other topics could be created the same way. To view the subtopics for a particular topic, the user just needed to double click the topic title. To see a detailed description and discussion for a particular subtopic, double clicking the title of the subtopic would bring up the discussion window, a sample of which is displayed in Figure 5.4. Session participants could add descriptions of the subtopics under the "Specifics" tab and enter ideas and comments under the "Discussion" tab.

A questionnaire was used to collect data at the individual and team levels. Quantitative data collected at the individual level were goal congruence, goal understanding, cognitive effort, distraction, session process satisfaction, and session outcome satisfaction. We did not measure cognitive effort consumed by each process; instead, we measured the total cognitive effort consumed during group interaction, since we felt it might be more fruitful to do it this way since this is an exploratory study. Goal understanding was measured to check whether participants understood the team goal. Group productivity was measured at the group level. Focus Theory defines group productivity as the degree of goal attainment and has two components: team efficiency and team effectiveness. Team efficiency for each group interaction session was not measured because the interaction

Figure 5.4   **Discussion Window**

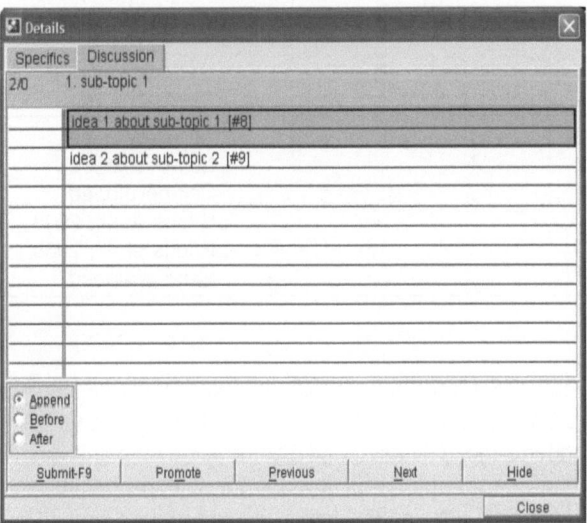

modes, tasks for each session, and team sizes were so different that measuring efficiency would generate little insight into group productivity. For example, a task that might take one group five minutes to finish in FtF mode might take twenty-four hours in asynchronous mode. The efficiency measure was not comparable across the modes and session.

If team effectiveness is a measure of degree of goal attainment, the quality of final deliverables produced by each team in this study could be used to estimate goal attainment. However, the final deliverables produced by each team were different. For example, the deliverable for the design team was the design of software, and the deliverable for the software development team was Java code. The two were not comparable. In addition, it would be more informative to have team effectiveness measured for each interaction session so that quantitative data and qualitative data of that session could be triangulated to provide insights into group interactions through the lens of Focus Theory. A more realistic measure, the number of fully discussed subtopics, was adopted to estimate group productivity for each session for a particular team. Before each group interaction session, the team leader listed subtopics under five standard topics: Tasks Completed Last Week, Tasks for This Week, Approaching Deadlines, Agenda Items, and Open Issues/Problems. After the session the team leader reported which subtopics had been fully or partially discussed, or not discussed at all. The number of fully discussed subtopics was used to measure interaction session productivity.

Satisfaction in this study also was measured as a kind of surrogate measure of group productivity because it is "a valenced affective arousal with respect to goal attainment" (Briggs et al., 2008). Group interaction process satisfaction and group outcome satisfaction were respectively estimated along a five-item scale. Measures of group process satisfaction and outcome satisfaction had been developed and verified by Briggs and his colleagues (Briggs et al., 2008). Measures for other constructs such as goal congruence, goal understanding, distraction, and cognitive effort were developed by us. Table 5.2 lists the number of items for each measure. Please see Appendix 5.1 for items comprising constructs.

Four types of data analysis were performed on quantitative data in this study: ANOVA (demographic data), construct inter-items reliability test, factor analysis of constructs (goal congruence,

Table 5.2

Table of Constructs

Measures/Variables	Number of items	Developed by
Goal congruence	4	Self-developed
Distraction	4	Self-developed
Cognitive effort	6	Self-developed
Process satisfaction	5	Briggs et al., 2008
Outcome satisfaction	5	Briggs et al., 2008
Goal understanding	3	Self-developed

cognitive effort, and distraction), and repeated measure analysis for constructs (e.g., goal congruence, cognitive effort, distraction). One assumption of ANOVA and repeated measure analysis is the independence of observations. Five students took Classes 1 and 2 at the same time and participated in GSS-facilitated project process tracking sessions twice a week. These five students were (by pseudo-name): LL, YH, AD, TD, and EK. YH was in the Class 1 SD and in the Class 2 DES team, both of which belonged to group B. TD was in the Class 1 FI team and the Class 2 MGN team, both in group B. The remaining three students participated in two different modes in the same week. In addition, all team leaders of FI, MM, PP, and SD also participated the PMT sessions and also experienced two different modes in the same week. Questionnaire data were collected after each of these sessions; data from these participants were treated differently than those from others.

Therefore, LL, AD, and EK were excluded from the Class 1 and Class 2 data files for ANOVA and repeated measure analysis. YH and TD were excluded from the Class 1 data file, but were retained in the Class 2 data file because these subjects had repeated experience with the same mode in a particular week. Four team leaders of Class 1 (FI, MM, PP, SD team leaders) were excluded from the ANOVA and repeated measure analysis. No assumption of independence of observations for reliability test and factor analysis was made. LL, YH, AD, TD, and EK were excluded from the Class 2 data file, but kept in the Class 1 data file. The team leaders for Class 1 FI, MM, PP, and SD were excluded from the MGN data file but kept in their individual team files. All statistical analysis was conducted by using SPSS 10.0.

Participants were required to fill out the same questionnaire after each interaction session. When data for six weeks were used for a reliability test, the inter-item reliabilities may have appeared to be higher than they actually were. The reliability test therefore was conducted each week to see whether there were substantial differences. Reliabilities for all constructs were above .77, which was acceptable.

Factor Analysis

Exploratory factor analysis was conducted for items that were intended to measure three constructs: goal congruence, distraction, and cognitive effort. Two frequently-used factor analysis methods are principal axis factoring or maximum likelihood. In this study, maximum likelihood with promax rotation was used to extract factors. Promax is an oblique rotation used when factors/constructs are supposed to be correlated, as in the cases of distraction and cognitive effort. We therefore used oblique rotation. Three important factors were extracted by examining the Eigen values, scree plots, and factor loading matrixes of the items.

Three factors had Eigen values above 1, and could explain 73 percent of the total variance. Examination of the screen plots explained three important factors and factor loading matrixes indicated all items had a pretty clear loading on three factors. All cognitive effort items were loaded nicely on Factor 1, cognitive effort with a loading correlation within the range of .52–.90. All other items were loaded very low on this factor, except for one goal congruence item that was loaded as .23. All four goal congruence items were loaded on the second factor nicely, ranging from .60 to .95. All other items were loaded very low on this factor except for one cognitive effort item that was loaded as .30. Factor 3 was distraction, for which all items were loaded at .81–.86 and all other items were loaded very low. We do not include figures or tables about factor analysis due to the limited space. As a result of factor analysis, all original items were included when the composite scores for goal congruence, distraction, and cognitive effort were calculated. The composite score was the mean of the individual items.

Focus Theory Constructs Manifestations

This section addresses research question 1: How are Focus Theory constructs manifested during group interactions, and why? Since the study is an action research and exploratory in nature, the purpose of quantitative data analysis is not hypotheses testing, as it would be in a strictly controlled experiment. For each construct measured in the study, repeated measure analysis was conducted to see how constructs were manifested quantitatively.

Repeated measure analysis, a type of ANOVA, was conducted for measures of goal congruence, goal understanding, distraction, cognitive effort, group session effectiveness, group session process satisfaction, and group session outcome satisfaction. Between-subject factor was group. Within-subject factors were week and mode. There were three interaction modes: FtF, synchronous, and asynchronous. Two weeks were devoted to using the same interaction mode. Three groups illustrated three sequences of interaction modes. The sequence for group A was FtF, synchronous, and asynchronous; the sequence for group B was synchronous, asynchronous, and FtF; the sequence for group C was asynchronous, FtF, and synchronous. The variables were measured by Likert format scales. All items except cognitive items were recoded so that 1 indicated lower and 7 indicated higher value.

Goal Congruence

Goal congruence measures the degree to which team goals are congruent with individual goals. It was expected that interaction modes would not affect goal congruence. In other words, participants were anticipated to have relatively identical levels of goal congruence in all three interaction modes.

Repeated measure analysis indicated that the measure of goal congruence was different for interaction modes $F(2, 54) = 3.96$, $p = 0.025$, partial $\eta^2 = 0.10$; and week*group $F(2, 27) = 4.68$, $p = 0.018$, partial $\eta^2 = 0.26$. A post-hoc Bonferroni test illustrated that the measure of goal congruence was higher for FtF than for synchronous (Mean Difference = 0.28, SD = 0.09, $p = 0.017$) mode. The measure of goal congruence was higher for FtF modes than for asynchronous mode, but the difference only approached significance (Mean Difference = 0.26, SD = 0.11, $p = 0.078$). There was no significant difference in the goal congruence measure between synchronous and asynchronous modes (Mean Difference = 0.02, SD = 0.13, $p = 1.00$).

The interaction between week and group is illustrated by Figure 5.5, which implied that the three groups had different change patterns of goal congruence. Groups A and C had relatively constant perceived goal congruence, whereas Group B had higher goal congruence in week 2 than in week 1 (Mean Difference = .36, Standard Error = .12, $p = .007$).

Figure 5.5   **Means of Goal Congruence for Week*Group**

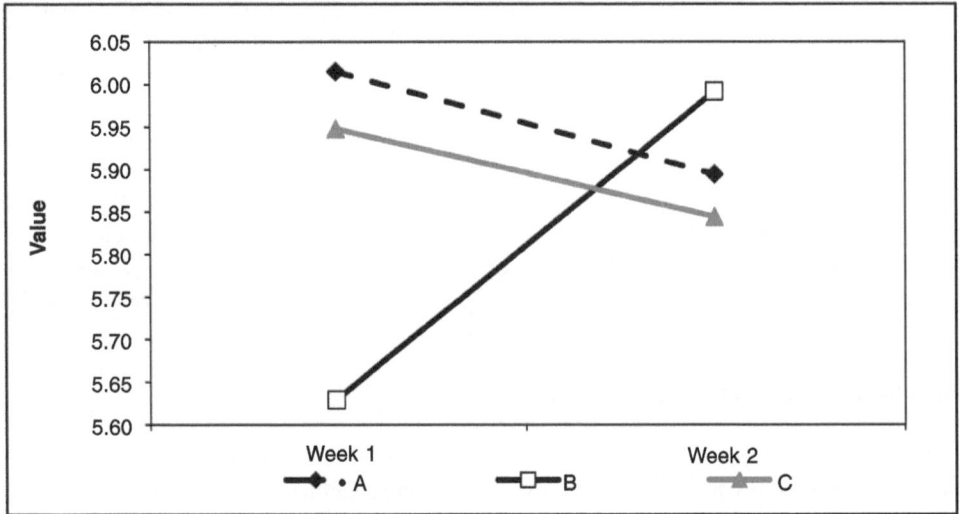

To examine why goal congruence was different for FtF and distributed interaction modes and explore what may affect goal congruence judgment, an analysis of goal understanding was undertaken to gain some insights about goal congruence, since it was impossible to observe goal congruence directly.

Team goal understanding is examined to estimate whether participants understand their team's goals. It was expected that goal understanding would be higher in FtF mode than in distributed modes, because participants might have more effective communication in FtF mode than in distributed modes.

Repeated measure analysis indicated that the measure of goal understanding was different for interaction mode $F(2, 54) = 10.86$, $p < 0.001$, partial $= 0.29$; week $F(2, 27) = 4.36$, $p = .046$, partial $\eta^2 = 0.14$, and week*group $F(2, 27) = 4.38$, $p = 0.004$, partial $\eta^2 = 0.25$. The post-hoc Bonferroni test indicated that the measure of goal understanding was higher for FtF than for synchronous (Mean Difference $= 0.66$, SD $= 0.17$, $p = 0.002$) and asynchronous (Mean Difference $= 0.68$, SD $= 0.13$, $p < 0.001$) modes. There was no difference between the measures for synchronous and asynchronous modes (Mean Difference $= 0.02$, SD $= 0.19$, $p = 1.00$). Participants appeared to have understood team goals better in week 2 than in week 1 (Mean Difference $= .23$, SD $= .11$, $p = .046$). The interaction of week and group is illustrated by Figure 5.6, which illustrates that participants in FtF mode did not experience much change in perceived goal understanding. However, participants in distributed mode were shown to have had better goal understanding in week 2 than in week 1.

The profile for goal understanding was somewhat similar to that for goal congruence, a result that seems to imply that perceived goal congruence was related to perceived goal understanding. If participants had had better understanding of team goals, they might have perceived more goal congruence between the team goals and personal goals. The correlation analysis between these two constructs supports this statement (Pearson's r $= .69$, $p < .001$).

Distraction

When participants interacted asynchronously, they did not have time pressure for the task, and could have chosen a time when there was little distraction to do the task. When participants interacted

Figure 5.6 **Means of Goal Understanding for Week*Group**

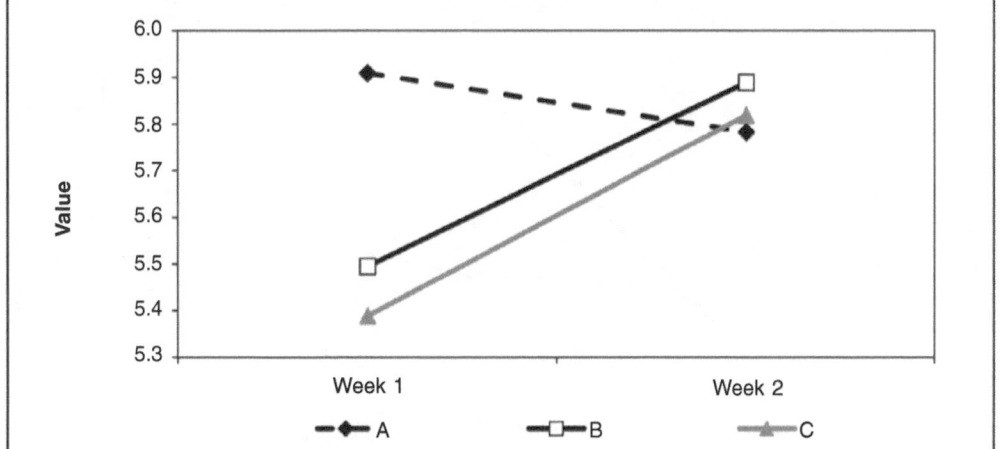

in FtF mode, they might have talked about things not relevant to group tasks and been distracted. When they interacted in synchronous mode, they had oral communication with other team members in the same room, but had to type ideas and comments into the system. Typing and talking at the same time can be very distracting and it was predicted that synchronous interaction would be more distracting than FtF interaction, which in turn is more distracting than asynchronous interaction.

Repeated measure analysis revealed no significant differences of distraction between modes, weeks, and groups. Neither were the interactions significant. Participants in synchronous interaction found that typing and talking at the same time could be distracting; however, it might be similar in FtF interactions. Just like one participant in FtF mode said: "It was hard to do talking and typing at the same time, sometimes, I thought that I had an idea, then I started to type. However, after typing, I kind of did not catch up with the group conversation" (quoted from the author's field notes of Class 2 SW Week 1 FtF). Some students suggested a need for specifying a person to act as a secretary to do note-taking for the team. According to their comments, the author suggested that every participant in FtF interactions log on to the system so the secretary could take the notes and all other participants could enter comments if they wanted to, allowing participants to focus on oral discussion and still keep a record of the group interaction.

However, there was another source of distraction in FtF interaction in relatively large teams, for example, a team of six people could have three conversations going on at the same time. There could be distractions when participants engaged in asynchronous communication, too. They could do multiple tasks at the same time, working on the task, and eating, drinking, listening to music, or talking to other people.

The result and observations suggested that different interaction modes may have different types of distraction; however, the level of distraction was more or less identical across three levels.

Cognitive Effort

Cognitive effort estimates the amount of attention resources used for communication, information access, and deliberation. If participants can communicate effectively, information access and

Figure 5.7   **Means of Cognitive Effort for Mode*Group**

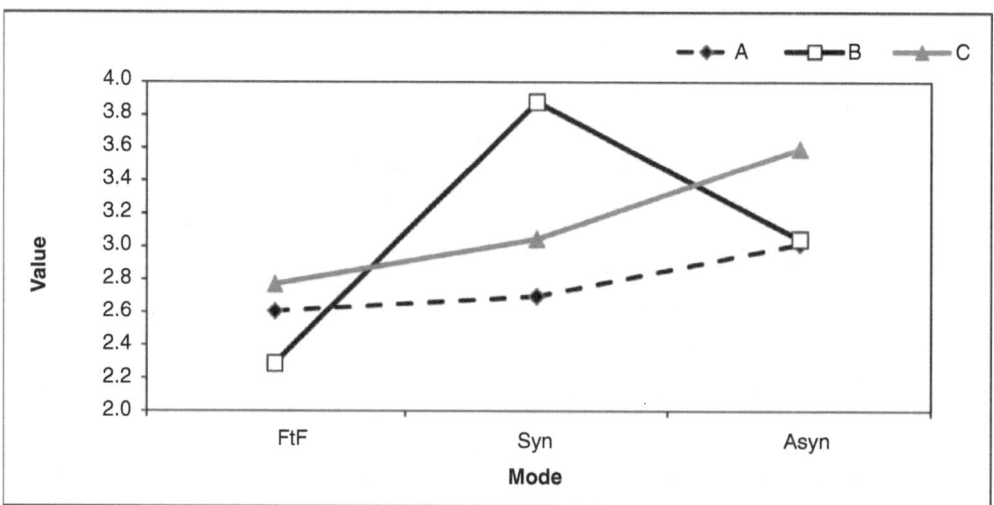

deliberation may become easier. FtF communication should provide the easiest communication because it supports all communication channels. Participants can encode messages in verbal and nonverbal channels, and message receivers can interpret messages from one or more channels. The distinction between synchronous and asynchronous communication is immediacy of feedback. In synchronous communication, participants can get feedback or response from team members immediately, and participants can get clarifications and responses in real time, thus reducing misunderstanding and waiting time. In contrast, participants in asynchronous mode must type ideas and comments into the system, and wait for minutes, hours or even days for a response or feedback. Delayed feedback makes it very difficult to engage in group discussion, negotiation, and consensus building. It had been predicted that participants would perceive relatively low cognitive effort for FtF mode, higher cognitive effort for synchronous mode, and highest cognitive effort in asynchronous mode.

Repeated measure analysis indicated that the measure of cognitive effort was different for interaction mode $F(2, 54) = 7.03$, $p = 0.002$, partial $\eta^2 = 0.21$, and mode*group $F(2, 27) = 4.47$, $p = 0.003$, partial $\eta^2 = 0.25$. The post-hoc Bonferroni test indicated that perceived cognitive effort was lower for FtF sessions than for synchronous (Mean Difference = $-.59$, SD = 0.19, $p = .012$) and asynchronous sessions (Mean Difference = -0.66, SD = 0.23, $p = .019$), there was no difference between synchronous and asynchronous sessions (Mean Difference = 0.07, SD = 0.17, $p = 1.00$).

The interaction of week and group is illustrated by Figure 5.7, which indicates that participants in Groups A and C experienced different patterns of cognitive effort change than those in Group B. Group B experienced more cognitive effort in synchronous mode than Group A and C in the same mode. However, the post-hoc Bonferroni pairwise comparison indicated that only the difference between Groups A and B in synchronous mode was significant (Mean Difference = -1.18, Standard Error = .39, $p = .016$). Group B experienced synchronous mode first, whereas Group A experienced FtF mode before employing synchronous-distributed mode. It was possible for Group A to have established the communication norms and familiarity with the software in FtF mode and therefore to have perceived less cognitive effort in synchronous mode than Group B, which had had no advance experience with the software.

It seemed that there were at least three major reasons why participants perceived synchronous interaction to be more difficult than FtF interaction. First, the system's interface did not clearly indicate who was discussing which topic, making it difficult for participants to locate the topic under discussion, especially when they were engaging in synchronous interaction for the first time. When the team got used to the interaction procedure, it was easier for them to locate the topic under discussion. This way interactions in week 2 were smoother than in week 1 for most teams.

Second, parallel input for this study could have created more than one conversation thread at a time, and this could have caused misunderstanding or confusion. Prior GSS research had indicated that parallel input of GSS was an advantage because group productivity could be increased by allowing multiple participants to enter input at the same time (e.g., Nunamaker et al., 1991). It is true for idea generation task, where ideas entered are independent from each other. In our study, participants usually needed to engage in focused discussion, ideas typed into the system were not independent from one another, and conversation was always built upon what had been said and understood. Existence of more than one conversation thread could cause misunderstanding or confusion, or at least make message interpretation more difficult.

The following messages/comments in italics illustrate this point. They were copied from interaction session minutes, and the notes inside brackets contain information about the interaction session from which the comments were copied. For the protection of participants' identities, all name tags were replaced with "*Tom*" for male participants, and "*Jenny*" for female participants. If a particular conversation involved more than one male or female participant, the name tag designates "*Tom1*," "*Tom2*," "*Jenny1*," "*Jenny2*," and so on. The capitalization of original name tags was retained. Most messages had a line number at the end, and this number was automatically appended by the system.

Where? [Tom2][#36]
why aren't the names showing up [Tom4][#37]
306 [Tom1][#38]
don't know [Tom1][#39]
—(Class 2 TST Week 3 Syn)

Statement 3 was the answer to statement 1, and statement 4 was the answer for statement 2.

Third, synchronous group interactions in text format tended to have created information overload for several reasons: the existence of more than one topic at a time; parallel input; limited time to read input, think, and type an appropriate response. Sometimes, one participant might still have been thinking and typing a response after other participants had moved to another topic, making the response seem irrelevant to the current topic.

Group Interaction Session Effectiveness

Group session effectiveness was used as the surrogate measure of group productivity. It was measured by the number of fully discussed agenda topics. Since FtF communication is easier and usually more effective than distributed communication, it was expected that FtF group interaction session would be more effective than distributed group interaction sessions. Being able to get immediate feedback during synchronous interactions should have facilitated discussion, negotiation, and consensus building. In contrast, delayed responses in asynchronous interactions should have made group discussion very difficult. It therefore was expected that synchronous interactions would be more effective than asynchronous interactions.

Repeated measure analysis revealed no significant difference in session effectiveness or in interactions between modes, weeks, or groups. There might be several reasons for this. First, the session sample size was small, thirty-nine sessions altogether. It was difficult for such a small sample size to detect a session-effectiveness difference even if there had been one.

Second, there may actually have been no difference in session effectiveness across three modes. Participants had felt it to be easier to have FtF interactions, but the group tasks might generally be so easy that participants could have effective distributed interactions even if they are not efficient as with FtF interactions. However, field observations and participants' feedback did not support this explanation and the interactions notes indicated that synchronous discussion tended to be more extensive and thorough than asynchronous discussion.

Third, the session effectiveness measure may not have been accurate. Group interaction session effectiveness was estimated from the number of fully discussed agenda items, but some agenda items may have been more complex than others and taken more time and effort to thoroughly discuss. In previous GSS research, group interaction effectiveness was usually measured by the quality of the final decision/report, the completeness of the information sharing, and the number of ideas/solutions generated. However, these measures were not applicable to this study. Future study that develops more accurate measures for effectiveness and group productivity is needed.

Group Session Process Satisfaction

Group session process satisfaction was estimated as how satisfied participants were with the group interaction process. This is closely related with communication. Therefore, it was expected that participants would be more satisfied with FtF interaction process than with distributed interaction. When participants become familiar with software usage and a particular distributed interaction mode, they may be more comfortable and confident to communicate in that mode. It is expected that participants are more satisfied with the same distributed interaction mode in week 2 than in week 1.

Repeated measure analysis indicated group session process satisfaction was different for interaction mode $F(2, 54) = 15.49$, $p < 0.001$, partial $\eta^2 = 0.37$; week $F(1, 27) = 13.86$, $p = .001$, partial $\eta^2 = 0.34$; mode*week $F(2, 54) = 4.98$, $p = .010$, partial $\eta^2 = 0.16$; and mode*week*group $F(4, 54) = 6.41$, $p < 0.001$, partial $\eta^2 = 0.32$. The post-hoc Bonferroni contrast test indicated that session process satisfaction was higher for FtF sessions than for synchronous (Mean Difference $= 0.88$, SD $= .20$, $p = .001$) and asynchronous sessions (Mean Difference $= 1.25$, SD $= .26$, $p < .001$). There was no difference between results for synchronous and asynchronous sessions (Mean Difference $= 0.38$, SD $= 0.22$, $p = .318$).

Participants generally appeared to feel more satisfied during the second-week interaction session than during the first-week session using sessions of the same mode (Mean Difference $= 0.43$, SD $= 0.12$, $p = 0.001$). The interaction of mode and week is illustrated by Figure 5.8. Participants had relatively constant process satisfaction in FtF mode; however, in distributed modes, they were more satisfied in week 2 than in week 1.

Group Session Outcome Satisfaction

Group session outcome satisfaction was used to estimate how satisfied participants were with group interaction outcomes. Because group session outcome satisfaction is closely related with process satisfaction, it was predicted that FtF participants were more satisfied with interaction outcome than participants using distributed mode, and participants would be more satisfied when using the same distributed format in a second week.

Figure 5.8   **Means of Session Process Satisfaction for Week*Mode**

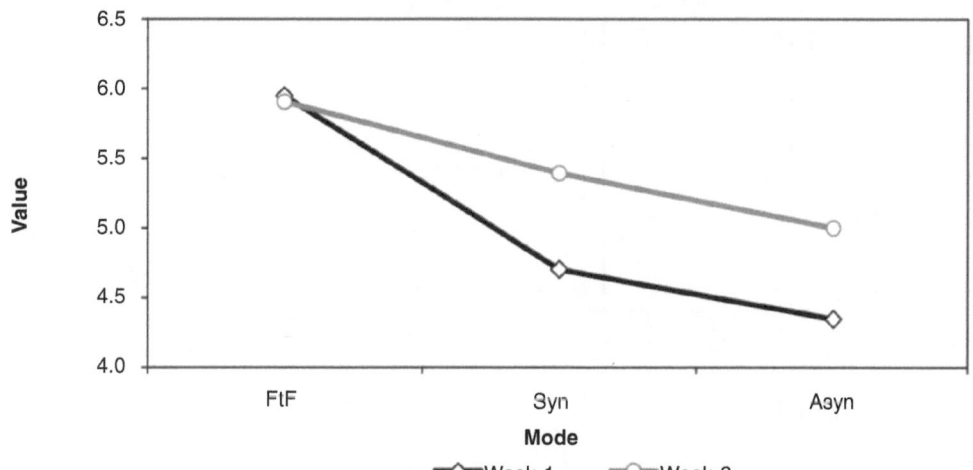

Figure 5.9   **Means of Session Outcome Satisfaction for Week*Mode**

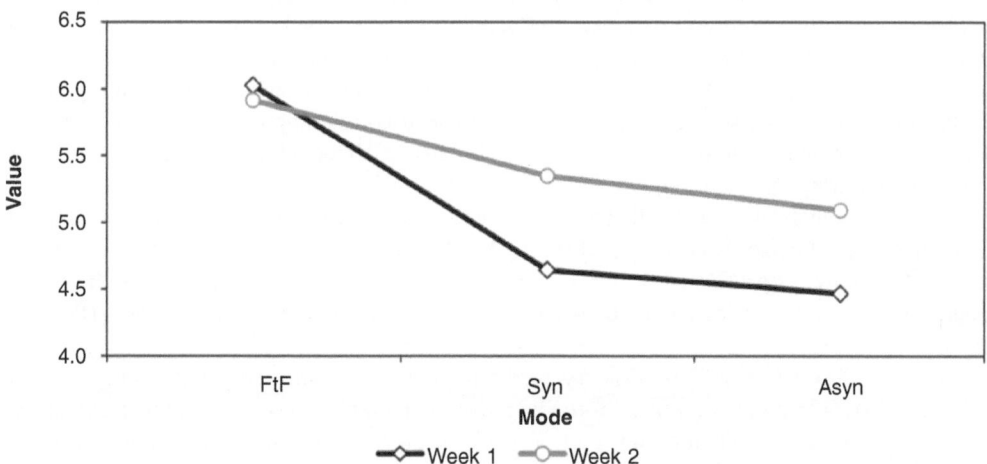

Repeated measure analysis indicated that group session outcome satisfaction was different for interaction mode $F(2, 54) = 13.31$, $p < 0.001$, partial $\eta^2 = 0.33$; week $F(1, 27) = 11.34$, $p < .001$, partial $\eta^2 = 0.30$; mode*week $F(2, 27) = 6.51$, $p = .003$, partial $\eta^2 = 0.19$; and mode*week*group $F(4, 54) = 4.39$, $p = 0.004$, partial $\eta^2 = 0.25$. The post-hoc Bonferroni test indicated that session outcome satisfaction was higher for FtF mode than for synchronous (Mean Difference = 0.98, SD = 0.20, $p < 0.001$) or asynchronous (Mean Difference = 1.19, SD = 0.27, $p = 0.000$) sessions. There was no difference between results for synchronous and asynchronous sessions (Mean Difference = 0.22, SD = 0.26, $p = 1.00$). Participants generally felt more satisfied with the second week than with the first week using the same communication mode (Mean Difference = 0.41, SD = 0.12, $p = 0.002$). The interaction of week and mode is illustrated by Figure 5.9. Just as in group session process satisfaction, participants indicated relatively constant outcome satisfaction in FtF sessions; however, they were more satisfied with the outcome in week 2 than with that in week 1.

Figure 5.10   **Distraction, Cognitive Effort, and Cognitive Load**

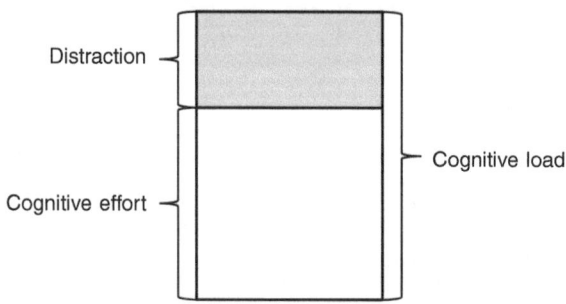

Correlation Analysis

Focus Theory implies that there should be a positive correlation between the constructs of goal congruence and cognitive effort, a positive correlation between cognitive effort and group productivity, and a negative correlation between distraction and cognitive effort. Group productivity was estimated by group session effectiveness in this study, and the relationship between the constructs of cognitive effort and of group productivity was estimated as the relationship between the measures of cognitive effort and group session effectiveness. Individual scores were used to calculate the correlations among distraction, cognitive effort, and goal congruence. An aggregation at the team level of the scores for cognitive effort was used to compute the correlation between cognitive effort and group session effectiveness, because each team had only one score for group session effectiveness.

Correlation analysis indicated that there was negative correlation between goal congruence and cognitive effort (Pearson's $r = -0.34$, $p < 0.001$, $N = 274$) and positive correlation between distraction and cognitive effort (Pearson's $r = 0.20$, $p = 0.001$, $N = 274$). The analysis also indicated that there was no significant correlation between cognitive effort and session effectiveness (Pearson's $r = 0.13$, $p = 0.13$, $N = 78$).

A closer examination at Focus Theory and group interactions showed that the study measured cognitive load instead of cognitive effort. Cognitive load refers to all the attention resources used for a task and includes attention resources used for irrelevant diversions taking place during the time allocated to accomplish a task. Cognitive effort refers only to attention resources that are used for task-related thinking or activities. For example, in a very noisy and crowded environment, it would be very difficult for a person to concentrate on reading a serious book; cognitive load may be high because some of the attention resources must be used to overcome distraction. Cognitive load for the same person to read the same book in a quiet environment might be lower, although cognitive effort used for reading the book might be the same. In other words, cognitive load includes cognitive effort and distraction. The difference between cognitive effort and cognitive load is illustrated by Figure 5.10.

Since cognitive load includes distraction, there should be a positive correlation between cognitive load and distraction, a relationship supported by correlation analysis. The term *cognitive load* will be used later to designate the cognitive effort measured in this study. Differentiation between cognitive load and cognitive effort also explains the negative correlation between cognitive load and goal congruence. When participants perceive team goals are congruent with their personal goals, they are willing to invest cognitive effort for the task, and they evaluate cognitive load against cognitive effort that needs to be invested. The higher the goal congruence, the more cognitive effort they were willing to invest and the smaller a cognitive load was perceived to be, given a constant cognitive effort. Focus Theory posits that there is a positive relationship between the constructs of cognitive effort and group productivity, but such a relationship could not be tested by the correlation between perceived cognitive load and group session effectiveness.

Reflection about Focus Theory

This section addresses research question 2, which investigated the ways in which Focus Theory is useful and in what ways it is limited in terms of explaining observed phenomena, and suggesting how can it be improved.

This study suggested that Focus Theory has some explanatory power for the observed phenomena. Group interaction seemed to involve all three processes that are specified by Focus Theory, and facilitating any of the three was likely to increase perceived satisfaction of interaction process and outcome, which could be surrogate measures of group productivity.

Focus Theory specifies that the group engage in three processes in interactions: communication, information access, and deliberation. Communication process can be directly observed. The author's observation and participants' feedback indicated that communication was a very important process for group interaction. When communication was smoother, participants were more satisfied. Communication in FtF was more efficient and effective than distributed communication. When groups engaged in synchronous interaction, since they could only communicate in text from different locations, it was difficult for them to locate the topic under discussion, and there could be more than one conversation at the same time; as a result, communication in synchronous mode was not as smooth as in FtF interaction. Participants made fewer contributions to asynchronous interactions, however, and feedback to a contribution was delayed. This made group discussion and negotiation difficult.

As a result, participants were more satisfied with FtF interaction than distributed interaction.

GSS supported information access by displaying comments and ideas on the computer screen promptly and by saving these comments and ideas for future access. The study indicated that information access was necessary for group interactions. The author's observation indicated that the effect of information access was confounded with the effect of communication. If participants could communicate more effectively and efficiently, they should have been able to access, and understand more information about, their tasks. It was seen that in asynchronous interactions delayed feedback made some information unavailable and prevented participants' continuation of their discussion tasks.

When participants were asked what they liked about GSS-facilitated interactions, and what system features they liked, some reported that they liked being able to take notes by using the system. All comments that mentioned recorded interaction notes (eleven in number) indicated that recorded notes were useful to track what had been said and decided. These comments did not state that information access was important for group interaction; however, the comments implied that keeping interaction notes was important. The underlying implication was that participants read the notes during and/or after group interactions as a form of information access.

Although deliberation is a process that is nearly impossible to observe with the naked eye, group process structure was supposed to facilitate group deliberation. Many prior GSS studies had used a structured process for decision making: understand the problem—brainstorm the solutions—organize solutions—vote on the solutions—discuss and select the optimal solution. This process structure allows a group to experience both divergent thinking and convergent thinking in an organized procedure. Divergent thinking (brainstorm activity) allows participants to explore as large a solution space as possible, calling upon organization and voting tools to help participants narrow down the number of solutions and evaluate and select solutions according to certain criteria. In this study, a project process tracking template was used instead of this structure. The session template listed five standard agenda topics: tasks completed in the past week, tasks in this week, approaching deadlines, agenda items, and open issues/questions. Team leaders created subtopics for these standard topics, and groups usually started with the first subtopic and moved through all subtopics sequentially. This template provided structural support for all three interaction modes. The template clearly listed all items that need to be discussed in a particular session, and it helped focus participants' attention on one small topic at a time.

When participants were asked what they liked about GSS facilitated interactions, eight mentioned that the structure and outline of the meeting were helpful. The comments and notes did not specify that deliberation was an important process in group activity. However, Focus Theory specifies that group deliberation could be a structured process (understand the problem—brainstorm the solutions—organize solutions—vote on the solutions—discuss and select the optimal solutions) or a chaotic process (understand the problem, get one solution, and use this solution). Consequently, it is reasonable to argue that, if participants like the organization or structure of an interaction, the structure may be a useful feature and may facilitate a group deliberation process.

However, there are several issues with Focus Theory that need to be addressed before testing the validity of Focus Theory in empirical settings. The first issue is that Focus Theory does not explicitly differentiate between cognitive effort and cognitive load, which is a measurement issue. Whenever perceived cognitive effort is measured, it seems that we in fact are measuring cognitive load. Without being able to measure cognitive effort accurately, investigation of the relationship between cognitive effort and productivity cannot proceed.

The second issue is how to measure the cognitive effort consumed by three processes, respectively, assuming that we could measure the cognitive effort. Focus Theory specifies three processes involved in group activities—communication, information access, and deliberation—and they are tightly interwoven. Communicators can access task-relevant information when they communicate with their team members, and if they do not communicate, deliberation won't move to anywhere. As the theory proposes that three processes are correlated, it is very difficult to separate them. For example, when participants communicate very successfully, it is likely that they will access more relevant information and can deliberate or think about the task more effectively. When participants cannot communicate well, they may not have enough information to think about. Allocating more cognitive effort to communication may improve communication effectiveness, and make information access and deliberation much easier, permitting participants to allocate less cognitive effort to information access and deliberation and still be able to increase group productivity.

Moreover, not all three processes can be easily observed. In the study, the process of communication could be observed, and so could some formats of information access. Information access was manifested as reading agenda items and notes, reading documents related to the group task, conducting online searches for task-related information, and requesting information from team members and instructors. Requesting information from others always involved communication, and it was very difficult to differentiate between communication and information access. It was impossible to observe deliberation directly; we could observe only some manifestations or effects of the group deliberation process. For example, structured problem solving usually facilitates a group deliberation process, letting researchers observe whether a problem solving structure makes the group deliberation process more efficient/effective or less so. The fact that three processes may be tightly interwoven and that some processes are difficult to observe gives rise to a measurement issue: How can one measure cognitive effort that is consumed by three processes, respectively?

The third issue is that the proposition that allocation of attention resources to three processes interferes with one another may not be valid. Focus Theory proposes that allocation of attention resources to three processes interferes with one another. For example, allocating more attention to communication makes less attention available for information access and deliberation. However, a closer examination of daily-life communication reveals that three cognitive processes may not interfere with one another if the threshold of cognitive load has not been reached. For example, allocating more cognitive effort to communication does not necessarily reduce cognitive effort available for deliberation, if the cognitive load threshold or ceiling has not been reached. Since this study did not collect empirical data about attention resources allocation to three processes, future study of this issue is needed.

The fourth issue is that the weights of three cognitive processes are not specified by the theory. The author's observations and student feedback in this study indicated that information access and deliberation were not as important as communication. In most cases, when participants communicated very clearly, the interaction was more effective and/or efficient, and participants were more satisfied. What should be the weights of cognitive processes in terms of their impact on group productivity? Which process is most important when considering group productivity? In other words, which process may be a bottleneck for group productivity for a particular interaction scenario? For a simple group activity such as deciding a meeting date and time, participants who communicate well can easily get results without any other information access, and with very little deliberation. In this scenario, communication may be the only process that is important.

STUDY LIMITATIONS, CONTRIBUTIONS, AND FUTURE RESEARCH

Readers may point out that there are three major limitations in the study. The first is that the study used students as subjects. Since students may have had little working experience, it may be difficult to generalize the study results to personnel in a working environment. However, the students in this study were juniors and seniors whose average number of full-time working years was approximately four. Many had had some working experience. Moreover, there is the debate about whether students should be used as surrogates for working personnel in various decision making situations (e.g., Briggs et al., 1996; Enis et al., 1972; Ferber, 1977; Hughes and Gibson, 1991; Remus, 1986; Shuptrine, 1975). Enis et al. (1972) state that students may only be appropriate surrogates when internal validity is more important than external validity. Shuptrine (1975) and Ferber (1977) suggest using students for exploratory research or pretesting of experimentation. Our study investigates how Focus Theory constructs are manifested during group interactions; it therefore focuses on internal validity instead of external validity. In addition, the study is exploratory. Therefore, it is appropriate to use students as subjects for this study.

The second limitation was that the project teams were not working in a real distributed environment and the simulation of asynchronous interactions may not have been sufficiently realistic. In a real distributed environment, team members would be expected to communicate only via the system. In the study, because participants were on the same campus, they had opportunities to engage in discussions outside the classroom. This may have affected the validity of results summarized from asynchronous interactions. However, this limitation would not invalidate the results as a whole, because the study was more interested in how Focus Theory constructs are manifested during group interactions than in the outcomes of group interactions.

Another possible limitation that readers may point out is that our research design is not a strictly controlled experiment; there may be confounding variables that affect the results. As we have explained earlier in the paper, the study is exploratory; it helps with understanding and building the theory, not testing the theory. Therefore, we think the study design should not be a concern.

Understanding the mechanism of group productivity should prove useful to team leaders and participants in a distributed environment because they might be helped to select and configure appropriate collaboration technology, and improve group interaction efficiency and/or effectiveness. It also should assist collaboration technology designers in determining what system features need to be implemented and improved to support more productive group interactions. The phenomenon of group productivity for group interactions supported by collaboration technology had not previously been fully addressed, even though studies in GSS had examined group productivity to a certain degree. This study added knowledge about this topic, even though more work needs to be done in order to test Focus Theory.

Future study needs to address all issues discussed in this section before we can put Focus Theory in test in an empirical setting.

CONCLUSION

Many prior studies that investigated group productivity and technology explicitly or implicitly adopted an input-process-output model (Dennis et al., 1988; Nunamaker et al., 1991; Nunamaker et al., 1993) to study how input factors affect process, which in turn affects output. It is very difficult to examine how thousands of different combinations of input factors might affect group process and outcome. Therefore, a parsimonious, bounded, general causal theory of team productivity is needed to substantially advance the research work of group collaboration. Focus Theory has been proposed as such a theory. This study was an exploratory study to understand Focus Theory in group interactions facilitated by collaboration technology. The study indicated that Focus Theory had some explanatory power and theoretical limitations. Focus Theory specifies that three processes consume attention resources to accomplish a group task: communication, information access, and deliberation. The study indicated that three processes consumed attention resources. However, several issues need to be addressed before Focus Theory could be put into empirical test: the theory needs to differentiate between cognitive effort and cognitive load, specify which process is more important in what conditions, and find a method to measure attention resources consumed by each of the processes separately. More research is needed to understand both Focus Theory in particular and group productivity in general.

ACKNOWLEDGMENTS

We sincerely thank Dr. Gail Corbitt, Dr. James Sager, and Dr. Stanley C. Gardiner for their help with data collection.

REFERENCES

Argyris, C.; Putnam, R.; and Smith, D.M. 1985. *Action Science*. San Francisco, CA: Jossey-Bass.
Benbasat, I., and Lim, L.H. 1993. The effects of group, task, context, and technology variables on the usefulness of group support systems: A meta-analysis of experimental studies. *Small Group Research,* 24, 4, 430–462.
Briggs, R.O. 1994. The focus theory of group productivity and its application to the design, development,

and testing of electronic Group Support Technology. Dissertation, MIS Department. Tucson: University of Arizona.

Briggs, R.O.; Balthazard, P.A.; and Dennis, A.R. 1996. Graduate business students as surrogates for executives in the evaluation of technology. *Journal of End User Computing*, 8, 4, 11–17.

Briggs, R.O.; Reinig, B.A.; and de Vreede, G.-J. 2008. The yield shift theory of satisfaction and its application to the IS/IT domain. *Journal of Association of Information Systems*, 9, 5, 267–293.

Dennis, A.R., and Gallupe, R.B. 1993. A history of group support systems empirical research: Lessons learned and future directions. In L.M. Jessup and J.S. Valacich (eds.), *Group Support Systems: New Perspectives*, 59–77. New York: Macmillan.

Dennis, A.R.; George, J.F.; Jessup, L.M.; Nunamaker, J.F. Jr.; and Vogel, D.R. 1988. Information technology to support electronic meetings. *MIS Quarterly*, 12, 4, 591–624.

Dennis, A.R.; Nunamaker, J.F. Jr.; and Vogel, D.R. 1990–91. A comparison of laboratory and field research in the study of electronic meeting systems. *Journal of Management Information Systems*, 7, 3 (Winter), 107–135.

Enis, B.B.; Cox, K.K.; and Stafford, J.E. 1972. Students as subjects in consumer behavior experiments. *Journal of Marketing Research*, 9, 1 (February), 72–74.

Ferber, R. 1977. Research by convenience. *Journal of Consumer Research*, 4, 1 (June), 57–58.

Fjermestad, J., and Hiltz, S.R. 1999–2000. An assessment of group support systems experimental research: Methodology and results. *Journal of Management Information Systems*, 15, 3, 7–149.

———. 2000–2001. Group support systems: A descriptive evaluation of case and field studies. *Journal of Management Information Systems*, 17, 3, 115–161.

Fjermestad, J.; Hiltz, S.R.; and Turoff, M. 1993. An integrated theoretical framework for the study of group decision support systems. In *Proceedings of the 26th Annual Hawaii International Conference on Systems Science*, Waikoloa, Hawaii, January 3–6.

Hughes, C.T., and Gibson, M.L. 1991. Students as surrogates for managers in a decision-making environment: An experimental study. *Journal of Management Information Systems*, 8, 2, 153–166.

Jessup, L.M., and Valacich, J.S. (eds.). 1993. *Group Support Systems: New Perspectives*. New York: Macmillan.

McCleod, P.L. 1992. An assessment of the experimental literature on electronic support for group work: Results of a meta-analysis. *Human-Computer Interaction*, 7, 3, 257–280.

Miller, G.A. 1956. The magical number seven, plus or minus two: Some limits on our capacity for processing information. *The Psychological Review*, 63, 81–97.

Nunamaker, J.F. Jr.; Dennis, A.R.; Valacich, J.S.; Vogel, D.R.; and George, J.F. 1993. Group support systems research: Experience from the lab and field. In L.M. Jessup and J.S. Valachich (eds.), *Group Support Systems: New Perspectives*, 3–7. New York: Macmillan.

———. 1991. Electronic meeting systems to support group work. *Communications of the ACM*, 34, 7, 40–61.

Pinsonneault, A., and Kraemer, K.L. 1989. The impact of technology on groups: An assessment of the empirical research. *Decision Support Systems*, 5 (Special Issue on Group Decision Support Systems), 197–216.

———. 1990. The effects of electronic meetings on group processes and outcomes: An assessment of the empirical research. *European Journal of Operational Research*, 46, 2, 143–161.

Remus, W. 1986. Graduate students as surrogates for managers in experiments on business decision making. *Journal of Business Research*, 14, 1, 19–25.

Romano, N.C.; Briggs, R.O.; Nunamaker, J.F. Jr.; and Mittleman, D. 1999. Distributed GSS facilitation and participation: Field action research. In *Proceedings of the 32nd Hawaii International Conference on System Sciences*, Maui, Hawaii, Jan. 5–8.

Shuptrine, F.K. 1975. On the validity of using students as subjects in consumer behavior investigations. *Journal of Business*, 48, 3 (July), 383–390.

Susman, G.I., and Evered, R.D. 1978. An assessment of the scientific merits of action research. *Administrative Science Quarterly*, 23, 4, 582–603.

Walsh, K.R. 1996. Generating insight for reengineering. Dissertation, MIS Department. Tucson: The University of Arizona.

APPENDIX 5.1. GROUP ACTIVITY EVALUATION SURVEY

Your class: _____ Your team: _____ Date: _____

Meeting mode: ☐ FtF ☐ Synchronous-Distributed ☐ Asynchronous-Distributed

Your Date of Birth (Month_Date_Year) _____ (e.g., if your birth date is August 5, 1967, your code is 08_05_1967)

Thank you for choosing to participate in this study. Your participation is optional. There are no correct or wrong answers for the questions. Please be forthright and candid with your answer. Please do not write your full name on the questionnaire. Please email questions to Fang Chen at fchen@email.arizona.edu.

A. Questions about Team Activity

```
1 = Strongly Agree
2 = Moderately Agree
3 = Slightly Agree
4 = Neither Agree nor Disagree (Neutral)
5 = Slightly Disagree
6 = Moderately Disagree
7 = Strongly Disagree
```

Circle one response for each question.

	Strongly Agree			Neutral			Strongly Disagree
1. I have lots of experience with computers.	1	2	3	4	5	6	7
2. Reaching the team goal gets me closer to something I value.	1	2	3	4	5	6	7
3. It may help me personally if the team succeeds.	1	2	3	4	5	6	7
4. I consider myself to be a power-user of computers.	1	2	3	4	5	6	7

	Strongly Agree			Neutral			Strongly Disagree
5. It was easy to work out solutions for team tasks.	1	2	3	4	5	6	7
6. I am happy with the results of today's meeting.	1	2	3	4	5	6	7
7. I understood the team goal.	1	2	3	4	5	6	7
8. I understood what the group was supposed to accomplish.	1	2	3	4	5	6	7
9. Accomplishing the team purpose helps me attain personal aim(s).	1	2	3	4	5	6	7
10. Other things took my attention away from team activities.	1	2	3	4	5	6	7
11. Our task-related problems were not hard to solve.	1	2	3	4	5	6	7
12. It took very little effort to accomplish our tasks.	1	2	3	4	5	6	7
13. I feel satisfied with the way in which today's meeting was conducted.	1	2	3	4	5	6	7
14. Distractions interfered with my efforts for the team.	1	2	3	4	5	6	7
15. I feel good about today's meeting process.	1	2	3	4	5	6	7
16. It did not demand much cognitive effort to get the team task done.	1	2	3	4	5	6	7
17. I liked the way the meeting progressed today.	1	2	3	4	5	6	7
18. Outside influences kept me from paying attention to team efforts.	1	2	3	4	5	6	7
19. The team goal was clear to me.	1	2	3	4	5	6	7
20. I feel satisfied with the procedures used in today's meeting.	1	2	3	4	5	6	7
21. I feel satisfied about the way we carried out the activities in today's meeting.	1	2	3	4	5	6	7
22. I liked the outcome of today's meeting.	1	2	3	4	5	6	7
23. The team task was easy to solve.	1	2	3	4	5	6	7
24. I feel satisfied with the things we achieved in today's meeting.	1	2	3	4	5	6	7
25. If the team achieves its goal, it moves me toward an outcome I want.	1	2	3	4	5	6	7
26. I experienced distractions when working on team tasks.	1	2	3	4	5	6	7
27. When the meeting was finally over, I felt satisfied with the results.	1	2	3	4	5	6	7
28. Our accomplishments today give me a feeling of satisfaction.	1	2	3	4	5	6	7
29. It did not require hard thinking to accomplish team tasks.	1	2	3	4	5	6	7
30. I am highly computer literate.	1	2	3	4	5	6	7

82

B. Demographic Questions

32. How many years of full-time work experience do you have? _____

33. How old are you? _____

34. Sex: ☐ Male   ☐ Female

35. For how many years have you used computers? _____

Goal congruence: 2, 3, 9, 25
Distraction: 10, 14, 18, 26
Cognitive load: 5, 11, 12, 16, 23, 29
Process satisfaction: 13, 15, 17, 20, 21
Outcome satisfaction: 6, 22, 24, 27, 28
Goal understanding: 7, 8, 19
Computer literacy: 1, 4, 30

CHAPTER 6

PATTERNS IN COLLABORATION

Gwendolyn L. Kolfschoten, Paul Benjamin Lowry,
Douglas L. Dean, Gert-Jan de Vreede, and Robert O. Briggs

Abstract: *Collaboration is a critical skill and a key driver of performance in organizations. While collaboration has been studied in a variety of contexts, this chapter will demonstrate and argue that there is a need to study collaboration in three specific levels of abstraction: the effects of entire collaborative processes, emerging patterns in collaboration, and interventions in collaborative effort. We will show that without the clear distinction between these levels of abstraction, research will result in conflicting findings and confusion. This chapter will present the results of a meta-analysis of literature, and a pattern analysis in a database of transcripts of collaborative sessions. The contribution of this chapter will be the presentation of six emerging patterns of collaboration: generate, reduce, clarify, organize, evaluate, and build consensus. We describe each fundamental pattern of collaboration with common subtypes of these patterns. This article clarifies these patterns and describes common subtypes. It also describes the key interventions required to evoke them, and the constructs used in the literature to measure these patterns (lower level of abstraction). Further it will present how these patterns can be combined in collaborative processes, and the patterns that can be found on this level (higher level of abstraction). Together, the emerging patterns, subtypes, and constructs used to measure these subtypes are combined into a framework for the explication and measurement of patterns in collaboration.*

Keywords: *Collaboration, Measurement, Metrics, Patterns of Collaboration, Group Support Systems, Collaborative Software*

Collaboration is a critical skill and competence in organizations. Frost and Sullivan surveyed 946 decision makers using a collaboration index, and found that collaboration is a key driver of performance in organizations (Frost and Sullivan, 2007). Collaboration can take place within or between organizations, local or globally, or within small teams and groups. However, despite the "size" of the group or organization represented by actors or stakeholders, collaboration, in the end, is between people. Collaboration is studied in a large variety of domains and outcomes studied are various and difficult to compare.

Collaboration is critical to the performance of organizations, but also challenging (free riding, dominance, group think, inefficiency, etc.) (Nunamaker et al., 1997; Schwarz, 1994). Especially when group size increases, productivity tends to decrease, and conflict tends to increase (Steiner, 1972). Furthermore, involvement of multiple actors and stakeholders in collaboration increases interdependency and the complexity of conflict resolution (Bruijn and Heuvelhof, 2007).

To understand and study collaboration, the focus of research has often been an entire collaborative process, which in most cases exists of several activities. Examples of such processes are the Delphi process for expert evaluation (Linstone and Turoff, 1975), the EasyWinWin process for requirements negotiation (Boehm et al., 2001), and collaborative risk management (Vreede and Briggs, 2005). Another way to study a collaborative process, or any other process, would be to break the overall process down into a sequence of steps and then to study the inputs, process, and outcomes of each step. Another approach would be to study the precise intervention in a collaborative process and to study its distinct effects on outcomes, but also on group members and their interaction. Given these different levels of abstraction and the variety of domains in which collaboration occurs, it is difficult to compare outcomes of research on collaboration. This is, for instance, visible in the research on collaboration support in which conflicting findings were found (Dennis et al., 2001; Fjermestad and Hiltz, 1999, 2001). Also on a higher level of detail in research on ideation and brainstorming researchers have reported conflicting findings for almost two decades (Diehl and Stroebe, 1987; Henninger et al., 2006; Paulus et al., 1993; Santanen, 2005; Vathanophas and Liang, 2007).

To study and to predict and explain collaboration research could benefit from a mediating level of abstraction, a layer between the highly detailed interventions in groups such as brainstorming rules, or the higher level interventions such as the use of group support systems (GSS) (Nunamaker et al., 1997) and the overarching processes such as Dephi (Linstone and Turoff, 1975), risk management (Vreede et al., 2005), and EasyWinWin (Boehm et al., 2001). In this chapter, we will present a framework based on a set of emerging, fundamental patterns of collaboration. We will show how these patterns were derived, how they emerge in various collaborative processes, and how they can serve as a basis to study and compare interventions in collaborative work.

This chapter provides three main contributions that extend previous research. First, we derive and define the fundamental patterns of collaboration. Second, we will show how these patterns can be used to link detailed interventions in collaboration to high-level collaborative processes. Third, we offer an overview of subpatterns that are instantiations of each pattern and the constructs that are measured by researchers during the study of these subpatterns. All of these are combined into a framework for research in collaboration. This framework will help researchers and practitioners in collaboration support to better understand choices among implementations and what measures will best assess the key outcomes of these implementations.

The remainder of this chapter is organized as follows. First, we summarize background research. Second, we will derive and define the framework. Third, we will show the use of the framework. Next, we describe the research approach to identify subpatterns and metrics. Last, we discuss our findings for each of the patterns of collaboration and describe common subpatterns for each pattern. The paper concludes with recommendations for further research.

BACKGROUND

The six fundamental collaborative patterns described by Briggs (Briggs et al., 2003; Vreede et al., 2006; Vreede et al., 2009) are the following: generate, reduce, clarify, organize, evaluate, and build consensus. Since these six patterns make up most, if not all, collaborative work, they are essential topics of study in their own right.

Three additional distinctions are important regarding research of these patterns. First, there are multiple approaches, or processes, for how each pattern can be accomplished. For example, in the case of the generate pattern, past research has shown that there are many interventions that stimulate a group to produce different outcomes including different types of questions (Dean et al., 2006; Santanen et al., 2004), other stimuli (Hender et al., 2002), processes (Dennis and Valacich, 1994; Pinsonneault et al., 1999), and motivational approaches (Shepherd et al., 1996). If research focuses on outcomes of multipattern processes (MPPs) in which generation is one step, it is difficult to study the specific effects of these variations on both the MPPs and the individual constituent patterns.

Second, even when the same process is used, the process may be supported by different types of media and tools such as flip charts, paper, sticky notes, a single computer, or some form of collaborative software. If the effect of different supporting tools is evaluated for MPPs (e.g., problem solving, risk assessment) researchers are unable to study the specific merits of each approach for each pattern.

Finally, single-user computer applications and collaborative work environments, such as GSS and online communities, are not all created equal (Briggs et al., 2003). Rather, different tools and different features of these tools offer different forms of support. It would be easier to understand the effects of these tools and features if researchers study these features in relation to each specific pattern rather than for MPPs.

In summary, by studying each fundamental pattern as the primary unit of analysis, researchers will be better able to discover the effects that different processes, media, and tools have on outcomes. This understanding will help produce more predictable, effective outcomes for each pattern of collaboration, allowing collaborative engineers to put these together to form more effective and predictable MPPs. Having said this, there are both advantages and disadvantages of studying an overall process as opposed to studying its fundamental components. There are two primary advantages of studying MPPs instead of fundamental patterns: First, larger overall processes are sometimes more interesting to practitioners and organizations and thus can be more interesting to researchers. Second, in terms of adoption by organizations, the overall process is typically the unit of analysis that managers manage and measure.

The disadvantage of using the overall process as the unit of analysis is that components of the process can be poorly understood and measured. Returning to the risk management example, it is common to generate a list of potential risks and to reduce this list to a smaller set of key risks that the organization should further analyze. Next, mitigation strategies for these risks may be generated and prioritized. Finally, these mitigation approaches may need to be elaborated on and adapted to the organization. While studying such an overall process can be beneficial, it can also obscure a clearer understanding of each of the parts. An understanding of the parts, however, is essential if designers of collaboration activities are to understand the pros and cons of different approaches for each pattern. The only way to assess these outcomes at the pattern level is through appropriate measurement. Unless research and measurement are conducted at the pattern level, it is virtually impossible to predict how the application of different processes and support approaches will benefit or impede MPPs.

A greater understanding of how implementations of each pattern produce specific outcomes can provide a many-fold benefit because a set of improved, understood implementations could be used in a myriad of larger end-to-end processes while making the overall process easier to manage, repeat, and optimize. Study at the individual pattern level will also help researchers focus on and refine measures for each pattern. Accordingly, we call for researchers to study implementations of fundamental patterns of collaboration.

Collaboration Engineering (CE) is an approach to designing collaborative work practices for high-value recurring tasks, and deploying those designs for practitioners to execute for themselves without ongoing support from professional facilitators (Briggs et al., 2003; Vreede et al., 2006; Vreede et al., 2009). To successfully design collaboration processes (CPs) with predictable outcomes, the designer must know how the implementation of collaborative patterns will produce specific outcomes (Kolfschoten and Vreede, 2009). By predictable group interventions, we mean

Table 6.1

Fundamental Collaborative Patterns

#	Pattern	Description
1	Generate	Move from having fewer to having more concepts in the pool of concepts shared by the group.
2	Reduce	Move from having many concepts to a focus on less that the group deems worthy of further attention.
3	Clarify	Move from having less to having more shared understanding of concepts and of the words and phrases used to express them.
4	Organize	Move from less to more understanding of the relationships among concepts the group is considering.
5	Evaluate	Move from less to more understanding of the relative value of the concepts under consideration.
6	Build consensus	Move from having fewer to having more group members who are willing to commit to a proposal.

an understanding of how a specific intervention, which evokes specific patterns of collaboration, will result in specific outcomes. Facilitation interventions for CE may be captured as design patterns called thinkLets (Briggs et al., 2003; Kolfschoten et al., 2006; Vreede et al., 2006), which are scripted, reusable, and transferable collaborative activities. ThinkLets are best practices and therefore to some extent predictable; however, the predictability of thinkLets can largely improve if we gain more understanding about the relation between facilitation interventions and the patterns of collaboration that emerge in the group as a result of these interventions.

Research in collaboration support has focused mainly on high level outcomes such effectiveness, efficiency, and satisfaction (Fjermestad and Hiltz, 1999). However, lab and field studies in collaboration support show conflicting results (Fjermestad and Hiltz, 1999, 2001; Santanen, 2005). Studies have shown that very small changes in the interventions to support brainstorming have significant effects (Santanen et al., 2004; Shepherd et al., 1996).

An area in which research has been focusing on a single intervention and pattern is the brainstorming literature. However, researchers in this area have reported conflicting findings for almost two decades (Diehl and Stroebe, 1987; Henninger et al., 2006; Paulus et al., 1993; Santanen, 2005; Vathanophas and Liang, 2007). There are two key reasons for conflicting results. First, the brainstorming processes and tools used are different, resulting in questionable comparisons (Santanen, 2005). Second, the metrics used to compare quantity and quality of the ideas generated are different (Briggs and Reinig, 2007; Reinig and Briggs, 2008). To resolve these conflicting findings with respect to the effects of collaboration support, we need to study interventions in collaboration in more detail, and with a focus on cognitive effects of these interventions (Henninger et al., 2006; Santanen et al., 2004).

Briggs et al. described the six fundamental patterns of collaboration that make up common collaborative activities (Briggs et al., 2003; Vreede et al., 2006; Vreede et al., 2009). These are shown in Table 6.1.

A number of meta-analyses have reported outcomes studied in collaborative or group settings (Baltes et al., 2002; Dennis and Wixom, 2002; Fjermestad and Hiltz, 1999, 2001; Hwang, 1998; McLeod, 1992; Tyran and Shepherd, 1998). Fjermestad and Hiltz offer the most complete overview

Table 6.2

Outcome Factors from Fjermestad and Hiltz

Pattern	Outcome Factors
Generate	Number of comments Idea quality Creativity/innovation
Reduce	[not addressed]
Clarify	Level of understanding
Organize	[not addressed]
Evaluate	Decision quality Depth of evaluation
Build consensus	Commitment to results Decision agreement Commitment

of outcome constructs that have been studied. Outcomes used to describe the success of collaborative activities are categorized as efficiency, effectiveness, satisfaction, and consensus. Efficiency is a measure of the resources spent on a task. Effectiveness relates to quantity and quality of outcomes and factors such as communication, focus, understanding, and goal attainment. Satisfaction includes factors reflecting the perceptions of participants about participation and outcomes. Finally, consensus and commitment are sometimes reported as outcomes.

Most of these outcome factors pertain to the results of MPPs, instead of a single pattern of collaboration. A notable exception is the generate pattern, which while frequently used in MPPs, has also been much studied as a stand-alone pattern. While some of the factors can be used to measure fundamental patterns of collaboration, most of the fundamental patterns are not covered or are only partially covered by these factors. Table 6.2 shows a mapping between the six patterns of collaboration and the outcome factors reported by Fjermestad and Hiltz (1999).

For *reduce* and *organize*, no outcome factors are reported. This is likely because these patterns are often interim steps in MP collaborations (Kolfschoten et al., 2004). Also, one reason reduction has received so little research attention is that it has sometimes been confused with convergence but, as we will explain later, it is not the same thing. Measurement of organization is likely omitted in the literature because it can be accomplished in many ways.

This overview shows that much GSS research has focused on MPPs. This is also visible if we look at some of the research models used in GSS such as Nunamaker's input-process-output model (Nunamaker et al., 1997), the adaptive structuration theory (DeSanctis and Poole, 1994), and the task-technology-fit model of Zigurs and Buckland (1998). While very useful, each of these models focuses on the effect of collaboration support on an entire task rather than a specific collaborative pattern.

RESEARCH APPROACH

To study ways in which fundamental patterns have been implemented, studied, and measured, we searched for articles that studied these patterns. Collaboration is a broad field, which is studied in a variety of disciplines, such as GSS research, human-computer interaction, organizational science, psychology, social psychology, decision science, education, and many others. To find articles related to patterns of collaboration, we searched for articles based on the names of the six fundamental patterns and synonyms for these patterns. We used a variety of search indices including Google Scholar, Scopus, IEEE Explore, PsycINFO, ACM Digital Library, EBSCO, and Web of Science. Where possible, we used articles that offered an overview of research regarding the pattern. In other instances, we had to explore different studies to derive subpatterns and different approaches used to create the pattern. We kept collecting articles until no new subpatterns and metrics were found. Furthermore, we examined the citations in the located papers to find additional papers describing similar interventions and metrics used. This search produced ninety-seven articles. From the articles, we captured the definition of the phenomena of interest, which reflected the pattern or subpattern, the approach to evoke the pattern, and the metrics used to assess the outcomes. This approach was used for all patterns except the generate pattern because one of the authors had recently published a comprehensive meta-analysis on measurement approaches for this pattern that included ninety journal articles in top journals from the 1990 to 2005 time period (Dean et al., 2006). We now discuss our findings.

MEASURING PATTERNS OF COLLABORATION

"Generate" Pattern of Collaboration

The generate pattern is defined as moving from having fewer to having more concepts in the pool of concepts shared by a group. *Generate* is a pattern in which the group creates content. Briggs et al. (2003) initially called this pattern diverge because it was conceptualized in the context of creativity and ideation. Subsequent discussion between the current authors and Briggs led to the renaming of the concept as generate because beyond ideation content is often generated by a group when collecting information. There are two types of generation: (1) new or creative ideas (solutions, problem solving); and (2) collection of expertise, facts, and explanations (knowledge sharing).

Ideation is by far the most researched form of generate. Early idea-generation research used quantity as a measure of quality, assuming that if a sufficient number of ideas were produced, the resulting idea pool would be more likely to contain high-quality ideas (Osborn, 1953). Briggs and Reinig (2007) state that the ratio between quality and quantity is especially important when assessing the success of creativity. The positive correlation between quantity and quality has been found in some studies (Diehl and Stroebe, 1987; Gallupe et al., 1992; Valacich et al., 1993), but a negative correlation has been found in other studies (Connolly et al., 1990; Gryskiewicz, 1980).

Studies that go beyond merely enumerating ideas require researchers to select a definition of one or more of the three constructs that are typically operationalized as the dependent variable(s): (1) idea quality; (2) idea novelty, which is sometimes referred to as rarity or unusualness; and (3) idea creativity. Dean et al. (2006) found that more recent studies tend to go beyond just counting the number of ideas produced by a group. Instead, they both count ideas and assess ideas on a number of dimensions. Recent meta-analyses have drawn a distinction between two fundamental views of creativity: the novelty-centric view, where ideas are considered creative if they are novel or rare, and the quality-centric definition of creativity, where ideas must not only be novel, but must also be feasible, effective in solving the problem, relevant to the problem, and clearly defined (Dean et al., 2006; Plucker et al., 2004). Moreover, Dean et al. (2006) found that some studies have focused on quality indicators such as effectiveness, relevance, and clarity but have excluded novelty.

Table 6.3

Subpatterns and Measurement Constructs for Generate

Generate	Creativity	• Number of contributions (per participant/time interval) • Number of unique contributions • Number of off topic/outside scope • Number of double • Number of purposeful • Quality • Uniqueness • Creativeness • Ratio quality/creativity/uniqueness/double/ purposeful/ off-topic vs. number of total or other criterion
	Gathering	• Completeness • Relevance • Clarity • Accuracy • Reliability • Timeliness • Purposefulness • Usefulness

The terms *quality* ideas, *novel* ideas, and *creative* ideas should be reserved for ideas that meet specific thresholds of the constructs included in these measures. To identify novel ideas, quality ideas, and creative ideas, Dean et al. (2006) recommend a threshold approach similar to that introduced in Diehl and Stroebe (1987) and later used by Dennis et al. (1997). In this approach, quality ideas should meet a specific threshold on workability and relevance. Creative ideas should meet a specific threshold on novelty, workability, and relevance. These threshold measures are noncompensatory measures in the sense that strength in one quality indicator should not compensate for weakness in another area. Finally, total quality, total novelty, and total creativity can be defined by summing the score for each of these dimensions.

Gathering or elaboration is the second form of the generate pattern. This subpattern has the objective to accumulate relevant information—as opposed to finding new or unique solutions. In this subpattern, the amount of information is less important than getting the relevant information required for the purpose of the decision at hand. The constructs of relevance, clarity, accuracy, reliability, timeliness, and intrinsic quality of information gathered (purposefulness, usefulness) are all important (Wand and Wang, 1996). Which of these factors are most relevant depends on the purpose of data gathering. Table 6.3 summarizes the subpatterns and measurement constructs for the generate pattern.

"Reduce" Pattern of Collaboration

The reduction pattern of collaboration deals with moving from having many concepts to a focus on fewer concepts that a group deems worthy of further attention. Although reduction has been studied less than generation, it is an essential pattern because it allows a group to both lessen and simplify the concepts that remain under consideration. In part, reduction is necessary because generation can produce a large volume of content of varying relevance. Moreover, generated content can be at multiple levels of abstraction and granularity.

Reduction has sometimes been confused with convergence, but it is not the same pattern. Briggs et al. (2003) described convergence as both reduction and the establishment of shared meaning. Briggs et al. (2006) later separated these two concepts into reduction and clarification. Reduction can be a step that can lead to further discussion, clarification, and evaluation—all of which are steps that a group can use to move towards convergence. The distinction between reduction and clarification is important because each can be accomplished independently. For example, it is possible to reduce information without achieving clarification and it is possible to accomplish clarification without reduction.

The aim of reduction is to keep only the information that meets a specific criterion or criteria. This can be achieved by either removing what is not wanted or selecting what is wanted. Metrics for this include the preciseness or match of selected item with respect to the information need, and the ratio between the amount of overall information and the amount of information that meets the information needs (Belkin and Croft, 1992). Another metric is the ratio between the amount of input information and the amount of information after reduction; in this case similar criteria can be used as in the generate pattern (e.g., number of unique before and after reduction, number of high quality before and after, etc.) (Kamal et al., 2007).

A second approach to reduction is a form of summarization. Rather than selection, the aim of this approach is not to select part of the information, but rather to capture the essence of information with less information elements. Namely, all redundant information is removed, but no choices are made about which remaining contributions are preferred over other contributions.

There are several approaches to summarizing. First, summarizing can be accomplished when only the unique information is selected. Second, similar contributions can be merged, to keep only unique contributions. Third, an instance of similar contributions can be selected to represent multiple instances. Last, extraction of the most important contributions can also be used as a summarizing method (Barzilay et al., 1999). In this instance, an evaluation pattern is used to accomplish reduction. Outcome metrics for the quality of summarization assess how well the summary represents the original set of contributions. Other key indicators are conciseness and consistency. An idea summarization would be both parsimonious and complete.

A third approach to reduction is to reduce information through abstraction. The purpose of abstraction is to make content more intellectually manageable by allowing group members to pay attention to relevant information and to ignore other details. Smith and Smith (1977) describe two approaches for abstraction: generalization and aggregation. *Generalization* refers to an abstraction in which a set of similar objects is regarded as a generic object, such as employed persons being abstracted as a generic object "employee." With this form of abstraction individual differences between employees—such as different names, job positions, and ages—can be ignored.

Aggregation refers to an abstraction in which a relationship between objects is regarded as a higher-level object. In such an abstraction, many details of the relationship may be ignored. For example, a certain relationship between a person, airplane, and a date can be abstracted as a "reservation" without bringing to mind all of the details of the underlying relationship—for example, the flight number, the date and time of the flight, and the airline. Metrics for abstraction are appropriate when they assess the appropriateness of the abstraction, whether the purpose is to retain the relevant information while omitting unneeded details in the form of aggregation or generalization. Moreover, abstractions should be complete in terms of the purpose they are intended to serve, be consistent, unambiguous, and without overlap. The difference between summarizing and abstraction is that in summarizing the same information is represented with less information elements while in abstraction the information is characterized by high level concepts that encompass

Table 6.4

Subpatterns and Measurement Constructs for Reduction

Reduce	Filtering	• Relevance of selected information • Amount of information selected • Amount of relevant information vs. total amount selected • Amount of information selected vs. initial amount of information • Amount of relevant in selected information vs. amount of relevant in initial information
	Summarizing	• Representativeness • Conciseness • Consistency • Completeness • Parsimoniousness
	Abstracting	• Representativeness • Completeness • Amount of ambiguity • Amount of overlap

relevant information in the original set. Table 6.4 summarizes the subpatterns and measurement constructs for the reduce pattern.

"Clarify" Pattern of Collaboration

The clarify pattern of collaboration deals with moving from having less to having more shared understanding of concepts, words, problems, and possible solutions. The clarify pattern can best be understood in terms of two subpatterns: development of shared understanding and sense making. Mulder et al. (2002) explain the notion of shared understanding as implying mutual knowledge, mutual beliefs, and mutual assumptions. Groups achieve shared understanding when the group comes to a common understanding of concepts and words that are germane to the task at hand. Sense making usually requires some development of shared understanding of concepts and terms but also includes the development of a common understanding of the problem, the context of the problem, and the possible actions the group might take to solve the problem. In other words, sense making is done to prepare the group to act in a principled and informed manner (Ntuen et al., 2005). Sense-making tasks often involve searching for ideas and input made by others in a group that are relevant for the purpose at hand and then extracting and reformulating the information so that it can be used (Weick, 1995).

Activities such as paraphrasing, summarizing, and explaining are part of developing share understanding and sense making. In line with shared understanding, there have also been a number of studies that have investigated the nature of mental models in being able to understand how learning takes place. In the context of the clarify pattern, mental models provide a means to specify relevant knowledge as well as the relationships between knowledge components through the use of concept relatedness ratings (Deshpande et al., 2006; Goldsmith and Johnson, 1990).

Table 6.5

Subpatterns and Measurement Constructs for Clarify

Clarify	Building shared understanding	• Conceptual learning • Validity • Clarity • Motivation • Relevance
	Sense making	

The same constructs can be used to assess both shared understanding and sense making. Table 6.5 summarizes the subpatterns and measurement constructs for the clarify pattern.

"Organize" Pattern of Collaboration

The organize pattern involves moving from less to more understanding of the relationships among concepts the group is considering. In other words, organize means to make complex ideas understandable (Briggs and Gruenbacher, 2002). Briggs et al. (2003) elaborate on the organize pattern as follows: The point of reducing complexity and making things more understandable is to reduce the effort of a follow-on activity.

When a group organizes a collection of concepts, they develop an understanding of the relationships among the concepts. They consider possible relationships among concepts, and determine which relationships exists among them. Briggs et al. (2003) provide the example that a group might organize a mixed list of ideas into a number of categories, or arrange them into a tree. They also emphasize that an "organize" pattern is typically not the end result of a group task—that organization is typically done prior to further divergence or elaboration.

Not surprisingly, categorization, sometimes referred to as classification, is the most common form of organization (e.g., Grisé and Gallupe, 2000), and is often used as a step after brainstorming. Categorization and classification are synonymous and represent the basic cognitive process of arranging into classes or categories. Collaborative software is explicitly used to represent the classes or categories. The quality of a categorization effort can be measured using several items, such as the number of ideas organized, the number of categories created, and the number of repeated items (or duplicates). Chen et al. (1994) provided an AI algorithm that tried to classify the most relevant ideas in a brainstorming session; they measured their attempts to automatically classify in terms of concept recall (the percentage of relevant meeting ideas that were properly captured) and concept precision (the percentage of the concepts in the lists that are deemed relevant to the actual meeting topics).

Whether more categories are better than fewer categories depends on the task; accordingly, there are two major types of categorization tasks: ones such as in brainstorming where the number of categories is not predetermined and others such as in software evaluation tasks where the number of categories is predetermined. Regardless, duplicates are counterproductive in virtually every group task.

Search for items that meet specific criteria is another form of organization. For example, research in software evaluation has focused primarily on software inspections (Rodgers et al., 2004; Tyran and George, 2002) and heuristic evaluation (Lowry and Roberts, 2003; Roberts et al., 2005). In both tasks, users are trying to find defects or violations of predetermined rules of how code should be written (software inspections) or violations of interface usability heuristics. The key difference with these types of tasks is that the categorization of potential violations is fixed and known in advance, as they are determined by predetermined rules and heuristics. Given this, these tasks involve search and the precise determination of whether a violation is correctly reported (correct reports) or incorrectly reported (false positives).

The third subpattern of organize that is common throughout the literature involves creating outlines with the purpose of creating an overall logical flow between the elements—not simple categorization. In other words, the order of the categories and subcategories highly matters in an overall thought-organization process. This subpattern is most commonly seen in outlining that is involved in collaborative writing (Lowry et al., 2004a; Lowry and Nunamaker, 2002, 2003; Lowry et al., 2004b; Lowry et al., 2005). Collaborative writing is a complex process that involves multiple collaboration engineering patterns (Lowry and Nunamaker, 2002). However, a key part of this task that has been included in collaborative writing research involves outlining the group's paper. In this type of organize task, the concern is not on the correct categorization of items, but the logical flow and organization of related content. Thus, assessment of document quality is the predominant measure when dealing with collaborative writing; other measures include length of document and time spent outlining.

The fourth organize subpattern pertains to developing sequence relationships among concepts; in other words, the sequencing of information and tasks (which is more common). This pattern of collaboration is generally found in workflow management (Gronemann et al., 1999), collaborative scheduling (Chan et al., 1999), collaborative project planning (Romano et al., 2002), and collaborative process planning (Kempenaers et al., 1996). Outcomes are often not focused on the sequencing task but on its effect on planning such as flexibility, number of scheduling conflicts, number of conflicts resolved, number of disturbances, responsiveness to disturbances, and schedule performance.

A fifth subpattern in organizing covers the causal relations between concepts. Causal modeling in collaborative setting is researched in Group Model Building literature (Rouwette et al., 2002) and in soft systems methodology (strategic options development and analysis) (Checkland, 1981; Eden, 1992). However, both systems mostly look at effects of the entire approach to problem solving and an interpretive research approach is used in most of these studies. Limited information is therefore available for specific outcomes and metrics used to evaluate the collaborative causal modeling activity. Rouwette et al. (2002) reports the size of the resulting model and its dynamic complexity (number of feedback loops), besides the metrics for collaborative modeling outcomes in general.

The sixth and last organize subpattern is found in literature on collaborative modeling. Collaborative modeling and Group Model Building are researched in different GSS research communities and in System Dynamics research (Dean et al., 2000; Hengst, 2005). Collaborative modeling is, like clustering, used to create shared understanding and to reduce complexity; however, since a modeling language is used, one of the quality dimensions of collaborative modeling is the consistency of the resulting model with modeling conventions or rules (Dean et al., 2000). Completeness and validity are other quality indicators (Dean et al., 2000; Hengst, 2005).

Further outcome measures are individual user comprehension of the models and the resulting efficacy of shared mental models (e.g., whether every group member has the same comprehension). These are very important because the purpose of modeling is to convey and facilitate meaning with multiple stakeholders—many of whom are not technical or capable of creating the models but need to understand them—such as business process managers, executives, and customers (e.g., Agarwal et al., 1999; Basu and Blanning, 2000; Kintsch, 1988). However, in collaborative modeling, strong individual user comprehension is not sufficient; the degree to which shared cognition or

Table 6.6

Subpatterns and Measurement Constructs for Organize

Organize	Categorizing	• Number of ideas organized • Number of categories created • Number of duplicates • Number of correctly categorized items • Number of relevant items • Correct reports • False positives
	Outlining	• External judged document quality • Participant perceived document quality • Length of document • Time spent outlining
	Sequencing	• Flexibility • Number of scheduling conflicts • Number of conflicts resolved • Number of disturbances • Responsiveness to disturbances • Schedule performance
	Building causal decomposition	• Model size • Dynamic complexity
	Modeling	• Arbitrariness • Clarity • Complexity • Consistency • Completeness/Parsimony • Validity • User comprehension • Modeling self-efficacy • Shared mental models

shared mental models accurately occurs is also a critical measure to evaluate—that is, the degree to which the stakeholders in the modeling effort are in alignment with their shared understanding of the model (Cannon-Bowers and Salas, 2001). Better task performance results when individual group members' mental models are aligned with task requirements into a cohesive, shared mental model (Cannon-Bowers and Salas, 2001). Table 6.6 summarizes the subpatterns and measurement constructs for the organize pattern.

"Evaluate" Pattern of Collaboration

The evaluate pattern involves movement from less to more understanding of the relative value of the concepts under consideration. The two purposes for evaluation are to support decision making and to support group communication (Briggs et al., 2005). Evaluation can be done through a voting or rating mechanism as well as through evaluative dialog. Voting and rating are the key approaches of nondialog evaluation. Both voting and rating include two key steps: collecting individual preferences and aggregating these into some form of a group preference (Gavish and Gerdes, 1997; Levin and Nalebuff, 1995).

The terms *voting* and *rating* overlap considerably because of a variety of voting and rating approaches. For example, group members may vote and be able to select one or more solutions from a larger set. Or group members may rate a set of items on one or more dimensions, so that the highest rated items move to the top. Depending on the situation, the ultimate decision can be made by the group or the preferences of a group can be used to inform a decision maker.

Evaluation is commonly used to support communication as a means of surfacing preferences, assumptions, agreement, and disagreements. This allows groups to explore the reasons for the agreement and disagreements while working towards some ultimate decision.

Many aggregation methods are found in the literature (e.g., Balthazard et al., 1998; Cheng and Deek, 2007; Gavish and Gerdes, 1997; Levin and Nalebuff, 1995). The various methods fall into one of the following three categories: (1) majority rule, (2) consensus rule, or (3) a selection based on expertise. Outcomes of voting are also various. An outcome can be in the form of a preference indication, a decision, or a measure of some property (e.g., the feasibility of a solution) (Balthazard et al., 1998; Cheng and Deek, 2007).

In the case of rational choice, correctness and the appropriate representation of participants' expertise are important metrics. When consensus is a group's objective, fairness, acceptance, and lack of postdecision regret are important (Balthazard et al., 1998). Consensus is often a metric of divergence of preference as will be discussed. Both in rational choice and consensus decisions, participant satisfaction and robustness of the result with respect to meeting some objective are important.

Other important indicators of evaluate are the complexity of the voting task (Cheng and Deek, 2007) and the complexity of the aggregation method (Carneiro, 2001). Complexity of the voting task drives the effort required by participants; too many items or too many dimensions can make voting tedious (Cheng and Deek, 2007). Moreover, the ability to combine votes in ways that are understood and meaningful for group members is important (Young, 1995).

Besides voting, qualitative evaluation can be performed by having group members textually comment on the desirability of different options. In effect, group members state pros and cons of different potential solutions. As opposed to generate, which may be focused on generating solutions, the focus in this pattern to evaluate solutions that are already produced. The generate pattern in this case has a more evaluative or reflective character that can help a group come to a more common view of the relative desirability of different options. This pattern is different from the gathering pattern in the sense that the gathering pattern is used for knowledge construction or sharing while qualitative evaluation is focused on reflection (Lowry et al., 2004a) or illumination and verification (Shah and Vargas-Hernandez, 2003). Qualitative evaluation is not about eliciting preference directly, but rather about explaining specific qualities of the concepts under consideration as a basis for (mostly) rational choice, such as evaluating the feasibility of solutions. When people review or offer feedback, a criterion often considered is that such feedback is constructive, thorough, and knowledgeable (McNutt et al., 1990). Completeness and clarity are also important indicators. Table 6.7 summarizes the subpatterns and measurement constructs for the evaluate pattern.

"Consensus Building" Pattern of Collaboration

Consensus is usually defined as an agreement, acceptance, or lack of disagreement or some other indication that stakeholders commit to a proposal (Briggs et al., 2005). Methods to achieve consensus are either though the aggregation of preferences as in social choice or through resolving different aspects of disagreement or conflict through negotiation, creating shared understanding or through the inclusion or exclusion of additional factors/stakes. Metrics for disagreement or divergence in preference are very numerous and range from standard deviation of voting results

Table 6.7

Subpatterns and Measurement Constructs for Evaluate

Evaluate	Choice	Social choice	• Consensus • Fairness • Satisfaction • Acceptance method • Lack of post decision regret • Robustness strategy • Robustness weight factors • Complexity aggregation • Effort/complexity voting
		Rational choice	• Correctness • Expertise • Robustness weight factors • Complexity aggregation • Effort/complexity voting
	Communication of preference		• Mutual understanding • Complete representation of preferences in results • Insight in disagreement/conflict
	Qualitative evaluation		• Thoroughness or completeness • Accuracy • Clarity • Constructiveness

(Martz and Shepherd, 2004) to fuzzy sets (Herrera et al., 1996) and Saaty's consistency ratio (Moreno-Jimenez et al., 2005). Another approach to measure consensus is to measure commitment or buy-in of the different stakeholders (Kolfschoten et al., 2009). Table 6.8 summarizes the subpatterns and measurement constructs for the consensus building pattern.

PATTERNS OF COLLABORATION: EFFECTS AND CAUSES

Briggs et al. (2006) provided a first decomposition of the patterns of collaboration into subpatterns. Based on the current research we have produced a more refined set of subpatterns as summarized in Appendix 6.1. The appendix further summarizes the subpatterns we identified and defines these patterns in terms of the effect created in the collaborative pattern of the group effort and line with the general pattern to which they belong. Note that these definitions often do not match the definition of the concept indicated with the pattern label, but only define the pattern of collaboration described by that label. Based on the patterns created in the group and the outcomes evoked, we show the key facilitation interventions required to create these patterns. We define these interventions as "rules" which offer the basis for the thinkLets used in Collaboration Engineering (Kolfschoten et al., 2006). Last, the appendix lists the metrics for the key outcomes that should be achieved. With this overview, the appendix offers collaboration engineers a detailed overview of the effects of the interventions they make: both the outcome and the pattern evoked. Furthermore, each pattern is now described as a cause and a fact, which offers a first basis for theory building in the tradition of logical positivism.

Table 6.8

Subpatterns and Measurement Constructs for Consensus

	Choice	• See evaluation choice
Consensus building	Building agreement visualizing divergence of preference	• Standard deviation • Kendall's coefficient • Fuzzy consensus • Saaty's consistency ratio • Perception of agreement/consensus/ commitment
	Building commitment	• Number of participants that commit • % of participants that commit • Satisfaction of participants

DISCUSSION

The six fundamental collaborative patterns described by Briggs et al. (2006), namely generate, reduce, clarify, organize, evaluate, and build consensus, make up most if not all collaborative work. To design collaboration processes with predictable outcomes, designers must know how the implementation of collaborative patterns will produce specific outcomes (Kolfschoten et al., 2006; Vreede et al., 2006). While these six collaboration patterns are well known in collaboration engineering, more research needs to be done to better understand the subpatterns involved in these patterns, and the primarily constructs and measures. Without constructs and measures to these subpatterns, it is virtually impossible for logical positivists to conduct empirical theoretical work that meaningfully explains and predicts outcomes for different collaboration patterns and contexts. This chapter addressed this gap in the literature.

The first major contribution of this chapter is that we offer a framework of the subpatterns that are common instantiations of each of the fundamental collaborative patterns. We presented a set of interventions that are likely to produce the patterns of collaboration and the outcomes intended in these patterns. Our second major contribution is that we describe the constructs that are measured during the study of these subpatterns in the literature. Together, these contributions result in a framework for future research that includes the patterns, subpatterns, and constructs that can be studied and measured by empirical logical positivists. This framework will help researchers create more specific effects in collaborative settings and better understand the variations in those effects and the interventions causing them. Better understanding of the choices among implementations and what measures will best describe the outcomes of these implementations will also help collaboration engineers to design more predictable collaboration processes.

From the appendix we can draw some interesting insights. Some interventions require only an instruction to the group while others require managing discussion and gaining commitment with respect to a group outcome, rather than simply visualizing or combining the results of the individual contributions of the group members. The latter is particularly the case in the generate pattern; while some generation patterns support participants to inspire each other or the help each other in striving to completeness or quality, they do not require the group to commit to a group result upon completion of the pattern. Similarly, they clarify and organize patterns to gain more understanding of the concepts under discussion and to gain insight in their relations. However, the focus of the pattern is increased understanding of the group members as opposed to a group outcome. Only in sense making, shared negotiated meaning can result as a group outcome. In reduce, evaluate, and consensus building patterns, choices are made and group members need to commit to the outcome of the pattern in order to gain a successful result. In these patterns the facilitation interventions are also less specific. Instead of a clear creativity instruction (generate pattern) "let the participants add ideas," these interventions often prescribe discussion based on some proposal that involves a choice. Such choices can be about the completeness of a summary or they can require consensus on a decision. However, when one or more group members reject the proposal, the outcome of the intervention is negative, or the activity is not finished. Naturally these patterns are therefore the most demanding patterns for a facilitator as was also concluded by Hengst and Adkins (2007).

CONCLUSION AND FURTHER RESEARCH

In this chapter, we presented a framework in which we describe the facilitation interventions to cause collaborative outcomes and the patterns that describe the group process that emerges as an effect of these interventions. This framework can be used by collaboration engineers to design predictable intervention in group process, but more important, it can be used by researchers to drill down one level and study collaboration on the elementary level of group interaction and single activities. On this level of analysis we can evaluate different methods, styles and approaches to intervention that enable us to resolve some of the paradoxes in collaboration and GSS research (Santanen, 2005).

GSS tools offer means to support groups in their collaborative activities. Many discussions have been focused on the appropriate use (Dennis et al., 2001; DeSanctis and Poole, 1994) of GSS and its effect on group effort (Fjermestad and Hiltz, 1999, 2001). Our framework does not focus on any technology. In our opinion, tools should be instrumental to the processes they support and should not determine the choice of methods to execute a task (Kolfschoten et al., 2006). For some of the processes presented here, tool support is limited, and could be further developed. Others can be supported by simple functionalities that are offered in a variety of tools. We hope that GSS developers use this overview of collaborative patterns and further expand their tools including functionalities to support each of the patterns discussed.

We further hope that this framework will serve as the basis for a new area in collaboration research in which researchers focus on collaborative activities on a deeper level, to gain understanding in the distinct collaborative activities that groups perform to achieve their goals, and the specific interventions required to evoke a more precise and predictable effect in collaborative effort.

ACKNOWLEDGMENTS

We appreciate general funding provided by the Information Systems Department and Kevin and Debra Rollins Center for e-Business, both at the Marriott School, Brigham Young University. We appreciate research assistance provided by James Gaskin and Aaron Bailey.

REFERENCES

Agarwal, R.; De, P.; and Sinha, A. P. 1999. Comprehending object and process models: An empirical study. *IEEE Transactions on Software Engineering,* 25, 4, 541–556.
Baltes, B.B.; Dickson, M.W.; Sherman, M.P.; Bauer, C.C.; and LaGanke, J.S. 2002. Computer-mediated communication and group decision making: A meta-analysis. *Organizational Behavior and Human Decision Processes,* 87, 1, 156–179.

Balthazard, P.; Ferrell, W.R.; and Aguilar, D.L. 1998. Influence allocation methods in group decision support systems. *Group Decision and Negotiation,* 7, 4, 347–362.

Barzilay, R.; McKeown, K.R.; and Elhadad, M. 1999. Information fusion in the context of multi-document summarization. Paper presented at the annual meeting of the Association for Computational Linguistics on Computational Linguistics, College Park, Maryland.

Basu, A., and Blanning, R.W. 2000. A formal approach to workflow analysis. *Information Systems Research,* 11, 1, 17–36.

Belkin, N.J., and Croft, W.B. 1992. Information filtering and information retrieval: Two sides of the same coin? *Communications of the ACM,* 35, 12, 29–38.

Boehm, B.; Grüenbacher, P.; and Briggs, R.O. 2001. Developing groupware for requirements negotiation: Lessons learned. *IEEE Software,* 18, 3, 46–55.

Briggs, R.O., and Gruenbacher, P. 2002. EasyWinWin: Managing complexity in requirements negotiation with GSS. In *Proceedings of the 35th Annual Hawaii International Conference on System Sciences,* Waikoloa, Hawaii, January 7–10.

Briggs, R.O.; Kolfschoten, G.L.; and Vreede, G.J. de. 2005. Toward a theoretical model of consensus building. Paper presented at the Americas Conference on Information Systems, Omaha, Nebraska, August 11–14.

Briggs, R.O.; Kolfschoten, G.L.; Vreede, G.J. de; and Dean, D.L. 2006. Defining key concepts for collaboration engineering. In *Proceedings of the 12th Americas Conference on Information Systems (AMCIS-12),* Acapulco, Mexico, August 4–6.

Briggs, R.O., and Reinig, B.A. 2007. Bounded ideation theory: A new model of the relationship between idea quantity and idea-quality during ideation. In *Proceedings of the 40th Annual Hawaii International Conference on System Sciences,* Waikoloa, Hawaii, January 3–6.

Briggs, R.O.; Vreede, G.J. de; and Nunamaker, J.F. Jr. 2003. Collaboration engineering with thinkLets to pursue sustained success with group support systems. *Journal of Management Information Systems,* 19, 4, 31–63.

Bruijn, J.A. de, and Heuvelhof, E.F. ten. 2007. Management in Netwerken Over veranderen in een Multi-actorcontext. Den Haag: Lemma.

Cannon-Bowers, J.A., and Salas, E. 2001. Reflections on shared cognition. *Journal of Organizational Behavior,* 22, 2, 195–202.

Carneiro, A. 2001. A group decision support system for strategic alternatives selection. *Management Decision,* 39, 3, 218–226.

Chan, W.T.; Chau, D.K.H.; and Lang, X. 1999. Collaborative scheduling over the Internet. *Computer-Aided Civil and Infrastructure Engineering,* 14, 15–24.

Checkland, P.B. 1981. *Systems Thinking, Systems Practice.* Chichester, UK: John Wiley and Sons.

Chen, H.; Hsu, P.; Orwig, R.; Hoopes, L.; and Nunamaker, J.F. Jr. 1994. Automatic concept classification of text from electronic meetings. *Communications of the ACM,* 37, 10, 56–73.

Cheng, K.E., and Deek, F.P. 2007. A framework for studying voting in group support systems. In *Proceedings of the 40th Annual Hawaii International Conference on System Sciences,* Waikoloa, Hawaii, January 3–6.

Connolly, T.; Jessup, L.M.; and Valacich, J.S. 1990. Effects of anonymity and evaluative tone on idea generation in computer-mediated groups. *Management Science,* 36, 6, 689–703.

Dean, D.L.; Hender, J.M.; Rodgers, T.L.; and Santanen, E. 2006. Identifying quality, novel, and creative ideas: Constructs and scales for idea evaluation. *Journal of the Association for Information Systems,* 7, 10, 646–698.

Dean, D.L.; Orwig, R.E.; and Vogel, D.R. 2000. Facilitation methods for collaborative modeling tools. *Group Decision and Negotiation,* 9, 2, 109–127.

Dennis, A.R., and Valacich, J.S. 1994. Group, sub-group, and nominal group idea generation: New rules for a new media? *Journal of Management,* 20, 4, 723–736.

Dennis, A.R.; Valacich, J.S.; Carte, T.; Garfield, M.; Haley, B.; and Aronson, J.E. 1997. Research report: The effectiveness of multiple dialogues in electronic brainstorming. *Information Systems Research,* 8, 2, 203–211.

Dennis, A.R., and Wixom, B.H. 2002. Investigating the moderators of the group support systems use with meta-analysis. *Journal of Management Information Systems,* 18, 3, 235–257.

Dennis, A.R.; Wixom, B.H.; and Vandenberg, R.J. 2001. Understanding fit and appropriation effects in group support systems via meta-analysis. *Management Information Systems Quarterly,* 25, 2, 167–183.

DeSanctis, G., and Poole, M.S. 1994. Capturing the complexity in advanced technology use: Adaptive structuration theory. *Organization Science,* 5, 2, 121–147.

Deshpande, N.; Vries, B. de; and Leeuwen, J. van. 2006. Collaborative design knowledge construction and measuring shared understanding. In J.P. van Leeuwen and H.J.P. Timmermans (eds.), *Progress in Design and Decision Support Systems in Architecture and Urban Planning,* 303–312. Eindhoven, NL: Eindhoven University of Technology.

Diehl, M., and Stroebe, W. 1987. Productivity loss in brainstorming groups: Toward the solution of a riddle. *Journal of Personality and Social Psychology,* 53, 3, 497–509.

Eden, C. 1992. A framework for thinking about group decision support systems (GDSS). *Group Decision and Negotiation,* 1, 199–218.

Fjermestad, J., and Hiltz, S.R. 1999. An assessment of group support systems experimental research: Methodology and results. *Journal of Management Information Systems,* 15, 3, 7–149.

———. 2001. A descriptive evaluation of group support systems case and field studies. *Journal of Management Information Systems,* 17, 3, 115–159.

Frost & Sullivan, Co. 2007. *Meetings Around the World: The Impact of Collaboration on Business Performance.* White paper sponsored by Verizon Business and Microsoft. https://e-meetings.verizonbusiness.com/maw/pdf/MAW_white_paper.pdf.

Gallupe, R.B.; Dennis, A.R.; Cooper, W.H.; Valacich, J.S.; Bastianutti, L.M.; and Nunamaker, J.F., Jr. 1992. Electronic brainstorming and group size. *Academy of Management Journal,* 35, 2, 350–369.

Gavish, B., and Gerdes, J.H. 1997. Voting mechanisms and their implications in a GDSS environment. *Annals of Operation Research,* 71, 1, 41–74.

Goldsmith, T.E., and Johnson, P.J. 1990. A structural assessment of classroom learning. In P. Schvaneveldt (ed.), *Pathfinder Associative Networks: Studies in Knowledge Organizations,* 241–254. Norwood, NJ: Ablex.

Grisé, M., and Gallupe, R. B. 2000. Information overload: Addressing the productivity paradox in face-to-face electronic meetings. *Journal of Management Information Systems,* 16, 3, 157–185.

Gronemann, B.; Joeris, G.; Scheil, S.; Steinfort, M.; and Wache, H. 1999. Supporting cross-organizational engineering processes by distributed collaborative workflow management—the MOKASSIN approach. Paper presented at the International Conference on Concurrent Multidisciplinary Engineering, Bremen, Germany, September 14–15.

Gryskiewicz, S.S. 1980. A study of creative problem solving techniques in group settings. Unpublished doctoral dissertation, University of London.

Hender, J.M.; Dean, D.L.; Rodgers, T.L.; and Nunamaker, J.F., Jr. 2002. An examination of the impact of stimuli type and GSS structure on creativity: Brainstorming versus non-brainstorming techniques in a GSS environment. *Journal of Management Information Systems,* 18, 4, 59–85.

Hengst, M. den. 2005. Collaborative modeling of processes: What facilitation support does a group need? Paper presented at the Eleventh Americas Conference on Information Systems, Omaha, Nebraska, August 11–14.

Hengst, M. den, and Adkins, M. 2007. Which collaboration patterns are most challenging: A global survey of facilitators. In *Proceedings of the 40th Annual Hawaii International Conference on System Sciences,* Waikoloa, Hawaii, January 3–6.

Henninger, W.G.; Dennis, A.R.; and Hilmer, K. 2006. Individual cognition and dual-task interference in group support systems. *Information Systems Research,* 17, 4, 415–424.

Herrera, F.; Herrera-Viedma, E.; and Verdergay, J.L. 1996. A model of consensus in group decision making under linguistic assessments. *Fuzzy Sets and Systems,* 78, 73–87.

Hwang, M.I. 1998. Did task type matter in the use of decision room GSS? A critical review and a meta-analysis. *International Journal of Management Science,* 26, 1, 1–15.

Kamal, M.; Davis, A.J.; Nabukenya, J.; Schoonover, T.V.; Pietron, L.R.; and Vreede, G.J. de. 2007. Collaboration engineering for incident response planning: Process development and validation. In *Proceedings of the 40th Annual Hawaii International Conference on System Sciences,* Waikoloa, Hawaii, January 3–6.

Kempenaers, J.; Pinte, J.; Detand, J.; and Kruth, J.P. 1996. A collaborative process planning and scheduling system. *Advances in Engineering Software,* 25, 3–8.

Kintsch, W. 1988. The role of knowledge in discourse comprehension—a construction integration model. *Psychological Review,* 95, 2, 163–182.

Kolfschoten, G.L.; Appelman, J.H.; Briggs, R.O.; and Vreede, G.J. de. 2004. Recurring patterns of facilitation interventions in GSS sessions. In *Proceedings of the 37the Annual Hawaii International Conference on System Sciences,* Waikoloa, Hawaii, January 5–8.

Kolfschoten, G.L., Briggs, R.O., and Vreede, G.J. de. 2009. A diagnostic to identify and resolve different sources of disagreement in collaborative requirements engineering. Paper presented at the International Conference on Group Decision and Negotiation, Toronto, Canada, June 14–19.

Kolfschoten, G.L.; Briggs, R.O.; Vreede, G.J., de; Jacobs, P.H.M.; and Appelman, J.H. 2006. Conceptual foundation of the thinkLet concept for collaboration engineering. *International Journal of Human Computer Science,* 64, 7, 611–621.

Kolfschoten, G.L., and Vreede, G.J. de. 2009. A design approach for collaboration processes: A multi-method design science study in collaboration engineering. *Journal of Management Information Systems,* 26, 1, 225–257.

Levin, J., and Nalebuff, B. 1995. An introduction to vote-counting schemes. *Journal of Economic Perspectives,* 9, 1, 3–26.

Linstone, H., and Turoff, M. (eds.). 1975. *The Delphi Method: Techniques and Applications.* Reading, MA: Addison Wesley.

Lowry, P.B.; Curtis, A.; and Lowry, M.R. 2004a. Building a taxonomy and nomenclature of collaborative writing to improve interdisciplinary research and practice. *Journal of Business Communication,* 41, 1, 66–99.

Lowry, P.B., and Nunamaker, J.F. Jr. 2002. Using the thinkLet framework to improve distributed collaborative writing. In *Proceedings of the 35th Annual Hawaii International Conference on System Sciences,* Waikoloa, Hawaii, January 7–10.

———. 2003. Using Internet-based, distributed collaborative writing tools to improve coordination and group awareness in writing teams. *IEEE Transactions on Professional Communication,* 46, 4, 277–297.

Lowry, P.B.; Nunamaker, J.F. Jr.; Booker, Q.E.; Curtis, A.; and Lowry, M.R. 2004b. Implementing distributed collaborative writing in traditional educational environments. *IEEE Transactions on Professional Communication,* 47, 3, 171–189.

Lowry, P.B.; Nunamaker, J.F. Jr.; Curtis, A.; and Lowry, M.R. 2005. The impact of process structure on novice, Internet-based, asynchronous-distributed collaborative writing teams. *IEEE Transactions on Professional Communication,* 48, 4, 341–364.

Lowry, P.B., and Roberts, T.L. 2003. Improving the usability evaluation technique, heuristic evaluation, through the use of collaborative software. Paper presented at the 9th Annual Americas Conference on Information Systems, Tampa, Florida, August 4–5.

Martz, Jr. W.B., and Shepherd, M.M. 2004. Group consensus: The impact of multiple dialogues. *Group Decision and Negotiation,* 13, 4, 315–325.

McLeod, P.L. 1992. An assessment of the experimental literature on electronic support of group work: Results of a meta-analysis. *Human-Computer Interaction,* 7, 3, 257–280.

McNutt, R.A.; Evans, A.T.; Fletcher, R.H.; and Fletcher, S.W. 1990. The effects of blinding on the quality of peer review. *Journal of the American Medical Association,* 263, 10, 1371–1376.

Moreno-Jimenez, J.M.; Joven, J.A.; Pirla, A.R.; and Lanuza, A.T. 2005. A spreadsheet module for consistent consensus building in AHP-group decision making. *Group Decision and Negotiation,* 14, 2, 89–108.

Mulder, I.; Swaak, J.; and Kessels, J. 2002. Assessing learning and shared understanding in technology-mediated interaction. *Educational Technology & Society,* 5, 1, 35–47.

Ntuen, C. A.; Leedom, D.; and Schmeisser, E. (2005). Performance of individuals and groups in sensemaking of information from computer decision aiding systems. In *Proceedings of the Human Factors and Ergonomics Society Annual Meeting,* 49, 292–296. Thousand Oaks, CA: Sage Publications.

Nunamaker, J.F. Jr.; Briggs, R.O.; Mittleman, D.D.; Vogel, D.; and Balthazard, P.A. 1997. Lessons from a dozen years of group support systems research: A discussion of lab and field findings. *Journal of Management Information Systems,* 13, 3, 163–207.

Osborn, A.F. 1953. *Applied Imagination.* New York: Scribners.

Paulus, P.B.; Dzindolet, M.T.; Poletes, G.; and Camancho, L.M. 1993. Perception of performance in group brainstorming: The illusion of group productivity. *Personality and Social Psychology Bulletin,* 19, 1, 78–89.

Pinsonneault, A.; Barki, H.; Gallupe, R.B.; and Hoppen, N. 1999. Electronic brainstorming: The illusion of productivity. *Information Systems Research,* 10, 2, 110–133.

Plucker, J.A.; Beghetto, R.A.; and Dow, G.T. 2004. Why isn't creativity more important to educational psychologists? Potentials, pitfalls, and future directions in creativity research. *Educational Psychologist,* 39, 2, 83–96.

Reinig, B.A., and Briggs, R.O. 2008. On the relationship between idea-quantity and idea-quality during ideation. *Group Decision and Negotiation,* 17, 5, 403–420.

Reinig, B.A.; Briggs, R.O.; and Nunamaker, J.F. 1998. Flaming in the electronic classroom. *Journal of Management Information Systems,* 14, 3, 45–60.

Roberts, T.L.; Lowry, P.B.; and Romano, N.C. Jr. 2005. Improving design artifact reviews with group support systems and an extension of heuristic evaluation techniques. In *Proceedings of the 38th Annual Hawaii International Conference on System Sciences,* Waikoloa, Hawaii, January 3–6.

Rodgers, T.L.; Dean, D.L.; and Nunamaker, J.F., Jr. 2004. Increasing inspection efficiency through group support systems. In *Proceedings of the 37th Annual Hawaii International Conference on System Sciences,* Waikaloa, Hawaii, January 5–8.

Romano, N.C. Jr.; Chen, F.; and Nunamaker, J.F. Jr. 2002. Collaborative project management software. In *Proceedings of the 35th Annual Hawaii International Conference on System Sciences,* Waikoloa, Hawaii, January 7–10.

Rouwette, E.A.J.A.; Vennix, J.A.M.; and Mullekom, T. van. 2002. Group model building effectiveness: A review of assessment studies. *System Dynamics Review,* 18, 1, 5–45.

Santanen, E.L. 2005. Resolving ideation paradoxes: Seeing apples as oranges through the clarity of think-Lets. In *Proceedings of the 38th Annual Hawaii International Conference on System Sciences,* Waikoloa, Hawaii, January 3–6.

Santanen, E.L.; Vreede, G.J. de; and Briggs, R.O. 2004. Causal relationships in creative problem solving: Comparing facilitation interventions for ideation. *Journal of Management Information Systems,* 20, 4, 167–197.

Schwarz, R.M. 1994. *The Skilled Facilitator.* San Francisco, CA: Jossey-Bass.

Shah, J.J., and Vargas-Hernandez, N. 2003. Metrics for measuring ideation. *Design Studies,* 24, 2, 111–134.

Shepherd, M.M.; Briggs, R.O.; Reinig, B.A.; Yen, J.; and Nunamaker, J.F., Jr. 1996. Social comparison to improve electronic brainstorming: Beyond anonymity. *Journal of Management Information Systems,* 12, 3, 155–170.

Smith, J.M.; and Smith, D.C.P. 1977. Database abstractions: Aggregation and generalization. *ACM Transactions on Database Systems,* 2, 2, 105–133.

Steiner, I.D. 1972. *Group Process and Productivity.* New York: Academic Press.

Tyran, C.K., and George, J.F. 2002. Improving software inspections with group process support. *Communications of the ACM,* 45, 9, 87–92.

Tyran, C.K., and Shepherd, M. 1998. GSS and learning research: A review and assessment of the early studies. In *Proceedings of the 31st Annual Hawaii International Conference on System Sciences,* Kohala Coast, Hawaii, January 6–9.

Valacich, J.S.; Wachter, R.; Mennecke, B.E.; and Wheeler, B.C. 1993. Computer-mediated idea generation: The effects of group size and group heterogeneity. In *Proceedings of the 26th Annual Hawaii International Conference on System Sciences,* Waikoloa, Hawaii, January 3–6.

Vathanophas, V., and Liang, S.Y. 2007. Enhancing information sharing in group support systems (GSS). *Computers in Human Behaviour,* 23, 3, 1675–1691.

Vreede, G.J. de, and Briggs, R.O. 2005. Collaboration engineering: Designing repeatable processes for high-value collaborative tasks. In *Proceedings of the 38th Annual Hawaii International Conference on System Sciences,* Waikoloa, Hawaii, January 3–6.

Vreede, G.J. de; Briggs, R.O.; and Kolfschoten, G.L. 2006. ThinkLets: A pattern language for facilitated and practitioner-guided collaboration processes. *International Journal of Computer Applications in Technology,* 25, 2/3, 140–154.

Vreede, G.J. de; Briggs, R.O.; and Massey, A.P. 2009. Collaboration engineering: Foundations and opportunities. *Journal of the Association for Information Systems,* 10, 3, 121–137.

Vreede, G.J. de; Fruhling, A.; and Chakrapani, A. 2005. A repeatable collaboration process for usability testing. In *Proceedings of the 38th Annual Hawaii International Conference on System Sciences,* Waikoloa, Hawaii, January 3–6.

Wand, Y., and Wang, R.Y. 1996. Anchoring data quality dimensions in ontological foundations. *Communications of the ACM,* 39, 11, 86–95.

Weick, K.E. 1995. *Sensemaking in Organizations.* Thousand Oaks, CA: Sage.

Young, P. 1995. Optimal voting rules. *Journal of Economic Perspectives,* 9, 1, 51–64.

Zigurs, I., and Buckland, B. 1998. A theory of task/technology fit and group support systems effectiveness. *Management Information Systems Quarterly,* 22, 3, 313–334.

APPENDIX 6.1. OVERVIEW OF PATTERN DECOMPOSITION: PATTERNS, SUBPATTERNS, INTERVENTIONS, AND KEY OUTCOMES

Pattern	Subpatterns	Pattern definition	Intervention	Key outcomes
Generate	Creativity	Move from having fewer to having more new concepts in the pool of concepts shared by the group	Participants add ideas within the scope of the topic	• # unique contributions • # off topic/outside scope
	Gathering	Move from having fewer to having more complete and relevant information shared by the group	Participants add information to describe the topic of interest	• Completeness • Relevance • Usefulness
	Reflecting	Move from having fewer to having more valid information, shared and understood by the group	Participants add comments to concepts under reflection, challenge the group questioning assumptions and intended qualities of the information	• Validity • Completeness • Knowledgeable
Reduce	Filtering	Move from having many concepts to fewer concepts that meet a specific criteria according to the group members	Derive criteria and let participant choose concepts from the list that meet these criteria	• Amount of information selected vs. initial amount of information
	Summarizing	Move from having many concepts to having a focus on fewer concepts that represent the knowledge shared by group members	Distill the key concepts that represent the information generated or remove information that overlaps or that is redundant	• Representativeness • Parsimoniousness
	Abstracting	Move from having many detailed concepts to fewer concepts that reduce the need to attend to details	Identify more abstract concepts that are useful for the group's purposes. Test whether these encompass the information under consideration and meet the objectives of the group	• Representativeness • Completeness

Pattern	Subpatterns	Pattern definition	Intervention	Key outcomes
Clarify	Sense making	Move from having less to having more shared meaning of context, and possible actions in order to support principled, informed action	Discuss the context and possible actions that can meet the group objective	• Retrospectiveness • Plausibility
	Building shared understanding	Move from having less to more shared understanding of the concepts shared by the group and the words and phrases used to express them	Discuss different meanings of concepts and words to achieve shared meaning	• Conceptual learning
Organize	Categorizing	Move from less to more understanding of the categorical relationships among concepts the group is considering	Participants identify categories and categorize concepts among the categories or let participants cluster concepts and label the clusters	• Number of duplicates • Correct reports • False positives • Number of categories created • Number of correctly categorized items
	Outlining	Move from less to more understanding of the logical connections among concepts the group is considering	Participants identify and label logical connections among concepts in discussion	• Participant perceived document quality • Time spent outlining • External judged document quality • Length of document
	Sequencing	Move from less to more understanding of the sequential relationships among concepts the group is considering	Participants discuss to determine the sequential order of concepts and visualize the resulting sequence	• Flexibility • # scheduling conflicts • # conflicts resolved • # disturbances • Responsiveness to disturbances • Schedule performance
	Building causal decomposition	Move from less to more understanding of the causal relationships among concepts the group is considering	Participants identify and visualize causal relations among the concepts	• Model size • Dynamic complexity
	Modeling	Move from a more to less complex overview of the concepts and relations the group is considering	Participants visualize relations among concepts and challenge the consistency of the resulting model	• Arbitrariness • Clarity • Complexity • Consistency • Completeness/parsimony • Validity • User comprehension • Modeling self-efficacy • Shared mental models

Pattern	Subpatterns	Pattern definition	Intervention	Key outcomes
Evaluate	Choice: social/ rational	Move from less to more understanding of the concept(s) most preferred by the group	Participants express their preference and aggregate a group vision, then discuss to build consensus or to determine the rational best choice	• Consensus • Satisfaction • Acceptance method • Correctness • Expertise
	Communication of preference	Move from less to more understanding of the preference of participants with respect to the concepts the group is considering	Participants express their preference and discuss differences, then discuss to gain mutual understanding of preferences and disagreement	• Mutual understanding • Completeness of perspectives in results • Insight in disagreement/ conflict
	Qualitative evaluation	Move from less to more understanding of the perspective of participants with respect to the preference of concepts the group is considering	Participants express their preference and perspectives on the concepts under evaluation	• Validity • Completeness • Knowledgeable
Consensus building	Choice	Move from less to more understanding of the concept(s) most preferred by the group	Participants express their preference and visualize the group result	• Consensus • Satisfaction • Acceptance method
	Building agreement/ visualizing divergence of preference	Move from less to more understanding of the difference in preference among participants with respect to concepts the group is considering	Participants express their preference and assess agreement and disagreements among the group, then resolve disagreements with respect to the outcomes	• Standard deviation • Perception of agreement/ consensus
	Building commitment	Move from less to more understanding of the willingness to commit of participants with respect to proposals the group is considering	Participants express their willingness to commit to a proposal, negotiate, modify the proposal or argue to increase commitment for a (modified) proposal	• % of participants that commit • Satisfaction of participants

PART II

PROOF OF VALUE

CHAPTER 7

MAINTAINING CREDIBILITY IN GROUP COLLABORATION

Detection of Deception

JUDEE K. BURGOON, JOEY F. GEORGE, JOHN KRUSE, KENT MARETT, AND MARK ADKINS

Abstract: While much has been written about deception and its detection in dyads, far less research has investigated deception in groups of size three or greater. Further, while most past research has focused on deception in oral face-to-face contexts, less research has examined deception in computer-mediated contexts, where participants are dispersed or otherwise. Growing reliance on distributed and mediated forms of communication warrant deeper exploration of both of these areas and their intersection.

To foreground this discussion, we first review several theories of deception along with an overview of the current status of deception and detection research. We then turn to an examination of deception in the context of group collaboration and mediated communication. We illustrate research at the nexus of these contexts by presenting results from one of the experiments we have conducted.

Keywords: Deception, Deception Detection, Collaboration, Computer-Mediated Communication, Group Interaction

It is a fundamental precept that human communication is founded on a presumption of trust—trust that people enter social interchanges from a stance of good will, trust that others' communication is sincere and honest, trust that others' motives are benign and transparent. In general, people trust each other to tell the truth (Levine, Park, and McCornack, 1999). Nowhere is this bedrock precept more pivotal than in the arena of collaboration, where cooperation, coordination, and consensus are keys to success. Yet a moment's reflection on the prevalence of deception in daily discourse reveals that group interactions are no less immune to hidden agendas, ulterior motives, exaggerations, misrepresentations, and falsehoods than other forms of human communication. Examples of deception in government, politics, sports, media, and business abound. A few famous examples:

- Scott Thompson, CEO of Yahoo, who resigned after it was discovered he had falsely claimed a computer science degree on his resume (Pepitone, 2012; Stewart, 2012);
- Attorney General Eric Holder's handling of "Operation Fast and Furious" (the program that put assault rifles in the hands of Mexican gun smugglers, guns that were ultimately used to kill a U.S. agent) that was described as somewhere between deception and flat-out lying;

- The Federal Trade Commission's fine of $12 million against LifeLock "to settle charges that the company used false claims to promote its identity theft protection services, which it widely advertised by displaying the CEO's Social Security number on the side of a truck" (Federal Trade Commission, 2010);
- Alex Rodriguez's announcement in early 2009 that he had indeed used steroids despite publicly denying it years earlier;
- Presidential candidate John Edwards lying to cover up his affair with Rielle Hunter and fathering her child while his wife, Elizabeth, was battling cancer.

More pernicious types of deception include financial fraud, as was so aptly illustrated by the massive pyramid schemes of Bernard Madoff ($50 billion lost) and Allen Stanford ($8 billion lost) (Carroll and Pilkington, 2009).

The prospect of deceit in all its many forms stands as a serious threat to the success of collaborative endeavors. Yet, little is known about how deception is played out in groups, particularly ones that are geographically dispersed. While much has been learned about how deception transpires among pairs of people in oral, face-to-face (FtF) communication, far less is known about deception when it occurs in larger groups of people, especially when they are geographically separated and communicate largely in electronic form. Collaboration, in today's world of virtual teams and group memberships that cross time zones and cultures, is increasingly transacted through computer-mediated communication (CMC) media. Thus, a timely issue in understanding collaborative technologies is the extent, form, and impact of deception under CMC.

One widely accepted finding from FtF literature is that individuals are not very adept at detecting deception, even when specially trained to do so (Ekman, O'Sullivan, and Frank, 1999; Frank and Feeley, 2002; Miller and Stiff, 1993). People can only correctly detect deception about half the time. We know little about how well people can detect deception when communication is mediated, and we know even less about situations where there are more than two people involved in the exchange. Is deception easier or harder to detect when communication is computer-mediated, or when people are meeting as a group and there is more than one person being deceived?

Both of these research questions have implications for collaboration among members of a group. Collaboration becomes more interesting as a practical and researchable problem when the process is mediated and as the number of people collaborating increases. When comparing collaborative communication between two people with the number of possible interactions among multiple participants, the amount of feedback and perceptions individuals must monitor increases dramatically as each new collaborator is added to the group (Nunamaker, Dennis, Valacich, Vogel, and George, 1991). This workload is heaviest when all members of the group meet at the same time and interaction is dynamic and spontaneous. CMC enables collaboration when group members are not physically in the same place, but it does not necessarily make the collaboration effort any less difficult. When deception is added to the collaboration picture, the workload for each individual group member increases even more (Anolli and Ciceri, 1997). For instance, if there is one deceiver in a group, and multiple receivers, the deceiver must monitor not only his or her communication with each individual receiver but also the potential interactions between receivers. If one of the receivers becomes suspicious, this belief could be transmitted to others as well, making successful deception more difficult.

The purpose of this chapter is to bring together research on deception and its detection with research on collaboration. The chapter will explain the mechanisms of deception and its detection, summarize key findings in deception detection research, and discuss the implications of this research for the design and deployment of collaborative processes and technologies. The chapter opens with the theoretical basis for studying deception and its detection. This is followed by a summary of major research findings from the deception literature. As an example of the type of research that can be done at the intersection of deception, CMC, and group collaboration, we describe one of our studies and its findings. The chapter ends with some speculation about collaborative processes and technologies that could be introduced to increase awareness of possible deception and even to thwart its effects during collaboration.

THE NATURE OF CREDIBILITY

Credibility is a multidimensional concept that refers to the judgments a given perceiver holds about the believability of another actor, in this case, another group member. In all human communication, people make implicit or explicit judgments of another's credibility. Such judgments frame message acceptance. For example, consider this eyewitness account of a pedestrian being hit by a car: "Well, you know, I think they were coming from over there and then, you know, the car just appeared, then there was a thud." Now consider an alternative version: "A male, approximate age early twenties, was walking due north on a green light when the red sports car turned right and hit him on the left side." The latter rendition engenders far more credibility, and is more likely to be believed because of the language used, even though the same event is being described.

The dimensions of judgment trace their roots to the early Greek philosophers' writings about *ethos* (one of the three canons of the Greek philosopher Aristotle's *Rhetoric*). Quintilian proposed that it could be defined as "a good man speaking well." Other conceptualizations emphasized two primary dimensions of judgment: competence or knowledge, and trustworthiness. Trustworthiness encompasses people's general character, including how truthful, honest, dependable, kind, and reliable they are.

Modern social science perspectives on credibility have established that people, messages, and institutions are judged not just according to their competence and character (which are the two dimensions that best reflect the original facets of ethos), but also other dimensions related to sociability or likability, composure, and extraversion or dynamism (Burgoon, 1976; McCroskey, Hamilton, and Weiner, 1974). Moreover, numerous analyses have decomposed trust into two constituents, one related to dependability, reliability, or predictability, and the other to honesty or truthfulness (e.g., Burgoon et al., 1999–2000; Jones and George, 1998). The latter presages the topic of the current chapter, namely how truthfulness and its polar opposite of deceptiveness affect credibility and collaboration in groups.

THEORIES OF DECEPTION

Theories of deception and its detection have run the gamut from those that emphasize physiological changes associated with deception to those that emphasize the verbal and nonverbal acts of deceivers and their detectability. Here we review three perspectives that have been influential in driving contemporary deception research.

The Leakage Hypothesis

This pivotal hypothesis refers to uncensored, telltale behavioral indicators of an individual's true internal state or deceptive intent. These indicators are thought to "leak out" of the body unknowingly and involuntarily. Articulated in Ekman and Friesen's (1969) seminal analysis of nonverbal deception and expanded upon in Ekman's later work (1992), this psychological perspective traces its roots to psychoanalytic views of human behavior, which indicate that internal experiences give rise to external manifestations of those states. Applied to deception, the hypothesis is founded on the assumption that the act of deceit is physiologically arousing and may lead to negative affective states (such as guilt, anxiety, and fear of detection), which are manifested involuntarily as indications that deception is taking place (deception clues) or revelations of the "true" state of affairs (called leakage, because it "leaks out" of the body unintentionally in the form of subtle nonverbal behaviors that reveal the deception to an alert observer). For example, behaviors such as fidgeting, facial micro-expressions, and changes in voice pitch may indicate that a person is engaging in deception. Although the terminology of leakage was—in contradistinction to other behavioral clues that deception is taking place—originally confined to signs of one's true emotional state of affairs, common usage now includes both forms of behavioral cues under the umbrella of leakage.

An important feature of the leakage hypothesis is the claim that channels (words, face, voice, body) differ in the availability of clues and controllability of leakage (Ekman and Friesen, 1969). Verbal features such as message content and language style, for example, are considered highly controllable, whereas nonverbal features are considered largely uncontrollable and uncontrolled, with the face being far more controllable, subject to self-consciousness and self-regulation, than the voice. According to the control hierarchy, people are also better at monitoring and controlling their upper body movements than their lower body and limbs.

The Four-Factor Theory

The four-factor theory of deception developed by Zuckerman, DePaulo, and Rosenthal (1981) incorporated much of Ekman and Friesen's (1969) leakage theory. The four-factor theory assumes that there is not one set of indicators that will reliably indicate deception, but rather several affective and cognitive processes that occur more or less often when deception is occurring. A receiver should be able to infer that deception is occurring by attempting to look for the cues that arousal, negative affect, cognitive effort, and attempted behavioral control may be taking place. Engaging in deception may cause deceivers to feel more generally aroused, and this arousal may be detectable from the nonverbal behavior of the deceiver. Among the indicators thought to signal deception-related arousal were greater pupil dilation, higher voice pitch, increased blinking, and more speech errors. Much like Ekman and Friesen (1969), Zuckerman et al. (1981) also believed that deception could cause the sender to experience negative emotions (such as guilt and fear of detection), and that these emotions could be indicated by behavioral cues. Cues indicative of negative affect included fidgeting, less pleasantness, and nonverbal distancing or "nonimmediacy," such as greater physical distance and avoidance of eye contact. The basic premise of the cognitive effort factor is that lying is more difficult (complex) than telling the truth; therefore, lying takes more cognitive effort than telling the truth because lying is believed to require more effort than simply recalling truthful information from memory, and liars must make their stories consistent and plausible with the facts as well as consistent with their own previous statements. Deceivers may manifest greater cognitive load through fewer illustrators (hand gestures that illustrate speech), longer response latencies, dilated pupils, and more speech hesitations than truth tellers (Zuckerman et al., 1981). Finally, deceivers may believe that showing unnecessary (nervous) nonverbal behaviors will betray their deceptive status and therefore, in an effort to appear truthful, may attempt to suppress these behaviors. The control of these behaviors can be difficult and may result in over control, such that deceivers exhibit fewer bodily movements and shorter response durations because they are attempting to control the amount of information that they are conveying. Vrij (2000) and colleagues (Caso, Gnisci, Vrij, and Mann, 2005) have reduced this to a three-factor theory that features emotional states, cognitive influences, and attempted control as the primary mechanisms driving deceptive displays. In this respect, arousal was conflated with emotionally charged activation. (In fact, their measurement of emotions includes the items, "Were you aroused when lying/truth telling?" and "Were you anxious when lying/truth telling?") The first two factors of emotion and cognitive load are, as in the original model, conceptualized as more reactive and uncontrollable or uncontrolled factors, whereas the third, attempted control, acknowledges deliberate actions by senders to manage their behavior.

Interpersonal Deception Theory

While embracing the leakage hypothesis and the four-factor theory to some extent, we have taken a different view not only on the prevalence and complexion of each class of cues during deceptive episodes, but also on whether deception-related cues are unintentional and involuntary or deliberate and voluntary. As postulated in *interpersonal deception theory* (IDT; Buller and Burgoon, 1996; Burgoon and Buller, 2008), profiles of deception indicators must include strategic (purposive, controllable, and goal-directed) as well as nonstrategic (unintentional, involuntary) acts, and strategic behavior implies that deception displays are adaptive and changeable, not static. Because humans are quite facile at "running off" deceptive routines, strategic activity should not be construed as requiring a high degree of cognitive awareness or mindfulness. Indeed, the general communicative strategies and associated specific behavioral tactics that are directed toward deception are the same strategies that may be employed in service of other nondeceptive purposes and therefore constitute overlearned and highly refined communicative routines, a factor that may account for receivers' poor success in detecting them.

Empirical evidence supports that deceptive behaviors may indeed be strategic and dynamic (e.g., Buller and Burgoon, 1994; Burgoon, Buller, Dillman, and Walther, 1995; Burgoon, Buller, White, Afifi, and Buslig, 1999; White and Burgoon, 2001). Deceivers deliberately construct their deceptions, and their deceptive messages are changeable as deceivers adapt them in response to feedback from their receiver. Whether these adjustments take the same form when adversarial behavior, hidden agendas, and other noncooperative behavior take place in groups is unknown.

Self-Presentation Theory

DePaulo (1992), in a departure from the more reactive view represented by the four-factor theory, has advanced a self-presentational theory that emphasizes deceivers' concern for, and active management of, their image so as to present themselves in the most positive light. Noting that liars may take their credibility less for granted than truth tellers, their actions should include efforts to repair their verbal and nonverbal behavior to improve their credibility and evade detection. In this respect, it shares some of the goal-oriented, communication-driven assumptions of IDT.

RELIABLE DECEPTION DISPLAYS

The various theories of deceptive displays have spawned an avalanche of empirical research attempting to confirm deceptive displays. Various summaries and meta-analyses (e.g., Buller and Burgoon, 1994; DePaulo, Lindsay, Malone, Muhlenbruck, Charlton, and Cooper, 2003; Vrij, 2000) have yielded far fewer reliable indicators than one might expect. Although deceivers tend to be more reticent, to tell less compelling lies, to show more evidence of heightened arousal and cognitive difficulty, to be more rigid and tense and inexpressive, and to use language differently when accessing real versus imagined events, these patterns are by no means uniform across situations, people, or cultures.

The lack of robust, reliable, and universal indicators is due in part to the subtlety of many indicators, the substitutability of various cues for one another, and a large number of moderators that alter what cues emerge in a given context. For example, Zhou, Burgoon, Nunamaker, and Twitchell (2004) conducted an experiment in which text messages were exchanged synchronously or asynchronously. When deceivers had the opportunity to take their time composing their messages and edit them before transmitting, they used more words, verbs, and sentences than did truth tellers—a pattern contrary to the previous conclusion that deceivers are reticent. In another examination that compared face-to-face, audio, and text messages during interviews about a possible theft of a wallet, modality exerted a main effect on a wide range of communication features (Burgoon, Blair, and Hamel, 2011).

Moreover, the empirical evidence that deceptive behaviors may indeed be dynamic and strategic (Burgoon, Buller, Floyd, and Grandpre, 1996; Burgoon, Buller, White, Afifi, and Buslig, 1999; Caso et al., 2005; White and Burgoon, 2001) implies that displays seen at the outset of an interaction may bear little resemblance to what deception looks like later in an interaction (Hamel, Burgoon, Humpherys, and Moffitt, 2007).

Whether potential deception indicators are applicable to adversarial behavior, hidden agendas, and other noncooperative behavior in groups has received only modest attention. As Marett and George (2004) rightly noted, group interactions are typically much more complex than dyadic ones. Deceivers must manage the perceptions and communication of two or more receivers at once. They may have to contend with shifting degrees of participation by other group members, making it more difficult to discern their level of acceptance of a deceiver's messages. The cognitive, emotional, and communicative demands on deceivers to manage this process, especially if other interactants might be suspicious and have ample time in the course of lengthier interactions, may evoke a variety of strategies to achieve one's ends while allaying suspicions and evading detection. Two distinctly different strategies might be employed, one a "flight" strategy of behaving passively in an attempt to be inconspicuous, only taking a more active role to opportunistically build upon others' errors and confusion. An alternative strategy is to adopt more of a "fight" or offensive strategy, attempting to exert leadership and persuade others to accept one's positions. In an investigation using a group simulation of an air operations center, deceivers opted for the latter approach, taking a more active and persuasive stance in attempting to convince their teammates to adopt the decision they were advocating (Burgoon, Wilson, Hass, and Schuetzler, in press). This shift to a more assertive stance replicates a finding from Dunbar et al. (in press) showing that the mere act of deceiving unsuspecting team members led deceivers to feel empowered and to adopt an active rather than passive stance in their interactions. Such strategies may enable deceivers to be convincing and to undermine group performance without their own culpability being recognized. This was the case in actual group collaborations in which distributed teams had to arrive at various strategies for improving a hospital's employee morale during the introduction of a smoking cessation campaign (Burgoon, Burgoon, Broneck, Alvaro, and Nunamaker, 2002). On the other hand, Fuller, Marett, and Twitchell (2012) conducted communication, command, control, intelligence, and surveillance simulation and found that although deceivers succeeded in impairing group performance, group members did perceive deception when it was present and correctly identified who the deceiver was. The presence of deception reduced the group's sense of mutuality and trust among team members, indicating that deception did not go unnoticed.

SUCCESS IN DECEPTION DETECTION

Extensive research has examined the ability of humans to detect deception. Several meta-analyses have arrived at very similar estimates: Humans do only slightly better than chance in their detection ability, averaging 54 percent accuracy (Aamodt and Custer, 2006; Bond and DePaulo, 2006; Vrij, 2000). That estimate, derived primarily from experimental subjects, combines accuracy at detecting the truth as well as accuracy in detecting deceit. The number drops to 47 percent when deceit is considered alone. The various meta-analyses summarizing results from hundreds of studies have also concluded that even people who work in occupations such as law enforcement that rely on the ability to detect deception were generally not more accurate than chance at detecting deception. Although deception detection accuracy rates have been as high as 82 percent in some studies in which judges have viewed videos of actual criminal interviews or professionals have been permitted to conduct longer interviews and to have access to contextual information (Blair and McCamey, 2002; Blair, Levine, and Shaw, 2010; Burgoon, Nunamaker, and Metaxas, 2010; Granhag and Vrij, 2005; Vrij, 2000), there is enough contrary evidence to suggest that detection accuracy is far from perfect under the best of circumstances.

One reason for suboptimal detection accuracy is that people commonly fall prey to exhibit a truth bias (Levine, Park, and McCornack, 1999). That is, receivers are more likely to judge both truthful and deceptive messages as truthful. This tendency makes people slightly more accurate at assessing truth and slightly less accurate at detecting deception. Other biases, such as the confirmation bias (seeking and attending more to information that fits one's preconceived notions), probing heuristic (believing someone more after asking the person a question, regardless of the answer), demeanor bias (believing certain people more often because of their nonverbal demeanor), visual bias (placing more faith in visual than other information), and expectancy violations heuristic (paying more attention to abnormal cues) may also lead to erroneous decisions (Burgoon, Blair and Strom, 2008; Dougherty, Franco-Watkins, and Thomas, 2008; Vrij and Baxter, 1999; Vrij, Fisher, Mann, and Leal, 2006).

Of interest here is whether moving to online collaborative environments exacerbates or ameliorates these biases. To answer this question requires considering two particularly salient aspects of online collaboration: the medium of communication and group size. We address each of these next.

Communication Medium

Media richness theory (Daft and Lengel, 1986; Daft, Lengel, and Trevino, 1987) posits that communication media can be characterized in terms of their "richness," where richness is defined as a medium's ability to reduce equivocality of information. According to MRT, the capacity of media to carry rich information is based on four criteria: speed of interaction, cue multiplicity, language variety, and personal focus. Rich communication is a key facilitator of effective collaboration and can provide the basis for "ambient awareness," the consciousness that collaborators have of one another's situations and contexts as they seek to synchronize their efforts. Increasingly, as groups rely on CMC to support some or all of their interactions and awareness, the importance of Channel Expansion Theory (CET) in describing the potential richness of these exchanges is amplified. Collaborative tasks that require the creation and maintenance of a rich, shared understanding and ambient awareness among all participants become increasingly difficult as additional participants become part of the process. These tasks can include work groups discussing and comparing potential strategies in business environments, strangers coming together online and working on open source programming efforts, and even groups working together in e-learning environments, such as WebCT (Kock and Nosek, 2005). In fact, such tasks are difficult even for groups predominantly using rich media, such as face-to-face meetings.

Research into the media selection process has generally relied on relating message requirements to media capabilities, positing that the most successful communication occurs when there is "fit" between these two aspects (e.g., Daft et al., 1987). For example, a manager who seeks to communicate with employees in an unambiguous fashion, leaving no room for confusion, would theoretically select a richer medium like face-to-face communication to do so.

CET (Carlson and Zmud, 1999) suggests that even lean media can be perceived or adapted to be "richer." CET identifies four key levels of experience or familiarity as driving the ability of an individual to richly communicate on a given medium: familiarity with the medium, familiarity with communication coparticipants, familiarity with the communication topic, and familiarity with the communication context. CET has generally received empirical support (e.g., Carlson and Zmud, 1999; Carlson and George, 2004). For example, Timmerman and Madhavapeddi (2008) found that, across three different media (email, phone, and face-to-face), familiarity with the medium, partner, topic, and context accounted for significant variance in perceptions of media richness. As communicators gain relevant experiences and familiarity, they perceive the media in use to be better able to handle rich, equivocality-reducing, socio-emotional communication (e.g., George and Carlson, 1999; Carlson et al., 2004). Other variables found to influence richness perceptions and the media selection process include social influences (Fulk, Schmitz, and Steinfield, 1990), participant experiences (Carlson and Zmud, 1999), and situational factors (Treviño, Lengel, and Daft, 1987).

The relevance of the medium to deception is twofold. First is the impact on media selection. Collaboration can only succeed to the extent that participants in a collaborative arrangement operate out of a spirit of good will and embrace communication practices that engender trust. To the extent that individuals enter into communication with hidden agendas and malicious intent, they may select communication media strategically to foster their own ends. The richness of the medium in terms of its potential to convey multimodal information is bound to be a deciding factor. It may be, for example, that manipulative and deceitful individuals select or manage media in a way that optimizes their personal objectives rather than those of the group and they may select media that reduce rather than enhance familiarity.

Second, the medium in use may influence the communication patterns displayed by deceitful and manipulative individuals as well as the detection ability of the targets of deception. Familiarity with the partner and context have been identified as important considerations in deception research (e.g., Buller and Burgoon, 1996; George and Carlson, 1999; Carlson et al., 2004) such that deceivers feel more confident and successful with targets who are unfamiliar with them, with their past history, or with deceptive cues in general. Thus, deceivers may prefer leaner media such as asynchronous email that allow them to control and edit the information that is transmitted, managing their self-presentation and minimizing receivers' access to those cues that create familiarity. For example, leaner media allow deceivers to focus more on the verbal content and style of their messages, which can have a significant impact on impression formation in computer mediated groups (Adkins and Brashers, 1995). Deceivers may feel that richer media, by giving receivers opportunities to become more "familiar," may put them at risk of being detected. In the case of situational familiarity, more familiarity does increase receivers' ability to detect deception (Reinhard, Sporer, Scharmach, and Marksteiner, 2011). However, relational familiarity works in the opposite direction. Although deceivers perceive more suspicion from friends than strangers, ironically, receivers are worse at detecting deceit from familiar others (Burgoon, 1992). They are more lenient in their judgments of acquaintances, friends, and family, brushing aside their suspicions and discounting possible indicators of duplicity (Bond and DePaulo, 2006; Buller, 1988; Burgoon, 1992; McCornack and Parks, 1988; Stiff, Kim, and Ramesh, 1992).

Familiarity is not the only consideration afforded by the communication medium. The speed of information transmission, usually captured in the concept of media synchronicity, also can exert influence. Burgoon, Chen, and Twitchell (2010) conducted an experiment that compared synchronous CMC (real-time chat) to asynchronous team interaction (exchanges that took place over several days). They hypothesized that compared to asynchronous CMC, synchronous CMC would foster more involvement and mutuality during the team interaction, would lead team members to regard each other as more credible, and hence they would be less likely to detect deception. Results confirmed the predictions for the synchronous mode increasing involvement, mutuality, and credibility. Deceivers also portrayed themselves as somewhat more credible than truth tellers, and teams with a deceptive member made poorer decisions than teams that were truthful. Thus, the deceivers could capitalize on the benefits of synchronous communication to further benefit their deceptive ends.

Finally, the physical proximity of group members may also influence perceptions of communication richness and affect one's ability to detect deception over CMC. While group member proximity is situational and not a characteristic associated with a medium, the possibility of transmitting communicative cues within a physical environment, beyond the cues related to the actual content being communicated, should not be overlooked. Environmental cues, such as laughter, sneezing, the sound of other group members typing, and other disruptive movements can influence group member behaviors and their perceptions of communication richness (Tung and Turban, 1998; Chidambaram and Tung, 2005). Physical proximity may also affect group members' suspicions, especially if one is prone to giving others the "benefit of the doubt." Proximal interaction has been found to promote feelings of mutuality between group members, which is important for establishing credibility between each other and building toward teamwork, something distant group members struggle with (Burgoon et al., 2002; Fuller, Marett, and Twitchell, 2012). Collaborative technologies can be found in both local and distance environments, and a deceiver who is physically collocated with other group members, even though using CMC, may be able to exploit such feelings to further his or her ends.

Group Size

In dyadic collaboration, participants are afforded the luxury of being able to fully tailor their own communication style and content to the particularities that they perceive in the other. As group size increases beyond the "simple" dyad, achieving rich communication in lean media becomes more challenging (Pinsonneault et al., 1999), and the tightly focused ability to tailor the message becomes less precise. Even in dyads, communicating richly may initially require considerably more effort and intentionality on the part of both participants to overcome and adapt to a constricted medium. Gaining familiarity and developing relational closeness in communication dyads does occur over lean media, albeit more slowly than in face-to-face (e.g., Walther and Burgoon, 1992). However, it is likely that the process of developing these relevant familiarities will become even lengthier as new group members are added.

In addition, as group size increases, participants experience additional process losses that detract from their ability to effectively address the group's given task (e.g., Nunamaker et al., 1991). Traditionally, a group size of five has been seen as the practical limit for effective communication (e.g., Shaw, 1981). However, this limit doesn't factor in the various supporting technologies that may be employed by groups today. The use of group support systems (GSS) may facilitate richer group collaboration (in the sense of enabling faster equivocality reduction) by helping to overcome these process losses (e.g., Nunamaker et al., 1991). CET would suggest that as GSS-supported groups gain relevant experience, they would be able to expand the medium's richness as well. Indeed, there is support in the literature that group experience facilitates performance (e.g., Guinan, Cooprider, and Faraj, 1998; Martz, 2002). As such, the benefits to group collaboration afforded by GSS and by the relevant experiences identified in CET may best be viewed as synergistic.

How the expansion of group size, with or without the benefit of GSS, affects deception displays and their detection has received little empirical or theoretical attention. One of the rare exceptions, a study by Zhou and Zhang (2006), compared dyads to groups of size three. They found several differences between deceivers and truth tellers related to group size. In three-person groups, deceivers experienced a higher level of cognitive complexity, but this did not dissuade them from active participation. In dyads, deceivers were less pleasant, had shorter response latencies, and used shorter words and noun phrases than truth tellers. These contrasting patterns suggest that the group setting was more conducive to deceivers engaging in successful, unimpaired communication that was the dyad.

As for the successful detection of deception in groups, very little is known. Given that individuals in dyadic communication are only as good as chance in detecting deception, success rates for detecting deception in groups may be even worse owing to the complexity of the task that occupies participants' attention. However, the complexity of maintaining credibility with multiple receivers may also be more taxing for deceivers, who must not only produce plausible messages but also monitor and respond to feedback from multiple receivers. Also, cross talk may take place between receivers, and a vigilant deceiver must also monitor this cross talk to fully gauge receiver reactions. IDT stipulates that successful deceivers must watch for signs of suspicion from others and then decide whether to continue lying or not. This may be more taxing when multiple receivers must be monitored for skepticism or acceptance.

A Model of Deception within a Collaborative Context

So far, our review of theories and empirical evidence regarding deception has underscored why it is so difficult to detect deception. Based on CET, we believe that the successful detection of a deceptive communication message is determined by the participants' involvement, their relationship, the design and delivery of the deception, and the medium in which it is conveyed. Both the deceiver and receiver are seen to possess several characteristics relevant to a deceptive interaction. These characteristics are motivation, intrinsic abilities, experiences, cognitions, and affect. As well, factors such as the characteristics of the task (as defined by each participant) and any support (technological or otherwise) being leveraged for task accomplishment will affect this process. Figure 7.1 presents a process model of deceptive communication which shows all of these elements and their relationships to each other (Carlson et al., 2004). The model should not be interpreted as causal. We are not suggesting, for example, that the deceiver causes the communication medium anymore than we are suggesting that the medium causes the outcomes.

The purpose of Figure 7.1 is to present in one place the most pivotal components that are involved in the deceptive communication process: the participants, features of their participation (motivation and so on), their relationship, the ongoing elements of the deceptive communication event itself, the medium, and finally, the outcomes. As this diagram is meant to show deception in the collaborative process, the box representing the receivers would include multiple receivers

Figure7.1   **A Model of Deceptive Communication in a Collaborative Context**

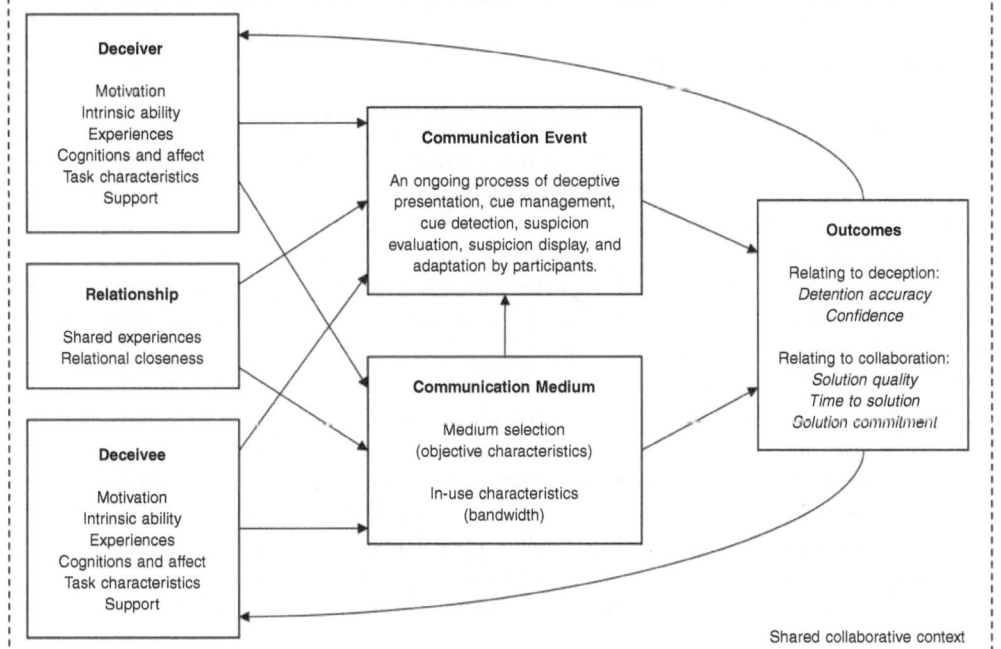

(and it would be possible to have multiple deceivers as well). The outcomes relate not only to deception detection but to the task outcomes of the collaborating group itself. Surrounding all of these elements is the shared collaborative context in which the group works, the nature of the work the group or organization performs, the relationship of the group to other groups both inside and outside an organization, and so on. Although the role played by medium is not static, as we saw in our previous discussion of CET, it does play an important role both in the formulation of the deception and in its potential detection. Each medium has its own limitations and advantages for deceivers and receivers. For example, under the right circumstances, face-to-face communication may well be the most supportive medium for deception, but it may also be the best to use for detecting deception. Giordano et al. (2007), for example, found that dyadic negotiators working face-to-face were better able to detect deception than were those communicating via instant messaging software. In an on-going deceptive communication event, the success or failure of the receiver to detect the deception serves as input for both the deceiver and the receiver for the next turns in the dialogue. The outcomes of this communication process include those directly describing the success (or failure) of the deceptive act as well as outcomes tied to the collaborative exchange that may be influenced by deception.

RESEARCH FINDINGS

Figure 7.1 has served as a useful depiction for us of the problem space associated with the deceptive speech act and the various parts of the process that influence both the act and its detection. As part of our work, we have conducted a limited number of studies that consider deception in a group context. We focus here on one study in particular, which varied technology support and proximity in three-person discussions in which there was one deceiver and multiple receivers.

Research Questions and Hypotheses

People working on a collaborative task typically assume that each person intends to work together toward a common problem or goal. However, role conflict, self-interest, power, and politics often contribute to one or more group members being motivated to be less than completely honest with their fellow group members. This possibility raises these questions:

How successful are deceivers at lying to others when there are multiple receivers (i.e., does group size affect deception success)? Does the setting or medium affect deception success? Finally, how likely are other group members to detect lies in those settings? These were the research questions we investigated in this study.

We hypothesized that receivers would be less successful detecting deception when using a computer-mediated modality and when the group was dispersed than with a non-CMC modality or when in a proximate location, due to the reduced number of communicative cues available by which to judge sender credibility. It was also expected that, due to deindividuation, deceivers using a CMC mode would submit more deceptive statements than deceivers not using CMC. Although it would be more difficult for deceivers to monitor the behaviors of others after a deceptive statement when using a GSS, deceivers would have to engage in other behaviors to make the deception believable, such as issuing more deceptive statements. Finally, it was expected that deceivers would be more successful at swaying the group decision when the group was collocated and when not using a CMC modality. Under these more traditional settings, group members were likely to develop a sense of mutuality with each other and to give each other the benefit of the doubt. Deceivers would likely thrive in such circumstances.

Sample

Sixty groups of three people each participated in the study, with fifteen groups meeting in each setting. The average age of subjects was 21.3 years, and 52 percent of the subjects were female. Subjects were randomly assigned to groups, and demographically, there was no heterogeneity among the four conditions.

Research Design and Procedures

The study was a laboratory experiment, with a 2×2 factorial design. The presence of computer-mediated communication and group member proximity were the independent variables. Groups met in one of four settings: a boardroom setting (proximate group members in a face-to-face discussion); a "decision room" environment (proximate group members utilizing a group support system); a teleconference setting (dispersed group members in a verbal discussion); and a virtual team setting (dispersed group members using a group support system).

The task required the groups to determine how to allocate funds of a charitable foundation across six causes. The deceiver's instructions included a particular cause to argue for, with the promise of a reward if he or she could convince the rest of the group to contribute the majority of the money toward that cause. The assigned cause was based on the results of a value assessment completed before the experiment, with the assigned cause aligning with the deceiver's lowest personal values and, therefore, necessitating the use of deception to provide arguments and personal support in the hopes of convincing the other group members to support the same cause. Groups met at the assigned location and were instructed on the task (and on the technology, if applicable). The average group discussion lasted a little more than ten minutes, and was followed immediately by a group vote on the allocation of funds, ending the task.

Dependent Measures

Once the task was completed, receivers completed a questionnaire asking them to identify any information from the task they thought to be dishonest. To verify that deceivers complied with instructions and to measure amount of deception taking place, deceivers were asked to review the transcript or recording of the discussion and identify specific deceptive statements they introduced into the dialogue that contained false information. Each individual statement or sentence was counted as one deceptive statement. Receiver detection accuracy was measured by dividing the number of deceptive statements correctly detected by a receiver into the total number of deceptive statements identified by the deceiver. Deception success was determined when the deceiver was able to sway the group decision toward his or her favor.

Results

Data analysis was conducted by a two-way ANOVA (see descriptive statistics in Table 7.1 below). Results largely supported the hypotheses. On average, deceivers contributed 1.82 deceptive statements during the group discussions. The modality used had a bearing on the interaction between deceiver and receivers. Deceivers in CMC-supported groups introduced more deceptive comments ($M = 2.20$, SD $= 1.06$) into the discussion than did deceivers communicating without CMC ($M =1.43$, SD $= 0.57$; $F[1,58] = 12.74$, $p <. 001$). Deceivers lied the most in the virtual team setting, contributing an average of 2.33 lies. Receivers, on the other hand, had very little success detecting lies in any setting. Overall, only 8.8 percent of the lies were detected, a finding similar to successful deception detection rates reported in Giordano et al. (2007) and George et al. (2008). Finally,

Table 7.1

Outcomes by Setting

Setting	CMC	Proximate setting	Number of deceptive statements	Percentage of deceptive statements detected	Percentage of groups successfully deceived
Boardroom		X	1.40 (.51)	8.3	90
Teleconference			1.47 (.74)	10.2	60
Decision Room	X	X	2.07 (.88)	3.3	87
Virtual Team	X		2.33 (1.23)	12.0	40

Note: Standard deviations in parentheses.

deceivers in proximate groups successfully affected the group decision 88 percent of the time, as opposed to a 50 percent rate of success in dispersed groups ($F[1,58] = 7.23$, $p < .01$). Deceivers were most successful in the boardroom setting, adversely affecting the group decision 90 percent of the time. This is compared to a 40 percent rate of success in the virtual team setting, which was the setting that featured the largest amount of deception. However, there was no significant relationship between amount of deception and deception success.

Although this experiment has its limitations, the findings here do strongly imply that deceivers are able to adapt their behavior to both the medium and group member proximity so as to improve their performance in fooling others and in avoiding detection of being deceptive.

COLLABORATIVE PROCESSES

The research findings on deception in communication and more specifically in collaboration have many implications for collaborative processes. How deception appears and is detected during collaboration depends upon the participants, their relationship, the design and delivery of the deception, and the communication medium in which it is transmitted. As per the expectations set by interpersonal deception theory, the deceiver can be expected to act strategically to maximize the effectiveness of the deception within the medium.

There are, nevertheless, specific attributes of collaboration that can affect deception. Most obviously, the nature of deception will depend upon the collaboration medium. Video teleconferencing (VTC), for example is considered to be a rich channel. Although quality varies (e.g., latency, sampling rates), VTC participants generally are subject to a higher degree of interactivity and observation than users of leaner media such as chat or email. As such, they may have to expend greater relative effort in maintaining credibility in relation to pressing forward with deception. On the other hand, such deceptions may be more practiced as they closely resemble day-to-day interaction. Moreover, we might expect that in an extension of channel expansion theory, that deceivers may grow more skilled at leveraging particular collaboration media in order to maintain credibility and evade detection.

The nature and mechanisms of deception are also influenced by the collaborative process. Collaborative processes vary greatly in their levels of complexity. As collaborative groups attempt higher levels of coordination and interdependence, collaborative complexity increases. Nunamaker et al. (1996) categorized collaboration activities and the associated group effort with three levels: individual work level, coordinated work level, and concerted work level.

At the individual work level, individuals act without coordinating their efforts, even if part of a collaborating group. Each participant works autonomously to provide work that will be integrated into the group's aggregated final product. The next level, coordinated work, requires that team members match up otherwise independent efforts. Nunamaker et al. (1994) likened the coordinated work level to running a team relay race where group performance requires team members to coordinate individual efforts.

The highest level of collaboration is the concerted work level in which participants must make a continuous, concerted effort in order to accomplish team goals. This effort is compared to a rowing crew in which each team member's concerted effort dovetails with the other group members. Each succeeding level of collaboration requires an increasing amount of interdependence and communication between the collaborators. As a result, deceivers in more complex collaborative circumstances—circumstances that are much more complicated than those in the experiment reported on above—may experience greater or more continuous group checks on their contributions. In such situations, collaborators may well know each other quite well, including each participant's skills, tendencies, and even language usage patterns. Under these conditions, this may make it more difficult to construct and convey effective deceptions.

Other process and contextual issues have also been shown to complicate deception detection in collaboration. For example, Zhou et al. (2004) attained findings that were counter to the initial expectations set by the literature. The study utilized a scenario in which collaborators worked together to select items useful to desert survival for their team. The deceivers were tasked with skewing the list of retained items towards a set that was poorer for living in the desert. Surprisingly, the deceivers were more likely to be more expressive and communicate more than truth tellers. The authors hypothesized that this was due to the persuasive nature of the task for the deceivers. Instead of evading detection of a past act, they were seeking to strategically lead their team via deception. Moreover, the authors surmised that the asynchrony provided by the email mode provided the deceivers with an advantage that they would likely not have in a more interactive form of collaboration:

> . . . virtually all of the differences between this experiment's findings and those of prior investigation can be laid at the feet of the unique characteristics of asynchronous, distributed, text-based communication and the specific task. Unlike interviews, in which respondents must construct answers spontaneously in real time, with little opportunity for prior planning, rehearsal, or editing, deceivers in this investigation had ample opportunity to create and revise their messages so as to make them as persuasive as possible. (Zhou et al., 2004, p. 99)

The communication context therefore can exert significant influence on how deception unfolds in collaborative contexts.

IMPLICATIONS

We reviewed the literature on the detection of deception and found that successful detection is difficult when communicating with only one partner. Indeed, detection accuracy is low, at, or slightly better than chance. In a group, created for a collaborative task, detection may be even more difficult. Trust is needed for successful collaboration, and people generally expect others to be truthful in their dealings with them. A group member entering into such a social situation with malintent and the desire to deceive can thus take advantage of that willingness to believe. While this is the case in dyadic communication, in a group setting, there is even more willingness to believe, given its importance to successfully accomplishing the group task. We also saw how deception detection can be affected by communication media, the collaboration process, and the context of the collaboration. In a computer-mediated setting, for example, it may be even easier to deceive group members, as many of the interactions between deceiver and partners predicted by IDT will be mediated and thus more difficult to execute properly. As we saw in our multiple receivers study, deceivers in computer-mediated settings lied more than those who did not communicate through computers. They had a more difficult time getting their deceptive messages through. However, the receivers in the study did not do very well at detecting the deception, despite the difficulty the deceivers had. The same barriers that made it difficult for deceivers to execute also made it difficult for receivers. Yet deceivers learned how to overcome those barriers and were successful at perpetuating their deception in a large proportion of the groups in the study.

Given the challenges to detecting deception in a group collaborative setting, it seems there are many different approaches that could be taken by those leading collaborative efforts and those designing collaborative technology. One could conceive of both social and technical approaches. Social approaches could include training members of new groups on the collaboration process and the role of the truth bias in it, while also increasing group members' awareness of the possibility of deceit and the effect it would have on collaboration. The danger here, of course, is to find the line between a healthy heightening of awareness, on the one hand, and the creation of too much suspicion and doubt, on the other. While the former could aid the group, the latter could help destroy it. However, the existence of such training may deter the group member who came into the effort with malintent and a plan to deceive. There are doubtless other social approaches that could be taken—this is only one example. From a technological perspective, designers of systems to support group collaboration would have many options. One option would be to design software that enforced adherence to collaborative processes less likely to be affected by deception, such as a system that enforced short messages, depriving deceivers of the advantages they enjoyed in the desert survival study described above. At the other extreme would be options that were less structured but that still disturbed efforts to deceive. For example, communication between group members could be analyzed in real time for the inclusion of certain text-based indicators of deception, such as the use of passive voice and negative language. If enough indicators were present, the system would then send messages to receivers, informing them of the suspicious nature of these messages. Receivers could then respond accordingly. Clearly, the success of any remedies aimed at reducing deception in groups, computer-mediated or otherwise, will ultimately depend on additional research in group process, media effects, collaborative process and collaborative context, where that research is specifically targeted to the study of deception in groups.

CONCLUSIONS

In this chapter, we've looked at the theoretical basis for why deception is detectable. The theories we reviewed include the leakage hypothesis, the four-factor theory, and interpersonal deception theory. All of these theories posit that deceivers give off cues to their deception, and we also reviewed five categories of cues: arousal-based, emotion-related, memory-related, message production processes, and communicator strategies and tactics. We then reviewed findings for deception detection related to each of these sets of cues. These theories, and these findings, however, are all related to either individual or dyadic (one receiver and one deceiver) face-to-face communication, where the receiver would first have to detect the cues and then interpret them correctly as indicators of deceit. What happens when the number of people involved in the communicative interaction increases beyond two, and you move from a dyad to a group? And what happens when communication moves from face-to-face to computer-mediated, as group members become dispersed? Looking at media richness theory and its extension through channel expansion theory, we pointed out the difficulties in achieving rich communication among group members in dispersed, computer-mediated settings. Add to these difficulties the additional challenges associated with detecting deception in groups, and you begin to see the scope of the problems associated with detecting deception in a dispersed collaborative group environment. The results of a study we conducted illustrate these problems and further show how well deceivers can adapt to the circumstances and continue to deceive successfully. They utilize the trust established among group members to their advantage. While there has been an increasing number of studies of deception in computer-mediated communication and among groups in recent years, clearly, there is much more work to be done in gaining an understanding of deception and its detection in collaborative group situations.

REFERENCES

Aamodt, M.G., and Custer, H. 2006. Who can best catch a liar? A meta-analysis of individual differences in detecting deception. *The Forensic Examiner,* 15, 7–11.

Adkins, M., and Brashers, B.E. 1995. The power of language in computer-mediated groups. *Management Communication Quarterly,* 8, 289–322.

Anolli, L., and Ciceri, R. 1997. The voice of deception: Vocal strategies of naïve and able liars. *Journal of Nonverbal Behavior,* 21, 259–284.

Blair, J.P.; Levine, T.R.; and Shaw, A.S. 2010. Content in context improves deception detection accuracy. *Human Communication Research,* 36, 423–442.

Blair, J.P., and McCamey, W.P. 2002. Detection of deception: An analysis of the behavioral analysis interview technique. *Illinois Law Enforcement Executive Forum,* 2, 165–170.

Bond, C.F. Jr., and DePaulo, B.M. 2006. Accuracy of deception judgments. *Personality and Social Psychology Review,* 10, 3, 214–234.

Buller, D.B. 1988. Deception by strangers, friends, and intimates: Attributional biases due to relationship development. Paper presented to the annual meeting of the Speech Communication Association, Boston, November.

Buller, D.B., and Burgoon, J.K. 1996. Interpersonal deception theory. *Communication Theory,* 6, 203–242.

———. 1994. Deception: Strategic and nonstrategic communication. In J.A. Daly and J.M. Wiemann (eds.), *Strategic Interpersonal Communication,* 191–223. Hillsdale, NJ: Lawrence Erlbaum.

Burgoon, J.K. 1976. The ideal source: A reexamination of source credibility measurement. *Central States Speech Journal,* 27, 200–206.

———. 1992. Applying an interpersonal communication perspective to deception: Effects of suspicion, deceit, and relational familiarity on perceived communication. Paper presented to the annual meeting of the Speech Communication Association, Chicago, November.

Burgoon, J.K.; Blair, J.P.; and Hamel, L. 2011. Factors influencing deception detection: Impairment or facilitation? Unpublished manuscript.

Burgoon, J.K.; Blair, J.P.; and Strom, R. 2008. Cognitive biases, modalities and deception detection. *Human Communication Research,* 34, 572–599.

Burgoon, J.K.; Bonito, J.A.; Bengtsson, B.; Ramirez, A. Jr.; Dunbar, N.; and Miczo, N. 1999–2000. Testing the interactivity model: Communication processes, partner assessments, and the quality of collaborative work. *Journal of Management Information Systems,* 16, 3, 33–56.

Burgoon, J.K.; Bonito, J.; Ramirez, A.; Dunbar, N.; Kam, K.; and Fischer, J. 2002. Testing the interactivity principle: Effects of mediation, propinquity, and verbal and nonverbal modalities in interpersonal interaction. *Journal of Communication,* 52, 3, 657–677.

Burgoon, J. K., and D. B. Buller 2008. Interpersonal deception theory. In L. Baxter and Dawn Braithwaite (eds.), *Engaging Theories in Interpersonal Communication.* Thousand Oaks: Sage Publications.

Burgoon, J.K.; Buller, D.; Dillman, L.; and Walther, J. 1995. Interpersonal deception: IV. Effects of suspicion on perceived communication and nonverbal behavior dynamics. *Human Communication Research,* 22, 2, 163–196.

Burgoon, J.K.; Buller, D.B.; Floyd, K.; and Grandpre, J. 1996. Deceptive realities: Sender, receiver, and observer perspectives deceptive conversation. *Communication Research,* 23, 6, 724–748.

Burgoon, J.K.; Buller, D.B.; White, C.H.; Afifi, W.A.; and Buslig, A. 1999. The role of conversational involvement deceptive interactions. *Personality and Social Psychology Bulletin,* 25, 669–685.

Burgoon, J.K.; Burgoon, M.; Broneck, K.; Alvaro, E.; and Nunamaker, J.F. Jr. 2002. Effects of synchronicity and proximity on group communication. Paper presented to the annual meeting of the National Communication Association, New Orleans, November.

Burgoon, J.K.; Chen, F.; and Twitchell, D. 2010. Deception and its detection under synchronous and asynchronous computer-mediated communication. *Group Decision and Negotiation,* 19, 346–366.

Burgoon, J.K.; Nunamaker, J.F. Jr.; and Metaxas, D. 2010. Noninvasive measurement of multimodal indicators of deception and credibility. Final Report to the Defense Academy for Credibility Assessment (Grant No. IIP-0701519), July 10.

Burgoon, J.K.; Wilson, D.; Hass, M.; and Schuetzler, R. In press. Interactive deception in group decision-making: New insights from communication pattern analysis. In M. Magnusson and D. McNeill (eds.), *T-patterns in Behavior and Interactions.*

Carlson, J., and George, J.F. 2004. Media appropriateness in the conduct and discovery of deceptive communication: The relative influence of richness and synchronicity. *Group Decision and Negotiation,* 13, 2, 191–210.

Carlson, J.; George, J.F.; Burgoon, J.K.; Adkins, M.; and White, C. 2004. Deception computer-mediated communication. *Group Decision and Negotiation,* 13, 1, 5–28.

Carlson, J., and Zmud, R. 1999. Channel expansion theory and the experiential nature of media richness perceptions. *Academy of Management Review,* 42, 2, 153–170.

Carroll, R., and Pilkington, E. 2009. Stanford charges spark run on banks. Guardian.co.uk, February 18. www.guardian.co.uk/sport/2009/feb/18/allen-stanford-banks-caribbean (accessed February 23, 2009).

Caso, L.; Gnisci, A.; Vrij, A.; and Mann, S. 2005. Processes underlying deception: An empirical analysis of truth and lies when manipulating the stakes. *Journal of Investigative Psychology and Offender Profiling,* 2, 195–202.

Chidambaram, L., and Tung, L.L. 2005. Is out of sight, out of mind? An empirical study of social loafing in technology-supported groups. *Information Systems Research,* 16, 2, 149–168.

Daft, R., and Lengel, R. 1986. Organizational information requirements, media richness, and structural design. *Management Science,* 32, 5, 554–570.

Daft, R.; Lengel, R.; and Trevino, L. 1987. Message equivocality, media selection, and manager performance: Implications for information systems. *MIS Quarterly,* 11, 3, 355–366.

DePaulo, B. M. 1992. Nonverbal behavior and self-presentation. *Psychological Bulletin,* 111, 2, 203–243.

DePaulo, B.; Lindsay, J.; Malone, B.; Muhlenbruck, L.; Charlton, K.; and Cooper, H. 2003. Cues to deception. *Psychological Bulletin,* 129, 1, 74–118.

Dougherty, M. R.; Franco-Watkins, A. M.; and Thomas, R. 2008. Psychological plausibility of the theory of probabilistic mental models and the fast and frugal heuristics. *Psychological Review,* 115, 199–211.

Dunbar, N.E.; Jensen, M.L.; Bessabarova, E.; Burgoon, J.K.; Bernard, D.R.; Robertson, K.J.; Kelley, K.M.; Adame, B.; and Eckstein, J.M. In press. Empowered by persuasive deception: The effects of power and deception on interactional dominance, credibility, and decision-making. *Communication Research.*

Ekman, P. 1992. *Telling Lies: Clues to Deceit in the Marketplace, Politics, and Marriage.* New York: W.W. Norton.

Ekman, P., and Friesen, W.V. 1969. Nonverbal leakage and clues to deception. *Psychiatry,* 32, 88–105.

Ekman, P.; O'Sullivan, M.; and Frank, M.G. 1999. A few can catch a liar. *Psychological Science,* 10, 263–266.

Federal Trade Commission. 2010. LifeLock will pay $12 million to settle charges by the FTC and 35 states that identity theft prevention and data security claims were false.www.ftc.gov/opa/2010/03/lifelock.shtm (accessed June 16, 2013).

Frank, M.G., and Feeley, T.H. 2002. To catch a liar: Challenges for research in lie detection training. *Journal of Applied Communication Research,* 31, 58–75.

Fulk, J.; Schmitz, J.; and Steinfeld, C.A. 1990. Social influence model of technology use. In J. Fulk and C. Steinfield (eds.), *Organizations and Communication Technology,* 117–141. Newbury Park, CA: Sage.

Fuller, C.; Marett, K.; and Twitchell, D. 2012. An examination of deception in virtual teams: Effects of deception on task performance, mutuality, and trust. *IEEE Transactions on Professional Communication,* 55, 1, 20–35.

George, J.F., and Carlson, J.R. 1999. Electronic lies: Lying to others and detecting lies using electronic media. *Proceedings of the 5th Americas Conference on Information Systems,* Milwaukee, WI, 612–614.

George, J.F.; Marett, K.; and Tilley, P. 2008. The effects of warnings, computer-based media, and probing activity on successful lie detection. *IEEE Transactions on Professional Communication,* 51, 1, 1–17.

Giordano, G.A.; Stoner, J.S.; Brouer, R.L.; and George, J.F. 2007. The influences of deception and computer-mediation on self-report measures of forcing negotiating, tension, satisfaction, and deception detection dyadic negotiations. *Journal of Computer-Mediated Communication,* 12, 2, 362–383.

Granhag, P.A., and Vrij, A. 2005. Deception detection. In N. Brewer and K.D. Williams (eds.), *Psychology and Law: An Empirical Perspective,* 43–92. New York: Guilford Press.

Guinan, P.J.; Cooprider, J.G.; and Faraj, S. 1998. Enabling software development team performance during requirements definition: A behavioral versus technical approach. *Information Systems Research,* 9, 2, 101–125.

Hamel, L.; Burgoon, J. K.; Humpherys, S.; and Moffitt, K. 2007. The "when" of detecting interactive deception. Paper presented to the annual meeting of the National Communication Association, Chicago, November.

Jones, G.R., and George, J.M. 1998. The experience and evolution of trust: Implications for cooperation and teamwork. *Academy of Management Review,* 23, 531–546.

Kock, N., and Nosek, J. 2005. Expanding the boundaries of e-collaboration. *IEEE Transactions on Professional Communication*, 48, 1, 1–9.

Levine, T.R.; Park, H.S.; and McCornack, S.A. 1999. Accuracy detecting truths and lies: Documenting the "veracity effect." *Communication Monographs*, 66, 125–144.

Martz, B. 2002. In search of GSS impact on groups: An exploratory field study. *Team Performance Management Journal*, 8, 3/4, 79–88.

Marett, L.K., and George, J.F. 2004. Deception in the case of one sender and multiple receivers. *Group Decision and Negotiation*, 13 (1), 29–44.

McCornack, S.A., and Parks, M.R. 1986. Deception detection and relationship development: The other side of trust. In M.L. McLaughlin (ed.), *Communication Yearbook*, vol. 9, 377–389. Beverly Hills, CA: Sage.

McCroskey, J.C.; Hamilton, P.R.; and Weiner, A.M. 1974. The effect of interaction behavior on source credibility, homophily, and interpersonal attraction. *Human Communication Research*, 1, 42–52.

Miller, G., and Stiff, J. 1993. *Deceptive Communication*. Newbury Park, CA: Sage.

Nunamaker, J.F. Jr., Briggs, R.O.; Mittleman, D.D.; Vogel, D.R.; and Balthazard, P.A. 1996. Lessons from a dozen years of group support systems research: A discussion of lab and field findings. *Journal of Management Information Systems*, 13, 163–207.

Nunamaker, J.F. Jr.; Dennis, A.R.; Valacich, J.S.; Vogel, D.R.; and George, J.F. 1991. Electronic meeting systems to support group work. *Communications of the ACM*, 34, 40–61.

Pepitone, J. 2012. Should Yahoo's CEO be fired for lying? CNNMoney, May 9. http://money.cnn.com/2012/05/09/technology/yahoo-ceo-resume-reactions/index.htm.

Pinsonneault, A.; Barki, H.; Gallupe, R.B.; and Hoppen, N. 1999. Electronic brainstorming: The illusion of productivity. *Information Systems Research*, 10, 2, 110–133.

Reinhard, M.-A.; Sporer, S.L.; Scharmach, M.; and Marksteiner, T. 2011. Listening, not watching: Situational familiarity and the ability to detect deception. *Journal of Personality and Social Psychology*, 101, 3, 467–484.

Shaw, M. 1981. *Group Dynamics: The Psychology of Small Group Behavior*, 3rd ed. New York: McGraw-Hill.

Stewart, J.B. 2012. In the undoing of a C.E.O., a puzzle. *The New York Times*, May 18. www.nytimes.com/2012/05/19/business/the-undoing-of-scott-thompson-at-yahoo-common-sense.html.

Stiff, J. B., Kim, H.J., and Ramesh, C.N. 1992. Truth biases and aroused suspicion in relational deception. *Communication Research*, 19, 3, 326–345.

Timmerman, C., and Madhavapeddi, S. 2008. Perceptions of organizational media richness: Channel expansion effects for electronic and traditional media across richness dimensions. *IEEE Transactions on Professional Communication*, 51, 1, 18–32.

Treviño, L.K.; Lengel, R.H.; and Daft, R.L. 1987. Media symbolism, media richness, and media choice in organizations. *Communication Research*, 14, 5, 553–574.

Tung, L., and Turban, E. 1998. A proposed research framework for distributed group support systems. *Decision Support Systems*, 23, 175–188.

Vrij, A. 2000. *Detecting Lies and Deceit: The Psychology of Lying and the Implications for Professional Practice*. Chichester, UK: John Wiley & Sons.

Vrij, A., and Baxter, M. 1999. Accuracy and confidence in detecting truth and lies in elaborations and denials: Truth bias, lie bias and individual differences. *Expert Evidence*, 7, 1, 25–36.

Vrij, A.; Fisher, R.; Mann, S.; and Leal, S. 2006. Detecting deception by manipulating cognitive load. *Trends in Cognitive Sciences*, 10, 4, 141–142.

Walther, J.B., and Burgoon, J.K. 1992. Relational communication in computer-mediated interaction. *Human Communication Research*, 19, 50–88.

White, C.H., and Burgoon, J.K. 2001. Adaptation and communicative design: Patterns of interaction in truthful and deceptive conversations. *Human Communication Research*, 27, 1, 9–37.

Zhou, L.; Burgoon, J.K.; Nunamaker, J.F.; and Twitchell, D. 2004. Automating linguistics-based cues for detecting deception text-based asynchronous computer-mediated communication. *Group Decision and Negotiation*, 13, 81–106.

Zhou, L., and Zhang, D. A 2006. Comparison of deception behaviour dyadic and triadic group decision making in synchronous computer-mediated communication. *Small Group Research*, 37, 2, 140–164.

Zuckerman, M.; DePaulo, B.M.; and Rosenthal, R. 1981. Verbal and nonverbal communication of deception. In L. Berkowitz (ed.), *Advances in Experimental Social Psychology*, vol. 14, 1–59. New York: Academic Press.

CHAPTER 8

ENABLING LARGE GROUP COLLABORATION

JOEL H. HELQUIST, JOHN KRUSE, AMIT V. DEOKAR,
AND THOMAS O. MESERVY

Abstract: *This chapter provides an overview of the difficulties and benefits associated with large group collaboration. The chapter presents the challenges of accommodating large groups given the current GSS paradigm. These challenges include the risk of the facilitator not being able to address the volume of information generated by large groups. Different methods for accommodating large groups are discussed. Participant-driven group support systems are presented as a means to accommodate large, distributed groups. This method of large group collaboration entails decomposition of collaborative tasks into discrete modules. These modules enable collaborators to work more autonomously in an iterative, parallel fashion, reducing the demands on the facilitator.*

Keywords: *Group Support Systems, Large Group Collaboration, Participant-Driven Group Support Systems*

Human capital provides competitive advantage in the information age, and all organizations have untapped human potential. This is especially true in larger organizations where silos, specializations, and divisions of labor are the norm. The size of the organization and the subgroups that comprise the organization preclude both the awareness of each member's skills and abilities and the opportunity to pool and leverage these resources. Large group collaboration is difficult, but may open up possibilities for increasing understanding, improving decision making, reaching consensus, and raising commitment to complex decisions with many stakeholders (Rasmussen et al., 2006).

Facilitated meetings and collaborative systems, including group support systems (GSS), have proven beneficial in increasing the efficiency and effectiveness of participants (Fjermestad and Hiltz, 1998). Such meetings and collaborative systems enable organizations to more fully leverage a greater breadth of human capital. It would be expected that such systems might also tap into "the long tail" of potential participants who have been previously untouched because of a combination of technological, process, cultural, and organizational barriers. By altering GSS technologies and practices, we hope to derive value from the marginal contributions of the large number of people who currently do not actively participate.

While collaborative systems have proven beneficial in relatively small group settings, they do not scale effectively to support large groups. In this chapter, we characterize a large group as having over fifty active participants. Although many systems may be able to accommodate large numbers of inactive users or passive "lurkers," the majority of collaborative systems, processes, and work-flows are not able to scale and accommodate these larger numbers of people as active participants.

GSS have been found to effectively support and enhance collaborative group work by providing: (1) a structured process to decompose problems into manageable units of collaborative work; (2) an anonymous environment where ideas can be evaluated based on merit; (3) a parallel processing environment where ideas and information can be entered and shared simultaneously by the participants; (4) a system to collect anonymous feedback, comments, and alternatives; and (5) a mechanism to evaluate, rank, and select from a pool of alternatives (Nunamaker et al., 1991b).

While the above mentioned benefits are also desirable in large group collaboration, organizing and facilitating collaborative meetings with large groups presents numerous challenges stemming from a variety of sources. First, it may not be economically feasible to bring all members of the group together at the same time and place. Second, it may be too disruptive for the organization to pull key personnel together for a traditional meeting. Third, there may not be sufficient computer and network hardware for each participant to be able to individually utilize the GSS. Fourth, political barriers may exist to prevent the use of a facilitator in a group deliberation. Fifth, current GSS designs do not scale well to large groups. Finally, information overload may present a problem as a large group may generate more information than can be synthesized and utilized by the group within limited time and cognitive constraints (Hiltz and Turoff, 1985).

This chapter addresses the benefits, challenges, and possible means of mitigating some of the challenges associated with large group collaboration. The goal of this chapter is to highlight some changes to the current GSS paradigm. These changes are needed in order to enable a more flexible GSS capable of leveraging the intellect, skills, and experiences of large groups.

BENEFITS OF LARGE GROUP COLLABORATION

The Internet fostered a new, more collaborative, environment that is exhibited in many of today's most popular web pages. Web 2.0, as it is called, refers to the proliferation of sites that aim to improve information sharing and collaboration among the users. In this paradigm, the users are typically the primary means of creating, editing, remixing, and validating content. The goal of these websites is to capture input and other information from end users and then leverage that information to benefit the larger community. As Tim O'Reilly stated, the collaborative system "... gets better the more people use it, consuming and remixing data from multiple sources, including individual users, while providing their own data and services in a form that allows remixing by others, creating network effects through an architecture of participation" (O'Reilly, 2005, p. 1). The goal of these systems is to build an intellectual repository that is contributed by groups of users. As the size of the group increases, so does the probability that more complete and valid information will be made available to the group. However, as group size grows, so does the probability that misinformation may be introduced into the system. This probability is mitigated by the number of individuals screening and reviewing the content

Many examples exist today of these collaborative websites. Arguably, one of the largest and most successful of these is Wikipedia, a free, online encyclopedia. What is interesting about Wikipedia is that the content contained within the site is largely generated by a large group of diverse individuals without remuneration. While Wikipedia certainly contains errors and inaccuracies, it is nonetheless a prime example of leveraging the power of a large group of individuals. The success of Wikipedia depends on its ability to attract a large, diverse set of users to contribute and validate information.

Wikipedia is just one of many examples of crowdsourcing, which is defined as taking a task and having it performed by an undefined, generally large group of people. Some corporations have successfully utilized crowdsourcing to gather information from large groups of people. For example, in 2006, Google launched an effort to leverage the human resources of a large group to label or tag a repository of images. Google created a game and incentives for people to label images for use in Internet indexing and search results. The result was a supply of free labor that improved Google's data repository and ultimately the number and quality of their service offerings.

Other websites leverage the resources of their readers to identify interesting content on the Internet and aggregate that information to share new and interesting information with all users of the website. For example, Digg.com uses a process whereby readers submit stories that they deem interesting or worthwhile to read. If enough readers agree with the original submitter, the story is placed on the front page of the website where the story is brought to the attention of all. If not enough readers agree that the story is interesting or worthwhile, the submission is discarded. In this paradigm, a democratic process allows participants to determine which stories and what content should be displayed or made available to website users. This democratic process mitigates the dependence on editorial staff and lessens the chances of management bias, selection, and intervention. Sites like Digg.com empower the end user to share information and aggregate judgment in order to identify quality content on the Internet.

Though these examples demonstrate the power of large group collaboration, interestingly, they also illustrate the difficulties in achieving more complicated, or unpredictable outputs. Wikipedia, for instance, is a very useful tool, but one might argue that it is only made possible because a Wikipedia article, the basic focus of a given group, (1) has a tacitly agreed-upon structure, and (2) requires relatively low levels of collaboration. In other words, most people contributing to a Wikipedia article generally understand the structure and goals of an encyclopedia article and collaborating on writing a given section does not require high levels of communication and coordination between collaborators. The users understand enough to "self-synchronize" their actions. The amount of collaborative interaction demanded from Digg users is even smaller. In essence, users perform a single role—"digging" (nominating/voting) content they find interesting or valuable.

A number of unique examples exist where concerted collaboration is desired in large group settings. For instance, in dealing with complex societal issues (Alabdulkarim and Macaulay, 2007), typical approaches for reaching consensus include surveys/polling; town hall meetings as public forums for discussion; government committees/task forces; lobbying; and social commentary. However, these methods do not harness the potential large number of stakeholders and often arrive at suboptimal and politically biased solutions. Given the large numbers of people affected by these problem domains, technology enabled large group collaboration has the potential of enabling increased citizen participation in the democratic process, resulting in efficient and improved decision making on issues of importance.

These examples illustrate the principle that groups may perform well by aggregating the judgments and abilities of the diverse constituents of a group. Again, the ability to leverage the skills, knowledge, and abilities of the group depends in part on the size and diversity of the group. Achieving quality results within the group context requires certain conditions to be met. Beyond diversity, Surowiecki (2004) posits that diversity, independence, decentralization, and aggregation are requirements for optimal group performance.

- *Diversity of opinion:* Diversity of opinion can throw different perspectives on a problem, bringing to surface certain pros and cons that would have been difficult to analyze by individuals thinking more similarly. Such diversity could even be just an eccentric interpretation of the known facts.
- *Independence:* People's opinions are not determined by the opinions of those around them. The lack of independence leads to phenomena such as groupthink that reduce the efficacy of the group.

- *Decentralization:* People are able to specialize and draw on local knowledge rather than common sources. Context specific information is often important in analyzing the problem and the implications of potential solutions. Decentralization promotes a diversity of opinion that accompanies independence.
- *Aggregation:* Some mechanism exists for turning private judgments into a collective decision. In other words, there must be some mechanism in the group work process whereby each individual can voice his or her opinion and the majority opinion is tabulated.

These four characteristics promote the effective harnessing of group intellect. Failure to comply with the four characteristics increases the risk of the group underperforming or completely failing to achieve the group's objectives. These characteristics enable the group to more effectively leverage the abilities and power of the group. The power lies not in leveraging solely the experts but a variety of talents and intellects. Blinder and Morgan (2000), for example, unexpectedly found that groups are not dominated by high performers. As they said, "In the end, we are left to conclude that neither the average player, nor the median player, nor the best player determine the decisions of the group. The whole, we repeat, does indeed seem to be something different from—and generally better than—the sum of its parts" (p. 46).

James March (1991) expressed this sentiment with regard to diversity, "[The] effect does not come from the superior knowledge of the average new recruit. Recruits are, on average, less knowledgeable than the individuals they replace. The gains come from their diversity" (p. 79). Furthermore, homogeneous groups spend too much time exploiting and not enough time exploring alternatives (March, 1991). By increasing group size and commensurately group composition and diversity, groups may be better equipped to provide a more thorough, critical analysis of the task at hand.

Independence is another critical factor in group decision making. Groupthink is the common term for the lack of criticality that overly cohesive groups may experience. Without sufficient independence, group members may fall into information cascades, a state in which group members ignore their own local information to cue off of the group norms.

Decentralization is tightly linked to independence in that it is required to provide the group members with sufficient local information for each member to act upon. People situated in diverse environments are likely to bring to the table different perspectives on formulating and clarifying the problem at hand, provide varied solutions considering contextual factors, and also provide a test bed to validate the feasibility of various potential solutions proposed by the group.

Finally, aggregation provides the mechanism for pulling the group's judgments together. While other factors can be promoted in a relatively straightforward manner, aggregation is more difficult as it relies upon a marriage of process and technology. In fact, it forms the main thrust for current research in facilitating large group collaboration.

CHALLENGES OF LARGE GROUP COLLABORATION

Collaboration involving large groups presents numerous challenges to participants, facilitators, and collaborative tools (Millen and Fontaine, 2003). One major challenge is that of physical proximity. Working in a traditional, proximal collaborative setting requires geographically distant participants to travel to the GSS location. Large groups are often unable to meet at the same physical location, as economic concerns, scheduling conflicts, and travel considerations may be prohibitive. As a result, organizations may be unwilling to sponsor such collaborative activities.

GSS locations have a limited capacity with regards to the number of workstations and participants that can be accommodated. Physical space and computing resources dictate an upper bound on the number of participants in a proximal session. Typically, GSS installations provide resources for groups of fifty or less. Various workarounds have been identified to expand the capacity limitation. One such example is to enable participants the ability to share workstations, taking turns performing collaborative work (de Vreede, 1997; de Vreede et al., 2000). This type of scenario can be successful if there is adequate space for the participants and a central projector or display to allow those not actively participating to monitor the progress and activity of the group. As long as the GSS location contains adequate physical space, additional participants may be included. However, as the size of the group increases past the number of computing resources, the percentage of active participation declines. Depending on the nature of the collaborative work, inactive participants may provide a lower level of utility in the group work, potentially yielding a lower return on human capital.

Geographically distributed collaborative sessions can mitigate some of the travel costs associated with proximal group work. In this scenario, individuals are able to participate from varying geographical locations. However, distributed collaborative work, like proximal work, must negotiate the schedules of the individuals involved in the collaborative effort. As the group increases in number, so too does the difficulty associated with finding an available time for the group to convene. One common example of this is collaboration involving global management teams. Busy schedules and time zone differences hinder the ability of the group to meet and collaborate.

These physical and logistical constraints often hinder the ability of a large group to meet and work in a proximal, synchronous GSS session. In such scenarios, the collaborative work must be executed in an asynchronous, distributed environment. Tools that support geographic distribution allow collaborative participants to work in separate locations, reducing the amount of required travel. This geographic distribution can be represented on a continuum. On one end, the entire group meets face-to-face to collaborate. On the other end of the spectrum, each group member is distributed from the other participants. Many alternatives are possible along this continuum, including having several small groups that each meet proximally but are distributed from each other. This collaborative environment is manifested in large, international organizations that have distributed offices. Collaborative participants may each congregate in a specific location or office and collaborate with individuals that are located in different offices.

Tools that support asynchronous collaboration enable participants to collaborate at different times throughout the day. As with physical proximity, synchronicity can also be plotted on a continuum. On one end of the spectrum, everyone meets at the same time. On the other end of the spectrum, each person contributes to the collaborative work at different times. Along this continuum, various numbers of individuals may be working together at any given time.

Taken together, synchronicity and proximity present numerous contexts from which groups may collaborate. These contexts enable more flexibility and additional opportunities to leverage human capital via collaborative work. However, physical and logistical requirements are only part of the collaborative environment. The collaborative tools must be able to afford this level of flexibility.

IMPLICATIONS OF EXISTING APPROACHES FOR LARGE GROUP COLLABORATION

Levels of Collaborative Work

Research by Nunamaker et al. (1996) posits that there are three levels of group work: individual, coordination, and group dynamics level. Individual is the lowest level of collaboration, requiring the least amount of collaboration and coordination between the members of the group. Authors compare this collection to a group of sprinters, each exhibiting effort but in an uncoordinated and individual manner.

Group work at the coordinated level is harmonized between individuals, but the work is still done independently. The authors compare this level of group work to a relay team at a track meet. The members work together to an extent for the good of the team. However, each participant is still working on an individual basis.

Group dynamics, or concerted effort, is the highest level of collaborative group work and it requires individual effort and coordination between individuals. At this level, the group works in a concerted effort toward the end goal. This level of collaboration requires much more orchestration of the group members than the other levels, including a highly dynamic workflow where the participants and their input are quite dependent on each other. A good example of this would be a sailing crew. Although each member takes direction, much of the effort is also self-synchronized and is based on observations made by the individual crew members.

Most current GSS tools support collaboration at all three levels in a traditional, face-to-face context. However, when the group moves to an asynchronous, distributed environment, achieving the highest level of collaboration becomes problematic. People in these contexts can function in distributed teams and work together toward a common goal by sharing and pooling information. However, achieving true group dynamics in a distributed, asynchronous setting requires new tools and processes in order to be effective. Similarly, GSS tools are able to accommodate larger groups more easily at the lower two levels of collaboration. Achieving group dynamics with a large group becomes increasingly complex due to the higher level of coordination and interaction.

Group Support Systems Benefits and Group Size

GSS usage has shown both tangible and intangible benefits in both laboratory settings and field studies (Adkins et al., 2003; de Vreede et al., 2003). The tangible benefits include such things as reduced time and resources to complete the requirements as compared with traditional, non-technology supported meetings (Grohowski et al., 1990; Nunamaker et al., 1996; Post, 1992). Other tangible benefits include generation of higher quantities of quality brainstorming ideas (Dennis et al., 1990b; Gallupe et al., 1991; Gallupe et al., 1992). The intangible benefits are, obviously, more difficult to quantify. These benefits include improved levels of group cohesiveness, improved problem definition, and stronger group commitment to the final solution (Nunamaker et al., 1996).

Research has shown that positive effects from GSS usage increase with the size of the group (Fjermestad and Hiltz, 1998; Gallupe et al., 1992; Nunamaker et al., 1991a). Fjermestad and Hiltz (1998) reviewed 200 GSS studies that were published in 230 articles. Their meta-analysis indicated that the benefits of GSS usage became more pronounced as the size of the group increased. The studies reviewed showed that larger groups outperformed smaller groups in a variety of GSS environments. It is important to note, however, that most of the experiments reviewed had group sizes that were small to medium in size; the largest groups reported only included twenty-four members. While some research suggests the benefits may scale linearly (Dennis et al., 1990a), additional research is still needed to understand the marginal increase or decrease of benefits due to group size (Aiken et al., 1994; Nunamaker et al., 1989).

Experimentation and field work with large groups presents numerous challenges for researchers, practitioners, and the GSS tools themselves. As a result, not much research has been conducted that focuses on large groups.

Facilitation

A primary component of traditional GSS collaboration is the facilitator. The facilitator is typically an independent party that is designated as the individual to guide the group through the collaborative work. The facilitator provides expertise on the collaborative workflow by helping to design the various collaborative activities, and the collaborative tools. A major role of the facilitator is to monitor the group and to efficiently shepherd it through the collaborative process (Adkins and Schwarz, 2002; Beise et al., 1999; Schwarz, 2002). The skills, abilities, and experience of the facilitator can vary dramatically. Different techniques have been discussed on how to best train facilitators to effectively manage GSS sessions (Yoong and Galupe, 2001). These differences in facilitator skill sets can significantly impact the productivity and outcome of the group (Anson et al., 1995; Briggs et al., 2001; George et al., 1992; Griffith et al., 1998; Nunamaker et al., 1991b; Valacich et al., 1994).

The level of involvement of the facilitator can vary depending on the needs of the group (Dickson et al., 1993). Likewise, the design of the GSS and the requirements placed on the facilitator are linked (Hayne, 1999). Facilitator responsibilities can be classified according to the level of support provided. Nunamaker et al. (1991b) proposed three different levels of process support: chauffeured, supported, and interactive styles.

The chauffeured style refers to a GSS session where only one person, generally the facilitator, uses the GSS tool. However, collaborative participants can observe the work being done. This context minimizes the hardware required and the level of technical involvement of the users in the collaborative session. This approach is typically used in proximal, synchronous meetings where most of the collaborative work and interaction is conducted verbally.

In the supported style, each participant is located at a GSS workstation and is responsible for interacting with the tool to complete the collaborative work. Communication within the group is now handled both verbally and through the GSS tool. In this context, the facilitator must provide instruction on how to use the collaborative tools and technical support during the collaborative work. The facilitator is also responsible for guiding the verbal discussion and moving the group through the designated workflow.

The third level of process support is the interactive style. Like the supported style, each member of the collaborative group has a GSS workstation and is responsible for interacting directly with the tool. However, communication and other aspects of collaboration are executed primarily through the GSS tool rather than verbal discussion and interaction.

Utilizing the skills and abilities of a large group mandates the use of the interactive style. As the size of the group increases, the verbal channel becomes too narrow to accommodate the group's communications. Similarly, large groups often necessitate the use of an asynchronous, distributed meeting. In this context, verbal exchanges are impractical or unfeasible and many nonverbal aspects are absent, decreasing the quality of the interaction (van Laere et al., 2000). Moreover, as the size of the group grows, and as the collaborative work becomes distributed and asynchronous, the ability of the facilitator to monitor, guide, and execute the collaborative workflow becomes constrained. The size of the group and the content generated by the group increases the cognitive load on the facilitator. Likewise, the facilitator may not have the tools available to effectively monitor and guide a large group through a complex collaborative workflow. As a result, the GSS tools and processes must be modified to accommodate these scenarios.

Different techniques and process changes have been implemented to accommodate large group scenarios. One way to handle the challenges of large groups is to implement additional structure or controls in the collaborative activities. For example, the participants may be required to craft their input and contributions according to some prespecified criteria. The criteria may include the content of the message or the way in which the contribution is consolidated or aggregated within the overall workflow. Klein and Iandoli (2008) present an example of this increased level of imposed structure in a collaborative tool. The authors require the participants to craft contributions following an argumentation method. In this approach, the participants are subjected to an increased level of cognitive load as their inputs and contributions must be specifically crafted and formatted; the level of requirement and commitment is increased for each of the participants. The result is a cleaner set of contributed information from which the participants may work. The authors posit that this approach enables large groups of individuals to collaborate more effectively. It should be noted that this approach may require additional help or guidance for the participants. In this study, several moderators were enlisted to help the participants formulate contributions. This approach may not be feasible without appropriate levels of oversight provided by these moderators.

Dividing the large group into subgroups has also proven to be an effective method for accommodating large groups. Work by de Vreede et al. (2000) examined the possibility of dividing a large group into subgroups. Each of the subgroups then completes one component of portion of the overall collaborative work. The overall workflow is conducted by different subgroups, each completing a specific portion and handing off their results to the next subgroup. The authors refer to this as a "relay" mode due to the analogs with runners on a track team. The performance of these "relay" teams yielded positive results. In certain contexts, subdividing large groups into specific subgroups may prove to be an effective way to accommodate large groups.

Collaboration Engineering

The collaboration engineering approach was proposed with a goal to design repeatable, predictable collaborative processes, such that the facilitator can play the role of a collaboration process designer, while a practitioner with leadership skills can follow the process design with guidelines to elicit the desired collaboration from the group. Underlying this approach is a prescriptive collaborative workflow conducted via GSS tools and methodologies. The workflow generally follows a nonspecific goal attainment process. For example, the collaborative work begins with the problem at hand or the task the group is engaged to complete. The problem is the impetus for the collaborative work. The group then works to create potential solutions or alternatives and refines and promotes shared understanding of these alternatives before selecting the best option. The solution is implemented and the results are monitored appropriately.

The following steps provide a specific illustration of a general goal attainment process (Kolfschoten et al., 2005):

1. Understand the problem
2. Develop alternate solutions
3. Evaluate alternatives
4. Choose an alternative
5. Make a plan
6. Take action
7. Monitor the outcome

This goal attainment process encompasses different collaborative tasks. The collaborative tasks can be categorized according to the six general patterns of collaboration (Briggs et al., 2006; Kolfschoten and de Vreede, 2007):

Figure 8.1   **Divergence and Convergence As It Relates to Collaborative Work**

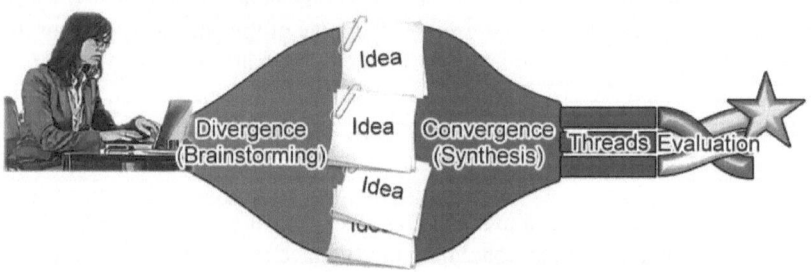

- *Generate:* Moving from having few concepts or ideas to having more concepts
- *Reduce:* Focus on the concepts that are worthy of further attention
- *Clarify:* Enhance understanding of the ideas or alternatives
- *Organize:* Determine the relationships between ideas in the solution space
- *Evaluate:* Develop more understanding of the value of the ideas or alternatives
- *Build consensus:* Increase buy-in from the members of the group

Roughly speaking, these patterns of collaboration incorporate two different broad ideas: divergence and convergence. First, the group generates ideas or alternatives that are presented to the group. The goal of a traditional brainstorming session is to generate as many ideas as possible, without concern for feasibility or plausibility at the time (Couger, 1995; Osborn, 1953). During divergence, the group creates new information (Briggs et al., 2003); the end result is a set of unsorted and uncategorized list of ideas that need to be synthesized by the group. This synthesis process is part of the overall convergence of the group. During convergence, the group moves from having a large quantity of ideas to focusing on a few, highly valuable ideas. Convergence entails many of the patterns of collaboration as the group works to refine, examine, organize, and clarify the information generated during divergence (see Figure 8.1).

The convergence activities represent one of the challenging aspects of GSS work. As stated by Briggs et al. (2003), considerable work has been performed to examine the divergence activities. However, convergence has not been well researched. Convergence represents a challenge due to the increased level of cognitive demand, process orchestration, and the requirement of achieving some level of consensus within the group.

Collaboration with large groups exacerbates the problems associated with convergence. As the size of the group increases, so does the quantity of content generated during divergence activities. This content must subsequently be synthesized and organized; the size hinders the ability of the group to converge. The collaboration engineering approach does not prescribe specific guidelines to deal with challenges in managing large groups. This approach relies primarily upon either a facilitator or the practitioner administering the process to monitor and guide the group. Collaboration engineering is suited well for traditional, face-to-face meetings but may require extensions or modifications to accommodate differing contexts.

ADDRESSING LARGE GROUP COLLABORATION CONSTRAINTS

Collaborative tools, including GSS, must be able to accommodate the requirements of large groups in a variety of contexts within which collaborative work may be executed. First and foremost, the collaborative tools must be able to accommodate distributed collaborative work. This means that the architecture of the collaborative tools must support remote network connectivity. The tools and the collaborative workflow must also be supportive of users that are working from disparate locations. This requirement implies that firewalls and network connections must allow remote traffic to reach the GSS servers. The collaborative tools and the collaborative workflow must also be able to scale to accommodate a sufficiently large group. Scalability thus includes such things as software architecture, server hardware (e.g., processing power and RAM), network bandwidth, and workflow processes that allow large groups to work.

Second, the tools and the processes must be able to accommodate asynchronous work. In these scenarios, participants are able to log in to the system and contribute to the group effort at various times. Tools must be able to structure the data so as to provide a clear and efficient way for participants to contribute. Additionally, tools must enable means whereby the facilitator or group leader can provide clear, explicit instruction to direct the efforts of the group. Moving from a synchronous, proximal group hinders the ability of a leader to provide face-to-face instruction and leadership. The tools must enable additional structure and instruction to compensate for this lack of face-to-face guidance.

Large group collaboration is also susceptible to information overload. As the size of the collaborative group increases, the amount of input generated (e.g., brainstorming ideas) dramatically increases (Chen et al., 1996; Chen et al., 1994). The facilitator or group leader, as well as the participants themselves, must synthesize an enormous quantity of information. The quantity of information increases the risk of information overload and the probability that the generated information will not be used (Dennis, 1996). As a result, the large quantity of information generated increases the time required to complete the collaborative work.

Participant-Driven Group Support Systems (PD-GSS)

Accommodating large groups presents numerous challenges for the facilitator and GSS tools. Some of these difficulties can be addressed by moving to an asynchronous, distributed meeting. Other difficulties can be addressed by appropriately utilizing specific GSS tools. However, the current set of GSS tools and methodologies are still not able to effectively handle a large group. A new framework is needed to leverage the skills and abilities of each group member to further the collaborative work. Participant-driven GSS (PD-GSS) seeks to utilize crowd sourcing to enable collaboration in more contexts and with large groups (Helquist et al., 2006a).

As the name implies, the participants themselves are placed in a position of increased responsibility and thus play an integral part in determining the collaborative process. The group members each provide the work and effort necessary to propel the group through the various collaborative activities. In this fashion, a group is able to self-direct much of the collaborative work, reducing demands on the facilitator. The name PD-GSS may imply that the facilitator is no longer needed or useful. However, PD-GSS still requires an actor (which could be a facilitator, a host, a leader, or a system) to make certain decisions regarding the workflow and activities of the group that are not appropriate for the participants. This decision-making actor can also set parameters for the time and effort spent on different aspects of the process. Additionally, an actor is still needed to configure and initialize the GSS tool.

The PD-GSS workflow is composed of separate, discrete modules that can be executed independently from each other. As system users log in, they are directed to modules or activities where work is needed. The responsibilities placed on each of the participants serve to improve some of the problems associated with large, distributed, asynchronous collaboration (Helquist et al., 2007).

As previously mentioned, one of these problems is information overload. In a synchronous, proximal session, the facilitator may lead the group in reviewing information produced during the divergence phase in an effort to clarify and improve the understanding of ideas. Due to the nature of brainstorming, input is often entered that is not thorough, complete, or refined. Facilitators can engage the group in a discussion to refine the input, clarify ambiguous definitions, and improve the ability of the participants to understand the underlying meaning of a given input. Facilitators can also perform much of this work by themselves, reducing the amount of time the entire group must spend in the work meetings. However, as the group grows in size, the volume of input incurs too much overhead for these traditional approaches. The time required to clean up and organize the input becomes too onerous; a new approach is needed to scale larger groups and increase input.

One means to improve the convergence process and reduce the load on the facilitator is to engage the participants in reviewing the input. Processes can be put in place where each brainstorming idea is peer reviewed. In this review process, the input is critiqued and evaluated to improve readability, thoroughness, and ultimately comprehension. The goal of this peer review process is to improve the quality and coherence of the input, resulting in a set of input that is easier to synthesize (Helquist et al., 2006b).

Organizing the input into categories and defining relationships between inputs represents another challenge. Again, the facilitator engages the group to identify relationships. Similarly, as the quantity of input grows, the time required to group ideas or content into categories becomes too time intensive. This activity must be decomposed and assigned to the participants in the group. Members of the group receive some of the brainstorming ideas and identify relationships or categories between the ideas. This process is repeated iteratively among the participants with the system aggregating the responses and identifying the clusters of related concepts or ideas. In this manner, the group can divide the categorization task up into discrete units of work. The participants each iterate through subsets of the brainstorming ideas, identifying similar content. In the end, the solution space becomes organized and the relationships between inputs are established through aggregation of the individual contributions.

The decomposition of the collaborative process into discrete modules that are worked on iteratively by members of the collaborative group is illustrated in Figure 8.2.

The workflow in PD-GSS is dynamic in the sense that it allows for individuals to be placed in various activities depending on the status of the group. This dynamic workflow enables participants to contribute whenever schedules allow and the system gets value from even small contributions. As a result, this approach accommodates participants that are not able to contribute for the entire duration of the collaborative process. Also, for a facilitator or leader administering the collaborative workflow, the dynamic workflow allows changing the ordering, priority, and switching between different modules based on the status of the collaboration. This is particularly helpful where certain phases of the process may need to be reiterated, such as reviewing clusters of brainstorming ideas to have the desired level of abstraction. The collaborative process can thus be flexible to accommodate dynamic process structure.

ROLES AND RESPONSIBILITIES

The roles and responsibilities of the participants in a collaborative session must be well defined. Of particular importance for this discussion is the delineation of responsibility between the facilitator and the meeting host or leader. Past research has identified many of the roles and responsibilities assumed by the facilitator (Beise et al., 1999; Hayne, 1999). The facilitator has responsibility to direct and structure group processes; the facilitator must manage relationships between the

Figure 8.2   **Distributed, Asynchronous Participant-Driven Group Support System**

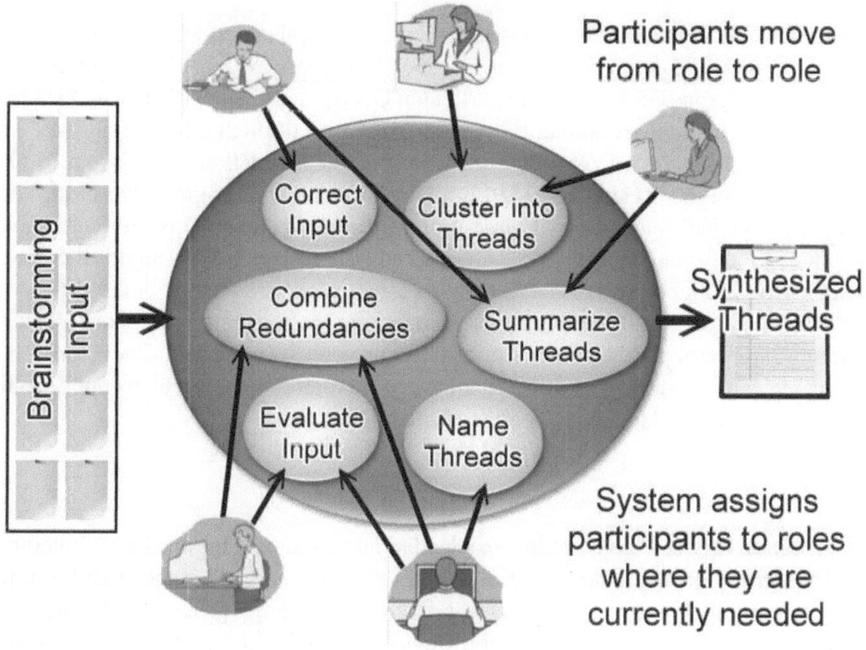

Source: Adapted from Helquist et al., 2008.

participants, the specific task, and the collaborative technology. The facilitator understands group dynamics as well as the exact details of the specific collaborative tools that are employed. To facilitate the collaborative workflow, the facilitator must appropriately structure the individual tasks into a logical process.

The facilitator is typically external to the collaborative group. In this manner, the facilitator is separated from the actual domain or content of the collaborative work. As such, the facilitator does not make content decisions for the group (Hayne, 1999). Instead, the facilitator focuses on the overall process and structure of the collaborative work.

In addition to the facilitator, a meeting leader or host is required. This individual is typically a subject matter expert within the content or domain of the collaborative work. The host is responsible for providing specific expertise and making content decisions. As such, the host works closely with the facilitator to plan, coordinate, and execute the collaborative work. Typically, it is this meeting host that provides the impetus for commencing the collaborative work, assembling the participants and the facilitator. As a result, the host has a vested interest in the proceedings and outcome.

As noted by Briggs et al. (2003), the presence of a facilitator may not be an option. Organizations may not have the resources to hire or employ a dedicated facilitator. In these scenarios, the host may be required to assume some of the facilitator roles and responsibilities. It is these scenarios that PD-GSS seeks to address. These modified GSS tools seek to alleviate some of the burden of the facilitator, enabling more hosts and practitioners to conduct some of the collaborative work. However, as noted previously, facilitation skills are still required of the host as these skills have direct impact on the productivity of a collaborative group.

THEORETICAL PERSPECTIVES

One of the criticisms of GSS research has been the lack of theoretical underpinnings. As illustrated by George (2007), this lack of theoretical foundation may be partially responsible for the conflicting results from the numerous GSS studies. In particular, George states that GSS researchers have typically ignored the vast small group theory that has developed through other disciplines. This rich literature provides numerous lenses through which group interaction and associated GSS involvement may be examined (George, 2007). Looking forward to large group work, the same need for a strong theoretical foundation of large group interaction exists. This literature should also form the foundation for large group collaboration and GSS research. Without this theoretical foundation, large group collaborative research runs the same risk of producing conflicting reports and results. Currently, a gap exists in the research regarding large group interactions. Specific theories regarding large groups, their interactions and dynamics, are needed. One approach to resolve this deficiency is to examine existing small group literature to determine its applicability to large group contexts. Considerable research is needed in this area.

CONCLUSION

Enabling collaboration between large groups may lead to increased benefits and better outcomes. As the size of the group grows, a larger set of skills, expertise, and experience can be drawn upon to complete the collaborative task. However, to this point, large group collaboration has been largely untouched due to the various complexities associated with it. One way to deal with these complexities is to enable the participants to fulfill some of the responsibilities of the traditional facilitator. By empowering participants, overhead and the workload are distributed across a large group. Empowered participants enable the group to self-direct their work and reduce the load on the facilitator. New GSS tools and methodologies are needed to enable this distributed, participant-driven facilitation as existing processes and tools are primarily equipped to handle smaller, proximal groups.

REFERENCES

Adkins, M.; Burgoon, M.; and Nunamaker, J.F. Jr. 2003. Using group support systems for strategic planning with the United States air force. *Decision Support Systems,* 34, 3, 315–337.
Adkins, M., and Schwarz, R. 2002. Embedded facilitation requirements using the skilled facilitator approach: With and across time and space. In *Proceedings of the 35th Annual Hawaii International Conference on System Sciences,* Waikoloa, Hawaii, January 7–10.
Aiken, M.; Krosp, J.; Shirani, A.; and Martin, J. 1994. Electronic brainstorming in small and large groups. *Information and Management,* 27, 141–149.
Alabdulkarim, A.A., and Macaulay, L.A. 2007. Facilitation patterns and citizen engagement. *International Journal of Technology, Policy and Management,* 7, 2, 122–133.
Anson, R.; Bostrom, R.; and Wynne, B. 1995. An experiment assessing group support system and facilitator effects on meeting outcomes. *Management Science,* 41, 2, 189–208.
Beise, C.M.; Niederman, F.; and Beranek, P.M. 1999. Group facilitation in a networked world. *Group Facilitation: A Research and Applications Journal,* 1, 1, 33–44.
Blinder, A.S., and Morgan, J. 2000. Are two heads better than one? An experimental analysis of group vs. individual decision making. NBER Working Paper No. W7909.
Briggs, R.O.; de Vreede, G.J.; and Nunamaker, J.F. Jr. 2003. Collaboration engineering with thinkLets to pursue sustained success with group support systems. *Journal of Management Information Systems,* 19, 4, 31–64.
Briggs, R.O.; de Vreede, G.J.; Nunamaker, J.F. Jr.; and Tobey, D. 2001. ThinkLets: Achieving predictable,

repeatable patterns of group interaction with group support systems (GSS). In *Proceedings of the 34th Annual Hawaii International Conference on System Sciences,* Waikoloa, Hawaii, January 3–6.

Briggs, R.O.; Kolfschoten, G.L.; de Vreede, G.J.; and Dean, D.L. 2006. Defining key concepts for collaboration engineering. In *Proceedings of the 12th Americas Conference on Information Systems (AMCIS 12),* Acapulco, Mexico, August 4–6.

Chen, H.; Houston, A.; Nunamaker, J.F. Jr.; and Yen, J. 1996. Toward intelligent meeting agents. *Computer,* 29, 8, 62–70.

Chen, H.; Hsu, P.; Orwig, R.; Hoopes, L.; and Nunamaker, J.F. Jr. 1994. Automatic concept classification of text from electronic meetings. *Communications of the ACM,* 37, 10, 56–73.

Couger, J.D. 1995. *Creative Problem Solving and Opportunity Finding.* Danvers, MA: Boyd and Fraser.

de Vreede, G.J. 1997. Collaborative business engineering with animated electronic meetings. *Journal of Management Information Systems,* 14, 3, 141–164.

de Vreede, G.J.; Briggs, R.O.; van Duin, R.; and Enserink, B. 2000. Athletics in electronic brainstorming: Asynchronous electronic brainstorming in very large groups. In *Proceedings of the 33rd Annual Hawaii International Conference on System Sciences,* Maui, Hawaii, January 4–7.

de Vreede, G.J.; Vogel, D.; Kolfschoten, G.; and Wien, J. 2003. Fifteen years of GSS in the field: A comparison across time and national boundaries. In *Proceedings of the 36th Annual Hawaii International Conference on System Sciences,* Waikoloa, Hawaii, January 6–9.

Dennis, A.R. 1996. Information exchange and use in group decision making: You can lead a group to information, but you can't make it think. *MIS Quarterly,* 20, 4, 433–457.

Dennis, A.R.; Heminger, A.R.; Nunamaker, J.F. Jr.; and Vogel, D. 1990a. Bringing automated support to large groups: The burr-brown experience. *Information and Management,* 18, 3, 111–121.

Dennis, A.R.; Valacich, J.S.; and Nunamaker, J.F. Jr. 1990b. An experimental investigation of the effects of group size in an electronic meeting environment. *IEEE Transactions on Systems, Man and Cybernetics,* 20, 5, 1049–1057.

Dickson, G.W.; Partridge, J.-E.L.; and Robinson, L.H. 1993. Exploring modes of facilitative support for GDSS technology. *MIS Quarterly,* 17, 2, 173–194.

Fjermestad, J., and Hiltz, S.R. 1998. An assessment of group support systems experiment research: Methodology and results. *Journal of Management Information Systems,* 15, 3, 7–149.

Gallupe, R.B.; Bastianutti, L.M.; and Cooper, W.H. 1991. Unblocking brainstorms. *Journal of Applied Psychology,* 76, 1, 137–142.

Gallupe, R.B.; Dennis, A.R.; Cooper, W.H.; Valacich, J.S.; Bastianutti, L.M.; and Nunamaker, J.F. Jr. 1992. Electronic brainstorming and group size. *Academy of Management Journal,* 35, 2, 350–369.

George, J. 2007. The gap between small group theory and group support system research. In J.M. Haake, S.F. Ochoa, and A. Cechich (eds.), *Groupware: Design, Implementation, and Use* (LCNS 4715), 1–14. Berlin: Springer-Verlag.

George, J.F.; Dennis, A.R.; and Nunamaker, J.F. Jr. 1992. An experimental investigation of facilitation in an EMS decision room. *Group Decision and Negotiation,* 1, 57–70.

Griffith, T.L.; Fuller, M.A.; and Northcraft, G.B. 1998. Facilitator influence in group support systems: Intended and unintended effects. *Information Systems Research,* 9, 1, 20–36.

Grohowski, R.; McGoff, C.; Vogel, D.; Martz, B.; and Nunamaker, J. 1990. Implementing electronic meeting systems at IBM: Lessons learned and success factors. *MIS Quarterly,* 14, 4, 369–383.

Hayne, S.C. 1999. The facilitators perspective on meetings and implications for group support systems design. *The DATA BASE for Advances in Information Systems,* 30, 3–4, 72–90.

Helquist, J.H.; Kruse, J.; and Adkins, M. 2006a. Developing large scale participant-driven group support systems: An approach to facilitating large groups. In Robert O. Briggs and Jayh F. Nunamaker, Jr. (eds.)., *Report of the HICSS-39 Symposium on Case and Field Studies of Collaboration,* 11–15. www.hicss. hawaii.edu/reports/39case_fieldstudies.pdf.

———. 2006b. Group support systems for very large groups: A peer review process to filter brainstorming input. In *Proceedings of the 12th America's Conference on Information Systems,* AMCIS, Acapulco, Mexico, August 4–6.

———. 2008. Participant-driven collaborative convergence. In *Proceedings of the 41st Annual Hawaii International Conference on System Sciences,* Waikoloa, Hawaii, January 7–10.

Helquist, J.H.; Santanen, E.L.; and Kruse, J. 2007. Participant-driven GSS: Quality of brainstorming and allocation of participant resources. In *Proceedings of the 40th Annual Hawaii International Conference on System Sciences,* Waikoloa, Hawaii, January 3–6.

Hiltz, S.R., and Turoff, M. 1985. Structuring computer-mediated communication systems to avoid information overload. *Communications of the ACM,* 28, 7, 680–689.

Klein, M., and Iandoli, L. 2008. Supporting collaborative deliberation using a large-scale argumentation system: The MIT collaboratorium. In *Proceedings of Directions and Implications of Advanced Computing; Conference on Online Deliberation* (DIAC-2008/OD2008), Berkeley, CA, June 26–29.

Kolfschoten, G.L.; Briggs, R.O.; Appelman, J.H.; and de Vreede, G.J. 2005. ThinkLets as building blocks for collaboration processes: A further conceptualization. In *Proceedings of the 38th Annual Hawaii International Conference on System Sciences,* Waikoloa, Hawaii, January 3–6.

Kolfschoten, G., and de Vreede, G.-J. 2007. The collaboration engineering approach for designing collaboration processes. In *Groupware: Design, Implementation, and Use: Proceedings of the Thirteenth International Workshop* (CRIWG'07), 95–110, Bariloche, Argentina, September 16–20.

March, J.G. 1991. Exploration and exploitation in organizational learning. *Organization Science,* 2, 1, 71–87.

Millen, D.R., and Fontaine, M.A. 2003. Multi-team facilitation of very large-scale distributed meetings. Paper presented at the Eighth European Conference on Computer Supported Cooperative Work (ECSCW), Helsinki, Finland, September 14–18.

Nunamaker, J.F. Jr.; Briggs, R.O.; Mittleman, D.D.; Vogel, D.R.; and Balthazard, P.A. 1996. Lessons from a dozen years of group support systems research: A discussion of lab and field. *Journal of Management Information Systems,* 13, 3, 163–207.

Nunamaker, J.F. Jr.; Dennis, A.R.; Valacich, J.S.; and Vogel, D.R. 1991a. Information technology for negotiating groups: Generating options for mutual gain. *Management Science,* 37, 10, 1325–1346.

Nunamaker, J.F. Jr.; Dennis, A.R.; Valacich, J.S.; Vogel, D.R.; and George, J.F. 1991b. Electronic meeting systems to support group work. *Communications of the ACM,* 34, 7, 40–61.

Nunamaker, J.F. Jr.; Vogel, D.R.; and Konsynski, B.R. 1989. Interaction of task and technology to support large groups. *Decision Support Systems,* 5, 2, 139–152.

O'Reilly, T. 2005. What is web 2.0: Design patterns and business models for the next generation of software. O'Reilly Media, September 30. http://oreilly.com/web2/archive/what-is-web-20.html.

Osborn, A.F. 1953. *Applied Imagination: Principles and Procedures of Creative Thinking.* New York: Scribner's.

Post, B.Q. 1992. Building the business case for group support technology. In *Proceedings of the 25th Annual Hawaii International Conference on System Sciences,* Maui, Hawaii, January 4–7.

Rasmussen, S.; Mangalagiu, D.; Ziock, H.; Bollen, J.; and Keating, G. 2006. *Collective Intelligence for Decision Support in Very Large Stakeholder Networks: The Future US Energy System.* SFI Working Paper No. 06-12-048. Santa Fe, NM: Santa Fe Institute.

Schwarz, R. 2002. *The Skilled Facilitator: A Comprehensive Resource for Consultants, Facilitators, Managers, Trainers, and Coaches.* San Francisco, CA: Jossey-Bass.

Surowiecki, J. 2004. *The Wisdom of Crowds: Why the Many Are Smarter Than the Few and How Collective Wisdom Shapes Business, Economies, Societies, and Nations.* New York: Doubleday.

Valacich, J.S.; Dennis, A.R.; and Connolly, T. 1994. Idea generation in computer-based groups: A new ending to an old story. *Organizational Behavior and Human Decision Processes,* 57, 3, 448–467.

van Laere, J.; de Vreede, G.-J.; and Sol, H.G. 2000. Supporting intra-organisational distributed co-ordination at the Amsterdam police force. *Proceedings of the 33rd Hawaii International Conference on System Sciences,* Maui, Hawaii, January 5–8.

Yoong, P., and Galupe, B. 2001. Action learning and groupware technologies: A case study in GSS facilitation research. *Information Technology and People,* 14, 1, 78–90.

CHAPTER 9

MOBILE COMPUTING AND COLLABORATION

JOSEPH S. VALACICH, CLAYTON A. LOONEY, RYAN T. WRIGHT,
AND DAVID W. WILSON

*Abstract: Over the past decade, significant progress in computing and telecommunications tech-
nologies has fostered the emergence of mobile computing. Today, mobile users can leverage various
wireless communications infrastructures to tap into computing resources and services through
portable devices that move with the user. Individuals, groups, and organizations communicate and
collaborate via mobile voice and data services, augmenting services offered in a wired computing
setting. The convergence of portability, power, and untethered connectivity promises to propel
computing into the new millennium by enabling users to collaborate from virtually anywhere at
any time. This chapter starts with a state-of-the-art review of the mobile computing architecture,
which is followed by a discussion emphasizing the value that mobile computing can deliver in
collaborative environments. Possible future research streams are outlined and discussed. Finally,
the chapter looks into trends that will likely have significant impact on the future of anytime/
anyplace computing.*

*Keywords: Collaborative Mobile Computing, Pervasive Computing, Mobile Computing Architec-
ture, Value of Mobile Computing, Challenges Facing Collaboration in Mobile Computing*

Imagine a world in which people can connect and collaborate with any communications infrastructure present in their vicinity. They would be capable of tapping into critical computing resources
and services from anywhere at any time, all accessed and controlled from a portable device carried by the user. Since the introduction of the first digital computer in 1946, significant progress
in devices, infrastructure, and application software has made this vision practical. Implemented
as a tool for making predictions for complex statistical problems such as weather forecasting and
artillery trajectories, the Electronic Numerical Integrator And Computer (ENIAC) was built at a
cost of $400,000, weighed 3 tons, and required a room 30×50 feet to house it. Today, a contempo-
rary smart device costs a fraction of the ENIAC, while possessing substantially more processing
power and storage capacity. Dramatic technological improvements, such as the reduction in form
factors and exponential advances in microcomputing capabilities, have pulled the computer out
of ventilated laboratories and into pockets (Lyytinen and Yoo, 2002). These advancements have
allowed individuals to carry portable, yet powerful computing devices with them as they move.

Paralleling this revolution, wireless communication technologies have rapidly progressed since
Marconi's transmission and reception of radio waves over a century ago. Through the convergence of portability, power, and untethered connectivity, the potent combination of computing
and wireless technologies promises to propel computing into the new millennium by enabling
users to collaborate from virtually anywhere at any time. This combination, referred to as mobile

computing, has created novel ways for businesses to innovate and gain competitive advantage by transforming the manner in which business can be conducted with employees, customers, and business partners. The competitive landscape across various industries continues to undergo significant changes as companies adapt business models to leverage these emerging technologies. For users, anytime/anyplace collaboration to critical computing services offers unprecedented levels of flexibility, convenience, and timeliness. Given mobile computing's potential to facilitate transactions efficiently and heighten productivity, these innovations promise to spawn new ways for users to connect to other users. Mobile computing has quickly grown in its scope and popularity, promising to usher in the next major paradigm in computing. According to a recent survey, three in four IT professionals indicate that their organization leverages some form of mobile computing. Respondents reported that mobile computing ranks among the top three areas of focus for future software development initiatives (IBM Corporation, 2011).

Unfortunately, there are several obstacles to overcome in order for this vision to become a reality. The greatest strength of handheld and mobile computing devices is ironically the root of two other problems: tiny and difficult to read screens, as well as input/output options that are either clumsy or imperfect. In addition to these basic problems, there are also issues concerning network privacy, network coverage, and infrastructure costs. Furthermore, unleashing users from temporal and spatial boundaries allows individuals to behave in novel ways, fundamentally transcending traditional forms of social interaction, collaboration, and organizational structures (Jessup and Robey, 2002). Thus, mobile collaboration currently wrestles with several technical, social, and organizational barriers to realizing its full potential.

This chapter attempts to provide a broad understanding of the operational, technical, and economic issues surrounding collaboration with mobile computing. First, a state-of-the-art review of the mobile computing architecture is presented, followed by a discussion emphasizing the value that mobile computing can deliver today. The obstacles that must be overcome to bring the potential of mobile computing to its fruition are then outlined. Finally, the chapter looks into prevailing ideas of how mobile coloration will evolve, as well as trends that will likely have significant impacts on the future of anytime/anyplace computing.

THE MOBILE COMPUTING ARCHITECTURE

How is mobile computing different from the traditional fixed, wired approach? First generation computers were bulky standalone machines, which were not designed to communicate with other computers. The emergence of wired networking technologies such as local area networks (LANs) and the Internet have greatly enhanced computing capabilities, allowing devices to utilize resources and data residing on other computers connected to the network. Simultaneously, the rapid size reduction in form factors and microprocessor technologies have made it possible to carry portable computing devices with us in our daily routines. By untethering computing devices from the wire, mobile computing has supercharged and extended these capabilities, acting as the catalyst for further innovation (Looney et al., 2004).

Yet, the mobile computing architecture presents a number of unique challenges. To seamlessly connect mobile users to the wide array of services traditionally reserved for wired platforms, the mobile computing architecture requires two additional components—mobile devices and applications specifically designed to run on them, as well as a wireless communication infrastructure, which provides connectivity (see Figure 9.1). This architecture, which now includes technologies such as virtualization and cloud computing (Kovachev et al., 2010), allows mobile devices to leverage the vast resources and data residing on traditional LANs and the Internet.

Figure 9.1   **Mobile Computing Architecture**

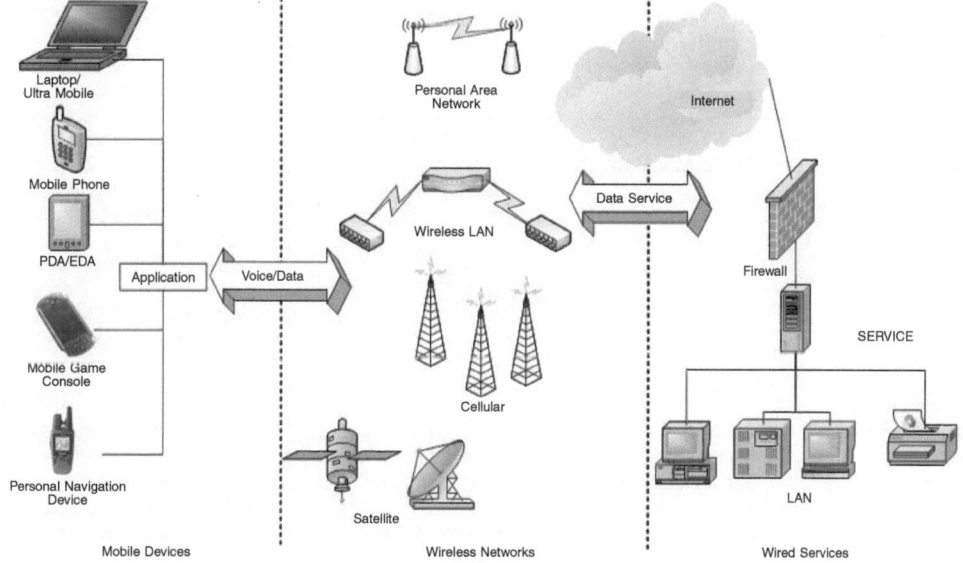

In terms of devices, many types have emerged as popular vehicles for conducting collaborative activities. Contemporary mobile devices range in size and functionality from relatively bulky
laptop computers to handheld smartphones. Likewise, wireless communication networks come in
a variety of forms—cellular networks, wireless LANs, personal area networks, and satellite networks—and present a variety of infrastructure options for mobile devices to connect to traditional
computing services. The following subsections highlight the key characteristics of contemporary
mobile devices and wireless networking technologies used in collaboration (see also Panko, 2008).

Mobile Devices

In 1982 Compaq Computer introduced the first viable mobile computer to the consumer market.
Weighing 28 pounds in a form factor the size of a sewing machine, users could take the Compaq
Portable with them while maintaining performance comparable to a desktop computer of its day.
Today, many types of lightweight, powerful, cost effective, and highly portable devices have
emerged as popular vehicles for conducting mobile computing tasks. Contemporary mobile devices range in size and functionality and include relatively large, full-function laptops and smaller,
ultra-mobile laptops, handheld tablet computers, smartphones, and specialized devices designed
for gaming, reading, and music. Each type of device comes with its inherent strengths and limitations, which are detailed in Table 9.1 and discussed in the following paragraphs.

Many users find traditional and ultra-mobile laptops attractive, as they can be utilized as portable
surrogates to replicate the functionality of fixed desktop computers. Yet, cost and hardware limitations have precluded laptops from fully replacing desktops for users who need full functionality.
Laptops cannot effectively compete with desktop computing due to their limited battery life, which
normally lasts for four to six hours before needing to be recharged. Ultra-portable laptops tend
to achieve more impressive battery life, lasting up to seven hours of normal use (Smith, 2012).

Table 9.1

Mobile Device Comparison

Device type	Examples	Strengths	Limitations
Laptop/ Ultra-portable laptop	IBM Think Pad; Apple MacBook Air	• Approaches the full functionality of fixed desktop models.	• More costly than handhelds • Limited battery life (though ultra-portables are becoming increasingly power efficient) • Can be cumbersome to carry around and use expeditiously and conveniently
Handheld tablet computers	Apple iPad; Samsung Galaxy Tab; Microsoft Surface; Amazon Kindle Fire	• Large, multitouch screen offers seamless interaction with onscreen content • Rich third-party development community	• Limited functionality as compared to a desktop or laptop • Substantial duplicate functionality with most smartphones
Smartphones	Apple iPhone; Nokia Lumia; Samsung Galaxy Nexus	• Very portable • All-in-one functionality (phone, Web services, camera, GPS) • Internet-connected, and all carriers provide data and voice service packages. • Rich third-party development community	• Most phones have small screens • Limited processing power
Mobile gaming, reading, and music devices	PlayStation Vita; Nintendo 3DS; Amazon Kindle; Apple iPod Touch	• Easy portability • Varying Internet capabilities • Excellent battery life (eReaders only) • Rich third-party development community (iPod only)	• Game consoles limited for gaming use and only run proprietary applications • eReaders largely limited to reading functionality • Can only use wireless networks (except some eReaders)

Source: Adapted from Looney et al., 2004.

Although portable, laptops can also be cumbersome to transport and problematic to use expeditiously and conveniently due to their size and complexity. On the other hand, ultra-portable laptops can be transported more easily, but they sacrifice functionality to save space. To effectively use a traditional or ultra-portable laptop, users need to pull them out, power them up, and connect them to a wireless communications provider to access the desired resources and data. In addition, laptops' clamshell form factor requires a table (or lap) to most effectively interact with the device.

A recent, but highly disruptive, addition to the mobile computing market, the handheld tablet computer offers a compromise between the larger screen size and functionality of a laptop computer and the convenient interaction and portability of a smartphone. Ranging in screen size from about 7 inches to just over 10 inches diagonally, this form factor allows simple, touch-based interaction with the content displayed on the screen. Tablet computers generally provide excellent battery performance, and many companies offer models that can connect to cellular data networks for data access on the go. Tablets are more limited in functionality as compared to laptop computers, but an increasingly rich repository of installable applications allows the users to add almost any desired capabilities to the device. Tablet computers have seen explosive growth since the initial introduction of Apple's iPad in 2010. Within one year after the iPad's introduction, over 17 million tablets were sold. In the following year, the number more than tripled to over 60 million units sold, as other companies entered the tablet market to compete with the iPad. Analysts estimate annual sales to grow to more than 320 million by the year 2015 (Milanesi, 2011). Tablet computers (as well as other modern mobile devices) have been so successful that many analysts and media professionals have begun arguing that we have entered the "post-PC" era (Giles, 2011).

Beyond laptops and handheld tablets, the smartphone is quickly becoming the most prominent and versatile mobile device for a majority of users. Early devices, labeled as "smartphones," were essentially Internet-enabled mobile phones, with very limited browsing capabilities and primarily enterprise email and calendaring functionality. Smartphones have evolved considerably in the last decade. When Apple's iPhone and its competitors were introduced in 2007, a large jump in usability and functionality caused an expansion of consumer expectations for smartphone capabilities. As a result, these devices have quickly evolved into sophisticated, versatile tools that meet many different needs of their users. The modern smartphone is equipped with (relatively) powerful information and graphics processing capabilities, large amounts of solid-state memory for music, video, and other data storage, an array of wireless connectivity options (e.g., WiFi, Bluetooth, cellular networks), advanced applications (e.g., GPS capabilities), and high quality cameras, which rival the image quality of many standalone point-and-shoot cameras. Most smartphones provide sufficient battery life for a full day of heavy use, allowing users to depend on their smartphones for a large number of on-the-go tasks. Like the tablet computer, the smartphone reaps the benefits of a large and growing repository of installable applications, many of which allow users to leverage advanced functionalities that meet a wide variety of needs. Smartphones are quickly becoming the standard in the wireless phone industry, accounting for close to 50 percent of mobile phones used in the U.S. market. Trends indicate that adoption will continue to increase (Nielsen, 2012).

Other mobile devices include portable gaming devices such as the PlayStation Vita or Nintendo 3DS, electronic book readers (eReaders) such as Amazon's Kindle or Barnes and Noble's Nook, and Internet-enabled music players such as Apple's iPod Touch or Microsoft's Zune. These devices provide more specific functionality than the devices previously mentioned. The portable gaming devices, for example, possess strong graphics and processing capabilities in order to provide an optimal gaming experience. eReaders provide extremely long battery life and low power screens meant to be easy on the eyes for reading. Portable music players have large amounts of storage and are highly portable. Nearly all of these devices are Internet-enabled, but with varying capabilities. Some eReaders are equipped with cellular data antennas, but most of these devices are limited to WiFi connectivity. With the exception of the iPod Touch, which very closely resembles a smartphone's functionality (without the ability to place calls), the Internet browsing capability on these devices is rather limited and not nearly as useful as that provided on smartphones or tablet computers. In sum, these devices excel at performing their intended function, but they are limited in most other functionality.

Figure 9.2   **Mobile Devices and Their Interrelationships**

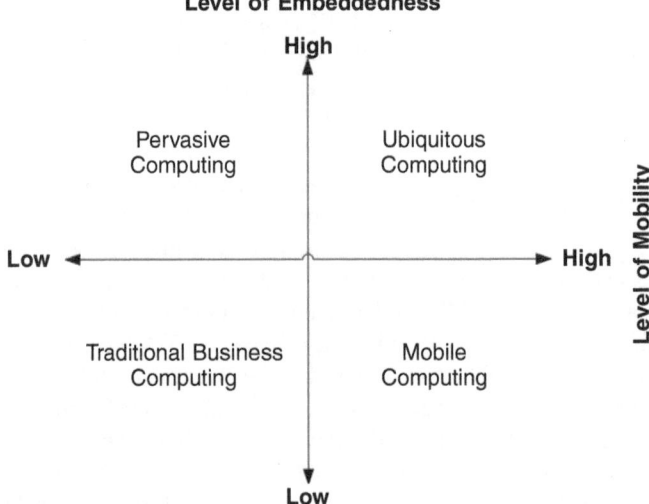

In summary, mobile devices can be broadly categorized into four groups: laptops, tablet computers, smartphones, and specialized devices. These categories and their interrelationships are summarized in Figure 9.2. While laptops provide the most functionality, they are less portable and more cumbersome. Trading some functionality for portability, users can choose to use a tablet computer, which provides an optimal user experience for a wide variety of typical, Internet-connected tasks. Smartphones provide even greater portability and remain very versatile mobile devices, thanks to an increasing tendency toward providing an all-in-one device with many key capabilities of other, previously separate devices. Finally, specialized devices such as portable gaming devices, eReaders, and portable music players perform specific functions very well and generally cost less than the other mobile devices, but users of these devices sacrifice additional functionality such as browsing or email.

Mobile Applications

Application software differs from mobile device to device. In addition, mobile applications diverge significantly from their desktop or laptop counterparts. While the majority of laptops replicate most of the functionality of desktop versions, due to their processing and battery limitations, mobile devices vary in the types of features they can support. Mobile applications can be categorized generally in two different groups. The first, increasingly less common group contains the proprietary, device-specific applications that are developed by a manufacturer for a specific device or group of devices. This type of mobile application is common on specialized mobile devices such as eReaders. A typical eReader has a few applications that provide Internet-based services, such as web browsing capabilities and weather updates. These applications tend to be clumsy and lack sophisticated features, largely because they fall outside of the core functionality of the specialized device.

Over the last several years, a more intriguing class of mobile applications has emerged. These applications parallel the rise in popularity of modern smartphones and tablet computers. Almost exclusively developed by third-party developers, these applications are organized into a searchable, categorized marketplace through which users can browse to see descriptions and screenshots of applications' functionalities. Individual applications can be purchased for a nominal fee (in many cases for free) and downloaded to the device. The applications are then installed and immediately available for use.

Each of the major mobile platforms (i.e., Apple's iOS, Google's Android, and Microsoft's Windows Phone) has one centralized marketplace, maintained by the sponsor of the platform, which houses approved applications. The centralized marketplace model has been immensely popular with both users and developers of third-party applications. In fact, Apple's marketplace (the "App Store") and Google's marketplace ("Google Play") currently house over 550,000 and 425,000 applications, respectively, with Apple claiming over 25 billion application downloads (Apple, 2012).

The application marketplace phenomenon has shaped the mobile computing industry significantly. Previous generation mobile devices, including early smartphones, were limited to a very few proprietary applications, and the available third-party applications required cumbersome installation procedures. In contrast, the modern smartphone and tablet marketplaces make development and distribution of third-party applications efficient and simple. In addition, application programming interfaces (APIs) allow developers to interact with and leverage the advanced capabilities of the smartphone or tablet computer hardware. For example, Apple has built extensive API support into the iOS operating system, giving developers access to a device's GPS, motion-detection, camera, and mapping capabilities. The Android and Windows Phone operating systems provide a similar array of APIs. Developers can easily access these and other APIs when developing third-party applications for mobile devices. The result has been a significant expansion in the capabilities of mobile devices, with the range of functionality in mobile applications limited only by hardware constraints and the developers' creativity.

Wireless Networks

The roots of wireless communications can be traced back more than a century to Guglielmo Marconi's 1894 transmission and reception of radio waves over long distances. Combined with the long-distance voice communications needs of two World Wars and the recognition of radio broadcasting as a commercially viable opportunity, the medium gained acceptance quickly. Today's wireless communications networks are built upon these foundational technologies. Contemporary networks transmit a combination of voice and data, seamlessly connecting mobile devices to terrestrial services. Wireless communications networks can be broadly classified as personal area networks, cellular networks, wireless local area networks, and satellite networks. The characteristics of each type of network differ in terms of capability and function, which are detailed in Table 9.2 and discussed in the following subsections.

Personal Area Networks

First generation mobile devices, such as the "brick" phone, were completely self-contained; these proprietary, analog devices allowed limited or no interaction with other devices (e.g., digital cameras, smartphones). The digital age has eliminated these barriers. The personal area network (PAN) arose from the need to connect all of these digital devices easily, so data can be transferred amongst devices. For example, Bluetooth represents a common PAN standard. This networking protocol enables devices to easily connect or "pair" with another Bluetooth-enabled device. For

Table 9.2

Wireless Network Technologies

Technology	Services/Features	Strengths	Limitations
Wireless Personal Area Networks (WPANs)	Communication among devices	1. Standards-based communication 2. Easy to setup and use	1. Reach is only a few meters 2. Security issues
Wireless LAN (WLAN)	Traditional LAN with wireless connectivity	1. Quick and easy to deploy 2. Relatively high data transfer speeds	1. Limited range
Cellular	Voice and data through mobile devices	1. Fast service in all large metropolitan areas	1. Inconstant bandwidth 2. Some areas lack service 3. Lack of transmission protocol standards
Satellite	Global positioning, voice, and data	1. Global availability 2. Provides advanced services such as Global Positioning Systems 3. Broadband	1. Expensive 2. Technologies still developing

Source: Adapted from Malladi and Agrawal, 2002.

example, a Bluetooth headset, when paired with a mobile device, can then transmit voice and data over very short distances. Currently, Bluetooth is the most ubiquitous of the protocols used in PANs.

The idea behind the PAN involves eliminating wires that connect peripheral devices, such as a camera or a printer. Although PANs have untethered the mobile device from its peripherals, security remains an issue. Improper PAN security allows others to easily gain access to important information via this wireless network. Security in PANs is relatively weak (e.g., a four digit code) compared to other more secure wireless means, such as wireless local area networks and cellular networks (e.g., 128-bit encryption). Another problem involves the limited range that PAN protocols allow. Typically, if two devices are not in the same room, it is unlikely that the devices will be able to connect and communicate. Applications leveraging PANs to engage users in collaboration and communication are now common. For example, users can exchange personal information seamlessly using an application such as LinkedIn's "bump." When two users are ready to exchange contact information they literately "bump" their mobile devices together which then enables the exchange of information via the PAN network.

Cellular Networks

First generation cellular networks were introduced by AT&T and Southwestern Bell, who built a viable radiotelephone service in 1946. Although the system proved feasible, technical barriers and a restricted spectrum on which signals could be transmitted precluded its usefulness. Engineers theorized about the creation of a wireless systems based on small geographic areas called cells with a low-powered transmitter in each. The transmission traffic in each cell would be controlled by a central switch and frequencies reused by different cells to maximize the number of available channels. In 1978 a ten-cell design covering 21,000 square miles in the Chicago area proved that mobile telephony via cellular technologies could work (Young, 1979).

Advancements in cellular technology have extended the capabilities of cellular networks by enabling the transmission of digital signals to support data. Currently, most major population centers, as well as most major roadways, are covered by one or more cellular providers, making it possible for mobile users to utilize cellular networks in many locations. However, carriers have shied away from sparsely populated areas mainly due to economic factors, leaving portions of the landscape disconnected. Furthermore, data transmission services are even more confined, with coverage concentrated in relatively populated areas. Data transfer rates are continually improving, with the most modern wireless infrastructures supporting transfer speeds that rival wired broadband access. Unfortunately, the rapid adoption of smartphones connected to the cellular data networks has caused many problems for carriers. Constantly connected smartphone users tend to consume large amounts of data. Some carriers have resorted to price increases and speed throttling in order to maintain reliable services for their customers (Troianovski and Bensinger, 2012). Mobile computing via cellular networks has also been hampered by the competing transmission protocols (Looney et al., 2004). In the United States, for example, two competing protocols still exist: Global System for Mobile Communications (GSM) and Code Division Multiple Access (CDMA). Fortunately, the most recent infrastructure investments from the major wireless carriers in the United States and elsewhere in the world have converged on a common standard, called Long Term Evolution (LTE). However, LTE tends to be available only in large metropolitan areas. As a result, CDMA and GSM incompatibilities will continue to pose problems for the foreseeable future. Many mobile devices adhere to specific protocols, rendering them useless when migrating to another cellular network that uses a different protocol.

Wireless Local Area Networks

Local area networks (LANs), a traditional wired technology, transmit data among computing devices through wired means such as fiber optic, twisted pair, or coaxial cable. In a typical LAN typology, devices are physically wired to switches, which in turn are wired to other switches and routers. A wireless local area network (WLAN) utilizes these same basic principles, yet transmits data through the air using radio waves (Panko, 2008). Relying on the IEEE 802.11 standard (also called WiFi), WLANs utilize access points, which broadcast radio signals to the surrounding area. Access points can also connect to traditional wired LANs, providing access to services available in traditional wired environments. Many mobile devices are WLAN compatible, meaning that they can be easily configured to connect to a WLAN via access point.

Many university campuses, hospitals, and office buildings have implemented WLANs to allow individuals to move freely about the premises with their computing devices while enjoying similar network connectivity and speeds of a traditional LAN. Most access points transmit several hundred feet and additional access points can be easily and inexpensively installed to extend the wireless network, further increasing the coverage area. In contrast, physically wiring a traditional LAN can be extremely expensive, especially in older buildings that do not have preexisting networking infrastructures. Additionally, a wired infrastructure provides far less flexibility and mobility since the physical wiring defines where computing devices can access the network. Considering their advantages as compared to traditional approaches, WLANs have seen mass adoption in personal and corporate networks.

Although WLANS are increasingly common in many public places including airplanes, airports, and shopping malls, WiFi networks are not currently pervasive. Whereas cellular networks can be accessed from any major population center around the globe, many applications of mobile computing can only be accomplished via WLANs in locations, called "hotspots," where they are installed. Due to its limited communication range of a few hundred feet, WiFi cannot service mobile users once they move too far away from the nearest access point. Thus, WLANs provide a reasonable solution for mobile users within the boundaries of network, yet suffer from the lack of pervasiveness.

Although Bluetooth is the most common PAN, there has been an explosion of WiFi wireless personal area networks that are being used for personal hotspots. These personal hotspots use a cellular (e.g., 3G or 4G) signal to provide local Internet connectivity to different devices via a WiFi data link protocol. The use case for this technology is for users to have wireless connectivity to several devices (e.g., laptop or tablet) via their cellular subscriber. This is a new generation of hybrid (e.g., cellular-local wireless) devices to connect devices to the Internet.

Satellite Networks

Satellite-based communication networks utilize a system of satellites orbiting the Earth, as well as ground stations to transmit radio waves to and from these satellites. One of the most intriguing aspects of satellite networks lies in their ability to transmit voice and data signals from anywhere on the globe. This is accomplished through the deployment of a constellation of low- or medium-orbit satellites connected wirelessly via line-of-sight. By relying on multiple satellites communicating with each other, signals can be transmitted from any point of Earth, uplinked to a satellite, and disseminated through the network to their intended destination.

While contemporary satellite infrastructures are extremely expensive to deploy and the technologies are still in their infancy, broadband satellite networks, which implement vast networks of satellites to enable global coverage, can provide coverage literally everywhere on Earth. Moreover, this communications network can potentially enable on-demand access to broadband Internet access, interactive multimedia, and high-quality voice. With projected uplink transmission speeds estimated up to 1.2 Gbps, satellite technologies will rival terrestrial wireless infrastructures.

Equipped with a satellite transceiver, mobile devices can connect to the satellite infrastructure in remote locations that remain uncovered by cellular providers or WLANs. In addition, these networks enable advanced services such as GPS, which can provide instantaneous positioning information including location, direction, and velocity to mobile devices suitably equipped to connect to these networks (Malladi and Agrawal, 2002).

THE VALUE OF MOBILE COMPUTING TODAY

Advances in traditional wired networking technologies, such as LANs and the Internet, have enabled individuals and organizations to disseminate information globally, interact more closely with other users, provide and receive customized information, streamline transactions, integrate disparate computing systems, and facilitate efficient collaboration (Looney and Chatterjee, 2002). The emergence of mobile computing promises to supercharge and extend these capabilities, acting as the catalyst for further innovation.

Wireless presents an attractive medium for conducting collaboration for two compelling reasons—*ubiquity* and *localization* (Looney et al., 2004). *Ubiquity* refers to the ability to access information from any location at any time. Users are no longer constrained by spatial and temporal boundaries. In contrast, users can complete their computing activities while out of the office or away from home. Ubiquity can be beneficial in cases where timely information is important, such as trading volatile stocks or verifying inventory levels during a sales meeting. Mobile computing is especially well suited for people on the go who need the capability of exchanging data and executing transactions whenever and wherever they are. This flexibility through mobility far outdistances traditional wired approaches in terms of convenience and responsiveness to changing environmental conditions.

Localization provides customized information based on physical location. Most modern smartphones are equipped with GPS functionality, which can be exploited as a means to commercial ends. Information can be delivered that is tailored to specific locales. For instance, firms can leverage localization to provide directions to the nearest branch office and customize directions from the user's current location. Another method of utilizing localization involves the tracking of fleets and employees, such as pinpointing the whereabouts of a lost package or contacting key personnel when situations arise that require their immediate attention.

By unleashing computing from the desktop, the ubiquity and localization that mobile computing offers can be used to transform the manner in which transactions are conducted and organizations function. These potential benefits include (1) enhanced collaboration, (2) transcending time and space constraints, (3) instant access to vital information and individuals, and (4) the ability to process rich streams of timely information (Davis, 2002).

A considerable portion of our daily lives involves communicating, coordinating, and collaborating with others. Mobile computing can facilitate dramatic reductions in time and effort to access key information and improve interactions with others. In essence, individuals are no longer constrained by time and place. With the aid of mobile computing, activities such as transmitting messages, conducting meetings, and exchanging information can be accomplished from anywhere at any time. These capabilities are especially critical for individuals who often conduct business outside of the office or travel frequently. Take, for example, the case of the traveling salesperson. During a sales call, the salesperson may need to verify inventory levels remotely before placing an order. Rather than phoning the home office or returning after the meeting to check inventory from a wired computer, the salesperson can request inventory status via a mobile device and the information can be instantaneously communicated in real time. If an inventory shortfall occurs, the mobile device can be used to access a supplier's system to order additional units and confirm delivery dates. In addition, the customer may need a customized product. The salesperson can use mobile computing to collaborate with designers and production managers by exchanging product specifications and schematics remotely. Thanks to mobile computing, the salesperson's activities can be accomplished more efficiently, streamlining business processes, and improving customer service.

Mobile computing can transcend time and space constraints. Traditionally, organizations have imposed specific work hours and physical locations for employees to perform their duties. As Davis (2002, p. 69) points out, "these constraints may be convenient for office support services, but they may not be optimal for productivity." Many individuals do not optimally work in a sequential fashion during customary working hours. In addition, distractions and interruptions within the organizational environment can reduce productivity. Mobile computing enables many work tasks to be carried out independent of physical locations, while providing the flexibility for workers to engage in these activities under the most productive conditions. These advancements have enabled individuals to effectively work from their homes. Furthermore, this flexibility can be leveraged to conduct business during nonbusiness hours with geographically dispersed people in other time zones.

Another benefit of mobile computing involves instant access to vital information and connection to individuals. In a traditional work environment, tasks may be delayed or postponed while waiting for key personnel to provide input. Although these individuals can likely be contacted via cellular phone, mobile computing allows critical information, such as spreadsheets and reports, to be shared expeditiously. In other words, the information needed for quality decision making can be put into the hands of the decision makers immediately, enabling business activities to be completed in a more timely fashion.

Mobile computing can also be utilized to process rich streams of timely information. Typically, managers receive summarized information contained in standardized reports, which can mask many important details. In a wired environment, if more detailed information were needed, it may take a substantial amount of time for personnel to retrieve and deliver it. Furthermore, this information is backward looking, meaning that it places managers in a reactive rather than proactive position. To detect early warning signals concerning problem areas, traditionally managers engaged in "walk arounds" in an attempt to gauge the organization's operational status (Davis, 2002). Mobile computing can facilitate the input of data and events as they occur, meaning that timely information can be captured instantaneously. These rich streams of detailed information allow managers to monitor activities, detect problems, and evaluate events in real time rather than sifting through less timely aggregated reports or expending time and effort inspecting operations.

THE FUTURE RESEARCH DIRECTIONS IN MOBILE COLLABORATION

Technical Issues

Since the mobile computing architecture requires more components compared to the fixed, wired approach, it inherently generates greater technical complexity. From a technical standpoint, a major hurdle facing mobile collaboration involves synthesizing disparate device, application, and wireless networking platforms. In the conventional wired environment, devices, applications, and networks are relatively mature and standardized. In contrast, common standards in mobile computing are still evolving. One of the major differences, for example, has to do with network protocols. Unlike wired transport mechanisms that rely on common networking standards such as Transmission Control Protocol/Internet Protocol (TCP/IP) and Hypertext Transfer Protocol (HTTP), cellular providers have (until recently) relied on two competing protocols as described above. Wireless LANs support the various 802.11 specifications and cellular data networks have still another. Each of these varies in speed, reliability, and coverage, which also pose significant barriers for mobile computing to reach its full potential. Thus, networking technologies will need to continue to evolve and stabilize so that mobile users can connect and stay connected, with adequate levels of bandwidth, anywhere on the globe for mobile computing to reach its full potential.

Additionally, as previously mentioned, mobile devices come in disparate forms, exacerbating heterogeneity. Each type has inherent strengths and liabilities in performing transactions, restricting the specific features and functions they can support. As mentioned, three separate and competing mobile platforms have emerged, each vying for third-party developer support and user adoption. While fostering healthy competition, developing applications that are compatible with the majority of mobile devices tends to be more difficult than the Windows-dominated desktop environment.

Although battery life has been improved, it continues to be a major technical hurdle. Many device manufacturers continue to enlarge the screen size and processing capabilities of mobile computing devices. However, advanced functionality can compromise battery life. For some devices, the battery capacity is not sufficient for even one day of normal use (Pierce, 2011). Manufacturers must continually balance a device's capabilities and features with practical usage scenarios, which can hamper expansion of device functionality in some cases.

One promising technology, called "electronic paper," that should help with battery life issues, is flexible and requires a fraction of the power needed to operate when compared to existing liquid crystal technologies. Since power consumption is largely driven by the display, e-paper-based designs require a fraction of the power. Additionally, with e-paper devices, users may be able to "fold out" or expand their display as needed. Several mobile device manufacturers have begun using the e-paper technology, with the widest application of the technology in popular eReaders such as the Amazon Kindle and the Barnes and Noble Nook. Though e-paper is praised for its low power consumption and flexibility, manufacturers continue to improve the technology to contend with several weaknesses, which include low refresh rates and residual coloring of areas of the display after an image changes. These drawbacks have prevented wider adoption of the technology in smartphones and other more advanced devices.

From a service design perspective, accommodating the differing capabilities of mobile devices involves increasing complex design, coding, and testing efforts. Functionality available on one device may be unavailable on another. Thus, services must be intelligent enough to identify the type of device to which they are transmitting. Furthermore, these applications need to deal with various bandwidth environments effectively, compensating for restricted throughput as needed. The evolving network, application, and device standards in the mobile environment make the transition from conventional wired approaches a challenging proposition.

Mobile computing environments introduce many new security threats. Given the hardware limitations of most mobile devices, code must be compact in order for it to be efficiently executed. Some operating systems fail to include robust security measures, such as certification, to protect devices from malicious code released into wireless networks. This situation can become particularly problematic with transportable code such as scripting languages, which can execute commands on mobile devices since the operating system cannot verify the legitimacy of the sender (Ghosh and Swaminatha, 2001).

Another source of security threats stems from the nature of certain mobile platforms. As mentioned previously, there are three competing mobile platforms. Apple's platform is relatively controlled, with limited hardware manufacturers (only Apple) and an Apple-controlled approval process for third-party applications. In contrast, Google's Android platform is more open, providing the operating system as an open source software solution to device manufacturers. Furthermore, Google's application marketplace, called Google Play, employs no approval process, allowing any application, malicious or not, to be promoted and sold. Such openness, particularly in the third-party software marketplace, has facilitated the exponential rise in mobile security threats within the platform. In the last half of 2011, for example, the number of malicious Android applications available in the Android marketplace increased by over 400 percent (Juniper Networks, 2011a).

Although size constitutes one of the greatest advantages of mobile devices, the small form factor lends itself to the risks of loss and theft. Unlike wired computers, mobile devices are not usually locked inside secured buildings and offices. In addition, mobile users may store personal or sensitive information about themselves, other individuals, or organizations on these devices. If stolen, the data can fall into the wrong hands, presenting the threat of identity theft and access to proprietary information. Since current technologies provide little protection via user-to-device authentication, corporate resources such as electronic mail systems and data repositories may be compromised (Ghosh and Swaminatha, 2001).

Behavioral and Social Issues

By enabling users to conduct computing tasks any time in any place, mobile computing enables novel forms of behavior. This empowerment has introduced some positive, as well as unanticipated negative, behavioral, and social side effects, such as decision-making degradation, evolving norms, and an inability to support rich communication.

The ability to process rich streams of real-time data can affect human decision making (Davis, 2002). By potentially inundating users with vast quantities of data, scarce attentional resources can be diverted to irrelevant pieces of information. It is well understood that humans tend to make errors in judgment based on recent events and extrapolating trends from small sets of data (Tversky and Kahneman, 1974). As information bombards mobile users, they will likely become more prone to decision-making fallacies. Judgment errors may be more pronounced in highly dynamic environments. For instance, individuals who utilize mobile computing as a means to trade stocks online can receive a wide array of real-time data such as stock quotes, breaking news, and alerts. Much of these data may not be relevant to the investment decision-making task and, thus, induce suboptimal decisions. As a user of mobile brokerage service admitted, "the worst trades I've ever done are the trades I've done on this [two-way] pager. This pager has brought out the least-disciplined elements of my trading personality" (Schmerken, 2000, p. 18).

Also, technology-based interruptions can degrade knowledge worker-decision performance when addressing complex tasks (Speier et al., 1999). Accordingly, as companies evaluate the widespread deployment of mobile computing devices, they may overlook the potential performance losses caused by employees receiving constant, interruptive updates via their mobile devices. More recently, we have seen how personal life is negatively impacted by mobile technologies, which cause personal work/life conflicts when an individual's coworkers are able to initiate interruptions in that individual's personal life (Chen and Karahann, 2011).

When novel behaviors are enabled, such as mobile collaboration, no social norms may be available to guide human behavior. For example, Jessup and Robey (2002) offer the story of the "Pied Piper of Concourse C" (pp. 88–89):

> Given the fixed positions of computers, furniture, and personnel at check-in counters in most airports, people have developed expectations and closely followed norms of checking in to get their boarding passes. They get in the back of the line and slowly make their way up to the person at the counter with the computer. In a European airport that had recently converted to wireless computers, airline personnel roamed freely throughout the concourse, checking in passengers with mobile computing devices. This posed a problem for passengers who did not understand how to behave. In an attempt to get checked in, people lined up behind the roving employee. The scene quickly took on the appearance of the Pied Piper as the employee with wireless computer walked around the concourse with a growing, snaking line of travelers desperately trying to follow the only norm they know for that context, forming a line behind her.

Additionally, the mobile computing medium may be unable to support sophisticated forms of social interaction. When individuals collaborate, they may need to leverage other technologies to successfully complete tasks. For instance, a virtual team may utilize mobile computing as a means to collaborate on the design of a new product. However, a complex design schematic may not be readily decipherable in electronic form alone. Technologies such as telephone, videoconferencing, or face-to-face meetings may be necessary to supplement these exchanges. In addition, it is not presently clear that virtual teams outperform traditional teams (Purvanova and Bono, 2009). Nor is it fully understood how these interactions can be structured to facilitate quality outcomes. Regardless, it is likely that mobile computing technologies will augment, but not replace entirely, traditional means of collaboration.

Further, with third-party application development capabilities on mobile platforms (e.g., iOS, Android, Windows 8), a proliferation of mobile educational software has occurred. Mobile learning represents a new area of interest for researchers and practitioners (Wang et al., 2009). Due to the different contexts in which education is delivered, different models and approaches to implementing such learning platforms need to introduced (Wang and Wang, 2008). The mobile environment presents several unique challenges, such as the social acceptability of mobile use in the classroom (Nickerson et al., 2008), privacy issues (Raento and Oulasvirta, 2008), and other possible contributions to knowledge transfer in mobility (Choi et al., 2007), all of which are strong candidates for future research.

Organizational Issues

Since mobile computing transcends spatial and temporal boundaries, conventional organization structures can be transformed. Virtual organizations, which have no physical presence, have emerged as a new breed of corporate structure (Staples et al., 1999). Coordinating, communicating, and collaborating via mobile computing enables firms to conduct business around the clock and across dispersed geographic regions. For instance, a virtual organization may coordinate the activities of a production facility in China, communicate through a customer service center in the United States, and collaborate with designers located in Spain, Australia, and Brazil. All of these activities can be conducted on a 24/7 basis. However, virtual organizations may be difficult for governmental agencies to monitor, posing the threat of unethical or even illegal business practices. With a virtual organization, corporate assets can be more easily hidden or moved because of their ephemeral nature (Jessup and Robey, 2002).

The ability to collaborate by exchanging voice and data with other organizational members and business partners at any time and from anywhere enables employees to work equally well from home, at the office, or while they are on the move. As such, mobility can blur traditional boundaries between work and play (Jessup and Robey, 2002). Traditionally, organizations specified the location and time where work would take place. With mobile computing, the conventional forty-hour, five-day workweek and physical office locations can be transcended by allowing employees to conduct their duties at any time and from anywhere. Although many positive effects can emerge, managers must be aware of the potential pitfalls. Work can become "all the time, everywhere" (Jessup and Robey, 2002, p. 90). Undesirable stress on individuals may surface (Ayyagari et al., 2011; Ragu-Nathan et al., 2008). Since people can be contacted remotely at any time via mobile computing, immediate, 24/7 responses may become the expected norm. Human beings require rest, relaxation, face-to-face social interaction, and a well-rounded personal life to maintain high levels of performance (Davis, 2002). Mobile computing can potentially engulf employees in work activities, causing them to ignore personal aspects that foster healthy individuals. On the other hand, employees operating outside the corporate boundaries can be influenced to a greater extent by nonwork distractions. Thus, work tasks may be "put on hold" in order to attend to peripheral matters. To promote long-term employee productivity, organizations need to establish clear boundaries that assist mobile employees in developing self-motivation and discipline.

Organizations may also experience other side effects from mobile computing including increased coordination and communications cost, centralization, and reductions in organizational development

(Davis, 2002). For example, because of the ease with which people can communicate and share information, increased "unnecessary" communication is likely to occur, just as email and instant messaging services on wired networks have led to widespread non-work-related communication in many organizations (Markus, 1994). The seemingly endless opportunities to multitask can disrupt normal business routines. Many people have expressed concerns about mobile users who display improper etiquette, devote their attention to their mobile device rather than the business at hand, and use devices for inappropriate purposes. For example, during a meeting an employee might check email on a mobile device rather than pay attention to the proceedings. Consequently, several organizations ban the use of mobile devices in public places, meetings, and social events (Naguchi, 2004).

Increased connectivity may also act to extend the span of control for a manager beyond a point of efficiency or effectiveness for the organization (see Huber, 1990). For example, managers will be able to track activities more easily, which may result in moving the locus of control higher in the organization. Many decisions could be decided at higher levels rather than being delegated to personnel performing the transactions. In other words, the "availability of information may provide the illusion of control: higher-level managers may misinterpret what is going on and make serious mistakes because of lack of local knowledge" (Davis, 2002, p. 71). Another unforeseen consequence involves the elimination of important personnel development and training opportunities for lower-level managers. In short, if supervisors make more decisions, subordinates will lack decision-making authority. Taken together, without careful organizational deployment, mobile computing could result in numerous negative organizational outcomes.

THE FUTURE OF MOBILE COLLABORATION

Due to the myriad of challenges facing the viability of mobile computing, certainly there are a number of breakthroughs to be made. Nonetheless, there is little doubt that the promise of any time/anywhere collaboration will be brought to fruition, given the pace at which mobile technologies are being developed and improved. This section looks to the future and investigates the forces that will likely impact mobile computing technologies.

Mobile Content Delivery

Wireless LANs are likely to continue to grow in popularity, further increasing wireless coverage areas in public places. For example, aircraft manufacturing companies such as Boeing and Airbus are delivering broadband 802.11 wireless networks into existing and future airplanes (Valacich and Schneider, 2010). Mobile devices configured with wireless networking capabilities can readily utilize this service. In addition, power outlets will be supplied to seats, mitigating issues concerning battery life. These advances will allow individuals to utilize these services for extended periods, such as during transcontinental and international flights.

Satellite technologies have yet to be fully deployed and will be expensive to utilize initially. Many satellite-based platforms focus on global positioning rather than voice or data communication (Maral and Bousquet, 2009). However, examining the historical record of new technologies, service costs will likely diminish. The modern implementations of broadband satellite services offer download speeds of up to 1.2 gigabytes per second (Murph, 2008). As service costs drop, satellite service might be viable and economical for mass consumption. Given its ability to provide connectivity on a global basis, satellite technology represents a powerful alternative for mobile users. As cellular, WLAN, and satellite providers continue to build out their infrastructure, mobile computing can only gain in popularity and usefulness. With global, cost effective connectivity, the wireless network can become transparent, as users could tap into whatever service is available at their location.

Standards in Mobile Computing

On the application front, dominant designs will be those that can leverage the most popular configurations of devices and infrastructure. Similar to wireless networks, application architectures are being shaped by the forces of standardization. At present, applications support specific platforms and devices, rendering them useless in the context of the broadest global marketplace. Best-of-breed solutions will allow various devices to communicate in both voice and data modes over disparate networks. Standardized XML-based markup languages such as Synchronization Markup Language (SyncML) and eXtensible Telephony Markup Language (XTML) have emerged to provide a comprehensive, flexible approach for delivering next-generation mobile services. SyncML and XTML offer the ability to create applications that seamlessly connect diverse devices and networks. This standardization and evolution in the application development platforms will speed development time and help to extend the useful life of many devices. Not only can these languages support a full range of current configurations, but they can also be scaled to enable new technologies as they emerge.

The next generation of collaboration software now focuses on mobile devices. For example, Microsoft's Office Communicator offers free calling from mobile devices via voice-over-Internet protocol (VoIP) technologies, which leverage the underlying Internet infrastructure to transmit phone calls. Any office user can make free calls from a web-enabled phone running on the Windows operating system. Several consumer-focused VoIP services, such as Skype (purchased by Microsoft in 2011) or Google Voice, provide popular mobile VoIP applications on all of the major mobile platforms. These mobile applications support standard calling functionality using only the phone's data connection, reducing the use of expensive minutes provided by the wireless carrier. VoIP technology clearly threatens the traditional revenue streams of mobile service providers. A switchover to free mobile VoIP calling means that mobile devices become instantaneously global, as users are no longer constrained by specific types of networks or service providers (Glover, 2006).

Devices are also converging. For example, modern smartphones such as the iPhone and the Samsung Galaxy Nexus, offer phone capabilities, video calling, mobile gaming, music and video playback, web browsing, and so on. For the foreseeable future, it is likely that both special purpose devices (e.g., mobile gaming devices) and all-in-one devices will continue to coexist in the marketplace because there is a clear set of size, cost, and functionality tradeoffs to consider. Nevertheless, as these technologies become increasingly powerful and standardized, mobile computing solutions can be designed and deployed more effectively since fewer platforms will need to be understood and supported.

Beyond these issues, socio-economic forces may preclude mobile computing diffusion. It may be unreasonable to expect high levels of adoption given the nascent nature of mobile technologies, especially considering coverage, cost, and usability. Yet, these issues do not eliminate the fact that mobile computing currently appeals to a specific market segment. Current adopters are those whose lifestyles require uninterrupted access to retrieve real-time information and exchange data from any locale at any time. In contrast, users working in fixed locations or those who do not need to continually exchange data will likely opt for conventional, wired approaches to computing. Those who perceive mobile computing as a method for realizing their computing goals will likely be adopters.

Figure 9.3   **Embeddedness and Mobility Matrix**

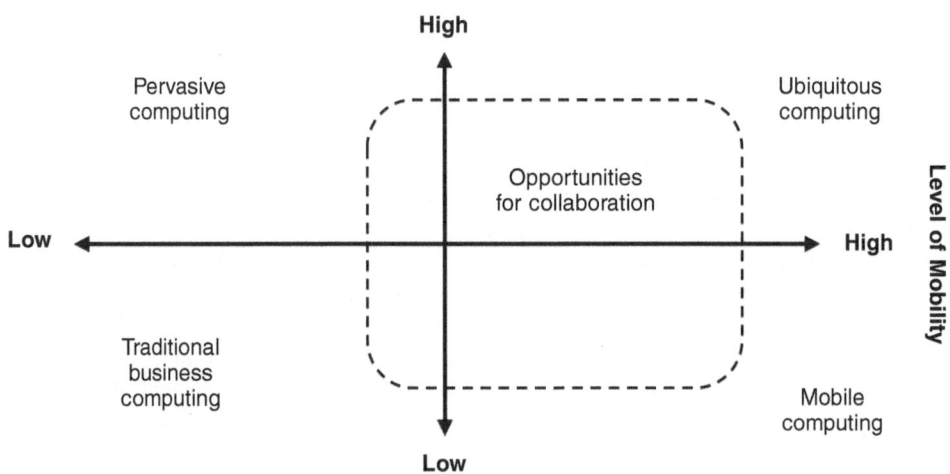

Source: Adapted from Lyytinen and Yoo, 2002.

Pervasive/Ubiquitous Computing

In the context of mobile collaboration in general, clearly there is a trend toward ubiquitous computing. As depicted in Figure 9.3, ubiquitous computing environments are the culmination of the advances from both mobile computing—the ability to move computing services with us—and pervasive computing—the ability to obtain information from the environment and dynamically configure services such that "any computing device, while moving with us, can build incrementally dynamic models of its various environments and configure its services accordingly" (Lyytinen and Yoo, 2002, p. 64). Although there are opportunities to increase a user's ability to collaborate using each of these means of communication, the opportunity to extend the ability to collaborate remains largely untapped in ubiquitous and mobile computing.

Pervasive computing is embedded within the environment and therefore does not have the portability as ubiquitous. For example, teleconference installation requires individuals to utilize stationary systems to collaborate. Over the past several years many organizations have moved away from expensive persuasive means of collaboration (e.g., Polycom) to nimble ubiquitous systems that allow users to connect with any device from anywhere (e.g., Cisco's WebEx). On the other hand, persuasive computing is expanding in some areas. For example, vending machines have the ability to sense the presence of humans in their surroundings, allowing the machine to conserve energy by "sleeping" and then "waking up" when a potential customer walks by. These devices can also be used in a variety of capacities including the detection of heat, light, motion, and various other pieces of environmental data that can be leveraged to trigger a broad range of actions. More elaborate technologies could build models of contextual environments dynamically. Applications that can make devices intelligent by allowing them to learn and adjust to their changing surroundings are complex and yet to prove fully operational (Lyytinen and Yoo, 2002).

Mobile devices are currently limited in that they cannot adjust to contextual factors. Mobile devices cannot sense environmental information like pervasive varieties, meaning that they are unable to compensate for the users' context. At present, users must manually control devices to compensate for environmental factors. The promise of combining the ability to carry computing devices with us as well as intelligent devices that can make contextual adjustments ushers in a new wave of functionality. Ubiquitous computing will further challenge developers, as devices will need to be aware of user factors such as state of mind, body temperature, and the like.

Independent Mobile Application Development

As stated previously, the development of mobile collaboration applications have undergone a transformation, with several platforms opening the door for independent, third-party application development. Mobile application marketplaces have allowed independent software to be sold and installed on millions of mobile devices. This new paradigm of application dissemination exposes users to applications, such as new collaboration tool, or the ability to expose traditional collaborative enterprise tools to mobile devices. This open architecture will likely propel mobile e-commerce, improve location-based software, and foster the mobile social networking phenomenon.

Mobile Social Networking

Some of the more interesting mobile applications relate to social networking. Social networking, which is used more and more for collaboration (e.g., Salesforce.com's Chatter), involves individuals, with similar interests or commonalities, using technology to interact virtually (Hampton and Gupta, 2008). Online social networks, such as Yammer, Facebook, and Twitter, provide extensive interaction capabilities via their mobile applications and APIs that enable third-party application development. Such a platform promotes explosive growth in mobile social networking activity. Users are constantly connected to their social networks anywhere and at any time, enabling them to easily update their friends with text, pictures, and video. Mobile social media users surpassed 650 million in 2011, and are expected to rise to 1.3 billion by the year 2016 (Juniper Networks, 2011b).

Location-Based Services

In 2001 the first global positioning systems (GPS) equipped mobile device was launched in Japan. Today, nearly all mobile devices come with GPS features. There are three components in the location-based system: (1) the mobile device, (2) GPS, and (3) the ability to access data services. By combining all three of these components, unique, location-based applications can be developed and utilized, allowing location-based services to flourish. Location-based software offers the ability to find someone or something (locating), to search for events or objects (searching), to ask directions (navigate), to ask questions about object locations (identification), and to look for nearby locations (checking) (Reichebacher, 2003). Some location-based services that have surfaced include weather, local dating, and recommendations (e.g., hotels, restaurants). As an example, one popular location-based service, called Yelp, provides user-generated reviews of services ranging from restaurants to auto mechanics to beauty spas. Yelp provides mobile applications for all of the major platforms. These applications leverage the GPS functionality of a device to allow users to quickly find reviews of local businesses. We are now just seeing the beginning of the ability of location-based software.

CONCLUSION

Over the past decade, significant progress in computing and telecommunications technologies has fostered the emergence of mobile collaboration. Today, mobile users can leverage various wireless communications infrastructures to tap into computing resources and services through portable devices that allow users the ability to collaborate in many different ways. Individuals, groups, and organizations collaborate via mobile voice and data services, while enjoying all the services offered in a wired computing setting. The convergence of portability, power, and untethered connectivity promises to propel collaboration into the new millennium by enabling users to perform computing tasks from virtually anywhere at any time, offering unprecedented levels of flexibility, convenience, and timeliness. Given mobile computing's potential to facilitate transactions efficiently and heighten productivity, these innovations promise to spawn new ways for users to conduct their daily activities.

However, the current state of mobile computing has been hindered by several obstacles, meaning that potential adopters should carefully weigh their options before selecting the device and networking configurations that best fit their mobile computing needs. Device heterogeneity, network security, coverage, and infrastructure issues must be addressed to enhance user ability to collaborate effectively. As technologies become increasingly standardized, mobile computing architectures will heighten efficiency and effectiveness.

Relatively little is understood concerning how best to deploy these technologies in social contexts especially in organizations. Mobile computing transcends traditional, temporal, and spatial boundaries, allowing individuals to behave in novel ways. Mobile users need to develop self-discipline and motivation to remain productive and organizations must learn how to effectively manage mobile users and data. Firms must develop the capabilities to recognize, assimilate, and fully leverage technological opportunities, while recognizing the potential for unanticipated consequences. Organizations will learn valuable lessons from the current rapid expansion into the mobile arena. No one is immune to the challenges facing mobile technologies. Mobile collaboration forces organizations to rethink the manner in which these technologies should be optimally distributed and supported to meet mobile users' needs. For instance, firms need to understand who these individuals are, what types of wireless devices they need to use, as well as how, when, and where users will likely utilize mobile wireless technologies in their business activities. By selecting the most appropriate options and configurations, firms can maximize productivity and more successfully integrate mobile collaboration into their existing operations. Firms that can cope with the rapidly evolving mobile environment will likely be more successful in the long run.

Over the next several years, technological advances will enable ubiquitous computing by leveraging pervasive and mobile computing technologies. Ubiquitous computing will evolve from concepts and designs to functional systems. As this evolution occurs, individuals, groups, and organizations can either wait on the sidelines until fully functional systems become available to users, or they can immediately inject themselves into the foray to help shape its future.

REFERENCES

Apple. 2012. Apple's App Store downloads top 25 billion. Press release, March 5. www.apple.com/pr/library/2012/03/05Apples-App-Store-Downloads-Top-25-Billion.html (accessed May 13, 2012).

Ayyagari, R.; Grover, V.; and Purvis, R. 2011. Technostress: Technological antecedents and implications. *MIS Quarterly,* 35, 4, 831–858.

Chen, A.J., and Karahann, E. 2011. Personal life interrupted: Understanding the effects of technology-mediated interruptions from work to personal life. In *ICIS 2011 Proceedings*, AIS eLibrary. http://aisel.aisnet.org/icis2011/proceedings/hci/10/.

Choi, H.; Im, K.S.; Lee, M.; and Kim, J. 2007. Contribution to quality of life: A new outcome variable for mobile data service. *Journal of the Association for Information Systems*, 8, 12, 598–618.

Davis, G.B. 2002. Anytime/anyplace computing and the future of knowledge work. *Communications of the ACM*, 45, 12, 67–73.

Ghosh, A.K., and Swaminatha, T.M. 2001. Software security and privacy risks in mobile e-commerce. *Communications of the ACM*, 44, 2, 51–57.

Giles, M. 2011. Beyond the PC. *The Economist*, October 8. www.economist.com/node/21531109 (accessed May 8, 2012).

Glover, T. 2006. Microsoft free internet voice service challenges Vodafone. *SAP Mobile Secure*, February 22. www.mobilesecurityzone.com/news/2006/02/22/1397744.htm (accessed June 18, 2013).

Hampton, K.N., and Gupta, N. 2008. Community and social interaction in the wireless city: Wi-fi use in public and semi-public spaces. *New Media & Society*, 10, 6, 831–850.

Huber, G.P. 1990. A theory of the effects of advanced information technologies on organizational design, intelligence, and decision making. *Academy of Management Review*, 15, 1, 47–71.

IBM Corporation. 2011. IBM Tech Trends Report. www.ibm.com/developerworks/mydeveloperworks/blogs/techtrends (accessed May 8, 2012).

Jessup, L.M., and Robey, D. 2002. The relevance of social issues in ubiquitous computing environments. *Communications of the ACM*, 45, 12, 88–91.

Juniper Networks. 2011a. *Malicious Mobile Threats Report 2010/2011*. Hampshire, UK: Juniper Research. www.juniper.net/us/en/local/pdf/whitepapers/2000415-en.pdf (accessed May 8, 2012).

———. 2011b. *The Mobile Social Media Briefing*. Juniper Research, January 11. www.juniperresearch.com/reports.php?id=345 (accessed May 8, 2012).

Kovachev, D.; Renzel, D.; Klamma, R.; and Cao, Y. 2010. Mobile community cloud computing: Emerges and evolves. In *Eleventh International Conference on Mobile Data Management (MDM)*, 393–395. Kansas City, MO: IEEE.

Looney, C.A., and Chatterjee, D. 2002. Web-enabled transformation of the brokerage industry. *Communications of the ACM*, 45, 8, 75–81.

Looney, C.A.; Jessup, L.M.; and Valacich, J.S. 2004. Emerging business models for mobile brokerage services. *Communications of the ACM*, 47, 8, 71–77.

Lyytinen, K., and Yoo, Y. 2002. Issues and challenges in ubiquitous computing. *Communications of the ACM*, 45, 12, 62–65.

Malladi, R., and Agrawal, D. P. 2002. Current and future applications of mobile and wireless networks. *Communications of the ACM*, 45, 10, 144–146.

Maral, G., and Bousquet, M. 2009. *Satellite Communications Systems: Systems, Techniques and Technologies*, 5th ed. West Sussex, UK: Wiley.

Markus, M.L. 1994. Finding a happy medium: Explaining the negative effects of electronic communication on social life at work. *ACM Transactions on Information Systems*, 12, 2, 119–149.

Milanesi, C. 2011. iPad and beyond: The future of the tablet market. Stamford, CT: Gartner. www.gartner.com/technology/research/ipad-media-tablet/future-of-tablet-market.jsp (accessed May 8, 2012).

Murph, D. 2008. Japan launches Kizuna satellite, hopes it will deliver high-speed Internet. Engadget, February 23. www.engadget.com/2008/02/23/japan-launches-kizuna-satellite-hopes-it-will-deliver-high-spee/ (accessed May 13, 2012).

Naguchi, Y. 2004. No escape from e-mail: Wireless BlackBerrys push limit of etiquette. *Washington Post*, September 29, A01.

Nickerson, R.C.; Isaac, H.; and Mak, B. 2008. A multi-national study of attitudes about mobile phone use in social settings. *International Journal of Mobile Communications*, 6, 5, 541–563.

Nielsen. 2012. Smartphones account for half of all mobile phones, dominate new phone purchases in the U.S. Nielsen Wire, March 29. http://blog.nielsen.com/nielsenwire/online_mobile/smartphones-account-for-half-of-all-mobile-phones-dominate-new-phone-purchases-in-the-us (accessed May 8, 2012).

Panko, R. 2008. *Business Data Networks and Telecommunications*, 6th ed. New York: Prentice-Hall.

Pierce, D. 2011. LG Nitro HD review. *The Verge*, December 7. www.theverge.com/2011/12/7/2613319/lg-nitro-hd-review (accessed May 13, 2012).

Purvanova, R.K., and Bono, J.E. 2009. Transformational leadership in context: Face-to-face and virtual teams. *The Leadership Quarterly*, 20, 3, 343–357.

Raento, M., and Oulasvirta, A. 2008. Designing for privacy and self-presentation in social awareness. *Personal and Ubiquitous Computing,* 12, 7, 527–542.

Ragu-Nathan, T.S.; Tarafdar, M.; and Ragu-Nathan, B.S. 2008. The consequences of technostress for end users in organizations: Conceptual development and empirical validation. *Information Systems Research,* 19, 4, 417–433.

Reichebacher, T. 2003. Adaptive methods for mobile cartography. In *Proceedings of the 21st International Cartographic Conference: Cartographic Renaissance,* 1311–1321. Durban, South Africa, August 10–16.

Schmerken, J. 2000. Where is wireless headed. *Wall Street & Technology,* 18, 12, 14–20.

Smith, M. 2012. Thin and fast: How Ultrabook performance stacks up beside larger laptops. *Digital Trends,* May 10. www.digitaltrends.com/computing/thin-and-fast-how-ultrabook-performance-stacks-up-beside-larger-laptops/ (accessed May 11, 2012).

Speier, C.; Valacich, J.S.; and Vessey, I. 1999. The influence of task interruption on individual decision making: An information overload perspective. *Decision Sciences,* 30, 2, 337–360.

Staples, D.S.; Hulland, J.S.; and Higgins, C.A. 1999. A self-efficacy theory explanation for the management of remote workers in virtual organizations. *Organization Science,* 10, 6, 758–776.

Troianovski, A., and Bensinger, G. 2012. Users rip AT&T data curbs. *The Wall Street Journal,* March 5, B3.

Tversky, A., and Kahneman, D. 1974. Judgments under uncertainty: Heuristics and biases. *Science,* 185, 4157, 1124–1131.

Valacich, J.S., and Schneider, C. 2010. *Information Systems Today: Managing in the Digital World,* 4th ed. Upper Saddle River, NJ: Prentice Hall.

Wang, Y.S., and Wang, H.Y. 2008. Developing and validating an instrument for measuring mobile computing self-efficacy. *Cyberpsychology & Behavior,* 11, 4, 405–413.

Wang, Y.S.; Wu, M.C.; and Wang, H.Y. 2009. Investigating the determinants and age and gender differences in the acceptance of mobile learning. *British Journal of Educational Technology,* 40, 1, 92–118.

Young, W.R. 1979. Advanced mobile phone service: Introduction, background, and objectives. *Bell System Technical Journal,* 58, 1, 1–14.

CHAPTER 10

THE FUTURE OF WRITING TOGETHER

Emerging Research in Collaborative Writing Technologies

MARK KEITH, SEAN HUMPHERYS, TRENT J. SPAULDING,
AND PAUL BENJAMIN LOWRY

Abstract: Collaborative writing (CW) has become a common part of many business and organizational activities. The technologies and techniques that support CW have progressed remarkably and valuable research explaining CW success has emerged. Therefore, it is important for organizations to understand the process of CW in order to create efficiency and other positive returns for collaborative work. This chapter breaks down the fundamentals of CW including: (1) an overview of the seven common CW activities, (2) a review of related authoring and document control strategies, and (3) a description of recent advancements in CW tool features. This chapter contributes to the CW literature by summarizing the relevant research in CW, particularly as it relates to thinkLets and CW tools and by outlining specific future research questions related to CW group sizes, webpage authoring, and group awareness.

Keywords: Collaborative Writing, Collaboration, Group Writing, Group Support Systems, Computer-mediated Communication, ThinkLets

Collaboration has become a staple of business activities. Wikis are finding their way into virtual communities, support groups, and businesses in general. Engagement proposals, project updates, executive strategy documents, and many other products of knowledge work have become a collaborative writing effort (Barbour, 1990; Duin, 1991). Collaborative writing (CW) is widely performed in industry, academia, and government (Anderson, 1985; Baecker et al., 1994; Beck, 1993; Couture and Rymer, 1989; Mabrito, 1992). Understanding the process of CW can create efficiency and other positive returns for large organizations. This chapter provides a foundational discussion of the activities and strategies of CW and summarizes current research in the area of CW.

CW is a process through which a group of people produce a document. The CW process formally begins with the formation of a group and includes all the activities necessary to create a document through the post-final review. Often, collaborative writing is described in terms of writing activities such as brainstorming and drafting. Authoring strategies and document control strategies are used to govern these activities.

Modern work in CW research has focused around thinkLets. A thinkLet is a package of tools, configurations, and scripts used to provide a predictable, repeatable pattern of collaboration to work toward a goal. CW software tools can take advantage of thinkLets to implement support for each CW activity.

Figure 10.1   **Six Types of Collaborative Authoring Strategies**

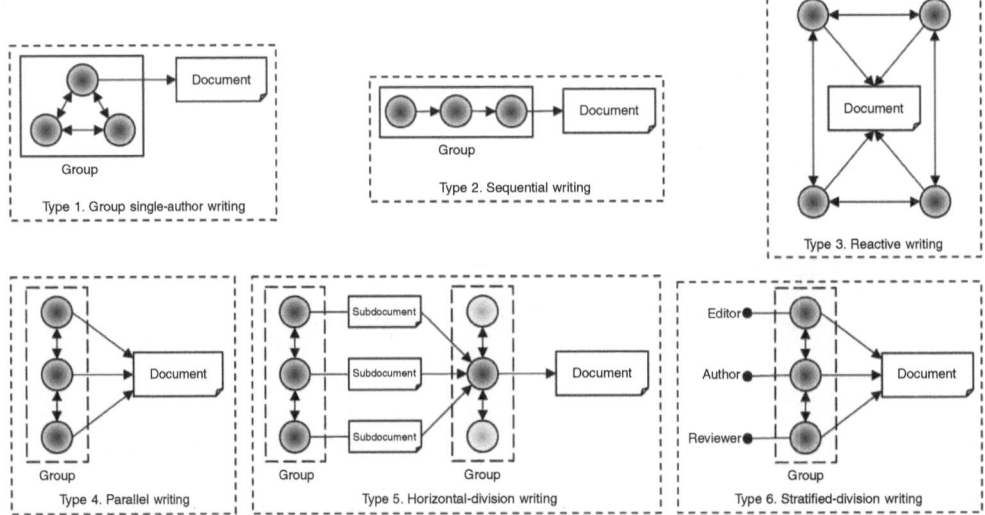

Source: Adapted from Lowry, Curtis et al., 2004.

Several different software tools have been implemented to support CW. Following previous work, we define three levels of collaborative writing software: individual work level, coordinated work level, and concerted work level. We focus our research summary on the concerted work level. With this frame we find that research focuses on three main areas. First, it compares modern CW tools to word processors. Second it looks at the effect of process structure on document quality and group dynamics. Lastly, current research focuses on the effect of proximity on productivity and group dynamics.

Our discussion points to three areas of future research. Much has yet to be discovered of the effect of process structure on CW outcomes (quality, productivity, satisfaction, etc.) in the context of different group sizes. This can be seen in particular in current interest in very large writing groups such as wikis (Libert and Spector, 2007). Second, the development of collaborative web authoring requires research in tools and standards for collaborative webpage creation. Finally, research on group awareness leaves many interesting gaps in the effect of awareness on CW outcomes.

TYPES OF STRATEGIES FOR COLLABORATIVE WRITING

CW strategies can be defined as a team's overall approach for coordinating the writing of a collaborative document. Each strategy has inherent strengths and is best applied in specific situations. To successfully complete a CW project, the team must choose authoring and control strategies that will help the team reach specific outcomes. Both authoring and control strategies are described below.

Writing collaboratively requires decisions regarding authorship strategy and document control. Who will write what and when? How will the document flow between authors? Who will manage document control and approve changes, and by what mechanisms? As authoring strategies often dictate control strategies, we start by discussing individual authoring strategies and their general purposes. Authoring strategies are usually separated into six different types, as depicted in Figure 10.1 and described in the next section.

Group single-author writing is a strategy in which a group elects one author to write for the group (Lowry, Curtis et al., 2004). This strategy is effective in the draft phases of a document.

Sequential writing occurs when each member of a group takes turns sequentially writing a document (Sharples, 1992). Sequential writing works well in writing and reviewing phases.

Reactive writing refers to a group of authors composing at the same time with instant access to each other's work, thereby reacting and adjusting to the content generated by each author (Sharples, 1993). Reactive writing is especially good for brainstorming and idea-gathering activities.

Parallel writing occurs when a team divides CW work into discrete units and works in parallel (Sharples, 1993). Parallel writing is often divided into two subcategories: horizontal-division writing and stratified-division writing. *Horizontal-division writing* is used when each participant generates a unique part of the overall document (Stratton, 1989). Horizontal-division writing can be used in many phases of the writing process. *Stratified-division writing* occurs when each member of the team fulfills different roles of the writing process such as writing the first complete rough draft versus revising an existing draft or performing the final copyedits (Stratton, 1989). Stratified-division writing is useful when a team desires to capitalize on individuals' strengths during different phases of writing.

Document control strategy is closely related to authoring strategies and is often broken into four modes: centralized control, relay control, independent control, and shared control. *Centralized control* occurs when one person controls the document throughout the writing activity (Posner and Baecker, 1992) and is most often used with group single-author writing. *Relay control* is when full control of the document is passed from one author to another (Posner and Baecker, 1992) and is used with sequential writing. *Independent control* occurs when individuals in the group have full control of their piece of the document (Posner and Baecker, 1992). Independent control is often related to horizontal-division parallel writing. Finally, *shared control* occurs when team members have simultaneous and equal access to writing privileges (Posner and Baecker, 1992) and is thus most often used with reactive writing.

COLLABORATIVE WRITING PROCESS AND THINKLETS

This section first focuses on the collaborative writing process itself, and then extends the discussion to thinkLets.

Writing Process

CW is often a complex, nonlinear process. For example, even though a group will likely use brainstorming near the beginning of a project, they might conduct another brainstorming activity to overcome a challenge in the middle or end of the process. Below is a list of common activities conducted during a CW project (see Table 10.1). The CW process can be divided into smaller activities that are used as needed to develop a document.

The nature of a group's document, along with associated processes and tasks, determine which activities are needed (see Table 10.2). For example, a progress report will require much less brainstorming and convergence on ideas than will an engagement letter. If an engagement letter is drafted, reviewed, and rejected, it may periodically return to the drafting or writing activity.

Besides the nature of the document, the size of a CW team also influences the tasks. Teams of six will likely take more time converging and communicating than will a team of two simply because of group size differences. Teams composing documents that could have a high impact on themselves or on their organizations are more likely to need better communication than teams

Table 10.1

The Common Activities of Collaborative Writing

Activity	Definition from research
Brainstorming	Developing new ideas for a paper draft (Posner and Baecker, 1992).
Converging	Deciding what to do with the brainstormed ideas as a group (Lowry, Curtis et al., 2004).
Outlining	Creating a direction the document will follow, including major sections and subsections (Adkins, et al., 1999).
Drafting	Writing the initial, incomplete text of a document (this is typically synonymous with the term *writing*, but the term *drafting* is used to convey incompleteness in the writing) (Galegher and Kraut, 1994; Horton et al., 1991). Also synonymous with composing (Odell, 1985).
Reviewing	Reading and annotating document draft sections for content, grammar, and style improvements (Galegher and Kraut, 1994).
Revising	Responding to review comments by making changes in the draft that reflect the review comments (Galegher and Kraut, 1994). Revising is used over editing to distinguish this activity more clearly from copyediting and from the editorial process of reviewing.
Copyediting	Making final changes that are universally administered to a document to improve consistency (e.g., copyedits, grammar, logic), usually made by one person charged with this responsibility. Often called editing (Posner and Baecker, 1992), which is a less descriptive term.

Source: Adapted from Lowry, Curtis et al., 2004.

working on low-impact projects. Teams with one authoritative figure may take less time on convergence than groups where participants are equal in authority.

ThinkLets

ThinkLets have been used to help practitioners and researchers reproduce positive results. According to Kolfschoten et al. (2004), a thinkLet is a named, packaged activity that produces a predictable, repeatable pattern of collaboration among people working toward a goal. ThinkLets are composed of three variables that can help bring about a desired outcome: tool, configuration, and script (Briggs et al., 2001).

- *Tool:* The type of software needed. For example, early in the CW process, a team may require a brainstorming tool. Later activities may require a voting tool.
- *Configuration:* How the software is configured to facilitate the group. Part of configuration is the document control strategy—managing who is allowed to edit the paper and for how long.
- *Script:* The scenario the facilitator gives to the group.

Simple changes in the script can have profound effects on the end product of a CW activity. In essence, thinkLets provide a mechanism whereby the knowledge and skills of a professional group facilitator (e.g., how to perform a task, what tools to use, and how to configure those tools)

Table 10.2

Examples of Documents Commonly Created Using CW

Category	Sample documents
Student projects	Term papers Position papers Discussion papers Decision papers
Academic work	Academic journal articles Books Monographs Case studies Instructional materials (Ede and Lunsford, 1990)
Manuals/Technical	Operating procedures Policy manuals User manuals Training manuals Operations orders and plans White papers
Business communication	Proposals Reports Memos Strategy documents Newsletters Goal statements Presentation notes (Ede and Lunsford, 1990) Progress reports Personnel reports (Wilds, 1989) Bulletins
Government and legal	Directives Legal briefs (Allen, Atkinson, Morgan, Moore, and Snow, 1987) Regulations Mission orders
Other	Short stories Action summaries Citations and recommendations for awards

can be explicitly defined into standardized units. As a result, one of the benefits of using thinkLets may be that self-organizing groups can gain some of the advantages of using a facilitator without actually having one.

Lowry and Nunamaker (2002) examined approximately sixty thinkLets—some of which are summarized in Table 10.3. The first column of Table 10.3 identifies ten specific group processes. Each process is comprised of multiple thinkLets (as seen in the second column). As defined by the thinkLet, the necessary tools are listed in the third column. Lastly, each thinkLet is designed to accomplish one of seven recognized patterns of CW: diverge, converge, organize, elaborate, abstract, evaluate, and build consensus (Briggs et al., 2001). These patterns appear in the fourth column of Table 10.3.

Table 10.3

ThinkLets Applied to General CW Process

Target script for group processes	ThinkLets, executed in the following order	Collaborative tool used	Primary patterns of thinking used
Group formation	• Execute ice breaker • Execute group formation and bonding	• Chat • Topic Commenter	• Organize
Planning	• Generate statement of purpose • Generate statement of scope • Generate specific objectives • Develop milestones on project plan • Assign roles and responsibilities • Vote on results • Discuss lessons learned	• Chat • Topic Commenter • Group Voter	• Organize • Abstract • Build consensus • Elaborate
Brainstorming	• Conduct anonymous brainstorming • Categorize brainstormed output • Prioritize brainstormed output • Decide on brainstormed output to use • Vote on results	• Brainstormer • Topic Commenter • Categorizer • Alternative Analyzer • Survey • Group Voter	• Diverge • Converge • Build consensus
Outlining	• Do group outlining • Vote on outline	• Group Outliner • Group Voter	• Elaborate • Build consensus
Research	• Do group research • Vote on research	• Group Outliner • Group Voter	• Elaborate • Build consensus

Drafting	• Do group drafting • Vote on draft • Discuss lessons learned	• GroupWriter • Group Voter • Topic Commenter	• Elaborate • Build consensus
Reviewing	• Do group reviewing • Group annotations • Vote on results	• GroupWriter • GroupAnnotations • Group Voter	• Evaluate • Build consensus
Revising	• Review, accept, and reject annotations • Group revisions • Decide if more drafting is needed—vote on results • Review open issues and develop action plan	• GroupWriter • GroupAnnotations • Group Voter • Topic Commenter	• Evaluate • Converge • Build consensus • Organize
Final draft	• Read document aloud • Vote on results • Final revisions • Final formatting	• GroupWriter • Group Voter	• Evaluate • Build consensus • Elaborate
Close project	• Conduct final discussion • Evaluate entire experience • Review open issues, decide on action plan	• Group Voter • Topic Commenter	• Elaborate • Evaluate • Build consensus

Source: Lowry and Nunamaker, 2002, 6.

RESEARCH ON COLLABORATIVE WRITING

Because CW is a prevalent form of group work that has many potential benefits and issues, CW research has been very interdisciplinary. Articles have been published on such topics as CW strategies (Ede and Lunsford, 1990), issues encountered by MBA students using basic CW technologies (Forman, 1991), CW processes and practices in the military (Rice and Huguley, 1994), e-government (Lowry et al., 2002), a research bibliography (Bosley et al., 1990), a case study on authority in CW groups (Loehr, 1995), a survey on CW in engineering co-op experiences (Kreth, 2000), CW in the workplace (Duin, 1991), large CW groups (McIsaac and Aschauer, 1990), an ethnographic study of large CW groups (Cross, 1998), CW experiments using computer-mediated communication (Galegher and Kraut, 1994), creating a CW course (Belanger and Greer, 1992), CW hypertext technologies (Rada and Wang, 1998), CW experiments using CW-specific software (Lowry and Nunamaker, 2003; Lowry, Nunamaker et al., 2004; Lowry et al., 2005; Olson et al., 1993), software development as a CW process (Bussell and Taylor, 2006), improving group awareness for CW (Lowry and Nunamaker, 2003; Tran et al., 2006), enabling concurrent editing for CW (Ho et al., 2006), and facilitating government policymaking via electronic CW (Lourenço and Costa, 2007). This section focuses on using specific tools designed to improve the CW process. We begin with an overview of these tools and then discuss the types of research questions that have been answered in regard to CW tools, including theory and methodologies. We finish by suggesting future research directions for CW.

Overview of Collaborative Writing Software

Technology has been demonstrated to play a significant role in group collaborative processes (e.g., El-Shinnawy and Vinze, 1998). As a result, a great amount of research has been dedicated to understanding these technology impacts. This section presents an overview of particular CW technologies.

Definition of Collaborative Writing Software

Collaborative writing software can be defined as a specialized form of group support system that allows CW groups to naturally perform the major CW activities—pre-meeting planning, brainstorming, converging on brainstorming, outlining, drafting, reviewing, revising, copyediting, and final wrap up—along with support of less predictable group activities such as researching, socializing, communicating, negotiating, coordinating, monitoring, rewarding, punishing, and recording (Lowry, Curtis et al., 2004). Clearly, CW software involves a high level of coordination and very complex communication.

Nunamaker et al. (1997) propose three categories of software that indicate the degree to which a software package involves group work:

1. *Individual work level* involves individual productivity software[1] that has no immediate group focus, such as word processors and spreadsheets (although individual productivity software can be used to support a group's work).
2. *Coordinated work level* involves group work that is largely made up of coordinated but independent contributions (similar to a relay team running a race). Most of the software in this category fits under traditional computer-mediated communications software (CMC)[2] such as email, instant messaging, and bulletin boards.

Figure 10.2   **Collaborative Writing Software in Context of Other Software**

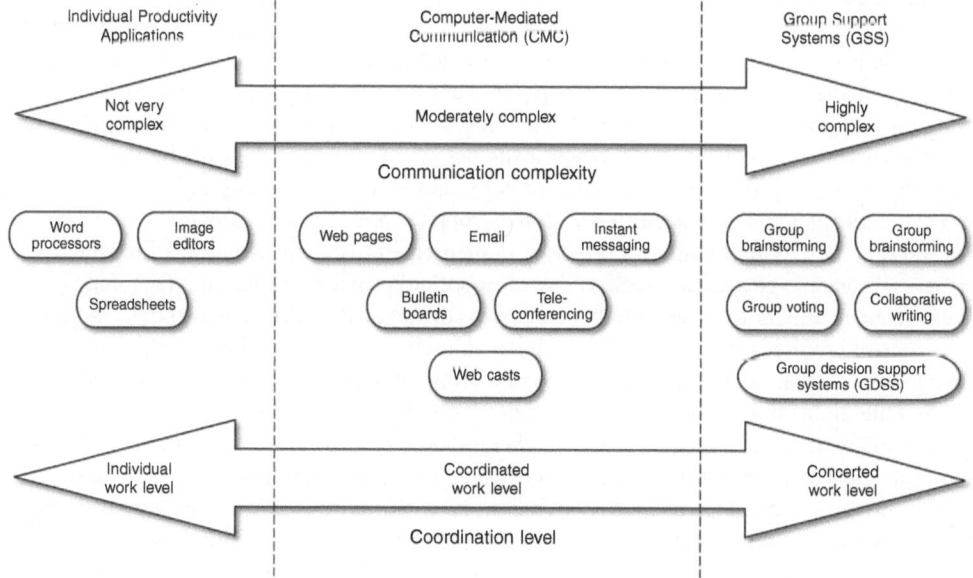

Source: Adapted from Lowry, Curtis et al., 2004.

3. *Concerted work level* represents the software that is most collaborative and requires concerted group effort and complex communication.

This is the traditional realm of group support systems (GSS) and where CW software resides. This overall framework is depicted in Figure 10.2.

Requirements of Collaborative Writing Software

How exactly should CW software be designed? *Media richness theory* can inform this important question (Daft and Lengel, 1986; Rice, 1992). While there is mixed support (Dennis and Kinney, 1998), the central proposition of media richness theory states that different communication media possess different levels of *richness*, which refers to the communication media's ability to transmit nonverbal cues, provide immediate feedback, convey personal traits, and support the use of natural language (Daft and Lengel, 1986). To understand, imagine a continuum of richness based on the above abilities. Face-to-face, synchronous communication is on the rich end of the spectrum and distributed, asynchronous communication is on the lean end. All of the various communication media fall somewhere along the continuum, with technology such as real-time video conferencing being rich and email being lean on their ability to convey knowledge and information. Selecting the media that best reduces or removes the uncertainties inherent in the collaborative task produces optimal results.

Media richness theory predicts that distributed CW groups will exhibit less-rich interactions than face-to-face groups. This lack of richness decreases the quality of communication and overall outcomes of distributed groups (Burke and Chidambaram, 1999). However, by developing software with the appropriate group communication interface, performance can be improved (Galegher and Kraut, 1994).

CW software must have strong coordination capabilities and group awareness to be effective. *Coordination* is the ability of group members to co-manage their work efforts toward a common goal. *Group awareness* is the ability of group members to know what other group members are working on—an ability that improves understanding of context, coordination, and overall communication (Kirby and Rodden, 1995). Group awareness varies based on the work mode employed because the underlying differences in synchronicity and proximity directly affect how much a person can understand what is occurring within a group (Schlichter et al., 1997).

Several specific CW tool features need to be implemented to enhance coordination and group awareness. Research shows that effective CW tools should provide a group interface that allows different team members to work simultaneously on different items of text without conflict or version control problems (Ellis et al., 1991). Such an interface should include group documents, group annotations that allow simultaneous commenting on a given annotation (Neuwirth et al., 1990), and hierarchical group outlines (Ellis et al., 1991; Kraut et al., 1988).

Support of parallel-partitioned writing is another important requirement to enhance coordination and group awareness that is not supported by word processors (Ellis et al., 1991). Parallel-partitioned writing allows group members to work synchronously or asynchronously on the same document and provides separate document sections that each member can work on yet allows each group member to be able to view or contribute to each other's work at any time. Parallel-partitioned writing also allows task decomposition, which has been shown to greatly increase coordination in collaborative groups (Kiesler and Cummings, 2001).

As mentioned above, selecting the optimal CW strategy is critical to group performance and success. Therefore, CW tools should support various roles and responsibilities to enhance coordination and group awareness. CW tools should support multiple collaboration roles that can be easily shifted throughout the writing process (Neuwirth et al., 1990). Writing tools need to allow participants to easily create, join, or leave CW sessions at any time without causing significant disruptions (Baecker et al., 1993). Typical roles include *writer, consultant, editor, reviewer, scribe,* and *facilitator* (Adkins et al., 1999; Posner and Baecker, 1992). CW tools should provide capabilities and security that change dynamically according to a user's role.

Not only should tools support parallel-partitioned CW and dynamic roles, they should also provide specific interfaces for the key activities of group writing. In particular, tools should provide features to support the aforementioned process of brainstorming, researching, planning, outlining, reviewing, revising, and final drafting (Kraut et al., 1988; Posner and Baecker, 1992). For example, brainstorming can be supported by an interface that allows participants to add ideas anonymously and that disallows participants from rushing ahead and writing document text. To support outlining, an interface can allow writers (but not consultants or editors) to create a hierarchical outline without detailed text. To support reviewing, the writing interface can prevent writers from making changes while editors are allowed to make annotations. By providing interfaces that are designed for specific CW activities, CW tools increase coordination by focusing group members on specific tasks.

How Collaborative Writing Tools Stack Up

The requirements listed above are difficult to implement, especially in distributed environments. Thus, it is not surprising that while historical attempts at creating CW tools showed promise, many documented issues still exist, especially since none of these tools has been designed to fully accommodate Internet-based, distributed work. Furthermore, too many tools ignore CW as a holistic process that involves heavy group communication and that can be conducted through many different strategies and work modes.

For two or three decades, CW tools have been developed for use in research. Some of the earlier and more prominent developments include Quilt (Leland et al., 1988), Grove (Ellis et al., 1991), MILO (Jones, 1993), Contact (Kirby and Rodden, 1995), Messie (Sasse and Handley, 1996), Instant Update (Tammaro et al., 1997), Aspect (Cerratto, 1999), Collaboratus (Lowry et al., 2002), and wikis (Noël and Robert, 2003).

Most of these tools were designed simply to test and support synchronous and asynchronous CW on small networks. Despite the coordination and group awareness features included in leading CW tools, limitations exist in supporting distributed groups because the tools have not been designed for Internet-based work—with a key exception of Collaboratus and wiki technology. Wiki technology, however, does not have built-in tools to support different CW processes. Though some work has been done to structure parallel wiki writing (Cosley et al., 2007), support for CW processes is still immature and technically difficult.

To support Internet-based work, CW tools need to allow large groups with little or no technical training to work via web browsers that use virtually any type of computer and operating system. These requirements are critical because it is unreasonable to expect large, distributed groups to have the same types of computers and operating systems. It is also unreasonable to expect writers to install and troubleshoot their own software—especially when they are working in different locations and time zones. Thus, Internet-based writing groups often resort to more primitive, inefficient methods, such as file sharing through email, which decrease the utility (and likely adoption) of CW tools.

Distributed CW environments naturally lack even more group awareness and coordination than face-to-face environments because teams in distributed environments are physically separated and have a restricted range of verbal and nonverbal cues (Schlichter et al., 1997). Such groups require specialized, distributed CW tools to accommodate these challenges. Collaboratus is the only tool listed above that is designed to meet the needs of distributed and diverse CW groups.

Overview of CW Tool Advancements

Given the need for better support of distributed CW, researchers from the Center for the Management of Information (CMI) at the University of Arizona set out to build a better tool. They designed Collaboratus to support Internet-based, distributed CW better than other CW tools. It builds on the taxonomy of CW by functioning as a tool that supports the activities (e.g., brainstorming, outlining, writing, and revising), strategies (e.g., sequential or parallel work), roles, document control modes, and work mode choices that are common to CW. Collaboratus is different from previous CW tools in that it is based on Java™ technology, which allows it to run through any Internet web browser, operating system, and hardware platform without requiring end-users to be aware of its technical details.[3] In fact, Collaboratus was designed so that users can work effectively even if they use low-speed modem connections. Collaboratus also supports a virtually unlimited number of users, depending on the speed of the network and computers.

Since the development of Collaboratus, the same features that support greater group awareness, team coordination, and distributed environments have been incorporated into the commercially available GroupSystems™ II software so that it can support CW, among many other activities (www.groupsystems.com). Recently, GroupSystems has evolved this product to use an Adobe Flash interface for smoother user interaction and uses the product name ThinkTank 2.0.

Figure 10.3   **GroupSystems Collaborative Writing**

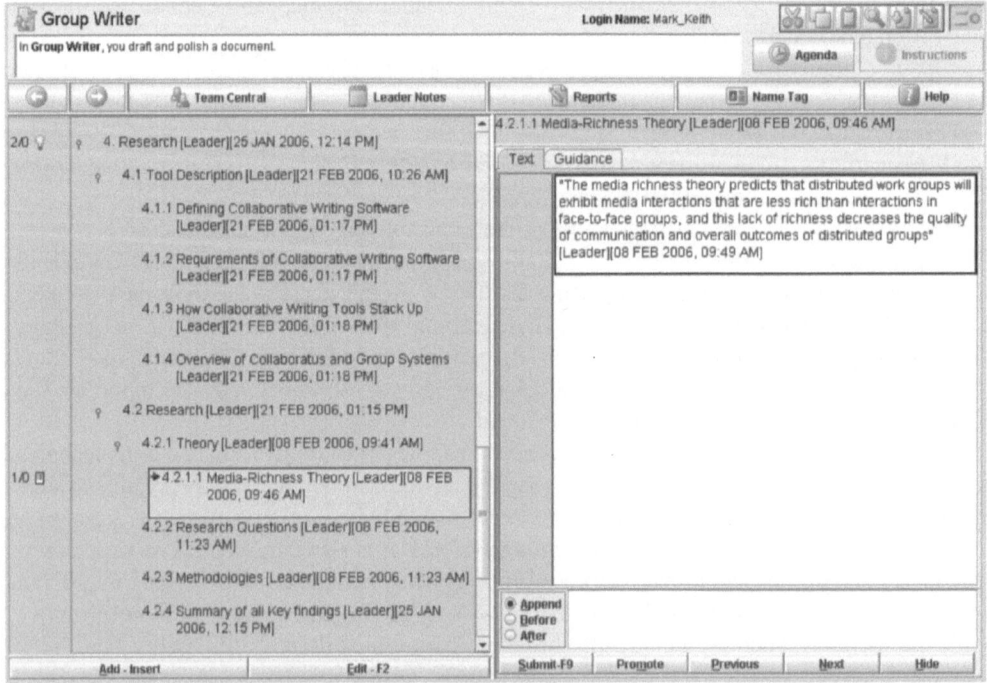

Collaboratus strongly supports group awareness and coordination. It builds on previous CW tools by supporting a full range of CW activities such as setting up user roles and rights, creating group agendas and plans, brainstorming paper contents, sharing group outlines, voting on group decisions, creating group papers, reviewing, and annotating. Collaboratus has a version control feature that allows participants to see the changes that have been made to a particular section of a document. It also supports specific CW roles and the ability to verify who is actively working on a CW document at any given time. Collaboratus also allows group members to work either asynchronously or synchronously in distributed work modes or to use a mixture of both work modes. Figure 10.3 depicts the CW features of GroupSystems II. On the left is the group outline; group members can access any portion of the outline and simultaneously write in the portion of the screen that appears on the right. This is an example of how theories such as media richness have been used in the development of collaborative software. By viewing a shared outline, GroupSystems users have fewer questions regarding who is doing what and when and thus will have fewer coordination and redundancy problems. GroupSystems users will likely identify issues and build off each other's work more rapidly because they can see the work of others in parallel.

Besides supporting CW, ThinkTank provides a variety of other collaboration services with real-time communication among distributed users. However, because of the relatively high cost and low availability of ThinkTank, a number of free or low-cost, web-based CW tools have emerged that can support real-time (or "near" real-time) collaboration. The newer alternatives can be broadly categorized as either desktop-based tools similar to ThinkTank (i.e., they must be downloaded and installed on each client computer) or web browser-based tools (e.g., Mozilla Firefox, Microsoft Internet Explorer, Apple Safari, etc.) that allow CW through "stateless" web pages. Examples of software-based tools include Gobby, ACE, and Groove. These tools do not have the extra features ThinkTank provides for group voting and analysis.[4] Because these tools are browser-based, users must reload the web page to capture the changes made by others. However, some of these tools, such as Google Docs, EditGrid, and SynchroEdit, can automate page reloading to make updates nearly in real-time.

Research Involving Collaboratus

The creation of Collaboratus was an interdisciplinary effort that has spawned a series of interdisciplinary CW research. Examples of Collaboratus-related studies include developing a taxonomy of CW (Lowry, Curtis et al., 2004), describing the evolutionary development of Collaboratus (Lowry, et al., 2002), using thinkLets to better support distributed work for specific writing tasks (Lowry and Nunamaker, 2002), proposing CW tool design requirements (Lowry, 2002a), improving asynchronous-distributed CW groups through increased process structure (Lowry et al., 2005), examining proximity effects in asynchronous-distributed CW groups (Lowry, 2002b), demonstrating Collaboratus's efficacy in providing enhanced group awareness and CW support in synchronous-distributed settings (Lowry and Nunamaker, 2003), and using Collaboratus to improve distributed education (Lowry, Nunamaker et al., 2004).

Studies have attempted to answer many types of research questions concerning CW tools, group process structure, and group proximity:

- Can CW tools improve group productivity better than word processing tools?
- Can CW tools produce higher quality results than traditional word processors?
- How do CW tools influence group satisfaction, relationships, and communication?
- How do varying levels of process structure affect document quality and group productivity, satisfaction, relationships, and communication?
- How does group proximity affect document quality and group productivity, satisfaction, relationships, and communication?

Table 10.4 summarizes the research addressed in three specific studies including the context, methodology, independent variables, and dependent variables that were used. In general, CW studies compare variables like synchronicity (synchronous vs. asynchronous), group member

Table 10.4

Examples of Research on Leading CW Tools

Study	Context	Independent variable	Dependent variable
Lowry and Nunamaker, 2003	Synchronous, distributed groups with constant process structure	CW tool (Word vs. Collaboratus)	1. Group productivity 2. Document quality
Lowry, Nunamaker et al., 2004	Asynchronous, distributed; Groups using Collaboratus	Process structure (high, moderate, and low)	3. Group member satisfaction 4. Group member relationships
Lowry, 2002b	Collaboratus-based groups with constant process structure	Proximity (distributed vs. FtF)	5. Group member communication

distribution (distributed vs. face-to-face [FtF]), CW tool (Microsoft Word vs. Collaboratus), and *process structure*, which refers to the rules and resources used to coordinate the flow of a group's processes (DeSanctis and Poole, 1994). Elements of process structure include agendas, organization norms, cultures, training, group experience, and knowledge.

In general, these studies found support for the hypothesis that CW tools that support the appropriate richness necessary for collaborative communication can improve the results of synchronous, distributed student writing teams (Lowry, Nunamaker et al., 2004). Group productivity, document quality, member relationships, and member communication were each significantly improved when CW teams used CW tools. However, the same was not true for group satisfaction. This result is not surprising since prior studies have found that first-time users of new technologies are often dissatisfied in the short run until they have become familiar with the technology (Olson et al., 1993; Watson, 1987). In fact, temporary dissatisfaction is predicted by theory on technology adoption and diffusion (Briggs et al., 1999).

Varying the amount of process structure was also found to have a significant effect on asynchronous, distributed groups (Lowry et al., 2005). High process structure groups outperformed low process structure groups on every measure. In addition, high process structure groups outperformed the moderate groups in terms of productivity, satisfaction, and relations, but not in document quality or communication. These results on the effects of process structure in CW tasks were fairly consistent with prior research on other collaborative tasks such as decision making (Ellis et al., 1991; Van de Ven and Delbecq, 1974).

And finally, a large body of research has demonstrated that distributed groups can suffer from process losses resulting from less opportunity for rich interactions (Herbsleb et al., 2000); less group awareness; less motivation to participate (Aytes, Johnson, and Frost, 1994); less attention; less familiarity; poorer norms, culture, and authority; less satisfaction; less productivity; a more abstract shared social setting (Kiesler and Cummings, 2001); fewer nonverbal channels; less trust and more difficulty with team building; more side conversations; and more restraint and responsibility from participants (Barile, 1998). However, as mentioned previously, Collaboratus was developed to provide a communication medium with the richness necessary to minimize or remove many of these issues. Lowry's (2002b) proximity study found no significant difference on any dependent measure (performance, quality, satisfaction, relationships, and communication) between Collaboratus-based FtF groups and distributed groups. Table 10.5 summarizes the results and findings of these three studies.

Future of Collaborative Writing Research and Tools

As demonstrated by the results of the above studies, there is great promise for media-rich CW tools like Collaboratus and ThinkTank. This chapter has made the case that CW is a highly complex form of collaboration that can benefit from specialized writing tools. This final section addresses future research opportunities in enhancing CW technologies and offers some potential research questions.

One way to frame the many research opportunities in CW is to extend the GSS foundation work by DeSanctis and Gallupe (1987) into an overall CW research framework. DeSanctis and Gallupe (1987) emphasized the need to look at different key inputs in collaborative work, such as task, tool, group, and context. This framework fits nicely with CW when it is customized to the proposed taxonomy of CW, along with the key processes, mediators, moderators, and outcomes of CW—as depicted in Figure 10.4. This figure combines several theoretical perspectives on CW into an overall model. On the left are DeSanctis and Gallupe's (1987) inputs with examples leading into a model of the CW task steps (team formation, team planning, document production, wind up),

Table 10.5

Summary of Three Collaboratus-based Studies

Study	Description	Work mode	Sample	Time	General finding
One	Collaboratus vs. Word groups in educational setting (Lowry and Nunamaker, 2003)	Synchronous-distributed (SD)	47	Four weeks	Distributed student CW teams can benefit from specialized CW software that provides parallel work, group awareness, and coordination.
Two	Collaboratus writing groups with variations in process structure (Lowry, Nunamaker et al., 2004)	Asynchronous-distributed (AD)*	550	Six weeks	High levels of process structure can be beneficial to distributed student writing groups; they need CW technologies and high levels of process structure.
Three	Collaboratus writing groups with variations in proximity (Lowry, 2002b)	Mixed-mode/asynchronous-distributed	550	Six weeks	AD CW groups did not have the expected process or outcome losses as compared to mixed-mode groups; AD work modes can be appropriate for distributed CW in education if they are provided the right tool and process support.

Source: Adapted from Lowry, Nunamaker et al., 2004.
*Asynchronous-distributed work mode refers to CW work that is performed at different times and in different places whereas synchronous-distributed refers to work that is accomplished at the same time and in the same place.

which includes examples of document production processes described above (e.g., brainstorming ideas, converging on brainstorming, outlining, drafting, reviewing, etc.). The outcomes of the CW task are also included as discussed above (quality, satisfaction, etc.). In addition, this model demonstrates the various types of process moderators found in the CW literature such as the level of group communication, rewarding and punishing strategies, recording, monitoring, researching, etc.

Based on this framework, we advocate research that takes into account the potential inputs as described by DeSanctis and Gallupe (1987). We will highlight some representative areas for research that appear to be most promising.

Task and Group Research Opportunities

Several research opportunities exist in exploring task and group considerations in CW groups. For example, little is known about the optimal size of CW groups for specific CW tasks. Likewise, more exploration needs to be done about the optimal mix of groups for specifics tasks. Moreover, additional research can focus on the effects of status differences in group work history.

As evidenced by the research by Lowry et al. (2005) on CW tasks among novices, document quality and group productivity, satisfaction, relationships, and communication can be significantly improved by providing more and better PS. Other collaborative activities, such as decision mak-

Figure 10.4   **Collaborative Writing Research Framework**

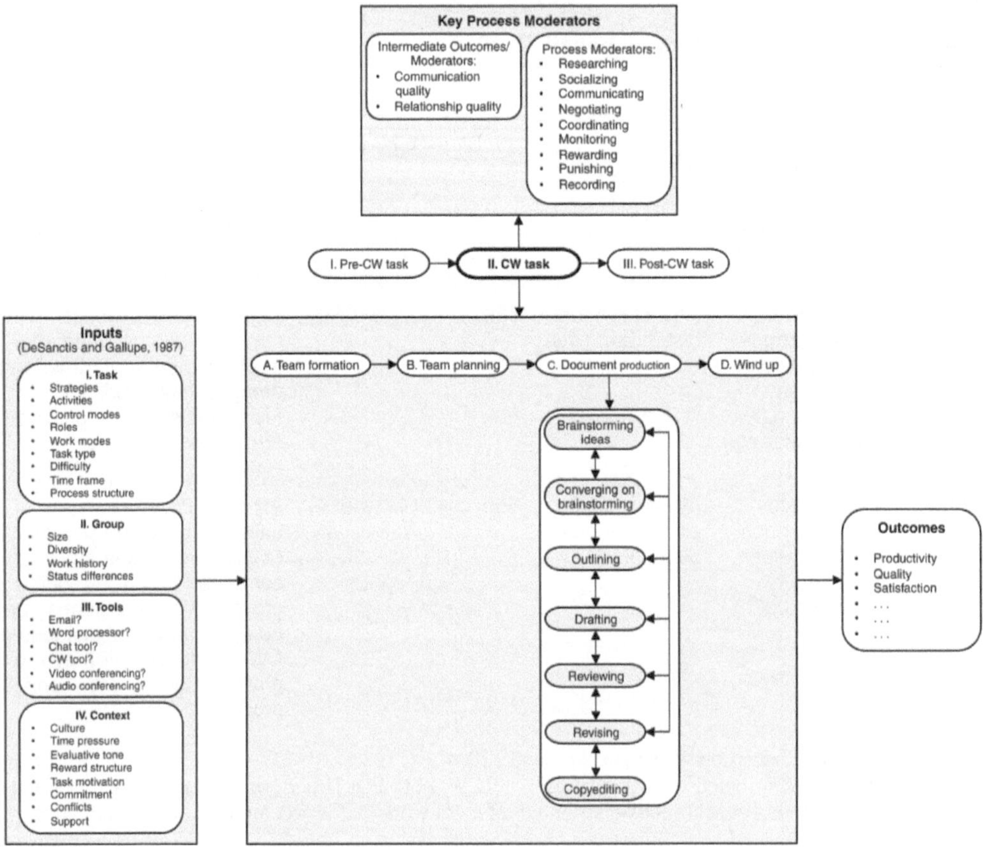

Source: Adapted and modified from Lowry et al., 2004a.

ing, benefit from the use of a trained and impartial facilitator who can professionally structure and execute group processes (Griffith et al., 1998). Typically, small writing groups such as those used in the Collaboratus experiments cannot afford or would not use such professional facilitators. This need for greater process structure in un-facilitated CW groups is an excellent area for future research.

A relatively recent development with great promise for improving process structure in novice CW is the concept of thinkLets (Kolfschoten et al., 2004). As mentioned earlier, a thinkLet is a named, packed activity that produces a predictable, repeatable pattern of collaboration among people working toward a goal. ThinkLets are conceptual building blocks in the design of collaborative processes. The purpose of a thinkLet is to capture the smallest unit of intellectual capital needed to reproduce collaboration patterns among people working toward a goal. ThinkLets have been successfully applied in other collaborative processes such as software code inspection (Koneri et al., 2005), quality-assurance techniques (Grünbacher et al., 2004), gathering end-user feedback for information system development (Bragge et al., 2005), and improving group brainstorming (Santanen et al., 2004). *Collaboration engineers* are people who design collaboration processes using thinkLets so the thinkLets are easily transferable to the practitioner (or group writer), which means the practitioner can execute the process without further assistance from the engineer or a professional facilitator (Kolfschoten et al., 2004). Experimental results indicate that, in the hands of collaborative engineers, thinkLets have become a powerful pattern language to describe and communicate sophisticated, complex process designs in a compact form (Briggs et al., 2003). A thinkLet framework has been developed to advance CW processes, facilitation, and techniques (Lowry and Nunamaker, 2002). But now, future research is needed to test whether novice CW groups using thinkLets can be more successful in their tasks and to what extent. In summary, we suggest the following as potential research questions[5]:

- What is the optimal size for CW groups for particular types of tasks?
- What determines the optimal sizes for CW groups?
- How should roles be divided among group members for various types of CW tasks?
- How does the use of thinkLets in designing CW tasks affect the process structure and general task uncertainty?
- What moderates the ability of thinkLets to improve process structure?
- How does the use of thinkLets to improve process structure affect the CW task performance, speed, and satisfaction?

Tool Research Opportunities

Many more research opportunities exist in CW tool research, since this research involves several aspects of group, task, and context considerations. For example, research can explore how CW tools mitigate group outcomes in terms of language barriers, geographic dispersion, and culture. There has been a strong research stream in terms of how technology can impact group polarization (El-Shinnawy and Vinze, 1998). For example, computer-mediated communication can reduce the normative influences which can negatively impact decision making by offering anonymity during brainstorming and discussion tasks. In addition, GSSs can offer certain analysis tools and features which would help to maximize the influence of informational influences. This issue should also be addressed in the context of CW where many decisions must be made concerning context, structure, etc.

Moreover, there is an interesting overlap between CW and web page authoring that merits more exploration. The World Wide Web Consortium (W3C) is developing standards for annotation, change tracking, and so forth, of web pages. Thus, it would be useful to explore what kinds of CW processes are involved in web page creation. For example, do web page authors encounter the same content-versus-formatting conflicts that traditional collaborative writers face? In other words, do web page authors spend too much "content development" time worrying about formatting issues? Can similar approaches and tools used to improve CW also be used to improve web authoring?

Related to web authoring, there are many research considerations involving the choice of Applets versus web-application interfaces in the creation of CW tools. Java, Flash, and HTML (DHTML, scripts, and so forth) provide interfaces that can run on a variety of operating systems and browsers. Thus, more work can be conducted to look at the tradeoffs involved in choosing different user interface technologies.

Another area of opportunity is research involving the creation of self-sustaining CW teams that work in distributed settings. One goal in creating self-sustaining (or auto-facilitating) teams is to wean distributed CW groups from the need for professional intervention and to free facilitators from the significant time required to create custom process scripts for specific CW tasks. The research on thinkLets can make an important contribution in this area. While complete independence may not be possible for inexperienced groups, we believe that groups can become self-reliant over time by using generic process scripts, wizards, and process agents. Therefore, we suggest the following questions for future research:

- How can CW tools minimize the impact of language barriers, geographic dispersion, and culture differences?
- How can CW tools reduce the negative impact of social normative influences during CW tasks?
- How can CW tools be used to maximize the influence of objective informational influences during CW tasks?
- How do CW tools influence the CW process differently during web page creation?
- How can CW tools be created to support self-sustaining CW teams?

Group Awareness and Coordination Research Opportunities

Group awareness and coordination can also open up many research opportunities that involve choices on tasks, groups, tools, and different contexts. One key area of research is to look for additional ways to increase group awareness and coordination for distributed CW environments. Several technologies should be considered for this enhancement, including multicasts, video conferencing, video phones, virtual meeting rooms, IP telephony, and collaborative virtual environments, which allow the use of avatars to represent each collaborator.

To enhance group awareness and coordination in distributed CW classrooms, researchers could explore the use of interactive, shared whiteboards where FtF and distributed participants could work together. To further help educational groups and novice writers, it may be useful to develop writing templates and wizards for different CW tasks (e.g., strategy documents vs. academic journal article) and work modes (e.g., FtF, synchronous distributed, and asynchronous distributed).

In addition, Dourish and Bly (1992) presented the concept of "portholes," which can be expanded by CW research. Portholes are video clips of group members and work locations, similar to a monitor showing a store's various video cameras. This concept could be extended to create "virtual portholes" that provide different graphical representations of what is currently happening with a group's members and work locations. For example, if a member is eating lunch, an animated avatar representing the group member could be shown eating lunch. If a member is on the phone, an animated avatar could show the member on the phone. If a member is working at the computer, an animated avatar could show the member at the computer.

In addition to "virtual portholes," awareness could be enhanced by status bars that show the progress of participants and groups against predetermined milestones from a project plan. It could also be useful to show participants the changes that have been made since their last logins. Automatic agent support could also send events and messages (e.g., form routing and email messages) as certain deliverables are completed.

Another research opportunity is to further improve group awareness and coordination for CW groups that have offline members or members that are not always connected through a network (e.g., they use mobile devices or have poor connectivity). This opens up difficult considerations that are partially addressed by technologies such as CVS or Lotus Notes™ replication capabilities. However, much more needs to be done to address sequential, conflicting off-line updates.

- Can features designed to increase the media richness of the communication during CW tasks (e.g., multicasts, video-conferencing, IP telephony, etc.) raise group awareness?

- How do these particular mechanisms to increase group awareness affect CW task performance?
- How does the use of portholes affect group awareness during CW tasks?
- Does the use of virtual portholes affect the awareness of CW groups working in a distributed, asynchronous environment?
- How do various methods for addressing off-line, conflicting updates affect CW group quality, speed, and satisfaction differently?

CONCLUSION

CW is a rapidly changing and progressing area of research and practice with applications in organizations, governments, and social systems in general. Using strategies, processes, and thinkLets in designing CW projects will improve experiences and outcomes. As the CW-supporting tools continue to develop and create new possibilities, research will be valuable in testing their value and influence. In addition, researchers should analyze the current uses for and needs of CW and suggest avenues for tool development.

NOTES

1. The term *office productivity software* is typically used to refer to the set of tools found in an office productivity suite such as Microsoft Office, Lotus Notes, Open Office, etc.

2. CMC systems are traditionally designed to enhance basic communication, as is seen with email or threaded chat boards. However, CMC systems do not provide support for advanced coordination, shared document updating, complex forms of communication, detailed decision making, or advanced levels of task and process structure.

3. Collaboratus requires only that users have a recent version of the Java client installed on their computers.

4. Other popular examples of web browser-based tools include Google Drive, ZOHO Write®, Writeboard™, Near-Time®, Socialtext, QuickTopicSM, EditGrid, SynchroEdit, PleaseReview, Coventi, Open Effort, and WE+.

5. Certainly, this list is not meant to be exhaustive, but only to provide ideas or a starting point for others.

REFERENCES

Adkins, M.; Reinig, J.Q.; Kruse, J.; and Mittleman, D. 1999. GSS collaboration in document development: Using GroupWriter to improve the process. In *Proceedings of the 32nd Annual Hawaii International Conference on System Sciences,* Maui, Hawaii, January 5–8.

Allen, N.J.; Atkinson, D.; Morgan, M.; Moore, T.; and Snow, C. 1987. What experienced collaborators say about collaborative writing. *Journal of Business and Technical Communication,* 1, 2, 70–90.

Anderson, P.V. (ed.). 1985. *What Survey Research Tells Us About Writing at Work.* New York: Guilford Press.

Aytes, K.; Johnson, J.; and Frost, J. 1994. Supporting distributed GDSS. *SIGOIS Bulletin* (Special Issue: Position Papers from the CSCW'94 Workshops), 15, 2, 18–20.

Baecker, R.; Glass, G.; Mitchell, A.; and Posner, I. 1994. SASSE: The collaborative editor. In *Proceedings of the Conference Companion on Human Factors in Computer Systems* (CHI'94), 449–460. New York: ACM.

Baecker, R.M.; Nastos, D.; Posner, I.R.; and Mawby, K.L. 1993. The user-centered iterative design of collaborative writing software. Paper presented at the ACM Conference on Human Factors in Computing Systems, Amsterdam, The Netherlands, April 24–29.

Barbour, D.H. 1990. Collaborative writing in the business writing classroom: An ethical dilemma for the teacher. *Bulletin of the Association for Business Communication,* 53, 3, 33–35.

Barile, A.L. 1998. Computer-mediated communication in collaborative writing. Unpublished doctoral dissertation, University of Oklahoma, Norman.

Beck, E. (ed.). 1993. *A Survey of Experiences of Collaborative Writing.* Berlin: Springer Verlag.

Belanger, K., and Greer, J. 1992. Beyond the group project: A blueprint for a collaborative writing course. *Journal of Business and Technical Communication,* 6, 1, 99–115.

Bosley, D.S.; Morgan, M.; and Allen, N. 1990. An essential bibliography on collaborative writing. *Bulletin of the Association for Business Communication,* 53, 2, 27–33.

Bragge, J.; Merisalo-Rantanen, H.; and Hallikainen, P. 2005. Gathering innovative end-user feedback for continuous development of information systems: A repeatable and transferable e-collaboration process. *IEEE Transactions on Professional Communications,* 48, 1, 55–67.

Briggs, R.O.; Adkins, M.; Mittleman, D.; and Kruse, J. 1999. A technology transition model derived from field investigation of GSS use aboard the U.S.S. CORONADO. *Journal of Management Information Systems,* 15, 3, 151–195.

Briggs, R.O.; de Vreede, G.-J.; and Nunamaker, J.F. Jr. 2003. Collaboration engineering with thinkLets to pursue sustained success with group support systems. *Journal of Management Information Systems,* 19, 4, 31–64.

Briggs, R.O.; de Vreede, G.-J.; Nunamaker, J.F. Jr.; and Tobey, D. 2001. ThinkLets: Achieving predictable, repeatable patterns of group interaction with group support systems (GSS). In *Proceedings of the 34th Annual Hawaii International Conference on Systems Sciences,* Maui, Hawaii, January 3–6.

Burke, K., and Chidambaram, L. 1999. How much bandwidth is enough? A longitudinal examination of media characteristics and group outcomes. *MIS Quarterly,* 23, 4, 557–580.

Bussell, B., and Taylor, S. 2006. Software development as a collaborative writing project. *Lecture Notes on Computer Science,* 4044, 21–31.

Cerratto, T. 1999. Supporting collaborative writing and its cognitive tools. Paper presented at the Third International Cognitive Technology Conference (CT'99) Networked Minds, San Francisco, California, August 11–14.

Cosley, D.; Frankowski, D.; Terveen, L.; and Riedl, J. 2007. SuggestBot: Using intelligent task routing to help people find work in Wikipedia. Paper presented at the International Conference on Intelligent User Interfaces, Honolulu, Hawaii, January 28–31.

Couture, B., and Rymer, J. 1989. Interactive writing on the job: Definitions and implications of collaboration. In M. Kogen (ed.), *Writing in the Business Professions.* Urbana, IL: National Council of Teachers of English; Association for Business Communication.

Cross, G.A. 1998. Collective form: An exploration of large-group writing. *Journal of Business Communication,* 37, 1, 77–100.

Daft, R.L., and Lengel, R.H. 1986. Organizational information requirements, media richness and structural design. *Management Science,* 33, 5, 554–571.

Dennis, A.R., and Kinney, S.T. 1998. Testing media richness theory in new media: The effects of cues, feedback, and task equivocality. *Information Systems Research,* 9, 3, 256–274

DeSanctis, G., and Gallupe, R.B. 1987. A foundation for the study of group decision support systems. *Management Science,* 33, 5, 589–609.

DeSanctis, G., and Poole, S. 1994. Capturing the complexity in advanced technology use: Adaptive structuration theory. *Organization Science,* 5, 2, 121–147.

Dourish, P., and Bly, S. 1992. Portholes: Supporting awareness in a distributed work group. Paper presented at the ACM Conference on Human Factors in Computing Systems (INTERCHI'92), Monterey, CA, May 3–7.

Duin, A.H. 1991. Computer-supported collaborative writing: The workplace and the writing classroom. *Journal of Business and Technical Communication,* 5, 2, 123–150.

Ede, L., and Lunsford, A. 1990. *Singular Texts/Plural Authors: Perspectives on Collaborative Writing.* Carbondale, IL: Southern Illinois University Press.

El-Shinnawy, Maha M., and Vinze, Ajay S. 1998. Polarization and persuasive argumentation: A study of decision making in group settings. *Management Information Systems Quarterly,* 22, 2, 165–198.

Ellis, C.A.; Gibbs, S.J.; and Rein, G.L. 1991. Groupware: Some issues and experiences. *Communications of the ACM,* 34, 1, 39–58.

Forman, J. 1991. *Computing and Collaborative Writing.* Urbana, IL: NCTE.

Galegher, J., and Kraut, R.E. 1994. Computer-mediated communication for intellectual teamwork: An experiment in group writing. *Information Systems Research,* 5, 2, 110–138.

Griffith, T.L.; Fuller, M.A.; and Northcraft, G.B. 1998. Facilitator influence in group support systems: Intended and unintended effects. *Information Systems Research,* 9, 1, 20–36.

Grünbacher, P.; Halling, M.; Biffl, S.; Kitapci, H.; and Boehm, B.W. 2004. Integrating collaborative processes and quality assurance techniques: Experiences from requirements negotiation. *Journal of Management Information Systems,* 20, 4, 9–29.

Herbsleb, J.D.; Mockus, A.; Finholt, T.A.; and Grinter, R.E. 2000. Distance, dependencies, and delay in global collaboration. Paper presented at the Conference on Computer-Supported Cooperative Work, Philadelphia, Pennsylvania, December 2–6.

Ho, K.S.; Leong, H.V.; Lam, W.; and Luk, R.W.P. 2006. Integrating XML and CORBA to support collaborative writing using off-the-shelf editing software. *Information Systems,* 31, 465–488.

Horton, M.; Rogers, P.; Austin, L.; and McCormick, M. 1991. Exploring the impact of face-to-face collaborative technology on group writing. *Journal of Management Information Systems,* 8(3), 27–48.

Jones, S. (ed.). 1993. *MILO: A Computer-Based Tool for (Co-)Authoring Structured Documents.* Berlin: Springer Verlag.

Kiesler, S., and Cummings, J.N. 2001. What do we know about proximity and distance in work groups? In P. Hinds and S. Kiesler (eds.), *Distributed Work.* Cambridge, MA: MIT Press.

Kirby, A., and Rodden, T. 1995. Contact: Support for distributed cooperative writing. Paper presented at the Fourth European Conference on Computer-Supported Cooperative Work, Stockholm, Sweden, September 10–14.

Kolfschoten, G.L.; Briggs, R.O.; Appelman, J.H.; and de Vreede, G.-J. 2004. ThinkLets as building blocks for collaboration processes: A further conceptualization. *Lecture Notes on Computer Science,* 3198, 137–152.

Koneri, P.G.; de Vreede, G.-J.; Dean, D.L.; Fruhling, A.L.; and Wolcott, P. 2005. The design and field evaluation of a repeatable collaborative software code inspection process. *Lecture Notes on Computer Science,* 3706, 325–340.

Kraut, R.E.; Galegher, J.; and Egido, C. 1988. Relationships and tasks in scientific research collaboration. *Human-Computer Interaction,* 3, 1, 31–58.

Kreth, M.L. 2000. A survey of the co-op writing experiences of recent engineering graduates. *IEEE Transactions on Professional Communication,* 43, 2, 137–151.

Leland, M.D.P.; Rish, R.S.; and Kraut, R.E. 1988. Collaborative document production using Quilt. Paper presented at the Conference on Computer-Supported Cooperative Work (CSCW'88), Portland, Oregon, September 26–28.

Libert, B., and Spector, J. 2007. *We Are Smarter Than Me: How to Unleash the Power of Crowds in Your Business.* Upper Saddle River, NJ: Wharton School Publishing.

Loehr, L. 1995. Composing in groups: The concept of authority in cross functional project team work. *IEEE Transactions on Professional Communication,* 38, 2, 83–94.

Lourenço, R.P., and Costa, J.P. 2007. Incorporating citizens' views in local policy decision making processes. *Decision Support Systems,* 43, 1499–1511.

Lowry, P.B. 2002a. Proposal of design requirements for collaborative writing tools for distributed work over the Internet. Paper presented at the Americas Conference on Information Systems (AMCIS), Dallas, Texas, August 9–11.

———. 2002b. Research on proximity choices for distributed, asynchronous collaborative writing groups. Paper presented at the Americas Conference on Information Systems (AMCIS), Dallas, Texas, August 9–11.

Lowry, P.B.; Albrecht, C.C.; Nunamaker, J.F. Jr.; and Lee, J.D. 2002. Evolutionary development and research on Internet-based collaborative writing tools and processes to enhance eWriting in an eGovernment setting. *Decision Support Systems,* 34, 3, 229–252.

Lowry, P.B.; Curtis, A.; and Lowry, M.R. 2004. Building a taxonomy of collaborative writing to improve interdisciplinary research and practice. *Journal of Business Communication,* 41, 1, 66–99.

Lowry, P.B., and Nunamaker, J.F. Jr. 2002. Using the thinkLet framework to improve distributed collaborative writing. In *Proceedings of the 35th Annual Hawaii International Conference on System Sciences,* Kona, Hawaii, January 7–10.

———. 2003. Using Internet-based, distributed collaborative writing tools to improve coordination and group awareness in writing teams. *IEEE Transactions on Professional Communication,* 46, 4, 277–297.

Lowry, P.B.; Nunamaker, J.F. Jr.; Booker, Q.E.; Curtis, A.; and Lowry, M.R. 2004. Creating hybrid distributed learning environments by implementing distributed collaborative writing in traditional educational settings. *IEEE Transactions on Professional Communication,* 47, 3, 171–189.

Lowry, P.B.; Nunamaker, J.F. Jr.; Curtis, A.; and Lowry, M.R. 2005. The impact of process structure on novice, Internet-based, asynchronous-distributed collaborative writing teams. *IEEE Transactions on Professional Communication,* 48, 4, 341–364.

Mabrito, M. 1992. Real-time computer network collaboration: Case studies of business writing students. *Journal of Business and Technical Communication,* 6, 3, 316–336.

McIsaac, C.M., and Aschauer, M.A. 1990. Proposal writing at Atherton Jordan, Inc. *Management Communication Quarterly,* 3, 4, 527–560.

Neuwirth, C.M.; Kaufer, D.S.; Chandhok, R.; and Morris, J.H. 1990. Issues in the design of computer-support for co-authoring and commenting. Paper presented at the Third Conference on Computer-Supported Cooperative Work (CSCW'90), Los Angeles, California, October 7–10.

Noël, S., and Robert, J.-M. 2003. How the Web is used to support collaborative writing. *Behaviour and Information Technology,* 22, 4, 245–262.

Nunamaker, J.F. Jr.; Briggs, R.O.; Mittleman, D.D.; Vogel, D.R.; and Balthazard, P.A. 1997. Lessons from a dozen years of group support systems research: A discussion of lab and field findings. *Journal of Management Information Systems,* 13, 3, 163–207.

Odell, L. 1985. Beyond the text: Relations between writing and social context. In L. Odell and D. Goswami (eds.), *Writing in Nonacademic Settings,* 249–280. New York: Guilford.

Olson, J.S.; Olson, G.M.; Storrosten, M.; and Carter, M. 1993. Groupwork close-up—A comparison of the group design process with and without a simple-group editor. *ACM Transactions on Information Systems,* 11, 4, 321–348.

Posner, I.R., and Baecker, R.M. 1992. How people write together. In *Proceedings of the 25th Annual Hawaii International Conference on System Sciences,* Kauai, Hawaii, January 7–10.

Rada, R., and Wang, W. 1998. Computer-supported collaborative writing phases. *Journal of Educational Technology Systems,* 26, 2, 137–149.

Rice, R.P. 1992. Task, analyzability, use of new media, and effectiveness: A multi-site exploration of media-richness. *Organization Science,* 3, 4, 475–500.

Rice, R.P., and Huguley, J.T. Jr. 1994. Describing collaborative forms: A profile of the team-writing process. *IEEE Transactions on Professional Communication,* 37, 3, 163–170.

Santanen, E.L.; Briggs, R.O.; and de Vreede, G.-J. 2004. Causal relationships in creative problem solving: Comparing facilitation interventions for ideation. *Journal of Management Information Systems,* 20, 4, 167–197.

Sasse, M., and Handley, M. 1996. *Collaborative Writing with Synchronous and Asynchronous Support Environments.* London: Academic Press.

Schlichter, J.; Koch, M.; and Burger, M. 1997. Workspace awareness for distributed teams. In W. Conen (ed.), *Lecture Notes on Computer Science,* vol. 1364, 199–218. Munchen, Germany: Springer.

Sharples, M. 1992. Representing writing: External representations and the writing process. In P. Holt and N. Williams (eds.), *Computers and Writing: State of the Art.* Oxford, England: Intellect; Kluwer Academic.

———. 1993. *Adding a Little Structure to Collaborative Writing.* London: Springer-Verlag.

Stratton, C.R. 1989. Collaborative writing in the workplace. *IEEE Transactions on Professional Communication,* 32, 3, 178–182.

Tammaro, S.G.; Moseir, J.N.; Goodwin, N.C.; and Spitz, G. 1997. Collaborative writing is hard to support: A field study of collaborative writing. *Computer-Supported Cooperative Work: The Journal of Collaborative Computing,* 6, 1, 19–51.

Tran, M.H.; Raikundalia, G.K.; and Yang, Y. 2006. Using an experimental field study to develop group awareness support for real-time distributed collaborative writing. *Information and Software Technology,* 48, 1006–1024.

Van de Ven, A., and Delbecq, A. 1974. The effectiveness of nominal, Delphi and interacting group decision-making processes. *Academy of Management Journal,* 17, 4, 605–621.

Watson, R.T. 1987. A study of group decision support system use in three and four person groups for a preference allocation decision. Unpublished doctoral dissertation, University of Minnesota, Minneapolis.

Wilds, N.G. 1989. Writing in the military: A different mission. In C.B. Matalene (ed.), *Worlds of Writing: Teaching and Learning in Discourse Communities of Work.* New York: Random House.

PART III

PROOF OF USE

CHAPTER 11

COLLABORATION SUPPORT TECHNOLOGY

Patterns of Successful Collaboration Support Based
on Three Decades of GSS Research and Use

GWENDOLYN L. KOLFSCHOTEN AND JAY F. NUNAMAKER JR.

Abstract: Collaboration has always been a cornerstone of success in organizations, and yet the importance of collaboration is dramatically increasing in our knowledge economy. With the development of the Internet and especially Web 2.0, a vastly growing amount of tools and technologies to support collaboration are emerging. This chapter will look back at three decades of group support systems (GSS) research, and will elicit patterns and lessons learned on important issues such as the types of problems that are solved with collaboration support technology, the characteristics and attributes of collaboration technology that create value, and the way in which collaboration technologies can be successfully employed in organizations. We discovered two parallel trends in collaboration support technology: the development of very generic multipurpose collaboration tools on one hand, and the development and use of very specific collaboration support tools that are tailored to a specific process or task. Furthermore, we sketch the efforts to support or even eliminate the facilitator, while at the same time we recognize that some facilitation skills will remain in demand, especially for tasks with high social or stakeholder complexity.

Keywords: Collaboration, Collaboration Support Systems, Collaboration Support Technology, Group Support Systems

Collaboration has always been a cornerstone of success in organizations, and yet the importance of collaboration is dramatically increasing in our knowledge economy. With the development of Internet and especially Web 2.0, a vastly growing amount of tools and technologies to support collaboration are emerging. This chapter will look back at three decades of group support systems (GSS) research, and will elicit patterns and lessons learned on three important questions

- What kinds of problems are solved by collaboration support technology?
- What characteristics of collaboration support technology create value?
- How can collaboration support technologies be successfully employed in organizations?

PROBLEMS SOLVED BY COLLABORATION SUPPORT TECHNOLOGY

Collaboration is challenging in several ways (Nunamaker et al., 1997; Schwarz, 1994). Early research showed that as group size increased beyond five people, productivity tended to decrease, and conflicts tended to increase (Steiner, 1972). Thus, collaboration involves several challenges.

Figure 11.1   **Collaboration Challenges**

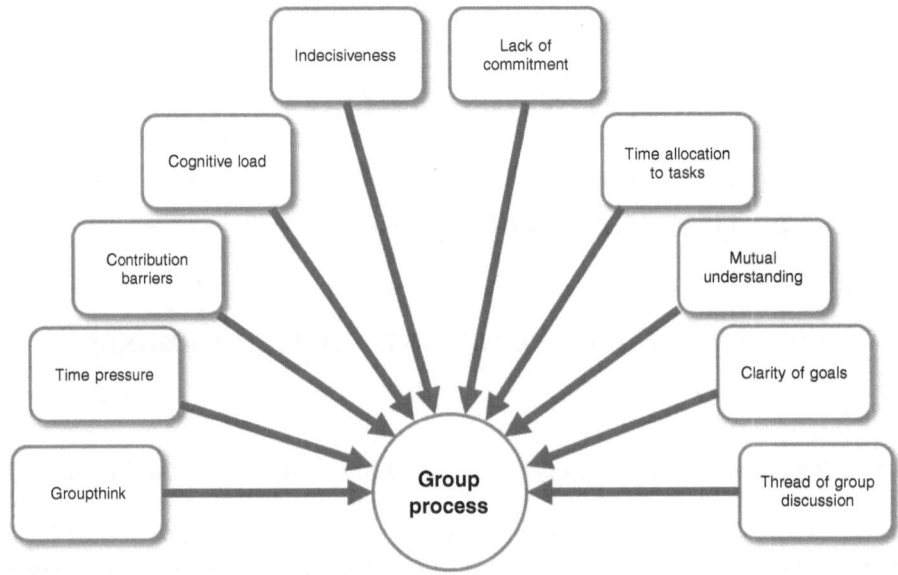

Source: Based on Nunamaker et al., 1991.

Nunamaker et al. (1991) identified these challenges three decades ago. Here we will discuss these challenges and new insights in group challenges in more detail around ten critical issues ranging from groupthink to cognitive load, and from time pressure to indecisiveness, as displayed in Figure 11.1.

We will further explain several of these challenges below.

Groupthink

Groupthink is a phenomenon described by Janis (1972). Groupthink is a state of group in which unanimity or loyalty to the group becomes more important than the content of the proposal, and thus a proposal is accepted without critical reflection. Groupthink can be seen as one of the strongest types of consensus, as all stakeholders are willing to commit. However, a lack of critical reflection can cause acceptance of proposals that are harmful to the group or its environment. Groupthink can be caused by many things including directive leadership, external stress or pressure, isolation, and strong homogeneity in the background of participants. To avoid groupthink, it is vital that a facilitator asks participants to challenge assumptions and to consider different perspectives and alternative explanations (Janis, 1972).

Time Pressure

When input of a group is required for a task, it is almost by definition costly. Spending an extra hour in a meeting with ten participants costs ten man hours. Therefore, in organizational settings there is a key pressure to keep meetings efficient. Efficiency can be thwarted by distraction and a lack of focus. Distraction comes from external sources, ranging from outside noise to personal problems of participants. A lack of focus can be caused by competing tasks. When participants in a process are working on multiple tasks, or have issues on their mind with respect to the joint task that are not the focus of discussion, this can consume attention, or even cause a drift in the focus of the interaction.

Contribution Barriers

When people collaborate, each participant is asked to contribute in some way to the joint product. Contributing in a collaborative setting can have several consequences besides the intended contribution. People in a group in some way depend on each other's input for the task, but also in the long run, when they have interdependent roles in the organization. In light of this they create a mental record of the persons they collaborate with, in which they store information about their competences, goals, behavior, and beliefs, and the alignment of those with their own worldview. When people share information, others will adjust their mental record of that person, especially when people have a more long term, and more interdependent relation. Therefore, when people share information explicitly, they might consider how this will affect the way other people perceive them. This can lead to various barriers in contributing, such as fear of negative judgment of contributions, dominance of some participants, with the intention to direct focus on a particular view on the task, and presumption of intent based on earlier contributions of a person.

Cognitive Load

When group members interact they are asked to send and receive messages, and to accommodate the information they receive to build on their understanding of the task. Furthermore, they are often asked to construct new knowledge from the information they receive. When working individually each of these tasks can also be required, but they can be performed in more distinct steps. Therefore, the limited cognitive attention an individual has can be focused to a single task, which enables higher performance. Collaboration demands that individuals allocate cognitive attention to multiple tasks, and thus requires more cognitive resources. Researchers assume that the cognitive capacity of an individual is limited (Bjork-Ligon and Bjork, 1996). Therefore, collaboration can easily result in cognitive overload; a situation in which participants cannot cope with the information they receive and therefore are forced to make choices in the cognitive tasks they perform, leading to lower overall performance. In different ways the cognitive load of a collaborative activity can be reduced; however, research to understand the precise sources of this "collaboration load" and the ways to structure tasks in order to optimize the use of cognitive effort is still in a preliminary phase (Dillenbourg and Betrancourt, 2006; Henninger et al., 2006).

Indecisiveness

Group discussions can be enduring when focus keeps changing. Some reasons for this can be that the goal of the group effort is unclear or not articulated. Even if the meeting goal is articulated, the meeting organizers can have a different perception of the stakeholder's goals, or the goal might be irrelevant for some stakeholders. It is also possible that stakeholders can, despite clear articulation of the goal, have conflicting expectations, or hidden agendas. While clarity of the goal can be resolved through sense making, hidden or changing agendas are more difficult to deal with. A lack of goal congruence is challenging as it disperses focus in the collaborative effort. It allows stakeholders to continuously change the proposal of consensus building. While it is useful to add issues to the conflict to create a win-win situation (de Bruijn and Heuvelhof, 2008) changing the overall purpose of the collaboration makes the process highly ineffective. In some conflicts, groups have to wait for a "window of opportunity": a state in which goals of the stakeholders are (temporally) aligned (de Bruijn and Heuvelhof, 2008).

Lack of Commitment

Willingness to participate in a collaborative effort requires that the goal of this effort is in some way instrumental to the stakeholders, and not conflicting with their personal goals. To achieve such goal congruence, a goal should be acceptable by all stakeholders. This can be achieved by formulating the goal broad enough to accommodate stakeholder's interests. In defining the proposal, the scope of the agreement can be further narrowed to find a consensus, keeping all stakeholders on board. Commitment has four key sources (Meyer and Allen, 1991): commitment to keep things the same, to preserve relations, commitment because the cost benefit analysis of the collaborative task is positive, and commitment because of pressure of others. To encourage participation, understanding and accommodation of individual stakes is important.

Time Allocation to Tasks

Besides these challenges of collaborative interaction, structuring collaboration can also be challenging. The most common way to structure collaborative effort is to set an agenda. An agenda is a plan, usually described in a document, that guides the activities of the group, or the topics they involve within the scope of their goal or target for the meeting (Niederman et al., 1996; Niederman and Volkema, 1996). Nunamaker et al. (1997) indicated that agendas are of vital importance when meetings are supported using GSS. de Vreede et al. (2003a) showed that not only the lack of an agenda, but also the choice of activities and topics can have an important impact on the success of the meeting. When topics are not important in the eyes of the participants, when they are unclear, or when topics are missing from the agenda, this can decrease participation and effort of participants. Also, when the time allocated to topics is not in balance with their relative importance, this might cause dissatisfaction of participants or poor results.

Mutual Understanding

In order to align goals and to jointly construct knowledge, the participants in a group process need some basis for shared understanding. The most extreme cases of misunderstanding occur when people do not speak the same language, or when their language skills are limited in the shared language. Furthermore, when participants have the same mother language, misunderstanding can occur due to different backgrounds such as education or expertise domains, education levels, and cultural backgrounds. A lack of understanding can cause disagreement and conflict which can result in poor outcomes and frustration (de Vreede et al., 2003a). It is therefore important to select participants that have some shared understanding, or spend time to construct a mutual understanding on key concepts. Also, it is important to verify mutual understanding in all key phases and steps of the process.

Clarity of Goals

When time is allocated to the appropriate tasks and goals, it needs to be communicated to the participants. This can happen both in advance or during the collaborative effort. However, in many ways, a lack of clarity about the goal of the meeting can cause failure or dissatisfaction (de Vreede et al., 2003a). First, when the goal is not clear, people might be disappointed about the results of the meeting, as their expectations are not met. Second, it might remain unknown that parts of the task have already been addressed or performed in other settings, causing the group to reinvent the wheel or do double work. Third, when the goal is unclear people might judge that it is not worth their effort and depending on when the goal is clarified, can cause a lack of participation before (no show) or during (free-riding) the collaborative effort. Finally, when confusion about the goal persists during the collaborative effort, effort is not focused, which can lead to poor results.

Threat of Group Decisions

Reaching agreement with a group of stakeholders is challenging, but when such agreement is achieved, it can be difficult to ignore or reverse. Group decisions have the buy-in and commitment of several stakeholders, are costly, and offer a basis for next steps. For a single individual it will be difficult to change a decision once approved or confirmed by a group. When a participant expects an outcome or decision that has a negative impact on stakes s/he represents, or on personal stakes, a strategy can be implemented to aim for no result or decision at all. When the consent of such a stakeholder is required, that stakeholder can have a blocking power (de Bruijn and Heuvelhof, 2008). When a stakeholder is not explicit about the intention to block a decision the process can become highly time consuming and frustrating for the other group members.

Given the challenges listed above, we can state that collaboration support is worthwhile and often necessary, not only to improve quality and efficiency, but also to support participation and feedback of larger groups such as users, customers, employees, or students. Collaboration technology can offer such support through a number of important characteristics. In the next section, these characteristics are discussed.

CHARACTERISTICS OF COLLABORATION TECHNOLOGY

The first generation of collaboration support technology was developed at universities, and called group support systems or group decision support systems. A *group support system* (GSS) is a suite of software tools for focusing and structuring group deliberation, while reducing the cognitive costs of communication and information access among teams making a joint cognitive effort toward a goal (Davison and Briggs, 2000). GSS are networks of hardware and software that support groups in their collaborative effort with a set of tools to coordinate their effort. GSS are a specific type of groupware. Typical tools in a GSS are brainstorming tools in which participants can add ideas to a shared page; structuring and commenting tools to reflect or elaborate on ideas; clustering and modeling tools, to organize ideas; and voting tools to evaluate and compare ideas, and to build consensus on the value of contributions. Some GSS only offer voting tools and can work with a voting system without workstations for each participant. Some screenshots of a GSS tool named Group Systems and the setting in which it can be used can be found in Figure 11.2.

GSS have a number of characteristics that since have developed in powerful collaboration support technology features.

Figure 11.2   **GSS Collaboration Room and Screen Shots of GroupSystems**

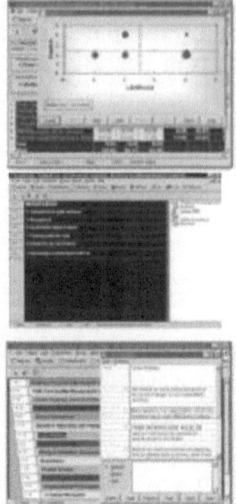

Parallelism

Participants can add, evaluate, and organize topics, ideas, or point of views simultaneously (Bostrom et al., 1992). This means that the disadvantage of waiting for a speaking turn is avoided. The result is a saving on meeting time (de Vreede et al., 2003b). Today, the added value of parallel communication is most apparent in Wikipedia, a large encyclopedia developed by contributions of the masses.

Anonymity

The software can enable participants to choose to work anonymously (Bostrom et al., 1992). This means that each idea is valued on content and not on the reputation of the author. Dominance in a meeting is avoided in this way (Nunamaker et al., 1997). Further, anonymity reduces barriers to participate, as it enables participants to contribute "half" ideas, or critical comments without losing face, or being accused. However, sometimes responsibility or the need for recognition might require identification of contributions. In social software the use of anonymity has emerged in very different ways. In some platforms identity is a critical driver of participation, and recommendation systems ensure that people gain status based on their contributions. An example of this is LinkedIn or Facebook. Another approach is found in platforms like Second Life, where one can explore becoming another personality. Especially in public and larger platforms, some level of identification is required to avoid "abuse" and commercial use.

Electronic Recording and Representation

Every idea, topic, or point of view is stored. This delivers more accurate and objective minutes and allows users to use the data processing capacity of computers to aggregate voting results or to analyze text (Bostrom et al., 1992). Traditional workshop leaders still make use of different types of sticky notes and markers to create this effect, adding a creative, active, and participative atmosphere. While this characteristic has become a true commodity, its capacity and strength is still rapidly developing. Today, artificial intelligence is used to mine text and large data streams to distill meaningful information and support decision making.

Deliberation Through Typing

When people type in ideas, they generally reflect slightly more on the formulation of their contribution than when they speak. This improves precision and supports shared understanding (Weatherall and Nunamaker, 2000). Often collaboration support systems can be customized to restrict or guide users in their contribution, requesting them to address specific information in their contribution to sharpen it, and ensuring sufficient detail.

Dual Communication Channels

Using the GSS in a face to face setting, the group has two separate communication channels at its availability: the computer network with a central screen and face to face communication. This enables the group to separate content and metacommunication, which is a very powerful way of structuring and focusing the discussion. Similar functionality is now also offered, for instance, through Skype voice and chat, and in collaboration environments such as SharePoint and Sametime.

Because of these characteristics, various advantages of group work (e.g., synergy, mutual stimulation, knowledge sharing, etc.) can be created. The effect of potential disadvantages (e.g., dominance, incomplete use of information) can be diminished. Because of this, a higher level of productivity and a better quality of results can be achieved (Nunamaker et al., 1997). Field studies on GSS show that they are often perceived to be more efficient and effective than manual meetings. Furthermore, participants are more satisfied in a GSS meeting than in a manual meeting (Fjermestad and Hiltz 2001). In a benchmark study where Boeing, ING-NN, IBM and EADS-M were compared, efficiency was improved with more than 50 percent both on meeting time and on project time, and "effectiveness compared to manual" and "user satisfaction" were rated 4.1 on average at a 5-point scale (de Vreede et al., 2003b). This increase in effectiveness, efficiency, and satisfaction is caused by a combination of the characteristics of GSS and facilitation. Users believe facilitation to be a critical success factor (de Vreede et al., 2002). While research has proven that the benefits of GSS are significant both in terms of quality improvement and in terms of efficiency and cost saving, implementing collaboration support in organizations is not trivial. It is difficult to create a business case for the implementation of collaboration support in organizations (Agres et al., 2005; Briggs et al., 2003; Post, 1993). Although the added value as described above is substantial, it is difficult to predict and document this added value. This difficulty may be due, in part, to the fact that collaboration support (facilitator and GSS hardware and software) poses highly visible costs, whereas improvements may be less visible and are difficult to measure and assign to specific budget categories. Many case studies reported that a single "champion" was responsible for the success of a GSS in an organization, with the consequence that once such a "champion" moves on or away, the facilities are abandoned. Collaboration often contributes to important processes in the organization, but not often to the central production process. Further, collaboration support is often required for "special" events, which do not occur on a frequent basis, making the generated value unpredictable in a budget plan. This makes it easier to eliminate such facilities during a budget crunch.

Summarized, the barriers for successful sustained use of GSS include:

- Skills required for facilitation.

- Need for a champion.
- Difficulty to visualize benefits.
- Lack of direct contribution to the primary production process.
- Unpredictable frequency of value.
- Difficulty to allocate costs to users.

In this last section we will demonstrate how we can guide the implementation and use of collaboration support to overcome some of these challenges.

IMPLEMENTATION AND USE OF COLLABORATION SUPPORT TECHNOLOGY

The challenges of implementing GSS can be seen as a pattern in social software and more in general in email and Internet use (Porter and Millar, 1985), as well as related fields such as Knowledge Management (Jennex and Olfman, 2004). For GSS, overwhelming evidence of success was recorded, and yet, researchers had to search for other means to guide and support successful implementation, as "proof of usefulness" was not sufficient to trigger a broad adoption and use.

Dennis et al. (2001) identified facilitation, training, and restriction as a mediator's successful appropriation of GSS tools. More recently, Collaboration Engineering has been presented as an approach to overcome the challenges of the implementation and use of Collaboration Support Tools, using thinkLets and Computer Supported Collaboration Engineering (CACE) suites to develop dedicated groupware for recurring collaborative tasks.

Training

Training for collaboration support can help teams by improving their communication skills and teaching them methods to overcome conflict. However, training would only be valuable if the trained team was to collaborate on a frequent basis, and even then it is costly to train all team members. Training is often focused on changing the behavior of collaborators. For instance, Schwarz (1994) offers a set of rules that instruct people to share information and to reduce the chance of personal conflict. Although these approaches are likely to increase the efficiency of the group, they are not specifically designed to support the group in accomplishing their goal. For this, specific methods for group work such as brainstorming and discussion techniques can be used. There are many such techniques and it would be very extensive to train teams in all of them along with their different applications.

Facilitation

A facilitator supports a group in achieving its goals by offering tools and techniques to support its collaborative effort. Facilitation is a process and task. As a process, facilitation can be described as a dynamic process that involves managing relationships between people, tasks, and technology, as well as structuring tasks and contributing to the effective accomplishment of the meeting's outcome (Bostrom et al., 1993). The facilitation task is a set of functions or activities carried out before, during, and after a meeting to help the group achieve its "own" outcomes (Bostrom et al., 1993). The tasks of a facilitator are numerous. Firstly, the facilitator prepares the meeting together with the client or problem owner. Preparation deals mostly with the logistics of the process, inviting participants, organizing location, and preparing resources, tools, and technology as instructed (Ackermann, 1996; Clawson et al., 1993; Dickson et al., 1996; Hayne, 1999; Niederman et al.,

1996; de Vreede et al., 2002). During the execution of the collaboration process, the task of the facilitator is to help the group to focus on the goal and outcomes, to give instructions, to guide discussion, to ensure participations, to maintain rules, and to support the use of technology. Finally, an important task for the facilitator is to deal with the dynamics of the group process, including managing conflict and emotions and supporting decision making and consensus building.

Restriction

It is reported that restriction of functionality to only the tools that are used for the specific task might be a way to offer guidance in the use of GSS, and constrain participants from activities that are "unfaithful" to the meeting agenda (Dennis et al., 2001; Silver, 1990). Traditionally, GSS have been built to enable users, particularly the "leader" or facilitator to configure a large set of user rights and access in order to improve the fit between tasks and tools. This high configurability makes the extent to which the functionality of the tool is restricted flexible. A current trend in GSS is to offer less configurability in order to reduce cognitive load of use for facilitators and users. Naturally, restriction works only when exactly those capabilities are offered that afford the activities in the agenda.

Research in the area of Collaboration Engineering has developed to avail groups with facilitation and restricted technology they can use for themselves without the use of professionals or technical experts. Collaboration Engineering is an approach to design and deploy collaboration support for high value recurring tasks (Briggs et al., 2003). To enable practitioners to use professional facilitation skills, design patterns called thinkLets are utilized. In addition, to enable the use and appropriation of collaboration technology, a new generation of GSS is currently available, which offers both Computer Aided Collaboration Support methods to guide the selection and configuration of tools for the specific task, and Collaboration Support Systems that offer a highly restricted end user environment that guides the group though the process.

ThinkLets

To design a predictable, transferable, reusable collaboration process the Collaboration Engineering approach uses design patterns called thinkLets. ThinkLets are design patterns collected in a pattern language for designing collaborative work practices. ThinkLets can be combined to create a sequence of steps that can be used by a group to execute the steps of a collaborative work practice in order to achieve collaborative goals. As with other pattern languages, thinkLets are used as design patterns, as design documentation, as a language for discussing complex and subtle design choices, and as training devices for transferring designs to practitioners in organizations (Kolfschoten et al., 2006; de Vreede et al., 2006). Research has shown that participant evaluations of satisfaction and efficiency of sessions run by practitioners using thinkLets was not significantly different than the scores obtained in similar settings by professional facilitators (Kolfschoten et al., 2009).

Computer Assisted Collaboration Engineering (CACE)

To support the rapid design of customized task specific collaboration support systems, a CACE tool could be developed (Briggs et al., 2010; Kolfschoten et al., 2009; Kolfschoten and Veen, 2005). Prototypes have been developed and current research projects are performed to further develop an environment that enables the rapid design of collaboration support environments that are focused on specific tasks. Such systems would offer users and groups more guidance in their collaborative tasks and therewith help groups to appropriate the tools in a way that makes them more effective.

CONCLUSION

In this chapter we described some patterns in the research on GSS, and how these patterns can be recognized in the more recent developments in collaboration support technology such as social software and new generation GSS. The chapter describes the important challenges of collaboration, the key characteristics of collaboration support technology, and the different ways in which adoption and use of these technologies is facilitated. We see a dual trend in these systems. On one hand very simple tools with a broad applicability are offered (e.g., Skype, SharePoint); on the other hand effort is made to design collaboration support that is highly tailored to the specific collaborative task, using restriction to ensure efficient and effective use of the technology. Finally, there will also remain a market for facilitated collaboration. While successful efforts have been made to transfer process guidance, facilitators also have a role in conflict mediation, team building, involving multiple perspectives and the stimulation of creative or critical thinking. These kind of effects can be supported by technology, but also require leadership and charisma, skills that cannot yet be coded in software.

REFERENCES

Ackermann, F. 1996. Participants' perceptions on the role of facilitators using group decision support systems. *Group Decision and Negotiation,* 5, 93–519.

Agres, A.; de Vreede, G.J.; and Briggs, R.O. 2005. A tale of two cities: Case studies of GSS transition in two organizations. *Group Decision and Negotiation,* 14, 4, 256–266.

Bjork-Ligon, E., and Bjork, R.A. (eds.). 1996. *Memory Handbook of Perception and Cognition.* San Diego, CA: Academic Press.

Bostrom, R.; Anson, R.; and Clawson, V.K. 1993. Group facilitation and group support systems. In L.M. Jessup and J.S. Valacich (eds.), *Group Support Systems: New Perspectives.* New York: Macmillan.

Bostrom, R.P.; Watson, R.T.; and Kinney, S.T. (eds.). 1992. *Computer Augmented Teamwork: A Guided Tour.* New York: Van Nostrand Reinhold.

Briggs, R.O.; Kolfschoten, G.L.; de Vreede, G.J.; Albrecht, C.C.; and Lukosch, S.G. 2010. Facilitator in a box: Computer assisted collaboration engineering and process support systems for rapid development of collaborative applications for high-value tasks. In *Proceedings of the 43rd Annual Hawaii International Conference on System Sciences,* Kauai, Hawaii, January 4–7.

Briggs, R.O.; de Vreede, G.J.; and Nunamaker, J.F. Jr. 2003. Collaboration engineering with thinkLets to pursue sustained success with group support systems. *Journal of Management Information Systems,* 19, 4, 31–63.

de Bruijn, J.A., and ten Heuvelhof, E.F. 2008. *Management in Networks: On Multi-Actor Decision Making.* London: Routledge.

Clawson, V.K.; Bostrom, R.; and Anson, R. 1993. The role of the facilitator in computer-supported meetings. *Small Group Research,* 24, 4, 547–565.

Davison, R.M., and Briggs, R.O. 2000. GSS for presentation support: Supercharging the audience through simultaneous discussions during presentations. *Communications of the ACM,* 43, 9, 91–97.

Dennis, A.R.; Wixom, B.H.; and Vandenberg, R.J. 2001. Understanding fit and appropriation effects in group support systems via meta-analysis. *Management Information Systems Quarterly,* 25, 2, 167–183.

Dickson, G.W.; Limayem, M.; Lee Partridge, J.; and DeSanctis, G. 1996. Facilitating computer supported meetings: A cumulative analysis in a multiple criteria task environment. *Group Decision and Negotiation,* 5, 1, 51–72.

Dillenbourg, P., and Betrancourt, M. 2006. Collaboration load. In J. Elen and R.E. Clark (eds.), *Handling Complexity in Learning Environments: Theory and Research,* 142–163. Oxford, UK: Elsevier.

Fjermestad, J., and Hiltz, S.R. 2001. A descriptive evaluation of group support systems case and field studies. *Journal of Management Information Systems,* 17, 3, 115–159.

Hayne, S.C. 1999. The facilitator's perspective on meetings and implications for group support systems design. *DataBase*, 30, 3–4, 72–91.

Henninger, W.G., Dennis, A.R., and Hilmer, K. 2006. Individual cognition and dual-task interference in group support systems. *Information Systems Research*, 17, 4, 415–424.

Janis, I.L. 1972. *Victims of Groupthink: A Psychological Study of Foreign-Policy Decisions and Fiascoes.* Boston, MA: Houghton Mifflin Company.

Jennex, M.E., and Olfman, L. 2004. Assessing knowledge management success/effectiveness models. In *Proceedings of the 37th Annual Hawaii International Conference on System Sciences,* Waikoloa, Hawaii, January 5–8.

Kolfschoten, G.L.; Briggs, R.O.; and de Vreede, G.J. 2009. A technology for pattern-based process design and its application to collaboration engineering. In S. Rummler and K.B. Ng (eds.), *Collaborative Technologies and Applications for Interactive Information Design: Emerging Trends in User Experiences,* 1–18. Hershey, PA: Information Science Reference.

Kolfschoten, G.L.; Briggs, R.O.; de Vreede, G.J.; Jacobs, P.H.M.; and Appelman, J.H. 2006. Conceptual foundation of the thinkLet concept for collaboration engineering. *International Journal of Human Computer Science,* 64, 7, 611–621.

Kolfschoten, G.L.; Duivenvoorde, G.P.J.; Briggs, R.O.; and de Vreede, G.J. 2009. Practitioners vs. facilitators a comparison of participant perceptions on success. In *Proceedings of the 42nd Annual Hawaii International Conference on System Sciences,* Waikoloa, Hawaii, January 5–8.

Kolfschoten, G.L., and Veen, W. 2005. Tool support for GSS session design. In *Proceedings of the 38th Annual Hawaii International Conference on System Sciences,* Waikoloa, Hawaii, January 3–6.

Meyer, J.P., and Allen, N.J. 1991. A three-component conceptualization of organizational commitment: Some methodological considerations. *Human Resource Management Review,* 1, 61–98.

Niederman, F.; Beise, C.M.; and Beranek, P.M. 1996. Issues and concerns about computer-supported meetings: The facilitator's perspective. *Management Information Systems Quarterly,* 20, 1, 1–22.

Niederman, F., and Volkema, R. 1996. Influence of agenda creation and use on meeting activities and outcomes: Report on initial results. Paper presented at the ACM SIGCPR/SIGMIS Conference on Personnel Research, Denver, CO, April 11–13.

Nunamaker, J.F. Jr.; Briggs, R.O.; Mittleman, D.D.; Vogel, D.; and Balthazard, P.A. 1997. Lessons from a dozen years of group support systems research: A discussion of lab and field findings. *Journal of Management Information Systems,* 13, 3, 163–207.

Nunamaker, J.F., Jr.; Dennis, A.; Valacich, J.; Vogel, D.; and George, J.F. 1991. Electronic meeting systems to support group work. *Communications of the ACM,* 34, 7, 40–61.

Porter, M.E., and Millar, V.E. 1985. How information gives you competitive advantage. *Harvard Business Review,* 63, 4, 149–160.

Post, B.Q. 1993. A business case framework for group support technology. *Journal of Management Information Systems,* 9, 3, 7–26.

Schwarz, R.M. 1994. *The Skilled Facilitator.* San Francisco, CA: Jossey-Bass.

Silver, M.S. 1990. Decision support systems: Directed and non-directed change. *Information Systems Research,* 1, 47–70.

Steiner, I.D. 1972. *Group Process and Productivity.* New York: Academic Press.

de Vreede, G.J.; Boonstra, J.; and Niederman, F.A. 2002. What is effective GSS facilitation? A qualitative inquiry into participants' perceptions. In *Proceedings of the 35th Annual Hawaii International Conference on System Sciences,* Waikoloa, Hawaii, January 7–10.

de Vreede, G.J.; Briggs, R.O.; and Kolfschoten, G.L. 2006. ThinkLets: A pattern language for facilitated and practitioner-guided collaboration processes. *International Journal of Computer Applications in Technology,* 25, 2/3, 140–154.

de Vreede, G.J.; Davison, R.; and Briggs, R.O. 2003a. How a silver bullet may lose its shine—learning from failures with group support systems. *Communications of the ACM,* 46, 8, 96–101.

de Vreede, G.J.; Vogel, D.R.; Kolfschoten, G.L.; and Wien, J.S. 2003b. Fifteen years of in-situ GSS use: A comparison across time and national boundaries. In *Proceedings of the 36th Annual Hawaii International Conference on System Sciences,* Waikoloa, Hawaii, January 6–9.

Weatherall, A., and Nunamaker, J.F. Jr. 2000. *Getting Results with Electronic Meetings,* 3rd ed. Chichester, UK: St. Richards's Press Ltd.

CHAPTER 12

GROUPSYSTEMS IN THE U.S. ARMY

JAMES GANTT

Abstract: In the early 1980s, the U.S. Army started using collaborative tools such as GroupSystems. This paper traces the use and development of GroupSystems across more than a twenty year period. Looking at early successes and failures, lessons are drawn on how to apply collaborative tools in an organization. The role of GroupSystems in preparing for Year 2000 Problem or Y2K and the development of the army for the war on terrorism (Afghanistan and Iraq) is also examined.

Keywords: GroupSystems, Collaborative Tools, Military Applications

In the early 1980s the U.S. Army Communications Command at Fort Huachuca, Arizona, started supporting research being conducted at the University of Arizona in collaborative decision making. Early versions of GroupSystems were used for varied applications. Use was limited because the software was available only for use in a room at the University of Arizona. Because of the limited availability, the army uses tended to be one time meetings that were unique in their purpose. While the benefits of such meetings were easily seen even with early versions of the software, acceptance of collaborative decision for day-to-day activities was not practical.

This paper traces the use of GroupSystems in the army across more than a twenty year period. Looking at early successes and failures, lessons are drawn on how to apply collaborative tools in an organization. The role of GroupSystems in preparing for Y2K and the development of the army for the war on terrorism is also examined.

GroupSystems is one example of a class of collaborative tools that allow many people to work on the same problem. Initially, support of groups during face-to-face meetings was the only mode of use. The tools in the GroupSystems provided support for brainstorming, ranking, voting, writing, and similar tasks. The ability of people to work on the same problem at the same time provided a multiplier of effort that was measurable. Over the years GroupSystems moved out of fixed facilities and became mobile and able to go to the customer. While these sessions were still face-to-face, the need for distributed, asynchronous sessions became obvious. The asynchronous sessions were especially appealing for follow-up work of an on-going group.

AIRMICS (1982–1992)

In 1982 the Army Institute for Research in Management Information, Communications, and Computer Sciences (AIRMICS) became the research group for the newly formed U.S. Army Information Systems Command (ISC). ISC was formed by adding most army computer and information resources to the Army Communications Command to expand the mission to manage all information resources in the army. AIRMICS had been the research arm of the U.S. Army Computer

Systems Command which became the U.S. Army Information Systems Engineering Command (ISEC). ISEC was a subordinate command under the ISC. The first Commanding General of ISC was Lieutenant General (LTG) Emmett Paige. LTG Paige was a visionary leader given the task of creating a unified information infrastructure. He was faced with moving a military culture from a communications focus to an information focus. He was extremely supportive of research and introduced AIRMICS to the group decision-making research being done at the University of Arizona.

AIRMICS worked with the University of Arizona to demonstrate the power of electronic meetings. Typical applications involved brainstorming, ranking, and voting. While these were powerful sessions there was not a repeatable application that was important enough to create an urgent demand for the software. While there was value in doing a onetime event, the acceptance of the tools into an organization depended upon finding a significant process that needed to be done on an on-going basis. The investment in facilities and training of facilitators was not justified by a series of disjointed events. The University of Arizona added an additional room that allowed larger groups, and the software continued to evolve and expand. Demonstration sessions were held with many army groups. However, the search continued for that "killer" problem that required GroupSystems to successfully solve.

PROGRAM MANAGER INSTALLATION SUPPORT MODULES

The first significant repeatable use of GroupSystems within the army came when the approach was used to support the Program Manager Installation Support Modules (PM ISM). AIRMICS and the University of Arizona had identified the problem domain of software requirements definition as a potentially repeatable application of GroupSystems. Colonel (COL) Wayne Bird as PM ISM was charged with developing common application modules to be used at all army installations around the world. COL Bird was using a structured approach that included bringing a small number of subject matter experts to a location for a two to three week requirements definition workshop. Because of the lengthy process, it was difficult to get top people to attend and it also meant that the breadth of knowledge was limited by the relatively small number of people involved. When the concept of GroupSystems was shown to COL Bird he immediately agreed to try it on his definition process.

The use of electronic meeting software allowed a much larger (twenty-five or more people versus six to eight before) and more diverse group of subject matter experts to come together to share their experience and knowledge in defining the module requirements. It was evident at the first session that the potential was being fulfilled. Having a larger number of people involved in the process produced a more comprehensive product. It also meant that there was better organizational buy-in since more organizations were involved in the development process. In general, it was felt that the quality and quantity of work done exceeded what had been done in the requirement workshops. Even if all other things were equal, the change in workshop duration would have been sufficient to change to the new approach. With GroupSystems the process was completed in less than three days, or a five to one reduction in time spent in the requirement process.

In one of these sessions, for example, twenty people participated in producing a requirements document in three and a half days that participants who were experienced in similar nonsupported sessions estimated would have taken four to six weeks without the tools. A project manager who was one of the participants estimated cost savings to be between $75,000 and $125,000. Another of these sessions took four and a half days to develop a functional description for a management information system. Future sessions recommended by management were estimated to produce savings of over $1,250,000, including personnel salaries (Gantt, 1992).

Because of the initial successes, the process was institutionalized and repeated over an extended period of time. A limitation on the process was the requirement to go to the University of Arizona for all the sessions. This was a short-term problem that was solved when GroupSystems became commercially available and was championed by many Washington area consulting groups. The consulting groups were able to offer their own facilities and quality facilitators that enabled many groups to utilize the tools for a variety of processes. Some of the most successful companies remained in the information requirements definition area. While the application of GroupSystems to support PM ISM was successful, the ISM project did not succeed because of applications development problems and change management issues unrelated to GroupSystems.

OTHER USES OF GROUPSYSTEMS

AIRMICS continued to expand uses of GroupSystems by implementing a portable electronic meeting facility. Breaking the bond of having to take people to fixed facilities, at the University of Arizona, expanded the number of groups able to experiment with GroupSystems. The state-of-the-art in "portable" computers was primitive by current standards. The size, weight, and cost of "portable" computers were a limiting factor. However, a portable configuration was developed and resulted in a significant increase in the use of the technology. In many cases a successful use of GroupSystems using a portable system resulted in a fixed installation being developed.

There was even some experimentation with early wireless technology. These experiments were generally successful. The systems did tend to work but were much slower than what we would accept today. In normal size groups (ten to fifteen users) the speed of the wireless networks was not a problem. Larger groups did put a strain on the wireless system and resulted in problems with user acceptance of the technology. This confirmed the need for a good network whether it is wireless or wired.

ARMY RESEARCH LABORATORY (1992–2004)

In the fall of 1992 AIRMICS became part of a new organization called the U.S. Army Research Laboratory (ARL). The ARL group in Atlanta continued to support research in collaborative decision making and electronic meetings. At this time, GroupSystems was accepted by many consulting groups in the Washington, DC, area. The Department of Defense (DoD) was trying to accomplish on a department wide level the same type of requirement analysis that COL Bird had done for the army at the installation level. GroupSystems provided DoD with the same type of productivity improvements seen by PM ISM. It is interesting that the DoD project experienced a similar failure to produce lasting results in the form of implemented systems. However, since GroupSystems was now available as a commercial software product, it became possible to share the technology with various groups in DoD.

The portable systems initially developed by AIRMICS continued to be used to demonstrate the collaborative meeting technology and explore new ways to apply the technology. The portable system was taken to Germany to support simulation research and then applied to a project that developed the army structure that was used so effectively in the 2003 invasion of Iraq.

LOUISIANA MANEUVERS

In 1992 General Gordon Sullivan, Chief of Staff of the army, initiated a project called the Louisiana Maneuvers (LAM). LAM was named after a series of field exercises the army held in

Louisiana during 1940 when the Army Chief of Staff General George Marshall became alarmed by Nazi Germany's Blitzkrieg victory in France. The exercises helped develop leaders and tactics that enabled the United States to be victorious in World War II. In his biography General Franks points out that "General Sullivan intended to use the end of the Cold War, as the Army withdrew formations from Europe, to shape and hone a leaner, but more flexible and lethal, fighting force" (Franks, 2004, p. 167).

The Louisiana Maneuvers Task Force was set up at Fort Monroe, Virginia, with Brigadier General (BG) Tommy Franks as the director. In his biography, General Franks says that "the job of the LAM Task Force was to explore the potential of innovative technology, doctrine, procedures, and training to ensure that this leaner war-fighting force would also remain the world's most powerful" (Franks, 2004, p. 168). It is appropriate that General Franks would develop the future army that he would be called upon to lead into Afghanistan and Iraq in 2003.

The need for an electronic meeting environment was pointed out by BG Franks when he described his job in his biography. "My position as a brigadier general task force director was similar to that of a vice president in a large corporation. Its board of directors was comprised of the chief of staff and the Army's four-star generals. And, as in the corporate world, we had no shortage of consultants—a group of two-star generals with expertise in all facets of Army operations" (Franks, 2004, p. 168). The "consultants" were called the General Officer Working Group (GOWG). As General Franks said, the GOWG was made up of one and two star generals from around the army. The first meeting of this group was held at Fort Monroe, Virginia, and used a traditional meeting facilitator from a well-known think tank. The result from the two day brainstorming session was a set of briefing slides with nothing to back them up except the memory of BG Franks. One of the senior members of BG Franks' staff knew about the work done by ARL using GroupSystems and he convinced BG Franks to visit the ARL office on the Georgia Tech campus in Atlanta (the former AIRMICS group). A simple demonstration convinced the general that this was a tool that he needed to try.

When the fifteen generals walked into the conference room for the second LAM GOWG they were each faced with a computer. The first person that had to be convinced to use the tools was the facilitator from the think tank. This was not an easy task. She quickly realized that she was no longer the center of attention. She no longer controlled the speed or direction of the process. The process was now controlled by the participants. She was also no longer the filter that controlled the outcome of the process. All comments were now captured and could be synthesized into the final product. This approach contrasted with the previous method where she decided what was written on the flip chart. While she did not directly hinder the process of using the new technology, she was not asked back to facilitate any future sessions. One of the lessons we learned from this was that it is not always easy to take someone who is a good facilitator for a traditional meeting and convert them into a facilitator for a computer supported meeting, using tools like GroupSystems. It is also evident that it takes training in the computer supported tools to make someone an effective facilitator. It was also evident that very good facilitators eagerly accepted new tools because they saw that the increase in participation and productivity was worth the changes in the way they did things.

The experience level of the generals with computers covered the entire spectrum. Some generals were very experienced and took to the electronic process with ease. One of the generals had never touched a computer or typewriter. He was totally lost and embarrassed. It turned out that he had a computer in his office, but his secretary printed out all documents including email and he never touched his machine. Exposing senior leaders to computers was a side benefit that General Sullivan wanted from the process. Today all army senior leaders are totally reliant on secure computer connectivity. All generals carry wireless PDA's and are constantly in touch. It is not uncommon to see general officers reading or replying to email during meetings. GroupSystems worked as advertised and was used twice a year for all LAM GOWG meetings until the LAM Task Force completed its work.

The results from the sessions were impressive. Instead of ending the meeting with only a few slides and no backup, BG Franks had all of the input from two days of intense activity by fifteen skilled individuals. The group was able to move beyond brainstorming and ranking to use almost all the tools in the GroupSystems tool chest. Another side benefit of the approach was the ability to increase the size of the GOWG. As people became aware of the project more organizations wanted to have a voice in the products of the LAM Task Force. The GOWG grew to over forty general officers and senior civilians. The acceptance of the process was evident by the fact that the final few meetings were held at the Army War College in Carlisle, Pennsylvania, where a fixed electronic meeting facility had been built and was being used for many group meetings and classes.

General Tommy Franks used GroupSystems to shape the army of the future, the Army that he led into Afghanistan and Iraq. The LAM Task Force was leading a wide ranging look at how to transform the U.S. Army in light of the collapse of the Warsaw Pact. As he stated in his book, "The context for this wide-ranging reevaluation was the idea that America would no longer require a huge, expensive ground force based overseas. Instead the Army's war-fighting units would be stationed in the United States, and would be trained and equipped as a Power Projection force, able to deploy quickly anywhere in the world in time of crisis or conflict" (Franks, 2004, pp. 168–69). The transformed army worked as it was envisioned. Electronic meeting technology contributed to the development of the "new" army.

SYNTHETIC THEATER OF WAR-EUROPE (STOW-E)

Simulation was identified during the LAM Task Force work as a critical part of the process to transform the Army. A series of exercises were conducted called the Synthetic Theater of War (STOW). The STOW exercises blended real troops with simulated forces in a seamless fashion. In 1994 an exercise was conducted in Europe called STOW-Europe (STOW-E) that included NATO allies in the mix. Because of the success using GroupSystems with the LAM GOWG, ARL was invited to take the portable system to Europe to support STOW-E.

While almost all applications of GroupSystems in the army to this point in time had been face-to-face meetings, STOW-E provided a different application. A critical part of the STOW-E exercise was visits by VIPs. Each VIP was assigned an individual to accompany them and note questions and comments made by the VIP. As soon as the VIP left, the guide went to a GroupSystems station and entered the information. This process not only captured the feedback and questions immediately, it also made them available to all parties in a timely fashion. This continuous use also allowed the people in charge of STOW-E to capture on-going problems and proposed solutions as they were applied to the problems. Problems or issues were addressed during the visits and the result was a continuously improved demonstration for future visitors. This was a very different type of use for GroupSystems and helped to show the need for collaborative tools that could be used for anytime, anyplace problem solving.

The system was also used in face-to-face meetings each evening to capture what was happening and what needed to be accomplished. One of the major benefits of the use of the GroupSystems tools was that as soon as the STOW-E exercise was done everyone was able to leave. Everything needed for the development of an After Action Report (AAR) had already been captured and much of the information had even been organized for distribution. The resulting AAR was a complete timeline of happenings and the way issues were addressed.

OTHER USERS FROM LAM

The use of GroupSystems by the LAM Task Force introduced the technology to a generation of senior army leaders. Several of the leaders used the concepts when they went back to their regular jobs. One of these leaders was General (GEN) Eric Shinseki. At the time of the LAM GOWG meetings GEN Shinseki was a Brigadier General assigned to the Pentagon. GEN Shinseki would later become the Chief of Staff of the army during the invasions of Afghanistan and Iraq in 2003. While GEN Franks was the commander of the troops in the conflicts, GEN Shinseki was responsible for training, equipping, and providing the army that was going to war. Just as GEN Franks had to fight with the army he helped design, GEN Shinseki was an integral part of the design of the army he led as Chief of Staff. When asked about his recollections of the process used during the LAM GOWG, GEN Shinseki responded with the following thoughts:

> . . . I do remember . . . electronic meetings from LAM TF work ups. I've used the concept myself a number of times in the years since. I found it particularly useful for brainstorming with groups that involved broad ranges in age; in intellectual agility and risk taking; in rank and experience, especially visible rank; and in the willingness to share thoughts. The electronic meeting leveled the playing field and teased out the thinking of most everyone at a work station. An old First Sergeant once told me that getting 10 to do the work of 10 takes real leadership. The electronic meeting gets 10 doing the work of 10. What does it require? Set up time to insure the system buzzes and whirrs, when needed; a good facilitator, who's been given a well thought through work plan to guide the brainstorming session; and participants who can type in some fashion. I thought electronic meetings got the best thinking out of an audience in ½ day when other concepts might take three. These are quick thoughts that go back many, many years. (Shinseki, 2005)

The insights from GEN Shinseki illustrate what makes a senior leader want to use electronic meeting support such as GroupSystems. Even after some ten years the uses and benefits are still fresh on his mind. Indeed, on another occasion GEN Shinseki brought up the topic and proceeded to share with a group of senior army civilians how beneficial the approach was to group decision making.

Y2K

January 1, 2000, seems a long time ago and it might be easy to forget the level of concern and preparation that went into preparing for that moment in time. The Year 2000 or Y2K problem was a worldwide event that resulted in the expenditures of billions of dollars to "fix" computer and information systems. Many legacy computer systems and programs were not developed to properly handle the change from 1999 to 2000. The fear was that there would be massive computer and infrastructure failures. The Department of Defense was concerned about the potential problem and spent a lot of time and money getting ready for the event. One of the ways that DoD prepared for Y2K was the establishment of a DoD Decision Support Center (DSC) headed by Jeff Gaynor. He brought together all the different military services and even U.S. allies in a facility that was designed to monitor and respond to any negative event during Y2K. GroupSystems was an integral part of the tool box used by Gaynor to monitor and if need be respond to events. GroupSystems was used in the DSC to capture and share information in real time.

A more innovative use of the system was implemented by the DCS for use in the Pentagon. Major Rachael Borhauer and Robert Harder developed processes that provided structured sharing of information across many offices within the Pentagon. Prior to their approach much of this information would have been coordinated by having Reserve Officers carry paper between offices for coordination and approval. The approach by the team provided immediate, simultaneous access to all offices involved in an action. One of the critical problems it addressed was to allow all people to know about a problem and yet quickly identify who were the real players and who did not need to be involved. The time savings were significant and it also made sure that all the key players were involved to produce the best solution. In a paper reporting about the project (Barrick et al., 2000), the conclusion was that the "key lesson learned was that information shared with GroupSystems made monitoring and managing more efficient and effective for everyone."

Today, this type of approach would be expected, but in 2000 it was new and innovative. This implementation was also interesting since the players were geographically distributed around the Pentagon and Washington, DC. While no major negative events occurred during Y2K the application of GroupSystems was a success and influenced how future coordination was accomplished.

ACCEPTANCE

With over twenty years of varied uses what made the use of GroupSystems or electronic meetings successful? While there are many points that could be made, it seems that task, level of participation, process, and outcome (Gantt and Beise, 1993) remain as some of the most critical issues. The PM ISM application showed that there had to be an important task that was either going to be repeated many times or a single task that had such high visibility that the investment of time and resources demanded an approach like GroupSystems. Until we found that repeatable task, we simply had a string of individual events that did not create a decision to invest in the technology for the long term. GEN Shinseki pointed out the benefit of more equal participation. Senior officers have been known to get mad when an anonymous participant was critical of their ideas. The senior officers seemed to forget that no one knew it was their idea until they got mad and claimed the idea. There were many cases where a sergeant had better ideas than a colonel, perhaps because they were closer to the problem. If there is no process then it is difficult to have a collaborative meeting. Using the approach for an ad hoc meeting does not usually work. However, innovative facilitators like Robert Harder are able to apply the technology in unique ways that create value in ways that produce truly valuable products. The availability of quality facilitators is critical to acceptance. The LAM Task Force used GroupSystems while GEN Franks was the Task Force leader and continued to use the approach even after he departed. This continued use of the tools after the departure of GEN Franks resulted from an acceptance of the approach by the entire organization and not just the top leader. The ability to get buy-in by a broad group within the organization is critical to long term success of the approach. GroupSystems had become institutionalized and was viewed as a critical part of the approach being used to transform the army.

BARRIERS

Barriers to use of this type of technology can fall into short-term or long-term categories. A concern raised by users is the commitment to using the results of the group process (Gantt, 1994). Involvement of management in the process and a commitment to use the results of the group process, even when they do not agree with the results, is essential to long-term acceptance of the approach. There were several examples of an organization accepting GroupSystems based upon the support of a specific senior leader. As soon as the proponent moved to their next assignment the tolls were no longer used. Another barrier to acceptance is the lack of qualified facilitators.

Even as the technology moves from exclusively face-to-face to distributed mode, the need for facilitation in some form is still essential. While many barriers identified when the technology was in its infancy (Gantt, 1994) still apply, others have been addressed. The technology no longer requires a dedicated facility. Adequate examples of successes are available to help organizations identify ways to apply the technology for maximum benefit to the group.

CONCLUSION

The U.S. Army was an early adopter of electronic meetings as a technology and has had several very successful applications over the last twenty years. Innovative applications have been done that have gone beyond the standard uses of the technology. Use of the technology survived changes in senior leadership when an important process was being successfully supported. When the use of the technology was dependent on the senior leader the usage tended to cease when the champion departed. Senior level commitment and significant tasks where real benefit is easily seen are critical to long-term use of this or any new technology. A comparison of the usage of similar tools over this same time period can be found in a paper by de Vreede et al. (2003), where they explore implementations in the United States and Europe. Their review includes both military and industrial users.

REFERENCES

Barrick, A.E.; Heilman, E.G.; and Harder, R. 2000. Using a group decision support system for DOD Y2K consequence management. *Army Acquisition, Logistics, and Technology,* PB-70-00-5, September-October, 41–42.

Franks, T. 2004. *American Soldier.* New York: HarperCollins.

Gantt, J.D. 1992. Experiences with groupware: Benefits and limitations in a real-world context. In D.D. Coleman (ed.), *Proceedings of the Groupware '92 Conference,* 438–442. San Mateo, CA: Morgan Kaufmann.

———. 1994. Position paper—Groupware users experience panel. In D.D. Coleman (ed.), *Proceedings of the Groupware '94 Conference,* 224–226. Scottsdale, AZ: The Conference Group.

Gantt, J.D., and Beise, C.M. 1993. The public reacts to GDSS. *Byte,* 18, 3, 118.

Shinseki, E. 2005. Private email correspondence, August 16.

Vreede, G.J. de; Vogel, D.; Kolfschoten, G.; and Wien, J. 2003. Fifteen years of GSS in the field: A comparison across time and national boundaries. In *Proceedings of the 36th Annual Hawaii International Conference on System Sciences,* Waikoloa, Hawaii, January 6–9.

PART IV

FUTURE DIRECTIONS

CHAPTER 13

A SIX-LAYER MODEL OF COLLABORATION

ROBERT O. BRIGGS, GWENDOLYN L. KOLFSCHOTEN,
GERT-JAN DE VREEDE, CONAN ALBRECHT, STEPHAN LUKOSCH,
AND DOUGLAS L. DEAN

Abstract: Designers of collaboration systems address many interrelated issues in a social-technical context. The volume, complexity, and variety of issues can invoke cognitive overload, causing deficiencies in system designs which, in turn, can reduce the effectiveness of teams. We use inductive logic to derive six key areas of concern for designers of collaboration systems. We use deductive logic to argue that these areas address collaboration at differing levels of abstraction, and so may be organized into a six-layer model, affording separation of concerns at design time. The layers are: Collaboration Goals, Group Products, Group Activities, Group Procedures, Collaboration Tools, and Collaborative Behaviors. At each layer and between adjacent layers there are different outcomes of interest, different constructs, theories and metrics, different ways of modeling collaboration, and different design concerns and methods. The model provides for a separation of concerns at design time, which may reduce cognitive load for designers and may help to improve completeness and consistency of their designs, yielding higher productivity for collaborating groups.

Keywords: Collaboration, Collaboration Engineering, Facilitation, Collaborative Work Practice, Collaboration Technology, Design Methodologies.

Groups collaborate to create value that their members cannot create through individual effort. Collaboration, however, engenders a set of interpersonal, social, political, cognitive, and technical challenges. Multiple actors with diverse backgrounds must establish common understandings (Weick et al., 2005) and align their efforts (Ren et al., 2008). They must think creatively, sometimes quickly, to solve problems (Rudolph et al., 2009) in the face of potential barriers (Ren et al., 2008) and distractions (Laxmisan et al., 2007).

Research shows that, under certain conditions, groups can improve key outcomes using collaboration technologies. Any technology that can be used well, however, can also be used badly. The availability of good-quality IS/IT artifacts do not assure successful collaboration. The value of a collaboration technology can only be realized in the larger context of a *collaboration system*, which we define as a combination of actors, hardware, software, knowledge, and work practices to facilitate groups in achieving their goals, in an effective and efficient way.

Designers of collaboration systems must therefore consider social, psychological, cognitive, technical, and many other aspects of collaboration when creating a new collaboration system. A *collaboration system* is a combination of hardware, software, actors, knowledge, and work practices for advancing a group toward its goal.

Collaboration researchers across many disciplines have produced a substantial and growing body of exploratory, theoretical, experimental, and applied research that could inform design choices. Finding, assimilating, and using the concepts of collaboration science, however, can impose high cognitive load on designers, which in turn, can lead to design defects in collaboration systems. This, in turn, may result in lost productivity for system users. Designers of collaboration systems may therefore find it useful to have an organizing scheme for the concepts and methods of collaboration science. In this paper we derive a Six-Layer Model of Collaboration (SLMC) to serve that purpose and to afford a multidimensional separation of concerns to collaboration system designers. We identify design considerations at each layer and at the interface of each layer with the layer above it. We discuss phenomena that manifest at each layer, the theories surrounding these phenomena, and approaches to measuring them. We propose that the next generation of collaboration technologies could accommodate the mobilizing of understandings at all six layers of the model. We draw attention to caveats about the model as an organizing scheme for collaboration concepts.

METHODS

We use inductive logic to derive the six key areas of design concerns for collaboration systems. We gather the supporting evidence for the inductions from more than 400 collaboration research papers in the Information Systems domain, and from several of its referent disciplines, among them Computer Science, Psychology, Management, and Education. We use deductive logic to build an argument that these areas of concern address collaboration at differing levels of abstraction, and so may be organized into a six-layer model, affording separation of concerns at design time.

SIX AREAS OF CONCERN FOR DESIGNERS OF COLLABORATION SYSTEMS

In this section we survey collaboration science literature of interest to the designers of collaboration systems. We synthesize this literature into six key areas of concern. Table 13.1 summarizes those areas of concern.

Concerns Related to Collaboration Goals

Many of the key concerns for successful collaboration relate to group goals, private goals, and the relationships among them. A *goal* is defined as a desired state or outcome (Locke and Latham, 1990). Much research focuses on the role of goals in group formation (Hahn et al., 2008), motivation (Vroom, 1995), continuity (Lodewijkx et al., 2006), productivity (Wheelan, 2009), and success (Levi, 2007).

Key phenomena in collaboration science are defined in terms of group goals. Collaboration itself, for example, is defined as joint effort toward a group goal (Briggs et al., 2003). Definitions of the terms *group* and *team* often refer to the collection of people who have committed to work toward a group goal (e.g., Cohen and Bailey, 1997). The effectiveness of a group is defined in terms of the degree to which a group attains the goals toward which it works (Cohen and Bailey, 1997). Group efficiency is defined in terms of the degree to which a group conserves its resources during the attainment of a group goal (Veld, 1987).

Other collaboration concerns pertain to the private goals of individual group members. Group cohesion, for example, is sometimes measured in terms of the degree to which an individual group member desires (has a goal) to remain a member of a group (Evans and Dion, 1991). The Yield

Table 13.1

Six Areas of Concern for Designers of Collaboration Systems

Area of concern	Description
Collaboration goals	A *goal* is a desired state or outcome. Deals with group goals, private goals, and goal congruence—the degree to which individuals perceive that working toward group goals will be instrumental to attaining private goals. Collaboration is defined as joint effort toward a group goal. Addresses motivation, group formation, commitment, productivity, satisfaction, and other goal-related phenomena.
Group products	A *product* is a tangible or intangible artifact or outcome produced by the group's labor. Deals with issues of quality, creativity, effectiveness, efficiency, and other product-related phenomena.
Group activities	*Activities* are subtasks that, when completed, yield the products that constitute attainment of the group goal. Deals with what groups must do to achieve their goals: sequences of steps that constitute decision-making and problem-solving approaches.
Group procedures	*Group procedures* are the methods, strategies, and tactics a group uses to execute its work. A sequence of procedures characterizes how a group moves toward its goals. Procedures may be informal and emergent or formal and prescribed.
Collaboration tools	*Collaboration tools* are artifacts or apparatus used in performing an operation for moving a group toward its goals. Deals with designing, developing, deploying, and using technologies in support of group efforts.
Collaborative behaviors	*Collaborative behaviors* are the things people actually say and do as they collaborate. This area considers the observable actions and reactions of team members making joint effort toward a group goal.

Shift Theory of satisfaction (Briggs et al., 2008) predicts that individual team members will feel satisfied with their group to the extent that group processes and outcomes invoke shifts in the perceived utility of and likelihood of attaining private goals.

Other phenomena, such as motivation (Hayne, 1999), commitment, consensus, and willingness to change, relate to *goal congruence*—the degree to which individuals perceive that working toward group goals would be instrumental toward attaining salient private goals. Instrumentality, Expectancy, and Reasons theories of motivation, for example, posit that motivation to make effort toward group goals will be a function of the degree to which individuals perceive value or benefit in the outcomes of the behaviors the group considers enacting (Westaby, 2002). In a group setting, these perceptions pertain to the actions an individual contemplates toward helping a group attain its goals. The Instrumentality Theory of Consensus posits that individuals will only be willing to commit effort and resources toward a proposal for achieving a group goal to the extent that they perceive that outcomes of the effort would be instrumental to their salient private goals (Briggs et al., 2005). The Value Frequency Model (VFM) for Change of Work Practice posits that an individual's willingness to change to a new way of working (e.g., a new collaborative approach) will be a function of the overall positive or negative value the individual perceives in using the new work practice, and the frequency with which the individual perceives that value will be attained (Briggs et al., 2007). VFM posits six dimensions of value: economic, political, social, cognitive, affective, and physical. These dimensions pertain directly to the kinds of utility individuals anticipate from the attainment of their salient private goals.

Issues of group formation and cohesion, efficiency and effectiveness, satisfaction, consensus, willingness to change, and other goal related phenomena must be addressed by the designers of collaboration systems and related phenomena. We generalize these concepts into an area of concerns labeled, "Collaboration Goals."

Concerns Related to Products

Designers of collaboration systems must consider a number of aspects relating to the products a group will create through its joint efforts. A *product* is a tangible object or intangible state produced by the group's labor, the existence of which advances a group toward its goal. If the collaboration goal of an internal risk audit were, for example,

> to discover risks that have not yet been controlled or mitigated, and to develop controls to cover those risks

then the group product might be,

> a list of risks organized by organizational unit, evaluated for likelihood and impact, elaborated with plans to mitigate each risk, and signed off by an auditor to signify that the controls are in place and functioning properly.

The existence of this group product would constitute the attainment of the group goal for the risk assessment.

Meta-analyses covering more than 300 studies (Baltes et al., 2002; Dennis and Wixom, 2002; Fjermestad and Hiltz, 1999; Hwang, 1998; McLeod, 1992) in the collaboration literature identify a number of issues pertaining to the products of collaboration as studied in the lab and the field. Some of these issues pertain to attributes of tangible products, for example, quality of a decision (Kellermanns et al., 2008), and the quality, creativity, and number of solutions (Dean et al., 2006). Others pertain to intangible products like awareness of problems (Beegun and Leroy, 2009), participation (Saltz et al., 2007), or gaining multiple perspectives (Clawson et al., 1993). Still others focus on the degree to which variations in the attributes of the team (Van Knippenberg and Schippers, 2006), the task (Higgs et al., 2005), and in other aspects affect the attributes of group products. We generalize these concepts into an area of concerns labeled, "Group Products."

Concerns Related to Group Activities

Collaboration systems designers focus much effort on designing a sequence of activities by which a group can achieve its goals. *Activities* are the high-level steps that comprise *what* a group will do to achieve its goals. Activities decompose group work into manageable chunks, each with its own interim goals and interim products. Many researchers describe domain-specific models of generalized activities for goal attainment. Herbert Simon (1979) proposed an economic model for rational decision making based on the premise that people go through a series of activities when evaluating a decision. Management researchers decompose decision into variations on a set of activities typically including problem identification, alternative generation, evaluation, and selection, planning, execution, and review (e.g., Schwenk, 1984; Dean and Sharfman, 1996;

Mitroff et al., 1974). Psychology researchers also propose activities as a foundation for problem solving tactics. For example, D'zurilla and Goldfried (1971) defined problem solving as a behavioral process which includes problem definition and formulations, generation of alternatives, evaluation and selection, and verification of potential solutions. Variations on these activities can be found throughout many literatures. The logical design phase in systems analysis and design methodologies, for example, typically include activities for problem identification, alternative generation, evaluation, and choice (Whitten et al., 2007).

Collaboration technology researchers often discuss the capabilities of their systems in terms of the tasks or activities they support. DeSanctis and Gallupe (1987) propose that GSS should support planning, creativity, intellective, preference, cognitive conflict, and mixed motive tasks. Using Speech-Act Theory, Flores and Winograd model collaboration processes as sequences of speech-act combinations to form standardized team activity workflows (Flores et al., 1988; Winograd and Flores, 1986). Based on their modeling approach, various collaboration systems in the area of workflow management were proposed. From these related research streams we derive the area of concern we label "Activities."

Concerns about Group Procedures

Group procedures are the work methods, strategies, and tactics a group uses to execute an activity. Procedures represent *how* a group executes its work. Group procedures are characterized by the observable effects of group effort on the state of the group and the state of the concepts with which it works. A sequence of procedures characterizes how a group moves through its work. Procedures may be informal and emergent or formal and prescribed.

Procedures can be described at different levels of specificity, from abstract patterns of collaboration to detailed execution rules. Nunamaker et al. (1997), for example, identify four procedures supported by GSS software, among them idea generation, idea organization, idea evaluation, and idea exploration. Collaboration engineering researchers identified six patterns of collaboration that characterize group procedures (de Vreede et al., 2009). *Patterns of collaboration* are observable regularities of behavior and outcome that emerge over time in teamwork (de Vreede et al., 2006). The six patterns are defined in moving the group from some state to a different state as follows:

- *Generate:* To move from having fewer concepts to having more concepts in the set of ideas shared by the group.
- *Reduce:* To move from having many concepts to a focus on fewer ideas deemed worthy of further attention.
- *Clarify:* To move from less to more shared understanding of the concepts in the set of ideas shared by the group.
- *Organize:* To move from less to more understanding of the relationships among concepts in the set of ideas shared by the group.
- *Evaluate:* To move from less to more understanding of the instrumentality of the concepts in the idea set shared by the group toward attaining group and private goals.
- *Build Commitment:* To move from fewer to more group members who are willing to commit to a proposal for moving the group toward attaining its goal(s).

Most of the behaviors in which a group engages can be characterized by these six patterns. In a risk assessment, for example, to identify risks, they may *generate* candidate risk statements, then *evaluate* the likelihood and impact of each risk, and *reduce* the list to the risks that pose a credible threat to the organization.

Researchers study phenomena relating to each of the six patterns of collaboration. With respect to the *Generate* pattern, for example, studies report the number of ideas a group produces (Connolly et al., 1990), their originality, relevance, quality, effectiveness, feasibility, and thoroughness (Dean et al., 2006). People generate by creating new ideas (Reiter-Palmon et al., 1997), by gathering previously unshared ideas (Bock et al., 2005), or by elaborating on existing ideas with additional details (de Vreede et al., 2000).

With the *Reduce* pattern, researchers address, for example, the number of ideas in the reduced shared set, the degree to which a reduced idea set includes high-quality ideas and excludes low-quality ideas (Barzilay et al., 1999), and the degree to which reduction of idea sets yields reductions of actual and perceived cognitive load (Simpson and Prusak, 1995). Groups reduce idea sets through idea filtering (Chambless et al., 2005), generalizing ideas (Yeung et al., 1999), or selection (Rietzschel et al., 2006).

Researchers of the *Clarify* pattern focus on, among other things, reductions in ambiguity, reductions in the number of words required to convey meaning, and on establishing mutual assumptions (Mulder et al., 2002). Among the phenomena of interest for research on the *Organize* pattern of collaboration are shared understandings of the relationships among concepts (Cannon-Bowers et al., 1993), cognitive load (Grisé and Gallupe, 2000), and the simplicity or complexity of the relationships among concepts, and the semantics of relationships; for example, complex structures may signify sequence, hierarchy, and networks of relationships, which in turn may model, for example, semantics of chronology, composition, heredity, or causation (Dean et al., 2000).

Research on the *Evaluate* pattern addresses projections of the possible consequences of choices, and the degree to which those consequences would promote or inhibit goal attainment (Westaby, 2002). Rating, ranking, and inclusion/exclusion are often-studied means of evaluation (Gavish and Gerdes, 1997). Research on such techniques focuses, for example, on the degree to which participants can accurately project the likely outcomes of the proposals they consider (Laukkanen et al., 2002).

Phenomena of interest for the *Build Commitment* pattern pertain to the degree to which people are willing to contribute to the group's efforts (Montoya-Weisset et al., 2001). Issues of commitment arise in many phases of group work, starting with the formation of the group (Datta, 2007), and continuing through every proposed course of action and every choice group members make as they move through their activities (Saaty and Shang, 2007).

Researchers who develop and test prescriptive techniques report many reusable collaboration techniques that can be employed to improve group performance. A *collaboration technique* is a reusable procedure for invoking useful interactions among people working toward a group goal (de Vreede et al., 2006). Consider, as an example, research on ideation techniques. Osborn (1963) proposed the brainstorming technique as a way to invoke synergy, and so to improve the number and quality of ideas produced by groups. Several subsequent studies reported that groups following Osborn's technique do not outperform those using nominal group technique (Diehl and Stroebe, 1987). Losses from production blocking, free-riding (social loafing), and evaluation apprehension appeared to outweigh possible benefits from synergy (Collaros and Anderson, 1969; Diehl and Stroebe, 1987). Groups using electronic brainstorming techniques that mitigated evaluation apprehension by allowing anonymous contributions, however, were shown to outperform both manual and nominal teams (Connolly et al., 1990; Dennis et al., 1990; Fjermestad and Hiltz, 1999; Gallupe et al., 1992).

Techniques that allow group members to interact anonymously appear to reduce evaluation apprehension (Connolly et al., 1990; Valacich et al., 1992) but may encourage social loafing (Harkins and Jackson, 1985; Paulus and Dzindolet, 1993; Sanna, 1992). Social comparison interventions were shown to reduce social loafing (Shepherd et al., 1995). Techniques that incorporate a devil's advocate role appear to foster creativity (Schulz-Hardt et al., 2008) and improve idea quality (Schweiger et al., 1986) yet they may reduce collaboration process satisfaction (Schweiger et al., 1986; Valacich and Schwenk, 1995). Techniques that decompose the problem space and/or solution space also appear to increase brainstorming performance (Dennis et al., 1997; Santanen et al., 2004). There are similar bodies of literature surrounding techniques for other patterns of collaboration, for team building, and for other aspects of collaboration. Research suggests that different techniques impose different level of cognitive load on group leaders and members (Kolfschoten and de Vreede, 2007; Kolfschoten and de Vreede, 2009), and different collaboration techniques may require different levels of facilitation and technology skills (Kolfschoten and de Vreede, 2009).

Researchers have begun to collect and codify collaboration techniques as design pattern languages for various aspects of collaboration (Khazanchi and Zigurs, 2006; van Der Aalst et al., 2003; de Vreede et al., 2006). A design pattern

> describes a problem which occurs over and over again and then describes the core of the solution to that problem, in such a way that you can use this solution a million times over, without ever doing it the same way twice. (Alexander et al., 1977, p. x)

Collaboration engineering researchers have developed design patterns called thinkLets (Kolfschoten et al., 2006; de Vreede et al., 2006; de Vreede et al., 2009). ThinkLets are named, scripted collaboration techniques for predictably and repeatedly invoking known variations of the six abstract patterns of collaboration (de Vreede et al., 2009). They enable design and specification of coherent, multilayered collaboration processes that can improve the productivity and quality of work life for teams (de Vreede et al., 2006).

From these lines of research, we generalize an area of concern we label "Collaboration Techniques."

Concerns Relating to Tools

A great deal of research has been done about the design (Cataldo et al., 2006; Reinig et al., 2007), deployment (Agres et al., 2005), and use (Golder and Huberman, 2006; Kamrani and Abouel Nasr, 2008; Smith, 2007) of tools to support collaboration. Collaboration *tools* are instruments or apparatus used in performing an operation for moving a group toward its goals, for example, whiteboards, flipcharts, or collaboration software systems. Collaboration tools afford users the capabilities they require to execute their work. The collaboration technology market is burgeoning with new products appearing monthly. A number of authors have proposed schemes for making sense of the range of capabilities offered in the collaboration space (Bos et al., 2007; Mittleman et al., 2008; Penichet et al., 2007; Sahni et al., 2008). Researchers have developed and published a pattern language of design considerations for collaboration software. This work addresses ninety-six generalized solutions for a range of functions such as community membership, workspace creation, shared artifacts, multi-modal communication, awareness, access control, persistence, and identification (Schummer and Lukosch, 2007).

Researchers have produced hundreds of articles on the use of group support systems (GSS) to improve group productivity (see Fjermestad and Hiltz, 1999; Fjermestad and Hiltz, 2001; Pervan and Arnott, 2006) for thorough compendia of these works). These studies have addressed a broad set of topics such as anonymity (Valacich et al., 1992), group size (Gallupe et al., 1992), task type, task-technology fit (Zigurs and Buckland, 1998), and national culture (Watson et al., 1994). Other researchers report on a variety of phenomena pertaining to, for example, wikis (Ebersbach et al.,

2008), audio and video conferencing (Nguyen and Canny, 2007), and metaverses (e.g., virtual worlds like Second Life) (Davis et al., 2009), reporting ways that collaboration technology use can improve or impede group performance. From this literature, we derive an area of concern we label, "Collaboration Tools." We choose the term, "Collaboration Tools" over the term "technologies" because we intend that both computer-based and non-computer-based tools be included in this area of concern.

Concerns Relating to Collaborative Behaviors

A number of studies in the collaboration science arena address collaborative behaviors. Collaborative behaviors are the observable utterances, actions, and reactions of group members as they interact to attain a group goal. Collaborative behaviors may be ad-hoc, unstructured, and emergent, or may be recurring, structured, and planned (DeSanctis and Poole, 1994; O'Sullivan et al., 2007; Rodriguez et al., 2006; Sapateiro et al., 2008).

Some collaborative behaviors may be guided by internal scripts—procedural knowledge embedded in the cognitive schema of individuals (Abelson, 1981). Other collaborative behaviors may be guided by external scripts that provide team members with procedural guidance (Kollar et al., 2005; Kollar et al., 2006), structuring and sequencing what participants in various roles should say and do to move the group forward. In the thinkLets design pattern language, for example, the essence of each technique is embodied as a highly structured set of rules that specify a *sequence* of *actions* people in specific *roles* should take using certain *capabilities* under certain *constraints* (Kolfschoten et al., 2006). Documentation for each thinkLet includes a sample script that instantiates those rules. Designers of collaboration systems tailor the thinkLet script or replace it completely, yet still invoke the same patterns of collaboration, so long as the new script still invokes the rules of the thinkLet (Kolfschoten et al., 2006).

Subtle variations in scripts can produce substantial variations in collaborative behaviors. Simply instructing a brainstorming group to think creatively, for example, has been shown to significantly increase the number of creative ideas they produce (Runco et al., 2005). Instructing the group to engage in problem construction before brainstorming begins also increases their creativity (Reiter-Palmon et al., 1997). Shepherd et al. (1995) reported that adding an invocation of social comparison to a brainstorming script increased the number of ideas produced by an anonymous brainstorming group by about 30 percent (e.g., "An average group produces about *xxx* ideas during a session like this. If you produce fewer, you are below average."). They found further that if the invocation were delivered in a jocular tone to increase its salience (e.g., ". . . If you produce less than that, you are brain-dead . . .)" productivity increased by another 30 percent. Other research showed that varying the order of twenty brainstorming prompts covering five topics in a directed brainstorming technique could yield variations of as high as 300 percent in the number of creative ideas a group produced (Santanen et al., 2000). From this body of literature, we derive an area of concern that we label, "Collaborative Behaviors."

DERIVING A SIX LAYER MODEL OF COLLABORATION

In this section we use deductive logic to argue that these areas of concern address collaboration at differing levels of abstraction, and so may be organized into a Six-Layer Model of Collaboration (SLMC), affording separation of concerns for designers of collaboration systems. Designers may make choices at every level that affect the layers below. Constraints at any level may affect the choices designers make at layers above. Figure 13.1 illustrates the layers of the model.

Figure 13.1 **The Six-Layer Model of Collaboration**

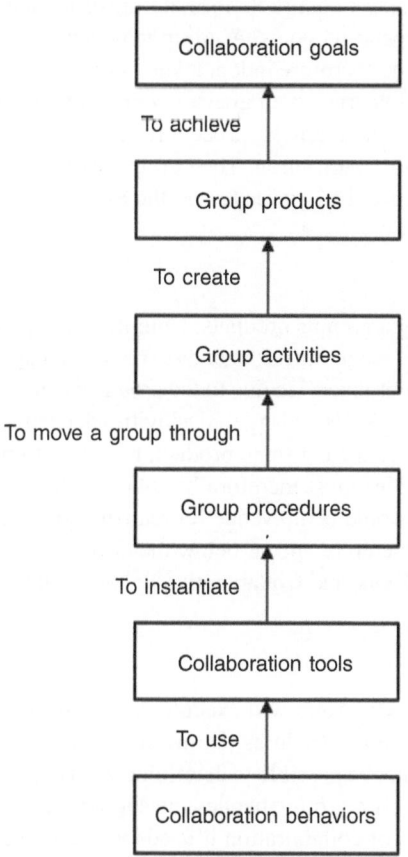

Note: Each layer deals with different collaboration concerns for the designer of collaboration systems. Each has different phenomena of interest, and therefore different methods for explaining, modeling and measuring collaboration.

The Collaboration Goals Layer

Without a goal, by definition collaboration does not exist. Unless the private goals of the individuals are congruent with the group goal, team members will not commit to collaborate, and so the group will not exist. If a group does not exist, then there is no need to address the other areas of concern. Concerns pertaining to goals must therefore comprise the top-most layer of the SLMC, because all other layers depend on the top layer.

The Group Products Layer

To achieve their collaboration goals, groups must create products—artifacts and outcomes that constitute goal attainment. Until a group goal exists, one cannot assert the need for a product, nor judge the degree to which a product fulfills a goal. If a group changes its goals, it may need to change the products it will create because products are the means by which a group goal is realized. If a group creates a product that does not attain its formal or instrumental goals, that product has no purpose. Products therefore depend on goals. A group may decide to attain the same goal by creating different products. Goals are therefore independent of products. Concerns about products must therefore be subordinate to concerns about goals. Lacking a product, however, there would be no need to address concerns about activities, procedures techniques, tools, or behaviors, because there would be no purpose to group action. The Group Products Layer must fall below the Collaboration Goals Layer, but above the other layers in the SLMC.

The Activities Layer

Activities are sub-tasks for creating a group's products. Until there is a product to create, activities have no purpose. If a group changes the product it intends to create, it may have to change its activities, because activities produce sub-products leading to the products that attain the group goal. If the product changes, the sub-products must also change, so activities depend on products. A group may decide to use different activities to create the same product, however, so products are independent of activities. Concerns about activities must therefore be subordinate to concerns about products. Lacking activities, however, there would be no venue for realizing group procedures or behaviors. The Group Activities Layer must therefore appear below the Group Products Layer, but above the Group Procedures, Collaboration Tools, and Collaborative Behaviors layers of the SLMC.

Group Procedures Layer

Group procedures characterize how a group will execute its activities. Patterns of collaboration are abstract building blocks for group procedures. Until sub-tasks have been identified and their sub-products articulated, it would not be possible to determine what combination of patterns might be useful for create a sub-product. If a group changes the sub-products it intends to create, then it may need to change the patterns of collaboration it needs to create them, because the patterns must give rise to the sub-products. Likewise, collaboration techniques specify procedures for moving through an activity. Concerns about techniques are therefore subordinate to concerns about activities. If a group changes the activities it wants to use to move to create its products, then it may have to change the procedures it uses. Concerns about procedures are therefore subordinate to concerns about activities. A group may execute the same activity with a variety of different procedures. Activities are therefore independent of procedures. The Group Procedures layer must therefore appear below the Group Activities layer in the SLMC. Lacking a procedure, however, it would not be possible to specify the tools required to instantiate the procedure, because each technique requires specific capabilities. Nor would it be possible to specify how people should use their tools to execute the procedure before the procedure is known. The Procedures layer must therefore appear above the Tools and Scripts layers of the SLMC.

The Collaboration Tools Layer

Tools afford the capabilities required to instantiate a group procedure. Until techniques have been selected, it would not be possible to select tools for instantiating the technique because each technique requires specific capabilities. Concerns about tools must therefore be subordinate to concerns about techniques. If a group changes the procedure it intends to follow, it may need to change its tools, because the techniques in the new procedure may require different capabilities.

Tools are therefore dependent on procedures. A group may decide, however, to use different tools to provide the capabilities their procedure requires. Procedures are therefore independent of tools. Lacking tools, it would not be possible to decide the behaviors group members should enact with their tools to instantiate a procedure. The Tools layer must therefore fall below the Procedures layer, but above the Collaborative Behaviors layer in the SMLC.

The Collaborative Behaviors Layer

Collaborative behaviors are things people in various roles do and say with their tools to instantiate the procedures selected for the group. Until tools have been selected, it would not be possible to decide how group members should use them. If a group changes the tools it uses, however, then it must change its behaviors to accommodate the new tools. Behaviors therefore depend on tools. Concerns about behaviors must therefore be subordinate to concerns about tools. The Collaborative Behaviors layer must therefore fall below the Collaboration Tools layer in the SMLC.

DISCUSSION

Concerns at the Interfaces Between SLMC Layers

In addition to the concerns for each of the six layers in the SLMC, there are concerns at the interfaces between each layer and the layer above it. Between the Products and Goals layer, for example, one must consider the degree to which products are valuable toward goal attainment. Because goals vary from group to group, there are no universal measures of product value; such measures must be derived on a task-by-task basis. It may be possible, however, to derive general measures of the perceived value of products, with questions such as, "The outcomes of today's efforts will (advance/inhibit) the achievement of our goals." Likewise, between the Goals and Activities Layers, a designer must take into account the degree to which activities create products that serve group goals. The purpose of the Procedures layer is to consider how a group moves through its activities. Of interest between the Group Activities and Group Procedures layers, therefore, is the effectiveness and efficiency with which the designed procedures would move a group through its activities to their interim goals and products. Between the Collaboration Tools and Group Procedures layers, a designer must consider the degree to which a given technology affords required capabilities for executing the procedure, and the degree to which those capabilities are afforded at a minimum of financial, political, social, cognitive, emotional, and physical cost. Of interest between the Tools and Behaviors layer would be the degree to which the group members use their tools in ways that faithfully the procedure chosen by the work practice designer.

Implications of the SLMC for Designing and Deploying Collaborative Work Practices

The six layers of the SLMC offer a framework for the many design choices that one must make when planning collaborative efforts. Collaboration Engineering researchers have developed a structured approach to designing collaborative work practices (Kolfschoten and de Vreede, 2009) consisting of six phases to address these design choices. This approach addresses all six layers of the SLMC. In the first phase the designer analyzes the task to understand the goals and deliverables of the work practice, the stakes of the individuals who will execute the work practice, and the resources available for the design effort. The next phase derives a set of activities for creating the deliverables. Based on this first blueprint of the process, the designer defines procedures by identifying a sequence of patterns of collaboration for each activity and selecting techniques (thinkLets) and the technologies to implement each activity. Having determined how the process will be executed, the designer adds further details, indicating the time frame for each activity and the information required for each activity (such as brainstorming questions or criteria for evaluation.) With this information the designer creates an agenda and develops prompts to guide group behaviors during the work practice. The process can be validated. In this step the relations between the layers become important: the guidance prompts should lead group members to enact useful behaviors with the selected tools, which should afford the capabilities required by the procedural techniques that should create the procedural patterns of collaboration that should move the group though activities to create deliverables that answer the goals of the group. Throughout the design effort, the collaboration process needs to be captured and documented in a more detailed prescription to make it transferable and reusable.

Implications of the SLMC for the Next Generation of Collaboration Technologies

The current generation of collaboration technologies focuses almost exclusively at the Tools layer of the SLMC. Users of collaboration technology, however, are not educated in the principles of collaboration science, and so may not know how to wield those tools to instantiate procedural techniques to invoke the patterns of collaboration that will move them through their activities to create the products that will achieve their goals. We propose that the next generation of collaboration technologies could present users not just with tools, but with well-designed work practices specified at all six layers. It might be useful if it were possible for a collaboration system designer to configure purpose-built task-specific software applications to help a group articulate its goals, and to move through a series of activities to create the deliverables by which they will attain their goals. For each activity the system should present the group with just the tools they need, configured to support the techniques they will use to complete the activity efficiently. Those tools should link to the data sets the group needs for the activity, and should provide the communication channels the group will need to interact effectively. These systems should provide practitioners with scripts and other guidance that will let them move through the activities together. We propose that this generation of practice-centric technologies be called *Process Support Systems* (PSS). A PSS would present practitioners with a library of collaborative applications tailored to their specific high-value recurring tasks. Practitioners could select the application they needed, instantiate it as a virtual work space, and move as a group through the activities in the work practice.

A Caveat

The Six-Layer Model of Collaboration conceives of collaboration as a *process* that may have economic, political, social, cognitive, physical, and technical dimensions. The model is, however, one of many ways one could frame collaboration. It will also be valuable to explore collaboration from other perspectives—from a resource perspective; a behavioral perspective; as a value network; as a communication network; as a network of power and influence. These and other perspectives are also worthy of research attention.

CONCLUSIONS

This paper draws from literature in five academic disciplines using both inductive and deductive logic to derive the Six Layer Model of Collaboration. It highlights key concerns for each layer, and discusses concerns that manifest between the layers. It discusses the realization of the six layers in a methodology for designing collaboration systems. Because the model provides for a separation of concerns at design time, it may reduce the cognitive load of designers who must address a complex set of interrelated issues, which may, in turn, lead to better designs.

NOTE

A previous version of this chapter was published as Robert O. Briggs, Gwendolyn Kolfschoten, Gert-Jan de Vreede, Conan Albrecht, Douglas R. Dean, and Stephan Lukosch, "A seven-layer model of collaboration: Separation of concerns for designers of collaboration systems," in J.F. Nunamaker Jr. and W.L. Currie (eds.), *Proceedings of the International Conference on Information Systems* (ICIS'09), paper 26. http://aisel.aisnet. org/icis2009/26.

REFERENCES

Abelson, R.P. 1981. Psychological status of the script concept. *American Psychologist*, 36, 7, 715–729.

Agres, A.; de Vreede, G.-J.; and Briggs, R.O. 2005. A tale of two cities: Case studies of GSS transition in two organizations. *Group Decision and Negotiation*, 14, 4, 267–284.

Alexander, C.; Ishikawa, S.; and Silverstein, M. 1977. *A Pattern Language: Towns, Buildings, Construction.* New York: Oxford University Press.

Baltes, B.B.; Dickson, M.W.; Sherman, M.P.; Bauer, C.C.; and LaGanke, J.S. 2002. Computer-mediated communication and group decision making: A meta-analysis. *Organizational Behavior and Human Decision Processes*, 87, 1, 156–179.

Barzilay, R.; McKeown, K.R.; and Elhadad, M. 1999. Information fusion in the context of multi-document summarization. In *Proceedings of the 37th Annual Meeting of the Association for Computational Linguistics (ACL'99) on Computational Linguistics,* 550–557. Stroudsburg, PA: Association for Computational Linguistics.

Beegun, R., and Leroy, P. 2009. Risk management challenges in UCITS III funds. *Journal of Securities Operations and Custody*, 2, 1, 37–52.

Bock, G.W.; Zamud, R.W.; Kim, Y.G.; and Lee, J.N. 2005. Behavioral intention formation in knowledge sharing: Examining the roles of extrinsic motivators, social-psychological forces, and organizational climate. *Management Information Systems Quarterly,* 29, 1, 87–111.

Bos, N.; Zimmerman, A.; Olson, J.; Yew, J.; Yerkie, J.; Dahl, E.; and Olson, G. 2007. From shared databases to communities of practice: A taxonomy of collaboratories. *Journal of Computer-Mediated Communication*, 12, 2, 652–672.

Briggs, R.O.; Davis, A.J.; Murphy, J.D.; Steinhauser, L.; and Carlisle, T. 2007. Transferring a collaborative work practice to practitioners: A field study of the value frequency model for change-of-practice. In J. Haake, S. Ochoa, and A. Cechich (eds.), *Lecture Notes on Computer Science,* 295–302. New York: Springer.

Briggs, R.O.; de Vreede, G.-J.; and Nunamaker, J.F. Jr. 2003. Collaboration engineering with thinkLets to pursue sustained success with group support systems. *Journal of Management Information Systems*, 19, 4, 31–64.

Briggs, R.O.; Kolfschoten, G.L.; and de Vreede, G.-J. 2005. Toward a theoretical model of consensus building. Paper presented at the Americas Conference on Information Systems, Omaha, Nebraska, August 11–14.

Briggs, R.O.; Reinig, B.A.; and de Vreede, G.-J. 2008. The yield shift theory of satisfaction and its application to the IS/IT domain. *Journal of the Association for Information Systems*, 9, 5, 267–293.

Cannon-Bowers, J.A.; Salas, E.; and Converse, S. 1993. Shared mental models in expert team decision making. In J. Castellan Jr. (ed.), *Individual and Group Decision Making,* 221–246. Hillsdale, NJ: Lawrence Erlbaum.

Cataldo, M.; Wagstrom, P.A.; Herbsleb, J.D.; and Carley, K.M. 2006. Identification of coordination requirements: Implications for the design of collaboration and awareness tools. In *Proceedings of the 2006 20th Anniversary Conference on Computer Supported Cooperative Work (CSCW'06),* 353–362. New York: ACM.

Chambless, P.; Hasselbauer, S.; Loeb, S.; Luhrs, S.; Newbery, D.; and Scherer, W. 2005. Design recommendation of a collaborative group decision support system for the aerospace corporation. In *Systems and Information Engineering Design Symposium (2005 IEEE),* 183–191. Charlottesville: University of Virginia.

Clawson, V.K.; Bostrom, R.; and Anson, R. 1993. The role of the facilitator in computer-supported meetings. *Small Group Research*, 24, 4, 547–565.

Cohen, S.G., and Bailey, D.E. 1997. What makes teams work: Group effectiveness research from the shop floor to the executive suite. *Journal of Management*, 23, 3, 239–290.

Collaros, P.A., and Anderson, L.R. 1969. Effects of perceived expertness upon creativity of members of brainstorming groups. *Journal of Applied Psychology* 53, 2 (Pt.1), 159–163.

Connolly, T.; Jessup, L.M.; and Valacich, J.S. 1990. Effects of anonymity and evaluative tone on idea generation in computer-mediated groups. *Management Science*, 36, 6, 689–703.

Datta, D. 2007. Sustainability of community-based organizations of the rural poor: Learning from Concern's rural development projects, Bangladesh. *Community Development Journal*, 42, 1, 47–62.

Davis, A.; Murphy, J.; Owens, D.; Khazanchi, D.; and Zigurs, I. 2009. Avatars, people, and virtual worlds: Foundations for research in metaverses. *Journal of the Association for Information Systems*, 10, 2, 90–117.

Dean, D.L.; Hender, J.M.; Rodgers, T.L.; and Santanen, E. 2006. Identifying quality, novel, and creative ideas: Constructs and scales for idea evaluation. *Journal of Association for Information Systems*, 7, 1, 649–699.

Dean, D.L.; Orwig, R.E.; and Vogel, D.R. 2000. Facilitation methods for collaborative modeling tools. *Group Decision and Negotiation*, 9, 2, 109–127.

Dean, J.W. Jr., and Sharfman, M.P. 1996. Does decision process matter? A study of strategic decision-making effectiveness. *The Academy of Management Journal*, 39, 2, 368–396.

Dennis, A.R.; Valacich, J.S.; and Nunamaker, J.F. Jr. 1990. Group, sub-group and nominal group idea generation in an electronic meeting environment. In *Proceedings of the 24th Annual Hawaii International Conference on System Sciences,* 1–25. Maui, Hawaii, January 8–11.

Dennis, A.R., and Wixom, B.H. 2002. Investigating the moderators of the group support systems use with meta-analysis. *Journal of Management Information Systems*, 18, 3, 235–257.

Dennis, A.R., Valacich, J.S., Carte, T.A., Garfield, M.J., Haley, B.J., and Aronson, J.E. 1997. Research report: The effectiveness of multiple dialogues in electronic brainstorming. *Information Systems Research* 8, 2, 203.

DeSanctis, G., and Gallupe, R.B. 1987. A foundation for the study of group decision support systems. *Management Science*, 33, 5, 589–609.

DeSanctis, G., and Poole, M. 1994. Capturing the complexity in advanced technology use: Adaptive structuration theory. *Organization Science*, 121–147.

Diehl, M., and Stroebe, W. 1987. Productivity loss in brainstorming groups: Toward the solution of a riddle. *Journal of Personality and Social Psychology* 53, 3, 497–509.

D'zurilla, T.J., and Goldfried, M.R. 1971. Problem solving and behavior modification. *Journal of Abnormal Psychology*, 78, 1, 107–126.

Ebersbach, A.; Glaser, M.; Heigl, R.; et al. 2008. *Wiki: Web Collaboration.* New York: Springer.

Evans, C.R., and Dion, K.L. 1991. Group cohesion and performance: A meta-analysis. *Small Group Research*, 22, 2, 175–186.

Fjermestad, J., and Hiltz, S.R. 1999. An assessment of group support systems experimental research: Methodology and results. *Journal of Management Information Systems*, 15, 3, 7–149.

———. 2001. Group support systems: A descriptive evaluation of case and field studies. *Journal of Management Information Systems*, 17, 3, 115–159.

Flores, F.; Graves, M.; Hartfield, B.; and Winograd, T. 1988. Computer systems and the design of organizational interaction. *ACM Transactions on Office Information Systems*, 6, 2, 153–172.

Gallupe, R.B.; Dennis, A.R.; Cooper, W.H.; Valacich, J.S.; Bastianutti, L.M.; and Nunamaker, J.F. Jr. 1992. Electronic brainstorming and group size. *Academy of Management Journal*, 35, 2, 350–369.

Gavish, B., and Gerdes, J.H. 1997. Voting mechanisms and their implications in a GDSS environment. *Annals of Operation Research*, 71, 1, 41–74.

Golder, S.A., and Huberman, B.A. 2006. Usage patterns of collaborative tagging systems. *Journal of Information Science,* 32, 2, 198.

Grisé, M.-L., and Gallupe, R.B. 2000. Information overload: Addressing the productivity paradox in face-to-face electronic meetings. *Journal of Management Information Systems*, 16, 3, 157–185.

Hahn, J.; Moon, J.Y.; and Zhang, C. 2008. Emergence of new project teams from open source software developer networks: Impact of prior collaboration ties. *Information Systems Research,* 19, 3, 369–391.

Harkins, S.G., and Jackson, J.M. 1985. The role of evaluation in eliminating social loafing. *Personality and Social Psychology Bulletin* 11, 4, 457–465.

Hayne, S.C. 1999. The facilitator's perspective on meetings and implications for group support systems design. *Database*, 30, 3–4, 72–91.

Higgs, M.; Plewnia, U.; and Ploch, J. 2005. Influence of team composition and task complexity on team performance. *Team Performance Management*, 11, 7/8, 227.

Hwang, M.I. 1998. Did task type matter in the use of decision room GSS? A critical review and a meta-analysis. *International Journal of Management Science*, 26, 1, 1–15.

Kamrani, A.K., and Abouel Nasr, E.S. 2008. Product design and development framework in collaborative engineering environment. *International Journal of Computer Applications in Technology*, 32, 2, 85–94.

Kellermanns, F.W.; Floyd, S.W.; Pearson, A.W.; and Spencer, B. 2008. The contingent effect of constructive confrontation on the relationship between shared mental models and decision quality. *Journal of Organizational Behavior*, 29, 1, 119–137.

Khazanchi, D., and Zigurs, I. 2006. Patterns for effective management of virtual projects: Theory and evidence. *International Journal of e-Collaboration*, 2, 3, 25–49.

Kolfschoten, G., and de Vreede, G.J. 2007. The collaboration engineering approach for designing collaboration processes. In J.M. Haake, S.F. Ochoa, and A. Cechich (eds.), *Groupware: Design, Implementation, and Use: Proceedings of the 13th International Workshop, CRIWG 2007*, Bariloche, Argentina, 95–110.

———. 2009. A design approach for collaboration processes: A multi-method design science study in collaboration engineering. *Journal of Management Information Systems*, 26, 1, 225–257.

Kolfschoten, G.L.; Briggs, R.O.; de Vreede, G.-J.; Jacobs, P.H.M.; and Appelman, J.H. 2006. A conceptual foundation of the thinkLet concept for collaboration engineering. *International Journal of Human-Computer Studies*, 64, 7, 611–621.

Kollar, I.; Fischer, F.; and Hesse, F. 2006. Collaboration scripts—A conceptual analysis. *Educational Psychology Review*, 18, 2, 159–185.

Kollar, I.; Fischer, F.; and Slotta, J.D. 2005. Internal and external collaboration scripts in web-based science learning at schools. In *Proceedings of the 2005 Conference on Computer Support for Collaborative Learning (CSCL'05)—Learning 2005: The Next 10 Years!* 331–340. Taipei, Taiwan, International Society of the Learning Sciences.

Laukkanen, S.; Kangas, A.; and Kangas, J. 2002. Applying voting theory in natural resource management: A case of multiple-criteria group decision support. *Journal of Environmental Management*, 64, 2, 127–137.

Laxmisan, A.; Hakimzada, F.; Sayan, O.R.; Green, R.A.; Zhang, J.; and Patel, V.L. 2007. The multitasking clinician: Decision-making and cognitive demand during and after team handoffs in emergency care. *International Journal of Medical Informatics*, 76, 11–12, 801–811.

Levi, D. 2007. *Group Dynamics for Teams*, 2d ed. Los Angeles, CA: Sage.

Locke, E.A., and Latham, G.P. 1990. *A Theory of Goal Setting and Task Performance*. Englewood Cliffs, NJ: Prentice-Hall.

Lodewijkx, H.F.M.; Rabbie, J.M.; and Visser, L. 2006. "Better to be safe than to be sorry": Extinguishing the individual–group discontinuity effect in competition by cautious reciprocation. *European Review of Social Psychology*, 17, 185–232.

McLeod, P.L. 1992. An assessment of the experimental literature on electronic support of group work: Results of a meta-analysis. *Human-Computer Interaction*, 7, 257–280.

Mitroff, I.I.; Betz, F.; Pondy, L.R.; and Sagasti, F. 1974. On managing science in the systems age: Two schemas for the study of science as a whole systems phenomenon. *Interfaces*, 4, 3, 46–58.

Mittleman, D.D.; Briggs, R.O.; Murphy, J.; and Davis, A. 2008. Toward a taxonomy of groupware technologies. In R.O. Briggs, P. Antunes, G.-J. de Vreede, and A.S. Read (eds.), *Groupware: Design, Implementation, and Use, Lecture Notes in Computer Science* (vol. 5411), 305–317. Berlin: Springer-Verlag.

Montoya-Weiss, M.M.; Massey, A.P.; and Song, M. 2001. Getting it together: Temporal coordination and conflict management in global virtual teams. *The Academy of Management Journal*, 44, 6, 1251–1262.

Mulder, I.; Swaak, J.; and Kessels, J. 2002. Assessing learning and shared understanding in technology-mediated interaction. *Educational Technology and Society*, 5, 1, 35–47.

Nguyen, D.T., and Canny, J. 2007. Multiview: Improving trust in group video conferencing through spatial faithfulness. In *Proceedings of the SIGCHI Conference on Human Factors in Computing Systems*, 1465–1474. New York: Association for Computing Machinery. http://portal.acm.org/citation.cfm?id=1240624.1240846 (accessed May 5, 2009).

Nunamaker, J.F. Jr.; Briggs, R.O.; Mittleman, D.D.; Vogel, D.D.; and Balthazard, P.A. 1997. Lessons from a dozen years of group support systems research: A discussion of lab and field findings. *Journal of Management Information Systems*, 13, 3, 163–207.

Osborn, A.F. 1963. *Applied Imagination*, 3d ed. New York: Scribner.

O'Sullivan, D.; Mulligan, D.; and Dooley, L. 2007. Collaborative information system for university-based research institutes. *International Journal of Innovation and Learning,* 4, 3, 308–322.

Paulus, P.B., and Dzindolet, M.T. 1993. Social influence processes in group brainstorming. *Journal of Personality and Social Psychology* 64, 4, 575–586.

Penichet, V.M.R.; Marin, I.; Gallud, J.A.; Lozano, M.D.; and Tesoriero, R. 2007. A classification method for CSCW systems. *Electronic Notes in Theoretical Computer Science* 168, 237–247. Amsterdam: The Netherlands: Elsevier Science.

Pervan, G., and Arnott, D. 2006. Key issues for GSS research. In S. Seifart and C. Weinhardt (eds.), *Group Decision and Negotiation (GDN) 2006 International Conference Proceedings,* 78–81. Karlsruhe, Germany: Universitätsverlag Karlsruhe.

Reinig, B.A.; Briggs, R.O.; and Nunamaker, J.F. Jr. 2007. On the measurement of ideation quality. *Journal of Management Information Systems,* 23, 4, 143–161.

Reiter-Palmon, R.; Mumford, M.D.; Boes, J.O.C.; and Runco, M.A. 1997. Problem construction and creativity: The role of ability, cue consistency, and active processing. *Creativity Research Journal,* 10, 1, 9–23.

Ren, Y.; Kiesler, S.; and Fussell, S.R. 2008. Multiple group coordination in complex and dynamic task environments: Interruptions, coping mechanisms, and technology recommendations. *Journal of Management Information Systems,* 25, 1, 105–130.

Rietzschel, E.F.; Nijstad, B.A.; and Stroebe, W. 2006. Productivity is not enough: A comparison of interactive and nominal brainstorming groups on idea generation and selection. *Journal of Experimental Social Psychology,* 42, 2, 244–251.

Rodriguez, H. Trainor, J.; and Quarantelli, E.L. 2006. Rising to the challenges of a catastrophe: The emergent and prosocial behavior following Hurricane Katrina. *The ANNALS of the American Academy of Political and Social Science* 604, 1, 82–101.

Rudolph, J.W.; Morrison, J.B.; and Carroll, J.S. 2009. The dynamics of action-oriented problem solving: Linking interpretation and choice. *The Academy of Management Review,* 34, 4, 733–756.

Runco, M.A.; Illies, J.J.; and Reiter-Ralmon, R. 2005. Explicit instructions to be creative and original: A comparison of strategies and criteria as targets with three types of divergent thinking tests. *Korean Journal of Thinking and Problem Solving,* 15, 1, 5–15.

Saaty, T.L., and Shang, J.S. 2007. Group decision-making: Head-count versus intensity of preference. *Socio-Economic Planning Sciences,* 41, 1, 22–37.

Sahni, D.; Van den Bergh, J.; and Coninx, K. 2008. Towards a collaboration framework for selection of ICT tools. *Proceedings of the Conference on New Approaches to Requirements Elicitation on Different Levels,* 33–39, Lund, Sweden.

Saltz, J.S.; Hiltz, S.R.; Turoff, M.; and Passerini, K. 2007. Increasing participation in distance learning courses. *IEEE Internet Computing,* 11, 3, 36–44.

Sanna, L.J. 1992. Self-Efficacy Theory: Implications for social facilitation and social loafing. *Journal of Personality and Social Psychology,* 62, 5, 774–786.

Santanen, E.L.; Briggs, R.O.; and de Vreede, G.-J. 2000. The cognitive network model of creativity: A new causal model of creativity and a new brainstorming technique. In *Proceedings of the 33rd Hawaii International Conference on System Sciences,* Maui, Hawaii, January 4–7.

———. 2004. Causal relationship in creative problem solving: Comparing facilitation interventions for ideation. *Journal of Management Information Systems* 20, 4, 167–197.

Sapateiro, C.; Antunes, P.; Zurita, G., Baloian, N.; and Vogt, R. 2008. Supporting unstructured activities in crisis management: A collaboration model and prototype to improve situation awareness. *Lecture Notes in Computer Science.* Berlin: Springer-Verlag. 5424:010.

Schulz-Hardt, S., Mojzisch, A., and Vogelgesang, F. 2008. Dissent as a facilitator: Individual-and group-level effects on creativity and performance. In C.K.W De Dreu and M.J. Gelfand (eds.), *The Psychology of Conflict and Conflict Management in Organizations,* 149–177. New York: Lawrence Erlbaum.

Schummer, T., and Lukosch, S. 2007. *Patterns for Computer-mediated Interaction.* Chichester, UK: John Wiley & Sons.

Schweiger, D.M., Sandberg, W.R., and Ragan, J.W. 1986. Group approaches for improving strategic decision making: A comparative analysis of dialectical inquiry, devil's advocacy, and consensus. *Academy of Management Journal* 29, 1, 51–71.

Schwenk, C.R. 1984. Cognitive simplification processes in strategic decision-making. *Strategic Management Journal,* 5, 2, 111–128.

Shepherd, M.M., Briggs, R.O., Reinig, B.A., and Yen, J. 1995. Social loafing in electronic brainstorming: Invoking social comparison through technology and facilitation techniques to improve group productivity. In *Proceedings of the 28th Hawaii International Conference on System Sciences*, Maui, Hawaii, January 3–6.

Simon, H.A. 1979. Rational decision making in business organizations. *The American Economic Review*, 69, 4, 493–513.

Simpson, C.W., and Prusak, L. 1995. Troubles with information overload—moving from quantity to quality in information provision. *International Journal of Information Management*, 15, 6, 413–425.

Smith, A.D. 2007. Collaborative commerce through web-based information integration technologies. *International Journal of Innovation and Learning*, 4, 2, 127–144.

Valacich, J.S.; Jessup, L.M.; Dennis, A.R.; and Nunamaker, J.F. Jr. 1992. A conceptual framework of anonymity in group support systems. *Group Decision and Negotiation*, 1, 3, 219–241.

Valacich, J.S., and Schwenk, C. 1995. Structuring conflict in individual, face-to-face, and computer-mediated group decision making: Carping versus objective devil's advocacy. *Decision Sciences*, 26, 3, 369–393.

van Der Aalst, W.M., Ter Hofstede, A.H., Kiepuszewski, B., and Barros, A.P. 2003. Workflow patterns. *Distributed and Parallel Databases*, 14, 1, 5–51.

Van Knippenberg, D., and Schippers, M.C. 2006. Work group diversity. *Annual Review of Psychology*, 58, 515–541.

Veld, J.I.T. 1987. *Analyse van organisatie problemen*. Leiden: Stenfert Kroese.

de Vreede, G.J.; Briggs, R.O.; van Duin, R.; and Enserink, B. 2000. Athletics in electronic brainstorming: Asynchronous electronic brainstorming in very large groups. In *Proceedings of the 33rd Annual Hawaii International Conference on Systems Sciences*, Maui, Hawaii, January 4–7.

de Vreede, G.J.; Kolfschoten, G.L.; and Briggs, R.O. 2006. ThinkLets: A collaboration engineering pattern language. *International Journal of Computer Applications and Technology*, 25, 2/3, 140–154.

de Vreede, G.J.; Briggs, R.O.; and Massey, A. 2009. Collaboration engineering: Foundations and opportunities. *Journal of the Association of Information Systems*, 10, 3, 121–137.

Vroom, V.H. 1995. *Work and Motivation*. San Francisco, CA: Jossey-Bass.

Watson, R.T.; Ho, Teck Hua; and Raman, K.S. 1994. Culture: A fourth dimension of group support systems. *Communications of the ACM*, 37, 10, 44–55.

Weick, K.E.; Sutcliffe, K.M.; and Obstfeld, D. 2005. Organizing and the process of sensemaking. *Organization Science*, 16, 4, 409–421.

Westaby, J.D. 2002. Identifying specific factors underlying attitudes toward change: Using multiple methods to compare expectancy-value theory to reasons theory. *Journal of Applied Social Psychology*, 32, 5, 1083–1104.

Wheelan, S.A. 2009. Group size, group development, and group productivity. *Small Group Research*, 40, 2, 247–262.

Whitten, J.L.; Bentley, L.; and Dittman, K. 2007. *Systems Analysis and Design Methods*. Boston: McGraw-Hill/Irwin.

Winograd, T., and Flores, F. 1986. *Understanding Computers and Cognition: A New Foundation for Design*. Norwood, NJ: Ablex.

Yeung, A.K.; Ulrich, D.O.; Nason, S.W.; and Von Glinow, M.A. 1999. *Organizational Learning Capability*. New York: Oxford University Press.

Zigurs, I., and Buckland, B.K. 1998. A theory of task/technology fit and group support systems effectiveness. *MIS Quarterly*, 22, 3, 313–334.

EDITORS AND CONTRIBUTORS

EDITORS

Jay F. Nunamaker, Jr. is Regents and Soldwedel Professor of MIS, Computer Science and Communication, and Director of the Center for the Management of Information at the University of Arizona, Tucson. He received his PhD in Systems Engineering and Operations Research from Case Institute of Technology, an M.S. and B.S. in Engineering from the University of Pittsburgh, and a B.S. from Carnegie Mellon University. Dr. Nunamaker received the LEO Award from the Association of Information Systems at ICIS in Barcelona, Spain, December 2002. This award is given for a lifetime of exceptional achievement in information systems. He was elected as a fellow of the Association of Information Systems in 2000. Dr. Nunamaker has over forty years of experience in examining, analyzing, designing, testing, evaluating, and developing information systems. He served as a test engineer at the Shippingport Atomic Power facility, as a member of the ISDOS team at the University of Michigan, and as a member of the faculty at Purdue University prior to joining the faculty at the University of Arizona in 1974. His research on group support systems addresses behavioral as well as engineering issues and focuses on theory and implementation. He has been a licensed professional engineer since 1965.

Nicholas C. Romano, Jr. is Professor of Information Systems in the School of Information Management, Faculty of Commerce, Victoria University, Wellington, New Zealand. Previously he was Associate Professor of Management Science and Information Systems, Spears School, Oklahoma State University. He earned his PhD at Arizona (1998) and worked for IBM. A 2006 *Business Research Yearbook* study ranked Romano third globally in electronic commerce journal articles (1998–2004). He has published over thirty refereed journal articles: *Journal of Management Information Systems, Communications of the ACM, European Journal of Information Systems, International Journal of Electronic Commerce, Group Decision and Negotiation*, and *Small Group Research*. In fall 2009 he received a Poole Research Excellence Award for publishing research in top-tier IS journals. Romano is Senior Associate Editor for *European Journal of Information Systems* and Senior Editor for *Electronic Markets* and has guest-edited more than sixteen special issues of IS and related-discipline journals. He has long been active in HICSS and AMCIS serving as minitrack chair and theme chair.

Robert O. Briggs is professor of information systems in the MIS department at San Diego State University. He researches the theoretical foundations of collaboration and learning, and applies his findings to the design and deployment of new collaboration technologies and new ways of learning and working. He has published more than 200 scholarly works on collaboration engineering, team productivity, technology-supported learning, creativity, satisfaction, consensus, and change. He is cofounder of the Collaboration eEngineering field and co-inventor of the thinkLets design pattern language for collaborative work practices. He lectures worldwide on collaboration theory and practice, and on the philosophy of science. He earned his doctorate in management information systems at the University of Arizona in 1994.

CONTRIBUTORS

Mark Adkins is a senior professional providing insight to leading corporations, governments, and agencies around the world. He is an authority on collaboration, cyber operations, information systems, network enabled operations, group decision making, human communication, and humanitarian assistance/disaster relief. Dr. Adkins works in industry and held a position as Director of Research at the Center for the Management of Information at the University of Arizona. His "cross-over" products provide information to Headquarters U.S. Army, Secretary of Air Force, Number Air Force and Fleet Commanders, and Chief of Naval Operations. Proven areas of achievement: leadership, business development, strategic planning, process and organizational engineering and facilitation. For over twenty-five years Adkins has established relationships and developed business across the defense, emergency management, homeland defense, and education sectors. Dr. Adkins is a thought leader as well as an action officer with many publications.

Conan C. Albrecht is a professor of Information Systems at Brigham Young University. He teaches classes in enterprise development, middleware, and business programming. Albrecht researches computer-based fraud detection techniques, ecommerce platforms, and online group dynamics. He is one of the primary authors of *Fraud Examination*, a fraud textbook used at many universities worldwide. He has published articles on fraud detection and information theory in *The Journal of Forensic Accounting, The Journal of Accountancy, The Communications of the ACM, Decision Support Systems, Information and Management*, and other academic and professional outlets. Albrecht is currently working on a platform to provide free and pay-for-upgrade, university-level textbooks to students. If successful, the effort will provide material to professors and students throughout the world, and it will still provide substantial compensation to book authors.

Judee Burgoon is Site Director for the Center for Identification Technology Research and Director of Research, Center for the Management of Information, at the University of Arizona, where she holds appointments as Professor of Communication and Family and Consumer Sciences. Dr. Burgoon has authored 8 books and nearly 300 articles, chapters, and reviews on such topics as nonverbal and relational communication, deception, and computer-mediated communication. Her current research—funded by the National Science Foundation, Department of Defense and Department of Homeland Security—is examining ways to automate analysis of nonverbal and verbal communication to detect deception and hostile intent. Her awards include the International Communication Association's Fisher Mentorship, Chaffee Career Achievement, and ICA Fellow Awards and the National Communication Association's Distinguished Scholar Award, Golden Anniversary Monographs Award, Woolbert Award for Research with Lasting Impact, and Knapp Award in Interpersonal Communication.

Fang Chen is an Assistant Professor of Management Information Systems in the Department of Accounting and Finance, University of Manitoba, Canada. She received her PhD in Management and Information Systems from the University of Arizona in 2004. Prior to joining the PhD program, Dr. Chen worked in industry as a database application developer. Her research interests include group collaboration, computer-mediated communication, virtual teams, and knowledge transfer. Her papers have been published in *Journal of International Technology and Information Management, Journal of Information Systems Education*, and *Group Decision and Negotiation*. Her teaching interests include data communication and networking, system analysis and design, and database management.

Douglas L. Dean is an Associate Professor of IS at the Marriott School of Management at Brigham Young University. He received his PhD in MIS from the University of Arizona in 1995. Dr. Dean's research interests include online communities, knowledge management, scientometrics, electronic commerce standards, and collaborative tools and methods. His work has been published in *Management Information Systems Quarterly, Management Science, Journal of Management Information Systems, Journal of the AIS, Group Decision and Negotiation*, and others.

Gert-Jan de Vreede is the Charles & Margre Durham Distinguished Professor and the Managing Director of the Center for Collaboration Science at the University of Nebraska at Omaha. He is also affiliated with Delft University of Technology in the Netherlands from where he received his PhD. He was a visiting professor at the University of Arizona and the University of Pretoria. His research focuses on social and organizational applications of collaboration technologies, the theoretical foundations of collaboration, Collaboration Engineering, and the facilitation of group work. He is cofounder of the collaboration engineering field and co-inventor of the thinkLets concept. He has published over 200 refereed journal articles, conference papers, and book chapters and was named the most productive Group Support Systems researcher world-wide from 2000–2005 in a comprehensive research profiling study. His research has appeared in journals such as *Journal of Management Information Systems, Journal of the Association for Information Systems, Communications of the Association for Information Systems, Small Group Research, Communications of the ACM, DataBase, Group Decision and Negotiation*, and *International Journal of e-Collaboration.*

Amit V. Deokar is an Assistant Professor of Information Systems in the College of Business and Information Systems at Dakota State University. His recent research interests are in business process management, collaboration processes and technologies, decision support systems, knowledge management, and healthcare informatics. His work has appeared in journals including *Journal of Management Information Systems, Communications of the AIS, Information Systems Frontiers*, and *IEEE Transactions*. He has also presented at national and international conferences and authored book chapters in the field of Information Systems. He holds a BE in Mechanical Engineering from V.J. Technological Institute, Mumbai, a MS in Industrial Engineering from the University of Arizona, and a PhD in Management Information Systems from the University of Arizona. He is a member of AIS, ACM, and AAAI.

James Gantt became the Director of the Center for Telecommunications Systems Management (CTSM) in February 2005. The CTSM is part of the Murray State University Program of Distinction in Telecommunications Systems Management. Dr. Gantt received a Bachelor of Science from Murray State University and a Master of Science degree from the University of Missouri at Rolla. He completed his PhD in Industrial and Systems Engineering at the Georgia Institute of Technology. In 2003 he was honored as a Distinguished Alumnus of Murray State University. During his thirty-two year career with the army, Dr. Gantt held a variety of positions in Research and Development. His personal research focused on collaborative decision making as applied to army applications. He was instrumental in the army research efforts supporting the development of GroupSystems. He progressed through a series of assignments culminating with his selection to become a member of the Senior Executive Service in 1998.

Joey George is a Professor of Information Systems and the John D. DeVries Endowed Chair in Business in the College of Business at Iowa State University. He is a Fellow of the Association for Information Systems (AIS), and he served as President of AIS in 2010–11. His research interests include the detection of deceptive computer-mediated communication, computer-based monitoring, and group support systems. His research has been funded by the U.S. National Science Foundation and the U.S. Air Force Office of Scientific Research. Professor George is currently a Senior Editor at *Information Systems Research*. From January 2006 until March 1, 2009, he served as Editor-in-Chief of *Communications of the Association for Information Systems*. He has served as both Senior Editor and Associate Editor for *MIS Quarterly*. He has worked extensively with the International Conference on Information Systems (ICIS). In 2001, he served as the Conference Co-Chair in New Orleans. In 2003 he was the co-chair of the Doctoral Consortium in Seattle. He will also be the Conference Chair for ICIS 2012, to be held in Orlando, Florida. Professor George earned his bachelor's degree at Stanford University in 1979 and his PhD in management at the University of California Irvine in 1986.

Joel Helquist is an Assistant Professor of accounting at Utah Valley University. Dr. Helquist graduated with a PhD in Business Management with an emphasis in Management Information Systems from the University of Arizona. Prior to completing his PhD, Dr. Helquist worked as a risk management consultant for Arthur Andersen, LLP and KPMG, LLP in Seattle, Washington. His research interests are primarily focused around risk management and processes and technologies to support collaboration.

Sean Humpherys is an Assistant Professor at West Texas A&M College of Business. He is published in *MIS Quarterly, Decision Support Systems, IEEE-TPC, Communications of the AIS,* and others. His primary research interests include: Computer-assisted deception detection, HCI, machine learning algorithms, data mining, and computational linguistics. He researches on projects funded by Department of Defense, Department of Homeland Security, National Science Foundation, Center for Identification Technology Research, National Center for Border Security and Immigration, and PwC. He received a PhD from the Eller College of Management, University of Arizona, and Masters of Information Systems Management (MISM) at the Marriott School of Management, Brigham Young University.

Mark Keith is an assistant professor in the Information Systems, Statistics, and Management Science department at The University of Alabama. His recent research focuses on service-oriented software development, organizational social networks, and the privacy risks of location-based services used in mobile computing. His research has appeared in the *Journal of the Association for Information Systems, Decision Support Systems, Decision Analysis, International Journal of Human-Computer Studies, Communications of the Association for Information Systems*, the *International Conference for Information Systems (ICIS)*, and other journals and conference proceedings.

Gwendolyn L. Kolfschoten is an assistant professor at Delft University of Technology in the Netherlands. Her research focuses on how teams, experts, or stakeholders can effectively collaborate, and use collaboration support tools, in problem solving tasks. She is an experienced facilitator of Group Support System workshops and sessions, having worked with numerous public and private organizations. Her current research focuses on cognitive perspectives on collaboration effectiveness, and implications for the design of collaboration support systems. She also works in several projects on the design of intelligent collaboration support systems, and worked on Collaboration Engineering and the thinkLet concept to capture patterns in effective collaborative effort. She has organized successful minitracks and tutorials at HICSS for the past five years, and organized the GDN 2010 conference in Delft. She was also a program chair for CRIWG 2010. Her research has been presented at e.g. HICSS, CRIWG, AMCIS, and GDN conferences and has been published in the *Journal of Management Information Systems, International Journal of Human-Computer Studies, Journal of the AIS, Computers and Education,* and *Group Decision and Negotiation.*

John Kruse is a Lead Information Systems Engineer at the MITRE Corporation. Previously, he was the Director of Systems Development at the Center for the Management of Information at the University of Arizona. He received his PhD in Management Information Systems with a minor in Management and Policy from the University of Arizona. He has worked extensively with a wide range of educational, governmental and military groups to help develop group processes, software that supports collaborative work and automated means for deception and intent detection.

Paul Benjamin Lowry is an Associate Professor of Information Systems at the Department of Information Systems, City University of Hong Kong. His research interests include behavioral security issues (e.g., interface design to improve security, IT policy compliance, deception, computer abuse, accountability, privacy, whistle blowing, fear appeals, intrusion detection, cyber terrorism, organizational justice, reactance, protection motivation, deterrence); HCI (e.g., mental-models based interface design, heuristic evaluation, self-disclosure, collaboration, national culture, individual-level culture, communication, entertainment, hedonic systems use, design for intrinsic motivations, affect); E-commerce and supply chains (e.g., interface design to improve Web presence, security, trust, distrust, branding, electronic markets, e-commerce protocols, model checking); and Scientometrics (e.g., citations analysis/bibliometrics, journal rankings, individual and institutional productivity analysis). He received his PhD in Management Information Systems from the University of Arizona. He has published articles in *MIS Quarterly; Journal of Management Information Systems; Journal of the Association for Information Systems; Information Systems Journal; European Journal of Information Systems; Communications of the ACM; Information Sciences; Decision Support Systems; IEEE Transactions on Systems, Man, and Cybernetics; IEEE Transactions on Professional Communication; Small Group Research; Expert Systems with Applications; Communications of the AIS;* and others. He serves as an associate editor at *European Journal of IS, Information & Management, AIS Transactions on HCI, Communications of the AIS,* and *Electronic Commerce Research and Applications.*

Clayton A. Looney is an Associate Professor and the Ron and Judy Paige Faculty Fellow in the School of Business Administration at the University of Montana. His research concentrates on electronic commerce, human-computer interaction, decision support systems, and judgment and decision making. This inter-disciplinary stream primarily focuses on the impact of technology designs on decision making processes and performance, particularly in situations involving risk and uncertainty. His research has appeared in several top practitioner and academic journals including *Management Science, Organizational Behavior and Human Decision Processes, Decision Sciences, Communications of the ACM,* and *Communications of the AIS.*

Stephan Lukosch is Associate Professor at the Delft University of Technology. His current research focuses on collaborative design and engineering in traditional as well as emerging interaction spaces, intelligent and context-adaptive collaboration support and design patterns for computer-mediated interaction. From 2003 to 2008 he was assistant professor at the FernUniversität in Hagen where he lead a research group that focused on environments for cooperative working or learning. His articles have appeared in various journals including the *International Journal of Cooperative Information Systems, International Journal of Human Computer Studies,* and *Journal of Universal*

Computer Science. Currently, he is a steering committee member of the special interest group on Computer-Supported Cooperative Work (CSCW) of the German computer science society and CRIWG conference on Collaboration and Technology. He further serves on the editorial board of the *Journal of Universal Computer Science (J.UCS)* and the *International Journal of Cooperative Information Systems (IJCIS).*

Kent Marett is an Associate Professor of Information Systems at Mississippi State University. He holds the PhD degree in MIS from Florida State University. His primary research interests include deceptive communication in computer-based media, the role of information technology in group and individual decision making, and the use of communicative technology within organizations and communities. His research has been published in several leading journals.

Thomas Meservy is an Assistant Professor of Management Information Systems at the University of Memphis. He graduated with his PhD in Management from the University of Arizona in 2007. His research interests include software development tools and methodologies, collaboration, and automated understanding of human nonverbal behavior. His dissertation focused on creating and validating systems to augment human capabilities in automatically detecting deception by observing nonverbal behavior. In 2001 Meservy graduated from Brigham Young University with a B.S. in Management and a Masters of Information Systems Management. Since the late 1990s he has worked as a software developer/engineer for small-medium sized businesses, as well as larger consulting firms. He enjoys systems development and has been an independent consultant advising firms on best practice software development techniques.

Daniel Mittleman is an Associate Professor at DePaul University's College of Computing and Digital Media. His research focuses on collaboration engineering, virtual teamwork, web 2.0/3.0 collaboration tools, and the design of both collaboration and learning spaces. His projects include investigation of collaboration aboard U.S. Navy ships; development of team processes to support architectural planning, collaborative writing, and brainstorming; and the design of technology-supported collaboration facilities. Dr. Mittleman holds an AB and MBA from Washington University (St. Louis) and a PhD from the University of Arizona. His blog on Virtual Collaboration is www.cdmblogs.net/work30.

John D. Murphy earned his PhD in Information Technology at the University of Nebraska Omaha. His research interests include the design and use of information technologies to support collaboration in virtual and face-to-face teams. His dissertation focused on understanding when people are willing to change work practices to integrate new technologies and processes into the workplace. He currently leads the IT Architecture and Engineering team supporting a globally-dispersed person workforce of 10,000 plus. He has published in the *Journal for the Association of Information Systems, Data Base for Advances in Information Systems,* and the *American Journal of Business.*

Trent J. Spaulding is an Assistant Professor in the department of Nutrition and Healthcare Management in the College of Health Sciences at Appalachian State University. Dr. Spaulding completed his PhD in Information Systems at Arizona State University in 2011. His dissertation work focuses on hospital information systems. He completed a dual Bachelors and Masters degree in Information Systems Management at Brigham Young University in 2006. Before starting his PhD, he worked as an ERP architect and engineer for Pace Symposia and as a systems analyst intern for the Church of Jesus Christ of Latter-Day Saints. In 2009 he led the development of a system to assist in the dissemination of the H1N1 vaccine in the greater Phoenix area. He specializes in the automation of business processes in the healthcare industry. This work benefits from the availability of data on thousands of hospitals from the Centers for Medicare and Medicaid Services, the Hospital Quality Alliance, the American Hospital Association, and the HIMSS Foundation. He has also researched the economics of online auctions and business use of virtual communities. His research has been published in *Health Affairs, Decision Support Systems (DSS), Electronic Commerce Research and Applications (ECRA), the Hawaii International Conference on Systems Science*, and the *International Conference on Information Systems*. He has also consulted on database development, management reporting, and website development.

Joseph S. Valacich is an Eller Professor of MIS in the Eller College of Management at the University of Arizona and a Fellow of the Association for Information Systems. He has had visiting faculty appointments at the City University of Hong Kong, Riga Technical University (Latvia), Norwegian University of Life Sciences, Buskerud College (Norway), and Helsinki School of Economics and Business. He received the PhD degree from The University of Arizona (MIS) (1989), and the M.B.A. and B.S. (computer science) degrees from the University of Montana. His primary research interests include human-computer interaction and information visualization, cyber security, deception detection, technology-mediated collaboration, individual and group decision making, and e-business. He has published more than eighty scholarly articles in numerous prestigious journals, including: *MIS Quarterly, Information Systems Research, Management Science, Academy of Management Journal, Journal of Management Information Systems, Decision Sciences, Journal of the AIS, Communications of the ACM, Organizational Behavior and Human Decision Processes, Journal of Applied Psychology*, and many others. He is a co-author of several leading textbooks. Prior to his academic career, Dr. Valacich worked in the software industry in Seattle in both large and start-up organizations.

David W. Wilson is a doctoral student at the University of Arizona in the Center for the Management of Information. He is a graduate of the Masters of Information Systems program of the Marriott School of Management of Brigham Young University, where he completed the Information Systems PhD Preparation Program. His research interests include online identity, privacy, trust, and HCI. His research has appeared in *Communications of the AIS*.

Ryan T. Wright is an Assistant Professor at the University of Massachusetts, Amherst. He holds a PhD from Washington State University in Management Information Systems and an MBA and Bachelor of Science in Business from the University of Montana. Ryan's research interests take a behavioral approach to understanding how current technologies can be used to enable secure and efficient e-business transactions. He is published in *MIS Quarterly, Journal of Management Information Systems, Communications of the AIS*, and other peer-reviewed publications. In addition to academic achievements, Ryan's professional experience includes tenure as CTO of a successful startup, time in management at Amoco Oil (now BP), consulting projects for the U.S. Department of Commerce and expert testimony on IS privacy and security. Ryan was in the 2008 ICIS Doctoral Consortium.

SERIES EDITOR

Vladimir Zwass is Gregory Olsen Endowed Chair and Distinguished Professor of Computer Science and Management Information Systems at Fairleigh Dickinson University. He holds a PhD in Computer Science from Columbia University. Professor Zwass is the founding editor-in-chief of the *Journal of Management Information Systems*, one of the three top-ranked journals in the field of information systems. He is also the founding editor-in-chief of the *International Journal of Electronic Commerce*, ranked as the top journal in its field. More recently, he has been the founding editor-in-chief of the monograph series *Advances in Management Information Systems*, the objective of which is to codify the field's knowledge and research methods. He is the author of six books and several book chapters, including entries in the *Encyclopaedia Britannica*, as well as of a number of papers in various journals and conference proceedings. He has received several grants, consulted for a number of major corporations, and is a frequent speaker to national and international audiences. He is a former member of the professional staff of the International Atomic Energy Agency in Vienna, Austria.

INDEX

Note: Italic page numbers indicate tables or figures.